THE
GOLD
STANDARD

An Alternative History
of the Twentieth Century

Saifedean Ammous

THE
SAIF
HOUSE

THE GOLD STANDARD: AN ALTERNATIVE HISTORY OF THE TWENTIETH CENTURY

ISBN: 979-8-9879755-3-4 *Hardcover*
      979-8-9879755-6-5 *Paperback*
      979-8-9879755-5-8 *eBook*
      979-8-9879755-4-1 *Audiobook*

Cover images:
Solidus of Constantine: © Classical Numismatic Group, Inc. http://www.cngcoins.com, (CC BY-SA 2.5)
The Bank of England: London - The City © Chunyip Wong/iStockphoto
Airplane image: Created with Grok (xAI).

To my father, who deserved to live in this golden century and wanted to see this book published, but did not. And to my younger daughter, who made him very happy.

Table of Contents

About the Author

Saifedean Ammous is one of the world's most widely read writers on economics. He wrote *The Bitcoin Standard* (2018), which sold more than one million copies worldwide in 39 languages; *The Fiat Standard* (2021), which is available in 22 languages; and *Principles of Economics* (2023), available in 11 languages.

Ammous teaches courses on bitcoin and economics in the Austrian school tradition on his online learning platform, Saifedean.com, and also hosts *The Bitcoin Standard Podcast*. Through The Saif House, he publishes high-quality hardcover books on bitcoin, fiat money, and Austrian economics.

From 2009 to 2019, Ammous served as a professor of economics at the Lebanese American University. He holds a PhD in Sustainable Development from Columbia University, a Master's in Development Management from the London School of Economics, and a bachelor's degree in mechanical engineering from the American University of Beirut.

Introduction

The invention of bitcoin has kindled interest in monetary history, offering people a historically unparalleled opportunity to experience firsthand the transformative potential of upgrading monetary technology. In 2018, I published *The Bitcoin Standard*, a book that focused on monetary history and monetary economics, explaining the problem of money over millennia in order to illustrate bitcoin's true potential and historical significance. In 2021, I published *The Fiat Standard,* which also focused on monetary history and economics to explain the functioning of fiat money and its far-reaching implications. In 2023, I published *Principles of Economics*, a book that explained the economics of human action and detailed how civilization emerges from the cooperation of individuals. All three books offered readers a departure from the usual approach of modern economics books, in that they challenged the inevitability and desirability of government-controlled money and illustrated its many devastating impacts on individuals and society. A central theme through all three books is that human civilizational progress is inextricably linked with the hardness of our money: the harder the money is to make, the less its supply will increase over time, the better it will hold its value, and the more it will allow its holder to provide for the future more effectively, decreasing the uncertainty surrounding the future, and causing us to discount the future less. In other words, hard money makes us more future-oriented, lowering our time preference, which is what initiates the process of civilization. As we increasingly value the future more, we defer immediate gratification in favor of long-term rewards. We save our resources for the future and invest them to increase our productivity. We control our base instincts and passions, subduing them to our reason, which calculates what is in our long-term interest. We cooperate and resolve differences peacefully because we recognize that the long-term benefits of peaceful cooperation far outweigh the short-term advantages of aggression. We engage in trade and build a highly sophisticated division of labor. If practiced over generations, this process of civilization manifests as a continuous increase in the material well-being of a society, with each generation living better than the previous generation.

The obverse is also true, unfortunately. The easier money is to produce, the more its supply increases and its value declines over time, the less it will allow us to provide for our future selves, increasing the uncertainty surrounding the future, and causing us to discount the future more. In other words, easy money makes us more present-oriented, raising our time preference, which is what destroys the process of civilization. As we discount the future more, we consume our resources with little regard for the future. Saving and capital investment decline. We are more likely to act to satisfy our present urges at the expense of our future well-being, since it matters increasingly less. We are less likely to cooperate and resolve differences peacefully, which compromises our division of labor and, in turn, our productivity. Much of the history of the past century has reflected this civilizational decline. The collapse of society witnessed under hyperinflation is just a faster and more noticeable version of the same process that slow fiat inflation brings about.

A contentious thesis for many, yet one that has found support among a growing worldwide readership with more than a million copies sold across 39 languages. I believe much of the books' success is due to their ability to explain to readers many of the phenomena they experience as they use different forms of money. The more I wrote and spoke about the impacts of money on time preference, the more stories I would hear from readers and listeners about their own personal experiences with inflation and how moving to bitcoin helped them become more future-oriented, as well as their countries' experiences with inflation and hyperinflation through the century of fiat money. Everywhere, there are countless stories to tell of how the destruction of money leads to the destruction of economic security and the destruction of civilization.

Pervading all three of my books is a deep sense of historical regret over a world that could have been—a world where money escaped the grip of the state, was chosen freely on the market, and constantly increased in market value, allowing savings, protecting from government and central bank debasement, and limiting government power by restricting its funding to transparent taxation. Countless times when examining one particular aspect of fiat's devastation of humanity, I would find myself wondering how different things could have been, how much prosperity was lost, and how much human suffering could have been averted. For years, I have found myself drifting off into lengthy thought experiments around the question: What would the twentieth century have looked like on a hard money standard? We can see how consequential the reduction in the value of money is in episodes of hyperinflation, high inflation, and even low inflation. We can see the impact upgrading from easy money to harder money has on individuals, as the stories of bitcoiners attest. And we can see how hard money is already showing signs of transforming President Nayib Bukele's El Salvador. Every time I observe one of these phenomena, I wonder how different the world would have been in the past century had it used hard money. In many interviews, I would be asked such questions and I would find myself overflowing with ideas for answers, my mouth unable to articulate them at the rate at which my mind produces them. That feeling is what puts fire in my fingers and gets them itching to pound them into my keyboard, systematically exploring and elaborating on them, culminating in the production of a book.

It would have been a natural continuation of my first two books on bitcoin and fiat to complete the series by writing a new book stretching back further in time to study the gold standard, its workings, and the implications for society. However, that book was already written in 2001 by the late Swiss banker

Ferdinand Lips, under the title *Gold Wars: The Battle Against Sound Money As Seen From A Swiss Perspective*. That book was one of my inspirations for writing *The Bitcoin Standard*, and I learned a lot from it; most of its important ideas have already been reflected in my three books. A more interesting question was to examine the failings of the gold standard and why it was replaced by fiat money. There were many imperfections in the gold standard during the nineteenth century. Even at its best, it fell short of the ideal form of a gold standard in which all monetary instruments are backed by 100% of their face value in gold in the vaults of the issuer. The classical gold standard still allowed for the creation of money and credit far in excess of the amount of gold held in reserve. What would happen if we had a perfect gold standard? What would the world look like if no entity were capable of creating money without opportunity cost? This question, along with the question of what the twentieth century would have looked like on hard money, inspired the writing of *The Gold Standard*.

This book builds upon the ideas from my three previous books on the importance of monetary soundness and applies them to a series of elaborate questions: What would the world look like if we had a gold standard in the twentieth century? What if, instead of downgrading from an imperfect gold standard to the catastrophic fiat standard at the beginning of the twentieth century, the world had upgraded to a better gold standard? Given everything we know about the impact of hard money, just how different would a hard money twentieth century have been? What would life be like with constantly appreciating money and declining prices? What would have happened if governments had not financed themselves through inflation in the last century without accountability? How much less blood would have been shed had governments had to fight their wars with their own treasuries without having recourse to inflation to rob all their citizens? How would living standards and wages change? How would the state and banking have evolved? What would have happened to education, technology, politics, and our production of energy?

The Gold Standard attempts to answer these questions with a fictional economic history of an alternative twentieth century in which the fiat money experiment fails in 1915. Since money is pervasive in all aspects of life, I endeavoured to make this as realistic as possible. Rather than simply assuming the monetary system I want and shaping the world around it, I chose to construct a history that could have conceivably led to this monetary transition taking place, thereby producing realistic historical developments throughout the century. When considering scenarios for an alternative history, there are many historical junctures where an author could take the liberty of choosing a different outcome from reality, thereby changing history. Franz Ferdinand's assassin's gun could have jammed, and the conflict between Serbia and Austria would have been averted, preventing the snowball of war that was to consume the planet. Austria's old Emperor Franz Joseph could have easily died a week before his crown prince nephew, Franz Ferdinand, traveled to Bosnia, making him emperor and potentially preventing his modernizing influence from causing conflict with Serbia and Russia altogether. However, such simple changes do not address the underlying historical and economic factors that led to the war, and thus would not offer a convincing rationale for the fundamental historical change. The same governments and central banks that went to war in 1914 could have gone to war a few years later with similar consequences. It was essential for me to alter a fundamental aspect of the monetary technology of the time to make this story engaging and realistic. Economists of the Austrian school have long emphasized the pivotal role entrepreneurship plays in changing history, and since this is an Austrian economist's book, I chose to make it a work of entrepreneurial fiction. It is an entrepreneur who creates a business that causes the world to undergo significant change, and the business idea draws inspiration from the creation of bitcoin, exactly 100 years later. In essence, this book asks: What would have happened if something like bitcoin had existed in 1911?

The fork in reality from which this book originates begins in February 1910, with an imaginary letter that was to advance the development of the aviation industry in the following years. A few entrepreneurs established an airplane-based international gold clearance service in 1911, and it would have a drastic impact on the world in 1915, during the war. Outside of the aviation industry, all of the world's major events remain the same in this story until September 1915, when the fiat money experiment fails and our alternative history begins in earnest. The years 1914–15 were of extraordinary historical importance, as they gave birth to the monetary system and world order in which we live today. By introducing developments that are not entirely out-landish to the aviation industry, this book derails the fiat money experiment in its infancy and strangles the fiat century in its crib, inviting you, dear reader, to teleport yourself via the power of imagination to this alternative world and think deeply about what it would have looked like.

When considering how best to write this thought experiment, I had con-sidered writing a fictional novel, a history book that's partly factual and partly imaginary, and a fictional economics textbook. Each of these three forms of writ-ing would have been ideal for some part of the thought experiment but would have been too cumbersome and unworkable for all of it. The history book can explain the political and economic realities of the world in the early twentieth century, which is essential for playing out the thought experiment for the cen-tury. The novel is a good tool to introduce and explore the technological and entrepreneurial story that changes the course of history by focusing on the piv-otal individuals involved. The economic textbook can provide an overview of the economic history of the alternative twentieth century. But each of these tools has its limitations. It would not have been very engaging to study the econom-ics of the twentieth century through a fake history book that takes the reader through fake historical events with anything close to the level of detail needed to explain real historical events, and I even think it would have been disrespectful to the reader's time to spend too much time dwelling on fake history, when the point is to get to the economics. Nor could the economics of the twentieth cen-tury have been fruitfully explained through a novel playing out over a century. An economic history book would not have been able to construct an elaborate and realistic story for why history changed in 1915, without getting into the personal stories of the pivotal individuals in the same way a novel can.

After much thought and consideration, my independent publisher self granted my author self the permission to do something strange, which, to my knowledge, has never been tried before: write a book that's a mix of a novel, a his-tory book, and an economics textbook. I hope the reader appreciates the variety!

The book is divided into five Parts. They are constructed as follows:

Part I: The Old World

Based on real-world history, covering events up to September 1915. All the facts presented here are historically accurate in our real world, to the best of my knowledge. Some of these facts may appear made-up and outlandish, but they are real.

Part II: Capital Flight

The story transitions to an alternative history of aviation, which begins in February 1910, and leads to a different outcome for World War I and the rise of a new world order. Events in this section are almost entirely fictional.

Part III: The Modern World

Examines how a modern gold standard would work and how states and banks might have evolved in this alternative timeline. This part contains a mix of real historical events, which are things that happened before September 1915, and fictional events, which happened after that date.

Part IV: The Century of Affluence

Explores changes in living standards, energy, technology, society, and education over the twentieth century under the gold standard.

Part V: Postscript from Fiat World

This final section overviews the story and timeline of the previous chapters, providing commentary from the perspective of our real world, comparing the economic outcomes of this thought experiment to our fiat world.

IMPORTANT NOTES:

All historical events happening before September 1915 are real, and all events happening from September 1915 onwards are fictional. Events in the history of the aviation industry are an exception, as these are real up to January 1910 but fictional from February 1910 onward.

All referenced quotes are genuine quotes by the quoted person. All quotes without references are fictional.

PART I

THE OLD WORLD

This part of the book is based on real history, and events here are real. The alternative history begins in Part II.

I.

The Classical Gold Standard

Gold is the money of kings, silver is the money of gentlemen, barter is the money of peasants, and debt is the money of slaves.

To understand the economic history of the twentieth century, we must first examine the monetary system that dominated at its inception. The classical gold standard era, from 1873 to 1914, represented the first time since antiquity that Western civilization was using the same monetary standard. And given European industrial and economic advancement over the rest of the world, by the end of the nineteenth century, the classical gold standard had arguably extended to the whole planet, as most of the world was now using gold as money, or gold-backed currencies, while only a few governments still clung to the silver standard and became increasingly marginalized economically, with the largest capital holders in their territories shifting to gold.

Why Gold?

But why did money concentrate in gold and silver, and then gold alone? The answer can be best understood with reference to these metals having the lowest growth rate of their stockpiles. A detailed study of monetary history shows that, at any time and place, whatever is used as money is whatever fungible, divisible, groupable, and transportable good happens to have the lowest stockpile growth rates. For instance, pre-industrial societies used seashells that were very hard to find. Societies that had not invented glass production used imported glass beads as money. Islands that had no limestone used limestone as money, because limestone could only be obtained at great risk and cost from other faraway islands, making their supply difficult to increase. Prisoners use cigarettes as money because they usually cannot be manufactured in prison, and getting new ones is difficult. As metallurgy began to spread, metals proved remarkably suited for serving as money, as they were fungible, divisible, groupable, and transportable. Iron, copper, silver, and gold had all been used as money, but over time, the first three metals gradually lost their monetary role to gold, the hardest-to-make monetary metal, because their supplies could be increased at rates faster than that of gold's supply.

It is remarkable that the rise of the gold standard did not occur through the efforts of any conscious designer or government mandate. The majority of the world had dealt with gold, silver, and copper as money for centuries. There was no international treaty between governments that would give gold monetary primacy and mandate the demonetization of silver. Individual governments had usually sought to maintain the monetary role of silver alongside gold, but they were powerless to do so in the face of overwhelming monetary incentives shaped by technological reality. Gold kept growing in prominence, and governments' regulations either facilitated its wider adoption to the benefit of their people, or impotently attempted to stymie its growth at the expense of their people's economic well-being.

Whether it was through rational consideration leading people to abandon alternative moneys for gold or through the holders of these moneys bleeding wealth to supply inflation far faster than gold holders, the end result has been the same everywhere in the world: the vast majority of wealth was concentrated in the hands of the holders of the monetary good that was the hardest to produce and had the lowest liquid stockpile growth rate.

Gold is distinct from the three other monetary metals in that it is chemically stable and practically impossible to destroy. It is the only one of these metals that does not corrode, disintegrate, rust, or tarnish. This means that all the gold humanity has produced over thousands of years remains available today, used as gold. Whereas the other metals' stockpiles are constantly disintegrating, gold's stockpiles just continue to grow. This means that, at any given time, the liquid stockpiles of gold held by people worldwide are orders of magnitude larger than any year's production. Data from the past century indicates the annual production of gold is usually in the range of 1.5%–2% of total stockpiles. Even if production were to increase through large discoveries of gold or increases in the productivity of mining processes, the increased supply growth rate will be transitory and self-defeating, as it is added to the existing stockpiles, making the denominator in the supply growth rate larger, bringing the supply growth rate down. Since silver, copper, and iron are constantly being consumed and ruined, their fungible liquid stockpiles are constantly declining, resulting in new production constituting a larger fraction of existing stockpiles as production becomes more efficient and as industrial uses increase.[1]

From the most primitive seashell to the most sophisticated modern gold bank, the choice of monetary medium has always been one determined by the market and subject to the iron forces of economic incentives. Governments enforced the market's choice, benefitting from obeying it and suffering when opposing it. By the start of the nineteenth century, money was gold and silver virtually everywhere, iron had lost its monetary role long ago, and copper's monetary role was confined to increasingly inconsequential small change. For millennia, under what came to be known as bimetallism, governments would mint gold and silver into fixed-weight coins and put their imprint on these coins to make them fungible and easy to trade, obviating the need for weighing and measuring irregular chunks of gold and thus making trade easier and less costly. However, the variations in the price of gold in relation to silver created a problem for monetary authorities, who would have liked to fix the price between their silver and gold denominations to facilitate trade, but the vagaries of supply and demand constantly shifted the price away from the desired fixed ratio.

---

1   Saifedean Ammous, *The Bitcoin Standard: The Decentralized Alternative to Central Banking* (John Wiley & Sons, 2018), 32; Saifedean Ammous, "Money," in *Principles of Economics* (The Saif House, 2023), 181–203.

Bimetallism and Its Discontents

The classical gold standard emerged from the increasingly unworkable nature of the bimetallic monetary system that had dominated the world for millennia. Both gold and silver were used as money. Gold's higher value per unit of weight gave it the leading role for larger transactions, whereas silver's lower value made it the dominant choice for lower-value transactions. The gold-silver ratio, which measures how many ounces of silver one needs to purchase an ounce of gold, has changed significantly throughout history, but nothing like its changes in the last century. Before 550 BC, we have records of the ratio varying between as little as 2 and as high as 21. Around 1000 BC the price was 3 in ancient Egypt thanks to the abundance of gold in the Nubian mines. In Phoenicia around 800–600 BC, the ratio was around 8 to 12. In the Levant, it was around 6 to 7; and in Mesopotamia and Anatolia, around 8 to 10. In the 7th century BC, the price in Persia was at 13 to 1. In Ancient Greece, the price was around 10 in the 4th Century BC. In the Roman Empire, Emperor Augustus fixed the price at 12 to 1 in the year 23 BC.[2] The debasement of the silver denarius led to the rise in desirability of gold and the rise of the GSR to 14 to 18, but the restoration of the Roman Empire in Constantinople led to the decline of the ratio to the range of 12 to 14. In the Islamic world, the ratio was closer to 10 to 15 from the 7th century AD, and under the Ottomans, from 1500 onward, the ratio was around 12 to 15. Medieval Europe saw silver appreciate to as little as a 9 to 4 GSR after the Black Death, but the ratio returned to the 12 to 15 range. The influx of silver from the new world to Europe around 1500–1800 stabilized the ratio around 15.[3]

As global trade became more advanced, cheaper, and widespread, the price harmonized globally. By the 17th century a global steady price of approximately 15 prevailed in the majority of the world's major markets and economies. But then, in the nineteenth century, modern banking, banknotes,

---

2   Louis C. West, *Gold and Silver Coin Standards in the Roman Empire*, Numismatic Notes and Monographs (American Numismatic Society, 1941).

3   James Ross and Leigh Bettenay, "Gold and Silver: Relative Values in the Ancient Past," *Cambridge Archaeological Journal* 34, no. 3 (August 2024): 403–20.

checkbooks, the telegraph and train, making trade more efficient, all conspired to undermine silver's monetary role. But the market rate had remained fixed around 15 because of many governments imposing that rate.

The intractable problem of bimetallism was that, being market goods, silver and gold would fluctuate in value as a result of variations in supply and demand conditions, causing them to diverge from any fixed exchange rate monetary authorities would set between their two denominations. If the exchange rate was set between the two and then the price of silver rose, the government's monetary standard presented an opportunity for arbitrage: any citizen could acquire gold coins and exchange them at the mint for silver coins at the fixed rate set by the government. In effect, the citizen was getting cheap silver from the government, which he could then export abroad and sell for gold at the prevailing foreign market rate, thus obtaining a larger quantity of gold than he had started with. By fixing the exchange rate, governments would necessarily undervalue one of the metals as soon as the market exchange rate between them moved slightly, which would drive the undervalued metal out of its borders and flood its markets with the overvalued metal.

It was through the process of bimetallic arbitrage that the classical gold standard emerged, thanks to the genius of the great English physicist Isaac Newton. Having dedicated his life to alchemy and developing a deep understanding of the processing of precious metals, Newton was appointed the warden of The Royal Mint. He set the bimetallic ratio to undervalue silver, as in the example above, which led to silver leaving Britain and gold flooding in. Newton described this process in a report to the Lords Commissioners of His Majesty's Treasury on 21 September, 1717.

And according to this rate [in England], a pound weight of fine gold is worth Fifteen pounds weight six ounces seventeen penny weight & five grains of fine silver ... Gold is ... in Spain and Portugal of Sixteen times more value [than] Silver of equal weight and allay ... In France a pound weight of fine Gold is [reckoned] worth Fifteen pounds weight of fine Silver ... In China and Japan one pound weight of fine Gold is worth but Nine or ten pounds weight of fine Silver; & in East India it may be worth Twelve

> ... And it appears by experience as well as by reason that Silver flows from
> those places where its value is lowest in proportion to Gold, as from Spain
> to all Europe & from all Europe to the East Indies, China & Japan; & that
> Gold is most plentiful in those places in which its value is highest in pro-
> portion to silver, as in Spain and England.[4]

By this overvaluation of gold compared to the global markets, Britain
was effectively on a gold standard, with silver progressively marginalized,
until 1816, when the Coinage Act defined the pound in terms of gold and
prohibited the use of silver for transactions larger than 40 shillings. As silver
continued to decline in value compared to gold, the British people's money
and wealth appreciated, as did the Spanish people's wealth, while countries
on silver became poorer through their money's devaluation. Asian countries
were harmed over the coming decades by their overvaluation of silver. They
lost their gold and accumulated a significant amount of silver, whose supply
increased at a higher rate than that of gold; as a result, it subsequently lost
value in relation to gold, particularly after 1870. It is impossible to understand
the economic supremacy of Europe over Asia during the nineteenth and early
twentieth centuries without this monetary context.

There are important technological factors to which the decline in silver
value can be attributed. Increased productivity, specialization, and division
of labor meant people were engaged in more trade, and physical coins became
increasingly inconvenient for an increasing number of trades. Coins are incon-
veniently expensive to divide into precise quantities for trade. It was far easier
to use paper notes backed by physical money, as these are lighter, cheaper to
transport, less conspicuous, and more easily exchanged for smaller or larger
denominations. Paper receipts for physical money became an increasingly
common medium of exchange, obviating the need for holding physical money
and increasing demand for holding gold in bank vaults while its receipts cir-
culated.

---

4   "The Rise of the Gold Standard, 1660–1819," in *The Monetary History of Gold: A
    Documentary History, 1660–1999*, 1st ed., ed. Mark Duckenfield (Routledge, 2004), 93–96.

Facilitated by the rise of industrial engines and electricity, the speed and distances at which trade takes place increased beyond the capacity of physical money to move with every physical trade. This led to a significant rise in reliance on banking institutions, with checks and bank transfers accounting for a progressively larger percentage of total trades. As these transactions all took place on bank balance sheets, there was little incentive to hold the easier silver money for conducting them, and demand for silver continued to decline compared to demand for gold. The market value of cash balances in gold continued to grow while balances in silver stagnated or declined. The greater the cash balances in a particular market good, the more significant its monetary role. Money, after all, is the good with the largest cash balances, and people spend as money the goods in which they have large holdings.

If silver's monetary role had relied on its lower value, making it more convenient for small transactions, paper and credit money obviated that role. Why use paper backed by silver for small denominations when you could just as easily use paper backed by gold, which holds its value better? Further, using the same metal for large and small transactions meant no fluctuating exchange rate between moneys. No longer were kings and nobility the only ones who could afford gold as their money; everyone could hold gold in the form of small-denomination paper backed by gold. The hardest money in the world became increasingly available to more and more people worldwide.

While the demise of silver was a centuries-long process driven by economic incentives, the decisive event that ended silver's monetary role was a clear historical moment: the Franco-Prussian War of 1871. At the end of the war, France was on a bimetallic standard of gold and silver, while newly united Germany was the world's largest silver-standard industrial economy. It was obvious that silver was declining, and Germany astutely seized the opportunity its victory presented by taking its indemnity from France in gold and using that gold as the new basis for its monetary cash balances. After officially adopting the gold standard in 1873, Germany experienced remarkable economic growth over the following decades, while silver's gradual decline accelerated. Also in 1873, the United States Congress passed the Coinage Act, which ended the minting of silver into monetary coins by the United States Mint and effectively put the US on a gold standard.

In 1900, the Gold Standard Act legally defined the dollar as 23.22 grains of fine gold and formalized the gold standard explicitly.

The Latin Monetary Union (LMU) was a monetary coinage convention adopted in 1865 between Belgium, France, Italy, and Switzerland to standardize the denominations of coins across these countries and their precious metal content. Greece joined in 1867, and many countries and colonies adopted all or some of the coin specifications without formally joining the LMU. The LMU specified the exchange rate between its members' silver and gold coins, making the two metals interchangeable at a price of 15.5 ounces of silver per ounce of gold. But in the wake of the American and German switch to the gold standard, the price of silver plummeted, making the LMU's gold/silver price unsustainable. Citizens of LMU countries could purchase silver and send it to the local mint to make coinage, and then convert that coinage to gold at the specified rate. Since the rate overvalued silver, they would end up with more gold than the amount they had used to purchase physical silver. This profit came at the expense of the government's mint. The LMU de facto switched to a gold standard in 1873, then formally limited the minting of silver coins in 1874. With the price continuing to decline, the LMU suspended minting silver coins completely in 1878.[5]

With Germany, the United States, France, Italy, Switzerland, Belgium, and Greece all practically going on a gold standard in the 1870s and joining Britain, Holland, and Sweden, the vast majority of the world's economic output and trade was now gold-based. This era also marked the emergence of economic globalization. Even countries that weren't formally on a gold standard used gold extensively in trade. Anyone, anywhere, could now trade with anyone, anywhere, using the same monetary unit, with no concern for exchange rate fluctuations or monetary instability. A gold coin could travel the world, and banks based on gold built ever-widening settlement and clearance networks, facilitating ever-cheaper trading by crediting transfers and settling them collectively with periodic rebalancing. This resulted in an unparalleled economic boom that was to last for decades, though it was punctuated by frequent severe financial crises.

---

5   Henry Parker Willis, *A History of the Latin Monetary Union: A Study of International Monetary Action* (University of Chicago Press, 1901), 266.

When goods flow peacefully across borders, bombs and armies become far less likely to cross them, and the end of the nineteenth century was relatively peaceful, although it too was punctuated by crises. After the Franco-Prussian War of 1871, there were no wars pitting the major European powers against each other except the Turkish-Russian war of 1877–78, but imperial ambitions meant a constant threat of major conflicts breaking out.

The Classical Gold Standard's Achilles' Heel

However, the classical gold standard had a major problem that prevented it from functioning optimally in its ideal form: the incessant extension of bank credit without corresponding savings. In 1912, at the young age of thirty, the Austrian economist Ludwig von Mises wrote *The Theory of Money and Credit*, which astutely identified the root of, and the enormous implications of, the problems with the classical gold standard. Mises identified two types of credit issued by banks. The first was commodity credit, which is credit for which the bank has full backing in terms of savings at the bank equal to the entire sum of the loan, and which is deposited for the entire duration of the loan. The second was circulation credit, where the bank has no savings matching the loan's sum and duration.

Should there be a discrepancy between the quantity of credit the bank borrows and the quantity it lends, or a discrepancy between the maturity dates, then the bank is no longer engaged in lending commodity credit, but rather in circulating credit. In this case, the bank is not merely transferring the money of savers to entrepreneurs; it is issuing credit that is being used as money, effectively inflating the money supply and causing substantial consequences.

Money, Mises explained, is unique in that it is the one good that is obtained purely to be exchanged for something else. It is not consumed, like consumer goods, nor is it used in the production of other goods, as capital goods are. Since its sole purpose is to be passed on and it performs no physical function for its owner, a claim on it, or a substitute for it, is capable of playing its role in a way that cannot be played by any substitute or claim on another consumer or capital good. A voucher for a steak cannot be eaten, and a receipt for a machine cannot produce the goods that the machine produces, but a receipt for money can be used to settle payment just like the money itself.

Due to the unique nature of money, monetary substitutes can apparently serve the functions of money. They can be acquired and spent as payment for goods or services without having to be redeemed for money at the issuing bank. The banknotes or bank accounts that the bank issues as circulation credit are themselves the medium of exchange, without requiring redemption for money. By producing credit and paper without full backing with savings, banks and central banks were effectively creating new money to add to the money supply. Even though the entire reason gold was money was that its supply is hard to increase, banks had managed to create monetary instruments that were as good as gold by generating credit without backing and then having their customers use this credit as money. Rather than long hours in labs trying to unravel the mystery of the philosopher's stone, alchemy in the nineteenth century was carried out every day by bankers issuing credit without corresponding savings.

But of course, there is no free lunch in economics, and the creation of more money had to come at a cost. In his masterpiece, Mises explained that the extension of credit without savings covering the entire sum of the loan results in the recurring financial and monetary crises that plagued both the nineteenth century and the early twentieth century. When a government allows banks to suspend redemption of their notes and credit for gold, it effectively turns these instruments into money themselves, causing a decline in their value compared to gold. As Mises concluded:

> Attempts to carry out economic reforms from the monetary side can never amount to anything but an artificial stimulation of economic activity by an expansion of the circulation, and this, as must constantly be emphasized, must necessarily lead to crisis and depression. Recurring economic crises are nothing but the consequence of attempts, despite all the teachings of experience and all the warnings of the economists, to stimulate economic activity by means of additional credit.[6]

---

6   Ludwig von Mises, *The Theory of Money and Credit* (1934; Yale University Press, 1953), 9–21.

Mises had astutely identified the Achilles' heel of the classical gold standard: banking monopolies could engage in inflationary credit expansion, which would cause recessions and financial crises and increase the supply of money substitutes on the market. This, in turn, would cause a decline in the value of money substitutes that offset the rise in their value caused by increased productivity. He would be proven correct in the most devastating way imaginable within three years of the publication of his book.

The primitive nature of the classical gold standard would become apparent as people engaged in the same predictable herd behavior every few years, with little awareness or ability to change course. "This time is different" was a constant refrain among people involved in financial markets, as inflationary credit expansion created several large and destructive speculative bubbles.

The pattern repeated frequently: banking monopolies would extend credit cautiously at first, increasing the money supply imperceptibly to most people, with little impact on prices. Instead of declining slightly (as would be expected due to gold's low supply growth rate), prices would increase slightly. Most people would neither notice nor understand why. Asset prices would also rise, which would drive speculative manias, particularly in new economic sectors. The more cautious the inflation, the longer the inflationary monetary policy could go on, which in turn encouraged banks to become more inflationary and walk too close to the edge of the monetary cliff, so to speak. A perverse competitive dynamic would then develop between the banks, wherein the most conservative and most honest would lose their market share to the most reckless and most inflationary. Banks would gradually increase their credit creation until they reached a point where they created speculative manias and bubbles in various sectors of the economy, typically in new sectors and industries with rapid growth. At a certain point, like chickens coming home to roost, an excess of outstanding bills would come back to the bank for redemption in gold. The banks' vaults would not have enough gold for this.

In normal times, this would be considered fraud, and the owners and managers of the bank would be held criminally liable for issuing redeemable financial instruments that cannot be redeemed. But in the nineteenth century, with this practice growing increasingly common, and with banks increasingly powerful and influential thanks to the centralization of gold in their vaults, banks, governments, and bank-financed media and academia came to see this as an inexplicable quirk of the gold standard, and a temporary problem which could be rectified with the correct policies.

The broad outlines of the deal between governments and banks under the classical gold standard went like this: governments would pretend to be regulating banks but, in reality, they would simply use their oversight to enforce banking oligopolies, which would allow the bank significant leeway in expanding credit beyond its gold holdings. In exchange, the banks would use their expanded credit to purchase government bonds, which government regulators would treat as being as good as gold for the purposes of the bank's reserve requirements. The quid pro quo was great for banks, as it allowed them to create money without an opportunity cost. It was great for governments, too, as they could finance their wars or projects with the credit the banks used to lend to them. Government money allowed banks to leverage their customers' deposits to create more credit money and lend it to the government. This was usually done in a surreptitious manner, or advertised as being some genius scheme for the purpose of "boosting the economy," "stimulating demand," "bolstering public finance," or various other euphemisms. As long as this arrangement held, the purchasing power of money declined, or it did not rise as much as it could. When the issue of credit money increased significantly and redemption requests strained the bank, a bank run would happen, and its resolution would be a complicated legal matter in which blame could be ascribed to particular individuals but *not* to the inherently unstable system. But the vast majority of people did not understand the very simple reality of what was going on: their wealth was being stolen by banks and governments.

By suspending the redemption of gold, providing money from the public treasury, or issuing more government bonds to finance the insolvent bank, the bank could continue to operate, its financial instruments could maintain value, and a painful collapse was avoided. But these measures effectively transfer the bank's liabilities onto the shoulders of future taxpayers. These practices constituted a highly rewarding form of 'punishment' for financial mismanagement, and they encouraged banks to engage in more and riskier inflationary credit creation. They also succeeded in portraying the suspension of redemption as a necessary corrective measure for markets to resume operations, rather than acknowledging that it is a sure sign of fraud, embezzlement, or catastrophic loss. This repeated pattern meant that the classical gold standard was plagued with financial crises throughout the nineteenth century.

The pattern was set for government intervention in the banking system, and for a political dynamic as dangerous as the dynamic of banking leverage excess. The more leverage the banks took on, the more they became insolvent, and the more the banks' arms in the media, academia, and politics would call for more government intervention and bailouts of the banks. This, in turn, served to encourage further irresponsibility on the part of the banks, which then led to even greater government intervention and support. The process inevitably culminated in the centralization of reserves into a central bank owned by the major banking cartels and granted monopoly status by governments.

The result of this constant inflation is that the money supply grew a lot more than the growth in the supply of gold. This expansion would accelerate until the bubbles burst and a solvency crisis hit the affected bank, causing the money supply to shrink. Asset prices would rise during the bubble phase and crash during the bust, and consumer good prices largely behaved similarly, though less extremely.

The fundamental distinguishing feature of the classical gold standard was its reliance on central banks to facilitate its operations. As communication and transportation advanced in the nineteenth century, making trade across distances increasingly common, bank reserves had to be increasingly centralized to facilitate trade quickly. The average distance between a man and his money grew steadily as bank reserves became more centralized. Not only was he no longer taking possession of his money, but increasingly larger fractions of it were not even held in his own bank. Instead, they were held in the bank's head branch or the regional or national central bank. Without a quick and cheap mechanism for moving gold, it had to be held away from transacting parties.

At the time, the Bank of England was the center of the financial universe, and its pound sterling was recognized worldwide for being as good as gold. The creditworthiness of the British government, its powerful military, and its unrivaled global payments settlement network had given it the supreme position in the global financial order, with around half of global foreign exchange reserves held in sterling.

The Bank of England operated a gold exchange standard for British colonies worldwide. Under the gold exchange standard, foreign central banks were relieved of the trouble of having to perform clearance of physical gold or take custody of gold by instead using the paper notes and credit lines of the Bank of England. As more remote territories joined the global economy and traded with one another, it became far more convenient for them to deal with the world through the Bank of England. Gold at the Bank of England was faster than gold outside it. As the British Empire expanded, the clearance market for the Bank of England grew larger and more liquid, making it increasingly sensible for global banks to rely on a balance at the Bank of England for global trade.

Since the colonies used the bank to settle their international payments, they were expected to hold significant amounts of these reserves at the Bank of England and not seek redemption in gold. Since taking custody of their gold was expensive, most central banks rarely did it. The more countries placed their gold at the Bank of England, the more the Bank of England could expand the supply of its paper and credit without commensurate gold backing. This allowed the bank a certain inflationary margin, to the point that by 1913, the ratio of official reserves to liabilities to foreign monetary authorities was only 31%.[7] As long as fewer than 69% of the liabilities were seeking redemption at any point in time, this arrangement worked fine. The Bank of England used its reserves to issue more liabilities, benefiting its shareholders and the British government, which borrowed from it at the lowest interest rates in the world. The bank had exported its inflation to the colonies, financing itself and the British government by devaluing the savings of people worldwide but placing itself in a precarious liquidity position. So long as most colonies, depositors, and paper holders did not ask to convert their bank accounts and notes to gold, liquidity would not be a problem.

---

7   Lawrence Officer, "Gold Standard," in *EH.Net Encyclopedia*, ed. Robert Whaples, March 26, 2008.

Even in the absence of an official central bank, the gold standard required the progressive centralization of reserves to facilitate clearance and settlement across increasingly long distances, as was the case in the United States, where major national banks held the lion's share of reserves. After Russia's central bank switched from a silver standard to a gold standard in 1897, the US became the last remaining major economy on a gold standard without a central bank. This anomaly would change on Christmas in 1913, as all the world's major economies then had central banks on a gold standard. Only nine months later, centralization of reserves, monopolization of banking, and the increasing tendency for inflation through credit creation would all add fuel to the fire of a war in the Balkans that would become humanity's most brutal and consequential, threatening to incinerate human civilization itself.

II.

The Great War

The relative stability of the monetary order from 1873 coincided with the stability of the political order. As the world traded one money, it also approached an ideal of one economic unit, with declining restrictions on trade and reductions in military conflicts. Relations between the major powers continued to improve over time, and the prospect of war became increasingly less likely. Britain and France, bitter rivals for centuries, signed the Entente Cordiale in 1904, an agreement that delineated British and French colonies in North Africa, prevented conflict between the countries, and led to growing cooperation between the two empires. Anglo-Russian relationships had also improved with the signing of the Anglo-Russian Convention in 1907, in which Britain and Russia delineated their Asian colonies to avoid conflict.

The Blaze of Splendor

Britain's relationship with Germany was also improving. Through royal marriages of her children to European monarchs, Britain's Queen Victoria was the grandmother of many royals across the continent, most notably the German Kaiser Wilhelm II, whose coronation in 1888 marked an auspicious moment for British-German relations, as he was the eldest of the forty-two grandchildren of Queen Victoria through her eldest daughter, Princess Victoria. At his birth, Wilhelm II was third in line for succession to the Prussian throne and sixth in line for succession to the British throne. When Queen Victoria was on her deathbed in 1901, Wilhelm II, who loved her dearly, traveled to be by her side. It is said that she passed away in his arms. He carried her coffin at her funeral.

After its victory in the Franco-Prussian War, Germany focused on consolidating its empire in the European mainland, and Britain expanded its empire everywhere else. The two countries approached the twentieth century with their interests harmonized and the threat of war subsiding. An alliance between the two great powers was even seriously considered at the end of the century.

Between 1890 and 1902, three potential problems arose in British-German relations. Kaiser Wilhelm II removed Bismarck as chancellor and ignored his advice to avoid pursuing a foreign empire, which inevitably aroused the distrust and discontent of the British, who had the world's biggest empire and did not want Germany competing with them for territories. Wilhelm II also became obsessed with building a navy to support the empire, provoking more animosity from Britain, which had the world's largest and most powerful navy, controlling the entrance to the North Sea, Germany's gateway to the world.

The death of Queen Victoria in 1901 and the ascension of her son Edward VII to the throne added to the friction in British-German relations. Kaiser Wilhelm II had a jealous rivalry with his uncle Edward, who had always looked down on him as a young man and his nephew, rather than treating him as an equal, the ruling monarch of a superpower. Known as "the possessor of the least inhibited tongue in Europe,"[8] Wilhelm II had suffered injury during

---

8   Barbara W. Tuchman, *The Guns of August: The Outbreak of World War I*, Barbara W. Tuchman's Great War Series (1962; Ballantine Books, 1990).

his birth, which gave him a withered left arm, and, some speculate, caused him to be erratic, impulsive, and emotional. His behavior created needless tension between Germany and Britain that threatened to sour the increasingly cordial and cooperative international order. In an infamous interview with *The Daily Telegraph* in October 1908, Kaiser Wilhelm II's attempts to win over British public opinion backfired, as his outbursts created resentment not only in Britain but also France, Russia, and Japan. Wilhelm's naval and imperial ambitions alarmed the British, and he grew increasingly concerned that Britain's rapprochement with France and Russia was meant to encircle and suffocate Germany.

These fears were alleviated in the second decade of the twentieth century. After King Edward VII's death, Kaiser Wilhelm II attended his funeral on May 20, 1910, which helped mend relations with the British people and royalty. A popular king at the zenith of his empire, Edward's funeral procession drew an estimated three to five million people, with 35,000 soldiers lining the funeral's route. From across Europe and the world, monarchs packed the palace in the largest gathering of monarchs to date. The astonishing spectacle and sense of solidarity and togetherness suggested the superpowers were entering a period of extended peace and friendship. Barbara Tuchman immortalized the occasion in a famous passage of her book, *The Guns of August*:

> So gorgeous was the spectacle on the May morning of 1910 when nine kings rode in the funeral of Edward VII of England that the crowd, waiting in hushed and black-clad awe, could not keep back gasps of admiration. In scarlet and blue and green and purple, three by three the sovereigns rode through the palace gates, with plumed helmets, gold braid, crimson sashes, and jeweled orders flashing in the sun. After them came five heirs apparent, forty more imperial or royal highnesses, seven queens—four dowager and three regnant—and a scattering of special ambassadors from uncrowned countries. Together they represented seventy nations in the greatest assemblage of royalty and rank ever gathered in one place and, of its kind, the last. The muffled tongue of Big Ben tolled nine by the clock as the cortege left the palace, but on history's clock it was sunset, and the

sun of the old world was setting in a dying blaze of splendor never to be seen again.[9]

The new king, George V, ascended to the throne in 1910 with his first cousin, Wilhelm II, ruling Germany, and his first cousins, Emperor Nicholas II and Empress Alexandra, ruling Russia. In June 1914, Britain and Germany arrived at an understanding that eased their differences over the Baghdad Railway. Even the naval rivalry between the two powers seemed like it could be resolved after extensive negotiations from 1912 to 1914.

In 1913, Kaiser Wilhelm II's daughter, Princess Victoria Louise, married. Her wedding was also a great gathering of European monarchs, suggesting further amicability. Any semblance of Anglo-German tension looked to have disappeared in the fateful final week of June 1914. The German Kaiser had joined the festivities of the annual Kiel Regatta Week, where he inaugurated the new Kiel Canal locks. That year's regatta was a historical occasion, for it saw the invitation of Britain's Royal Navy's Second Battle Squadron, which comprised the four newest and most powerful dreadnoughts in the world. As the German Navy had grown to become the second biggest navy in the world, the invitation of the biggest navy to this occasion signaled that the two navies had found a way to peacefully coexist, and the naval rivalry between them was coming to an end. Kaiser Wilhelm II, who was bestowed the rank of admiral in the British Navy by his grandmother, wore his British admiralty uniform to inspect the British warships. The evening of Saturday, June 27, saw raucous parties as British and German sailors visited each other's boats, drank together, engaged in friendly boxing matches, and partied into the morning of the fateful day of June 28. At 6 p.m. on that day, with sailors still nursing their hangovers, news would arrive of the assassination of Archduke Franz Ferdinand, heir to the throne of the Austro-Hungarian Empire. The world would never be the same.

The news would take the joy out of the events of the week and cause Kaiser Wilhelm to cut his visit short. He left Kiel the next day. King George V then

---

9   Barbara W. Tuchman, "The Death of Jaurès," in *The Proud Tower: A Portrait of the World Before the War, 1890-1914*, Barbara W. Tuchman's Great War Series (Random House, 1966), 451–515.

sent a message delivered by the commander of the British squadron leaving Kiel on June 30:[10]

> Friends Today
> Friends in Future
> Friends Forever

It was almost completely inconceivable for anyone in Kiel that these two friendly navies would be at war in a mere five weeks, but that is exactly what happened. It was an astonishing turn of events. Within the space of one week between July and August, Europe went from optimism that Austria and Serbia were going to find a diplomatic solution to their quarrel to an all-out war with the five major powers in conflict: Austria-Hungary, Russia, Germany, France, and Britain, and three more powers to follow over the coming months: the Ottoman Empire, Italy, and Japan. To get a sense of just how unlikely this was at the time, note that the Serbian-Austrian crisis had not been mentioned in the British parliament for four weeks after it happened. Hardly anybody had even thought this affair carried any significance for the British. On July 24, British Prime Minister Herbert Asquith wrote to his lover Venetia, "We are within measurable, or imaginable, distance of a real Armageddon. Happily there seems to be no reason why we should be anything more than spectators."[11] On July 27, a day before Austria-Hungary declared war on Serbia, Chancellor of the Exchequer David Lloyd George stated that there could be no question of taking part in any war, and he was aware of no minister who was in favor.[12]

---

10 Patrick J. Buchanan, *Churchill, Hitler, and "The Unnecessary War": How Britain Lost Its Empire and the West Lost the World* (Three Rivers Press, 2008), 85–87.

11 Herbert Henry Asquith, *H.H. Asquith, Letters to Venetia Stanley*, ed. Michael G. Brock and Eleanor Brock (Oxford University Press, 1982), 123.

12 Martin Gilbert, *First World War* (HarperCollins, 1995), 23.

The Sleepwalkers

On August 4, Germany invaded Belgium, and on August 5, the first battle of the Great War began: the Battle of Liège, which pitted the German army against the Belgian army. Liège fell on August 16, and the German army continued its march through Belgium on its way to France, where one of the most brutal warfronts in history awaited them against the French and British armies.

On August 12, 1914, the Austro-Hungarian military under the command of General Oskar Potiorek launched its first offensive into Serbia. Hundreds of thousands of soldiers were killed and injured on both sides as Serbia succeeded in fending off the Austro-Hungarian attack, in one of the greatest upsets in military history. Soon after, on August 17, Russia invaded Austrian East Galicia and East Prussia, where it suffered large losses in a successful German counter-attack. At the Battle of Tannenberg, which took place the following week, Germany achieved a crushing defeat of Russia, setting Russia on the wrong foot from the start of the war. On May 23, 1915, Italy declared war on Austria-Hungary, opening a new front.

Perhaps no better testament to the senselessness of this war existed than the Christmas Truce of 1914, when German and British soldiers on the Western Front both decided to stop fighting over the Christmas holidays (without having received orders to do so) and crossed enemy lines to socialize and exchange gifts. They even played a game of football together before going back to their trenches and resuming their attempts to slaughter each other. The absurdity of the war was palpable: German soldiers, many of whom had worked in England and grown fond of the country, had learned to play football there. They were now in France to fight the British army of King George V, their Kaiser's cousin. Germany had no plans to take over Britain, and Britain had no plans to take over Germany, so neither of these sets of soldiers felt a serious threat from one another. None of the soldiers could quite understand how things had spiraled so quickly into a large-scale war, nor could the diplomats and intellectuals in the respective countries explain it either. The Christmas truce laid bare the truth that these soldiers had nothing against each other, had nothing to gain from fighting this war, and could see no reason to continue it.

Whatever rivalry existed between these nations could very well be acted out peacefully on the football pitch at the cost of disciplined training rather than the blood of an entire generation.

In the aftermath of the war, virtually nobody could explain how the major powers had gone to war against each other. There was a sense that this was a disaster into which the major powers inadvertently sleepwalked, as historian Christopher Clark put it, "watchful but unseeing, haunted by dreams, yet blind to the reality of the horror they were about to bring into the world."

After the assassination of the Austrian crown prince in Sarajevo by Serbian nationalists, Austria seemed overconfident in its ability to bring Serbia to heel. Russians were extremely cavalier about smashing the Austrians in defense of Serbia. The Germans, gripped by paranoia that the British, French, and Russians were aiming to destroy Germany, seemed to think they could take on France, then Russia, and expect Britain to stay out. The French vastly overestimated their ability to fight the Germans and regain Alsace-Lorraine, and the British imagined their entry would decisively and quickly settle the war.

They were all unfathomably wrong.

There is a compelling case to be made that all parties deserve some blame for their overreaction and instigation. It is easy for historians to simply cast blame everywhere and virtue-signal about peace being good and war being bad. Yet, there was also a very real historical context in which this tragedy was born, one that has its roots in nineteenth-century military conflicts and alliances, as well as in the imperial ambitions of monarchs who had grown callous to the true cost of their ambitions in men and treasure, thanks to the enormous hoards of gold sitting in their capital city's central banks, close to their thrones, constituting the majority of their nations' liquid wealth. While the mass slaughter can never be justified, it can at least be understood with the benefit of hindsight and a treasure trove of secret documents released over the decades.

III.

Tsargrad

Whoever possesses Constantinople ought to rule the world.

— Napoleon Bonaparte

The Russian Empire was already in a precarious state as it entered the Great War. Tsar Nicholas II had taken over power at the young age of twenty-six, following his father, Alexander III's, unexpected death at forty-nine. Early in his reign, Nicholas complained to his Minister of Foreign Affairs, saying, "I know nothing. The late emperor did not foresee his death and did not let me in on any government business."[13] Throughout his reign, he seemed more interested in validating this statement than overcoming it. Tsar Nicholas II aroused discontent with his amateurish handling of Russia's war with Japan as well as his decidedly autocratic rule at home.

Witte's Golden Wisdom

Sergei Witte was an important and outstanding Russian statesman bequeathed to Nicholas II by his father, Alexander III, who had made Witte Minister of

---

13 Dominic Lieven, *Nicholas II: Emperor of All the Russias* (Pimlico, 1993), 42.

Finance in 1892. On his deathbed in 1894, Alexander told his son to heed the advice of Witte. Witte remained Minister of Finance until 1903, during which time he nearly doubled the government's revenue.[14] In 1897, he put Russia on the gold standard, redefining the ruble in terms of gold rather than its traditional denomination of silver, which had witnessed a significant reduction in its market price over the previous three decades. Moving to the gold standard led to a surge of international investment, and Witte oversaw the mass industrialization of Russia, including the building of the Trans-Siberian Railway. In 1900, Russia produced three times as much iron, and twice as much coal, as it had in 1890.[15]

Witte was adeptly managing Russian advances in the Far East, but Nicholas II would ignore his father's advice to listen to Witte, firing him in 1903 and letting his policy in Manchuria and Korea fall under the sway of ambitious, belligerent nationalists. After being fired as Minister of Finance, Witte was appointed Chairman of the Committee of Ministers, a role that was supposed to be more ceremonial. However, circumstances made it a very important role in the years to come. It was a catastrophic mistake to fire Witte, and it would set in motion the chain of events that would eventually cost Tsar Nicholas everything. While Witte constantly warned about the dangers of provoking Japan by extending Russian influence into Korea, Russia's affairs in its Far East were now handled by ambitious reactionaries who sought to acquire as many resources as possible from the region, while neglecting the threat of Japanese retaliation. They were very cavalier in their approach to Japan, not expecting what they viewed as an inferior race to attack a European power. After several Japanese proposals for an understanding over Korea and Manchuria were rebuffed by the Russians, Japan surprised the Russians by attacking their heavily outnumbered forces in Port Arthur and declaring war against Russia on February 8, 1904. Russia may have been a great terrestrial and naval power, but its military and navy were in Europe. Manchuria was a world away, and it would take the Russian Navy nine months to mobilize from Europe to China, around the Cape of Good Hope. Meanwhile, terrestrial supply lines consisted of a

---

14 Hugh Chisholm, ed., "Witte, Serge Julievich, Count," in *Encyclopædia Britannica*, 1911, 28:762–63.

15 David Warnes, *Russia: A Modern History* (Collins Educational, 1992), 6.

single railway track that ran 9,200 kilometers from St. Petersburg to Port Arthur in Manchuria. The Tsar's terrestrial ambition had exceeded his military's capacity to back it up, and he had not even planned for the contingency of a Japanese attack. The Japanese pounced mercilessly, destroying Russia's meager Pacific fleet and then laying siege to Port Arthur in August of 1904.

Even as the war continued decisively in favor of Japan, which won battle after battle and secured more Manchurian territory, the Tsar continued to delude himself, supremely confident that his military's racial superiority would guarantee him victory. He sent Russian soldiers to slaughter with little in the way of coherent plans, as his German cousin Wilhelm II egged him on and harangued him for considering peace. Wilhelm II repeatedly told Nicholas II how important it was for him to be the bulwark of the white race against the yellow peril and implored him to destroy the Asian races before they turned to Europe. Behind the racist, pugnacious rhetoric of Wilhelm II lay an ulterior motive. Wilhelm wanted Russia to expand in Asia, thereby bringing it into conflict with France. Doing so would result in the end of the alliance between Russia and France in Europe, which was Germany's existential nightmare. Nicholas II fell for his cousin's ruse and pushed on aggressively in East Asia, imagining Japan would not dare to challenge him.[16]

Tsar Nicholas saw war as an inevitable God-given victory, ignoring the enormous cost as well as American efforts for mediation.[17] Fearing the humiliation of signing a peace treaty on the terms of an inferior race, Tsar Nicholas continued to double down on a losing war, deciding to send most of his Baltic fleet to Japan to relieve the siege of Port Arthur. They left in October 1904, and after a tortuously long journey rife with obstacles, they were ambushed by the Japanese on May 27, 1905 in the Tsushima Strait between Korea and Japan. The Russian fleet was completely devastated. It would go down as history's only decisive battle between modern steel battleship fleets.[18]

---

16 Turner Collins, "Russo-Japanese War: How Racism Ended European Hegemony in Asia," TheCollector, April 12, 2022.

17 Rotem Kowner, *Historical Dictionary of the Russo-Japanese War* (The Scarecrow Press, 2006).

18 Milan N. Vego, *Joint Operational Warfare: Theory and Practice*, 1st ed. (Government Printing Office, 2009), V–76.

Tsar Nicholas was playing tennis when he received a telegram informing him of the destruction of his navy. He read the message, put it in his pocket, and continued his tennis match.[19] Russia had practically destroyed its expensive and critically important navy, months away from its European home, in pursuit of unimportant, faraway land. Only then did Tsar Nicholas accept American offers of mediation, and he appointed Sergei Witte as head of the Russian delegation. Two years after firing him had precipitated the war, Nicholas II went back to his father's sage advisor to extricate him and Russia from the consequences of his actions. US President Teddy Roosevelt arranged for the Portsmouth Peace Conference in August in New Hampshire, but Tsar Nicholas was initially very intransigent, instructing the delegates to agree to no territorial concessions or reparations. Eventually, Sergei Witte masterfully succeeded in securing a deal that ended the war while ceding some of the territory the Japanese wanted, without having to pay an indemnity. He had managed to stop the senseless sacrifice of Russian lives and treasure by disobeying Tsar Nicholas' instructions and avoiding too many concessions to the Japanese.

The failure of the unpopular war against Japan had increased opposition to Nicholas II. The people of Russia were angry at conscription, which had resulted in the deaths of tens of thousands, as well as the enormous expenditure on attempting to secure faraway Chinese territory, which was insignificant to their lives.[20] Protests increased around the country, culminating in the Bloody Sunday massacre in January 1905, when soldiers of the Imperial Guard opened fire on unarmed demonstrators seeking to present a petition to Tsar Nicholas at the Winter Palace in St. Petersburg, killing and injuring hundreds. The opposition was emboldened, and thousands of opposition groups and worker cooperatives across the country simmered with malcontent and revolutionary and Marxist ideas. Strikes, riots, and even military mutinies increased. In his palaces, Nicholas II remained serene in his misplaced confidence that he was divinely inspired and could do no wrong.

---

19 Lieven, *Nicholas II: Emperor of All the Russias*, 127.
20 Richard M. Connaughton, *The War of the Rising Sun and Tumbling Bear: A Military History of the Russo-Japanese War, 1904–5* (Routledge, 1988), 109, 342.

After the October 1905 strike paralyzed the Russian train network, Witte outlined the two options available to the Tsar: "Either he must put himself at the head of the popular movement for freedom by making concessions to it, or he must institute a military dictatorship and suppress by naked force for the whole of the opposition."[21] Witte was very clearly in favor of the first option.

Tsar Nicholas would write in his diary:

> Through all those horrible days I constantly met with Witte. We very often met in the early morning to part only in the evening when night fell. There were only two ways open: to find an energetic soldier to crush the rebellion by sheer force. There would be time to breathe then but as likely as not, one would have to use force again in a few months, and that would mean rivers of blood and in the end we should be where we started.

> The other way out would be to give to the people their civil rights, freedom of speech and press, also to have all laws confirmed by a state Duma—that of course would be a constitution. Witte defends this energetically. He says that, while it is not without risk, it is the only way out at the present moment. Almost everybody I had an opportunity of consulting is of the same opinion.[22]

Nicholas II, ever obtuse, would not listen to Witte, his father, or anybody he consulted. He wanted to impose a military dictatorship, and for it, he chose the man who had the combination of loyalty, popularity, and respect of the armed forces necessary for this crucial job. Grand Duke Nicholas Nikolaevich was the cousin of Nicholas II's father and a highly decorated officer who had been uninvolved with the Japanese war, thus preserving his popularity and respect among the military and the Russian people. To distinguish the two Nicholases, the Tsar was known as Nicholas the Short, while the Grand Duke was known as Nicholas

---

21 Sergei Witte, *The Memoirs of Count Witte*, trans. Abraham Yarmolinsky (Doubleday, 1921), 450–451.

22 Robert K. Massie, *Nicholas and Alexandra: The Classic Account of the Fall of the Romanov Dynasty* (Random House, 2000), 15.

the Tall, as he stood at 1.98 meters tall. The Grand Duke had urged the Tsar to implement the reforms suggested by Witte. But Nicholas the Short summoned the Tall to the palace and tasked him with becoming a military dictator instead. The Grand Duke drew his pistol and pointed it at his own head, and told the Tsar that he would shoot himself there and then if the Tsar did not accept Witte's plan and retract his plans to institute a military dictatorship. The Tsar succumbed to the Grand Duke's threat, sparing Russia a military dictatorship.[23]

The result of agreeing to Nicholas the Tall's ultimatum and Witte's reforms was the Tsar's October Manifesto, which provided for freedom of conscience, speech, meeting, and association. It also required Duma approval for new laws. However, it kept in the hands of the Tsar the power to dissolve the Duma, appoint ministers, and most importantly and tragically, declare war. The Tsar also created an upper chamber, the State Council, half of whose members he would nominate. The Tsar was not happy with the watered-down Duma, and so he dissolved it twice in quick succession. The radicals were also not appeased and continued to plot against the government. Witte became Russia's first prime minister, but his position was untenable; he resigned in April 1906 and was appointed to the upper chamber of parliament. A third and fourth Dumas fared slightly better than their two predecessors, but political unrest continued to plague Russia, and revolutionaries continued to become more emboldened in their demands. Separatist elements in border provinces became stronger and more emboldened, adding to the trouble of the Tsar. In his memoirs, Witte wrote of this period:

> The policy of converting all Russian subjects into "true Russians" is not the ideal which will weld all the heterogeneous elements of the Empire into one body politic. It might be better for us Russians, I concede, if Russia were a nationally uniform country and not a heterogeneous Empire. To achieve that goal there is but one way, namely to give up our border provinces, for these will never put up with the policy of ruthless Russification. But that measure our ruler will, of course, never consider.[24]

---

23 Greg King and Penny Wilson, *The Fate of the Romanovs* (John Wiley & Sons, 2003), 11.
24 Witte, *The Memoirs of Count Witte*.

Dreams of Tsargrad

Rather than seek to solidify his grip over the core of his empire, the Tsar continued to press for its expansion. Having seemingly learned nothing from the calamity of the Russo-Japanese war, the tensions in the Balkans offered Tsar Nicholas the opportunity to repeat the same mistakes, only this time, at a larger scale. On its face, the decision of Nicholas II to go to war seems the oddest among all European rulers. His empire, monarchy, navy, and military were not in their best shape when he recklessly drove them into a war against three of the world's largest militaries, and over a part of the Balkans with no direct borders with Russia, offering no credible threat to his empire. He had already suffered one devastating defeat during his reign, and he had no official defense treaty with Serbia obliging him to defend her. He had survived a revolution in 1905 and was becoming less popular as revolutionaries aimed to unseat him, and his trusted appointees and family members had grown increasingly bold in opposing him. To mobilize for a confrontation with Germany in that situation seemed insane. Whatever the fate of Serbia, it was hard to imagine Russia could emerge from such a war without enormous losses. But with military conscription compulsory and the gold standard centralized enough for the Tsar to suspend it, the cost seemed tolerable to Nicholas II in his palaces.

Describing Nicholas II, one of his biographers, Robert Warth, writes:

> His tolerance if not preference for charlatans and adventurers extended to grave matters of external policy, and his vacillating conduct and erratic decisions aroused misgivings and occasional alarm among his more conventional advisers. The foreign ministry itself was not a bastion of diplomatic expertise. Patronage and "connections" were the keys to appointment and promotion.[25]

---

25 Robert D. Warth, *Nicholas II: The Life and Reign of Russia's Last Monarch* (Praeger, 1997), 47.

While nowhere near justifying or validating the choice to go to war, historians would soon be able to explain and decipher the motivations behind this calamitous decision, thanks to the release of classified documents from the Russian Foreign Ministry after the war.[26]

Russia had taken a keen interest in the Balkans because of its long-term goal of seeking to control the Turkish straits, the Bosphorus and the Dardanelles, which connect the Mediterranean Sea with the Black Sea, where Russia's only warm-water seaports lay. Without the ability to send its navy through the Turkish straits, Russia's navy was immobile for half of the year, during which its Baltic seaports were frozen. By controlling these straits, Russia would be able to move its warships in and out of the Black Sea and grow its empire. With its position straddling two continents and controlling the Turkish Straits, control of Constantinople had been of enormous strategic importance for centuries, during which empires vied for it. Napoleon had famously remarked that controlling Constantinople would mean controlling the world, and the Great War was a testament to his foresight, as Russian attempts to conquer Constantinople would embroil the planet in its biggest war ever.

Conquering Constantinople was also a centuries-old religious dream for the Russian Orthodox Church, as it sought to reclaim the seat of the ancient Byzantine Empire from the Muslim Ottomans who had conquered it. Ivan III had married the niece of the last Byzantine emperor in 1472 and adopted the double-headed eagle of the Byzantine Empire as Russia's symbol.[27] Even though they never conquered it and no Russian Tsar ever ruled it, Russians referred to Constantinople as Tsargrad: "the city of the emperor." Nowhere in history has a foreign nation yearned for a city as much as Russia yearned to rule Constantinople. And it was the control of Constantinople that was the main driver of Russian foreign policy and their quest to rush into the Great War.[28]

In 1908, when Austria-Hungary sought to annex Bosnia-Herzegovina, Austria's Foreign Minister Alois Lexa von Aehrenthal met with Russian

---

26 In reality, it was the Bolsheviks who released all these documents as they discovered them in the late 1910s and early 1920s.

27 Cyrus Hamlin, "The Dream of Russia," *The Atlantic*, December 1, 1886.

28 Sean McMeekin, *The Russian Origins of the First World War* (Belknap Press, 2011).

Foreign Minister Alexander Izvolsky and offered a bargain: if Russia were to support Austrian annexation of Bosnia and Herzegovina, Austria would support the opening of the Turkish straits to Russia. The two men agreed on this in principle, but no official agreement was signed. Izvolsky said he would write the conclusions of the meeting and send them to von Aehrenthal, but he never did.[29] When Austria announced the annexation of Bosnia on October 6, 1908, it triggered an international outcry of condemnation, and even the Russian public was livid. This led Izvolsky to deny he had made such an agreement with his Austrian counterpart. Christopher Clark provided the context for Izvolsky's behavior in his book *The Sleepwalkers*:

> Yet the evidence suggests that the crisis took the course it did because Iz-volsky lied in the most extravagant fashion in order to save his job and reputation. The Russian foreign minister had made two serious errors of judgement. He had assumed, firstly, that London would support his de-mand for the opening of the Turkish Straits to Russian warships. He had also grossly underestimated the impact of the annexation on Russian na-tionalist opinion. According to one account, he was initially perfectly calm when news of the annexation reached him in Paris on 8 October 1908. It was only during his stay in London a few days later, when the British proved uncooperative and he got wind of the press response in St. Peters-burg, that he realized his error, panicked, and began to construct himself as Aehrenthal's dupe.[30]

With the Turkish straits not forthcoming, Izvolsky developed a deep op-position to the Austro-Hungarian annexation of Bosnia and Herzegovina. He called for an international conference to solve the crisis. This resulted in Germany threatening war in defense of its ally, Austria. With Russians still smarting from the Japanese defeat, they decided to back down to avoid a German confrontation. Izvolsky had humiliatingly discovered that the diplomatic path to opening the

---

29 Luigi Albertini, *The Origins of the War of 1914*, vol. 3 (Enigma Books, 2005), 207.
30 Christopher Clark, *The Sleepwalkers* (Harper Perennial, 2012), 86.

Turkish Straits was a dead end, blocked by the intransigent Germans. From that moment onwards, Russian foreign policy sought to acquire Tsargrad through military means. They set about laying the groundwork for the war that would neutralize German opposition and finally get them the jewel of Constantinople.

The debacle led to Izvolsky's resignation as foreign minister, and he was subsequently appointed Russian Ambassador to France. Although a demotion on the surface, the new appointment allowed Izvolsky to continue playing a leading role in the Russian quest to take Constantinople by recruiting France to the cause. The alliance with France was an important element of Russian foreign policy in this period, as they saw France as a natural enemy of Germany and Alsace-Lorraine as a great pretext to mobilize public opinion for war.

The increasing detente between France and Britain also meant that an alliance with France would help recruit Britain to a war in which Russia was involved. Only if France and Britain entered the war could Russia realistically expect to defeat the German and Austrian militaries, and Izvolsky worked tirelessly to that end. He secured large amounts of Russian funding for French agents in politics and the press.[31] Most significantly, Russia supported the election campaign of President Raymond Poincaré because he had been willing to go to war with them against Germany, while his opponent, Joseph Caillaux, favored staying out of war. Between 1900 and 1914, Russia had given more than 6.5 million francs per year to Arthur Raffalovich,[32] the Russian financial agent in Paris who distributed the money to the French Press, and to French Minister of Finance Louis-Lucien Klotz, to promote the candidacy of Poincaré and his pro-Russian policies, to provide favorable publicity for the many Russian loan requests from the French capital markets, and to push for the expansion of mandatory military service from two to three years.[33]

France had signed treaties with Russia in 1891 and 1893. In August 1912, when Poincaré was the Prime Minister, he made a trip to Russia with Izvolsky,

---

31 Jack Beatty, *The Lost History of 1914: How the Great War Was Not Inevitable* (A&C Black, 2012).

32 Eric Toussaint and Nathan Legrand, "The French Press in the Pay of the Tsar," CADTM, August 4, 2017.

33 McMeekin, *The Russian Origins of the First World War*, 50–52.

the mastermind behind the Russian-French alliance. On this trip, in a secret agreement, Russia convinced Poincaré to concentrate the French Navy in the Eastern Mediterranean to support the Russian fleet in the Black Sea, a tactic suggesting an attack on Constantinople was in the plans very early. France concurrently made an agreement with Britain, whereby France would withdraw its navy from its northern shores to the Mediterranean, and Britain would defend these shores against a possible German attack. This arrangement had two significant effects for Russia: it made the French navy available to help them take Constantinople, and it obliged Britain to enter a war against Germany, as Britain could not tolerate German control of the French northern coast. In September 1912, Poincaré assured Russian Foreign Minister Sergey Sazonov that if Germany helped Austria in a conflict in the Balkans, France would join Russia in a war against Germany and Austria-Hungary. In the same month, Izvolsky met with King George V and his Foreign Secretary, Edward Grey, and both confirmed that they stood ready to help Russia in a war against Germany.

On Poincaré's visit to Russia in July 1914 during the Serbian-Austrian crisis, Christopher Clark wrote:

> Poincaré had come to preach the gospel of firmness and his words had fallen on ready ears. Firmness in this context meant an intransigent opposition to any Austrian measure against Serbia. At no point do the sources suggest that Poincaré or his Russian interlocutors gave any thought whatsoever to what measures Austria-Hungary might legitimately be entitled to take in the aftermath of the assassinations.[34]

Because of Poincaré's trip to Russia, France played a relatively minor role during the escalation of the crisis in late July. With Germany disrupting their marine communications during their return from Russia between July 23 and 29.[35] But they had already done their part to stoke the flames.

---

34 Clark, *The Sleepwalkers*, 449–50.
35 David Fromkin, *Europe's Last Summer: Why the World Went to War in 1914* (Vintage, 2005), 194.

Izvolsky's Powder Kegs

American Colonel Edward House visited Europe in the spring of 1914. In his report to President Woodrow Wilson, he explained the situation as he saw it, astutely and prophetically:

> The situation is extraordinary. It is militarism run stark mad. Unless someone acting for you can bring about a different understanding, there is some day to be an awful cataclysm. No one in Europe can do it. There is too much hatred, too many jealousies. Whenever England consents, France and Russia will close in on Germany and Austria. England does not want Germany wholly crushed, for she would then have to reckon alone with her ancient enemy, Russia; but if Germany insists upon an ever increasing navy, then England will have no choice. The best chance for peace is an understanding between England and Germany in regard to naval armaments and yet there is some disadvantage to us by these two getting too close.[36]

One must stand in awe of the cunning of the Russian diplomats, particularly Izvolsky and Sazonov, who had set the stage by 1912 for the war they needed. They had managed to tailor the French-British relationship to their benefit, relocating the French fleet to the Eastern Mediterranean, where it could serve no function other than to help Russia take Constantinople, leaving the French northern coast exposed to Germany, forcing Britain to step in and defend France in the event of a German attack. Izvolsky and Sazonov had placed the powder kegs in place, and all that was needed was the spark to detonate them. But time was not on the Russians' side. As Germany and Britain reached agreements over the Baghdad railway, Russia saw the window of opportunity closing for it to recruit Britain to its desired war.

The assassination of Franz Ferdinand was the spark Izvolsky's powder kegs needed. Historians are still in dispute about the extent of Russian involvement

---

36　Edward Mandell House, "The Intimate Papers of Colonel House 1858-1938," Memo from May 29, 1914 to President Woodrow Wilson, ed. Charles Seymour (1971), 2.

in the assassination.[37] While it is indisputable that there was official Serbian involvement, Russian guilt has not been established beyond a shadow of a doubt, although the circumstantial evidence abounds, the motive exists, and Russia's extremely well-rehearsed reaction hints at it strongly. There were good relations between the Serbian and Russian militaries and intelligence services. It is also evident that Russia encouraged Serbian nationalism and pan-Slavic expansionism, which it viewed as an effective means to undermine the Austro-Hungarian Empire in the Balkans and help clear the way for Russian control of the Turkish Straits. Whatever the reality of Russia's involvement, what remains abundantly clear is that Russia was ready to capitalize on the assassination.

Although Russia had no treaties with Serbia obliging it to intervene, Russian media emphasized the importance of Slavic solidarity and the need not to abandon Serbia. Russian diplomats made it clear to Austrians that they opposed their attempts to launch a war against Serbia. Russia's secret alliances with France and England required that it would appear as if Germany had attacked first. Public opinion was still important in these countries, and the population, parliaments, and cabinets were highly unlikely to support a Russian war of aggression. The assassination, carried out by individuals with no official relation to Russia, seemed perfectly designed to invoke war on the terms Russia wanted.

The Austrian Crown Council was livid over the assassination, and the only debate was whether to launch a war or issue an ultimatum that Serbia would reject, which would justify the war. The only dissenting voice was the Hungarian Prime Minister, Tisza, who warned that a war would lead to Russian intervention, and that would result in a world war. His warnings fell on deaf ears and the Austrians marched determined to disaster.[38] On July 23, Austria-Hungary issued an ultimatum to Serbia with ten demands and an expiry day of July 25.

Before Serbia had even responded to Austria's ultimatum, the Tsar convened the Council of Ministers for a meeting on July 24 and 25, during which he put the Russian army on "alert." However, the Russian army had no plans

---

37 Fay, Sidney Bradshaw. *The Origins of the World War: Before Sarajevo: Underlying Causes of the War.* (Macmillan, 1929)

38 Fromkin, *Europe's Last Summer: Why the World Went to War in 1914,* 165.

for partial mobilization, and in practice, the military was put on full mobilization for war, which Nicholas confirmed on July 30, two days after Austria declared war on Serbia.

Chief of the Russian army's mobilization section, Sergei Dobrorolski, described the significance of the mobilization on July 25:

> the war was already a settled matter, and the whole flood of telegrams between the Governments of Germany and Russia represented merely the stage setting of a historical drama.[39]

Not only had Russia mobilized against Austria, but it had also mobilized its troops in Poland, which meant it was preparing for war with Germany. The French ambassador reported the mobilization to the French government on July 25.[40]

In those days, it was well accepted that mobilization meant war. It took a considerable amount of time to mobilize troops, and the logistics involved were extremely elaborate and costly. Once one country mobilized, its neighbors had no choice but to mobilize as well, because a mobilized army across the border is an unbearable menace. With both armies mobilized, it would be very difficult to get them to demobilize and avoid war. The plans for mobilization had a momentum of their own that could not be reversed, and both Kaiser Wilhelm and Tsar Nicholas would soon discover this as they attempted to backpedal on their mobilization, only to be told by their generals that it could not be done.[41]

On July 29, Nicholas exchanged telegrams with his cousin, Kaiser Wilhelm, in Germany, in what came to be known as the Willy-Nicky correspondence. Both monarchs expressed hope for peace and called on the other

---

39 Sergei Dobrorolski, *Die Mobilmachung der Russischen Armee 1914: Mit Beiträgen von Graf Pourtalès*, vol. 1 (Deutsche Verlagsgesellschaft für Politik und Geschichte mbH, 1922), 21–22. See translation in L. C. F. Turner, "The Russian Mobilization in 1914," *Journal of Contemporary History* 3, no. 1 (January 1968): 77.
40 Dobrorolski, *Die Mobilmachung der Russischen Armee 1914*.
41 Tuchman, *The Guns of August*, 100, 101; Maurice Paleologue, *An Ambassadors Memoirs*, 5th ed., trans. F. A. Holt O.B.E, vol. II (Hutchinson & Co. Paternoster Row, 1925).

to take steps to ensure it. Tsar Nicholas requested that the conflict between Austria and Serbia be submitted to the Hague, but the Kaiser did not respond to this suggestion. In an astonishing lapse of judgment, Tsar Nicholas II wrote a telegram in the early hours of July 30 to his cousin on the German throne informing him that "the military measures that have now come into force were decided five days ago," effectively confessing that Russia had started mobilization for war. Germany had also concluded that Russia wanted war because Russian mobilization came in spite of Germany twice warning Russia's foreign minister, Sazonov, on July 26 and July 29, that Russian mobilization would trigger German mobilization. Yet Russia continued with its mobilization anyway. Russia claimed to hope for peace talks but mobilized its army in preparation for a potential failure of the talks. Germany learned of the Russian mobilization and began to mobilize its army while issuing a twelve-hour ultimatum to the Russian military on July 31 to demobilize. After twenty-four hours had passed without a response, Germany declared war against Russia on August 1.

On hearing the news of war breaking out, Alexander Izvolsky, the Russian ambassador to France at the time, exclaimed, "This is my war!"[42] Given the role he played in setting the stage for the crisis in the Balkans, the years he spent coordinating and consolidating a Russian-French alliance, and the effort he put into securing a secret alliance with Britain, it is hard to argue with him.

Across the decades before 1914, Russia's moves formed a coherent strategy aimed at one supreme objective. From the annexation of Kars-Ardahan-Batum in 1878, the significant militarization and migration of Russians into the annexed region, the constant quarrels over the Turkish Straits, the Treaty of San Stefano and its revision at Berlin in 1878, the Bosnian annexation crisis of 1908–09, and the Balkan Wars of 1912–13, Russia's strategy was to contain Austria in the Balkans and defeat the Ottomans in Anatolia to open the path to the grand prize: Tsargrad and its waterways.

---

42 Dobrorolski, *Die Mobilmachung der Russischen Armee 1914.*

Military Reality Check

As in Manchuria, the Russian military was woefully unprepared for the war its reckless emperor had plunged it into. And as in Manchuria, Sergei Witte was the ignored voice of reason. But against the German, Austrian, and Ottoman armies, the price paid by Russia in men and money would be incomparably higher than that paid against the Japanese. And unlike in Manchuria, Tsar Nicholas would not escape punishment as his people suffered.

Tsar Nicholas appointed Grand Duke Nicholas Nikolaevich as supreme commander of the Imperial Russian Army, the same man who had threatened to commit suicide rather than become military dictator in 1905. Grand Duke Nicholas had never commanded an army in a war before, and he had no part in the planning of the war or the decision to enter it. The decision may have been popular, but it was indicative of a deep dysfunction on the part of Tsar Nicholas, who entrusted the military to a man with no input on the decision to go to war or its preparation. Hew Strachan writes of the Grand Duke's reaction to his appointment: "On receipt of the Imperial order, he spent much of his time crying because he did not know how to approach his new duties."[43]

Russia had been industrializing rapidly during the years leading to the Great War but was still significantly behind the major powers in terms of industrial military capacity. The Russian military was under-equipped compared to the German and Austrian militaries, but the Tsar and some of his trusted associates maintained ridiculous, anachronistic, and tragic faith in the power of numbers, failing to appreciate the realities of modern kinetic warfare, where soldiers are useless without modern equipment. With insufficient rifles, bullets, boots, artillery, and transport, the Russian soldiers were massacred in enormous numbers. Indifferent to their suffering, the Tsar and the military's top brass kept sending more ill-equipped soldiers to the front line, instructing them to arm themselves with the weapons of their slain comrades. The Russian military achieved victories against the Turkish and Austrian militaries, but against the Germans, their most formidable and geographically important

---

43 Hew Strachan, *The First World War: Volume I: To Arms* (Oxford University Press, 2001), 313.

enemy, they suffered brutal defeats and had to retreat drastically. Having sent his troops in a deluded attempt to conquer the Balkans, the Tsar saw them lose Poland, much of the Baltic states, and other large territories, retreating hundreds of kilometers east, and coming uncomfortably close to St. Petersburg. As they retreated, Russian soldiers burned down the villages and homes of peoples they suspected of being insufficiently loyal to the Tsar, in what would herald the breakdown of the multi-ethnic Russian Empire and the irreparable schism between it and its many minority populations. Hundreds of thousands of Jews, Germans, Poles, and Muslims were expelled from their homes, their villages were burned, and the economic and human toll of the war continued to grow.[44] The number of dead soldiers had quickly reduced the popularity of the war among the Russian people, and the enormous economic cost had completely destroyed it.

As Sean McMeekin explained, Russia missed the chance to strike decisively at Germany when Germany was preoccupied on its western front. Russia also came too late to Gallipoli to make a difference as British and French soldiers were dying to secure Tsargrad. As part of its grand strategy to secure the Turkish Straits, Russia also sought to defeat the Ottomans in Eastern Anatolia, but it failed to provide the Armenians with the support they needed, with tragic consequences. Russian military prowess proved no match for her imperial ambition and diplomatic cunning. As McMeekin put it: "A mere twelve months into the world war, Russia had failed on every important front but the diplomatic."[45]

The ruthless cunning of Russia's diplomats had—literally and figuratively—written checks which its bumbling military could not cash. Izvolsky, Sazonov, and the Russian foreign ministry had spent years plotting to set the stage for Russia to have the war and allies it needed to defeat Austria and Germany—the barrier standing between her and conquering the teetering Ottoman Empire and liberating Tsargrad from Muslim rule—only to then have

---

44 Peter Gatrell, *A Whole Empire Walking: Refugees in Russia during World War I* (Indiana University Press, 1999); Eric Lohr, *Nationalizing the Russian Empire: The Campaign against Enemy Aliens during World War I* (Harvard University Press, 2003).

45 McMeekin, *The Russian Origins of the First World War*, 173–74.

their military fail decisively at delivering the needed victory. Instead of achieving the dream of all the Tsars, Nicholas II had caused the murder of millions of Russians and endangered the empire's very survival.

To finance his doomed military adventure, the Tsar had suspended redemption of gold in 1914, effectively ending Witte's gold standard after a short eighteen years. At no point did the Tsar have to worry about collecting taxes from his subjects, or what they thought of their wealth going to fight foreign wars. With this suspension, the value of the ruble began to decline, which manifested in rising prices for goods and services. To make matters worse, millions of farm workers taken from the field to the front caused reductions in the production of essentials. The economic cost of the war was being felt sharply by the population. By every conceivable measure, the war was a catastrophe for the Russian Empire.

Watching helplessly from the upper house of the Duma, Witte had grown increasingly frustrated with Nicholas II and the devastation he had brought to Russia. He repeatedly emphasized to anyone who would listen that Russia must avoid war at all costs and instead work on fostering friendly economic relations with France and Germany to counter England's dominance.[46] In a frank discussion with the French ambassador, Witte stated that going to war was madness on the part of Russia, that Slav solidarity was nonsense, and that Russia could hope for nothing from the war.[47] He was also extremely concerned about the revolutionary movements growing in momentum thanks to the war. "There must inevitably break out in the conquered country a social revolution, which by the very nature of things, will spread to the country of the victor,"[48] he warned.

Things came to a head in Russia in the summer of 1915 following a series of defeats that forced the Russian military to begin its Great Retreat eastward. This strategy was meant to prevent further defeats and to prevent remote military units from being surrounded and cut off from supplies from the

---

46 Bernard Pares, *The Fall of the Russian Monarchy* (1939; Phoenix, 2001).
47 Richard Tames, *Last of the Tsars: The Life and Death of Nicholas and Alexandra* (Pan Books, 1972), 43.
48 Lionel Kochan, *Russia in Revolution* (Paladin, 1970), 174.

mainland. Tsar Nicholas II fired the Grand Duke from the supreme command and assumed the role himself. At the same time, prices in the local market were rising, and by July 1915, they were approximately 40% higher than they had been before the war.[49] It was clear to those who understood economics that the rise in prices was a result of an increase in the issue of money that followed the suspension of gold redemption—the latest in a long line of catastrophes to befall Russia as a result of ignoring Sergei Witte's sage advice.

---

49 Peter Gatrell, *Russia's First World War: A Social and Economic History*, 1st ed. (Routledge, 2014), 146.

IV.

Bismarck's Africa

Your map of Africa is very nice. But there is France, and here is Russia, and we are in the middle, and that is my map of Africa.

— Otto von Bismarck, to a colonial adventurer
trying to tempt him to colonize Africa

The Grandmaster

Otto von Bismarck was the grandmaster of European geopolitics in the nineteenth century, and his legacy—and its abandonment—are essential to understanding Europe's descent into The Great War. As Minister President of Prussia under Wilhelm I, Bismarck led Prussia to victory over France in 1870–71 with the aid of other German states, and then used the victory to unite 27 German states into the German Empire, under the Prussian crown of the House of Hohenzollern, whence he became Chancellor. Bismarck demanded an indemnity of 5 billion francs from France, an astonishing sum equal to 1,450 tons of gold, or 46 million troy ounces. In a stroke of economic genius rivaling his geopolitical genius, Bismarck used the substantive indemnity France paid Germany to establish the gold reserve needed to switch Germany from a silver standard to a gold standard, supercharging Germany's economic rise and industrialization which would make it rival—if not supersede—Britain as the world's leading industrial power by the beginning of the twentieth century.

After the triumphant conclusion of the Franco-Prussian War, Bismarck had presided over three wars in his first eight years in power as Minister President of Prussia, and you would have been forgiven for expecting more. Instead, Bismarck presided over two decades of peace, deftly manipulating and managing relations with Germany's neighbors and major powers to ensure the country's peaceful growth and advancement.

After Prussia and its German allies defeated France in the Franco-Prussian War in 1871, Kaiser Wilhelm's grandfather took Alsace-Lorraine from France against the advice of Bismarck, who thought this move would win Germany an eternal enemy that seethed to retake the territory.[50] Bismarck had little time for imperial fantasies overseas, which he saw as an expensive endeavor not worth its cost. Patrick Buchanan explains Bismarck's strategic thinking:

> Bismarck had engineered the wars on Denmark, Austria, and France, but he now believed his nation had nothing to gain from war. She had "hay enough for her fork." Germany should not behave "like a nouveau riche who has just come into money and then offended everyone by pointing to the coins in his pocket."[51] He crafted a series of treaties to maintain a European balance of power favorable to Germany—by keeping the Austro-Hungarian Empire allied, Russia friendly, Britain neutral, and France isolated. Bismarck opposed the building of a fleet that might alarm the British. As for an overseas empire, let Britain, France, and Russia quarrel over colonies. When a colonial adventurer pressed upon him Germany's need to enter the scramble for Africa, Bismarck replied, "Your map of Africa is very nice. But there is France, and here is Russia, and we are in the middle, and that is my map of Africa."[52]

Such was Bismarck's disdain for colonialism that he wanted to give the British German South West Africa, which he viewed as a burden and an

---

50 Winston S. Churchill, *The World Crisis 1911–1914* (1923; Bloomsbury Academic, 2015), 4.
51 Henrik Bering, "Prussian Maneuvers–Henrik Bering on Iron Kingdom: The Rise and Downfall of Prussia, 1600–1947 by Christopher Clark," Hoover Institution, April 3, 2007.
52 Buchanan, *Churchill, Hitler, and "The Unnecessary War"*, 8.

expense, rather than an asset.[53] Bismarck had one haunting fear: Russia and France uniting in a war against Germany. Uniting Germany and protecting it from an alliance of enemies that could destroy it was Bismarck's imperative, and expanding over hostile faraway territories was at best an expensive distraction, and at worst, courting disaster by cultivating enemies. When the Balkans was in another of its interminable crises in 1876, he told the German Reichstag (parliament):

> I am opposed to the notion of any sort of active participation of Germany in these matters, so long as I can see no reason to suppose that German interests are involved, no interests on behalf of which it is worth our risking—excuse my plain speaking—the healthy bones of one of our Pomeranian musketeers.[54]

As historian Eric Hobsbawm put it: "Bismarck, who remained undisputed world champion at the game of multilateral diplomatic chess for almost twenty years after 1871, devoted himself exclusively, and successfully, to maintaining peace between the powers."[55] In 1887, Germany under Bismarck signed the secret Reinsurance Treaty with Russia, which required both countries to stay out of each other's wars. The relationship between the two was on relatively friendly terms, which isolated and weakened France. Under Wilhelm, Bismarck, and the gold standard, Germany experienced peace and magnificent economic and technological advancement that enabled it to challenge and sometimes overtake Britain in many industrial output metrics, laying claim to being the world's leading industrial power.

Wilhelm's Folly

But change is the way of life, and the fortunes of nations change with the changing of the guard. Emperor Wilhelm would die in 1888, to be replaced

---

53 A. J. P. Taylor, *Bismarck: The Man and Statesman* (Vintage, 1967).
54 Emil Ludwig, *Bismarck: The Story of a Fighter* (Blue Ribbon Books, 1927), 511.
55 Eric Hobsbawm, *The Age of Empire: 1875–1914* (Vintage, 1989), 312.

by his son Fredrick III, whose reign would last only 99 days before he died, handing the reins of power to his son, the 29-year-old Kaiser Wilhelm II. Having only spent ninety-nine days as Crown Prince, Wilhelm II had not been properly prepared for power, and had not developed the wisdom required to successfully manage an empire as large as the German Empire. He had not even developed the ability to appreciate such wisdom in others, and so in 1890, he had the impetuousness to dismiss Bismarck, the storied mastermind of European geopolitics, and take a more direct role in managing his nation's affairs. Jealous of his maternal family's British Empire, Wilhelm II sought to make Germany a leading world power through imperialism and building a navy. His ambition, as is so often the case with leaders, laid the foundations of his demise. Wilhelm II let the Reinsurance Treaty with Russia lapse without renewal, probably because he thought his friendship with his cousin Tsar Nicholas II would be enough to resolve differences with Russia, and possibly because he wanted to pursue an alliance with his uncle in Britain, and he thought Britain's colonial conflicts with Russia would get in the way of an alliance with Britain.

By 1914, Germany was the third-largest global Empire,[56] an unwise overextension that antagonized the British over marginal territories the Germans could not defend effectively, since all their sea lanes required passage through British waters in the North Sea. To support his empire, the Kaiser became obsessed with building a modern navy. Wilhelm had come across the work of American naval historian A. T. Mahan, and it shaped his policies for the two decades before the Great War. Germany heavily invested in modernizing its navy, and this unnerved the British. Should the German Navy achieve superiority over the British Navy, Britain itself would be in danger—and not just its colonies. And since Germany had a small empire of largely insignificant land scattered all across the globe, the British could not easily believe that the point of the navy was to protect German shipping routes. They remained wary that the navy would be used to attack Britain.

---

56 "Colonialism and Addressing the Past," Federal Ministry for Economic Cooperation and Development, July 20, 2023.

In 1896, Bismarck revealed the existence of the Reinsurance Treaty and its non-renewal. He argued that the failure to renew it would inevitably draw Russia and France together,[57] and of course he was right. Russia and France became natural allies at that point, a marriage of convenience uniting the politically diametric opposites of Europe: the most progressive democratic republic and the most conservative and autocratic empire. Both believed a growing Germany was a threat they could not handle individually, and one that limited their territorial ambitions. Germany occupied Alsace-Lorraine while also supporting its Austrian ally's expansion in the Balkans, standing in the way of Russia's access to the Turkish straits.

At this point, it would have seemed natural that Britain would ally with Germany. France and Russia were Britain's serious rivals in their empires, and Germany's imperial ambitions were limited and not as important to it as an alliance with Britain to protect it from the threat of French and Russian unity. But the German foray into building a navy worried the British, and the Russian and French prioritization of Europe over their empires allowed them to tempt Britain into allying with them by offering colonial concessions. Germany, being a relatively new arrival to colonialism, could offer the British Empire little. Through relentless diplomacy, the French and Russians succeeded where the Kaiser failed, and Britain was drawn into a secret de facto military alliance with France and Russia. France and Britain signed the Entente Cordiale in 1904, in which they agreed not to challenge each other in their main North African colonies: Morocco for France, and Egypt for Britain. In 1907, Britain and Russia signed the Anglo-Russian Convention, which ended their rivalries in Central Asia by delineating their spheres of influence. Britain would have southern Persia, Russia would get the north, and they would split central Asia. The course was set, the Triple Entente of France, Britain, and Russia was drawing closer, and Germany felt its horror of encirclement draw nearer.

We can see the four long-term strategic mistakes the Kaiser and his grandfather committed and how they all contradicted the prophetic counsel of

---

57 Marcus Jones, "The Alliance That Wasn't: Germany and Austria-Hungary in World War I," in *Grand Strategy and Military Alliances*, ed. Peter R. Mansoor and Williamson Murray (Cambridge University Press, 2016), 284–312.

Bismarck. Taking Alsace-Lorraine left France angry, as it sought revenge and restitution, a long-term risk that was not worth the territory for an already burgeoning German Empire. Letting the Reinsurance Treaty with Russia lapse left Russia and France open to cooperating against Germany, making Bismarck's worst nightmare come true. Building an empire distracted Germany from focusing its effort on protecting its own borders, and it antagonized the British, who saw it as a challenge to their imperial ambitions. Building a navy also antagonized and worried Britain, making it open to the possibility of collaborating with the French-Russian alliance against Germany. The fatal error of Wilhelm II was to ignore the threat to his nascent terrestrial empire and chase dreams of a navy, overseas empire, and global leadership.

These four strategic mistakes laid the groundwork for the Kaiser to commit two further tactical mistakes in the summer of 1914, which would prove catastrophic to his Empire. Germany had developed its own triple alliance with Austria-Hungary and Italy, and the assassination of Archduke Franz Ferdinand thrust the country into the center of potential war. The Kaiser gave Austria an infamous blank check, in which he promised to support them against the Serbs regardless of the course of action they took. This would prove an extremely costly error that set the stage for war. The Austrians' inflamed ultimatum to Serbia seemed designed to elicit rejection and bring about a war, without much regard for the possibility of Russian intervention. Serbia accepted all of Austria's demands except for one part where Austria demanded its police could investigate the murder of Franz Ferdinand in Serbia and have the power to arrest Serbians, effectively ending Serbian sovereignty. The Serbs had instead requested that the International Court of Justice intervene.

The Austrians seemed foolishly emboldened by the promise of German support. Germany itself was foolishly wedded to its alliance with Austria, meaning its entire fate rested on the cantankerous decisions of an eighty-three-year-old Austrian monarch and his angry generals and diplomats. When word of the Serbian response reached Kaiser Wilhelm in Berlin on July 28, he was confident it had averted the possibility of war and relieved that he wouldn't be forced to back up his promise to support the Austrians:

A brilliant solution—and in barely 48 hours! This is more than could have been expected. A great moral victory for Vienna; but with it every pretext for war falls to the ground, and [the Ambassador] Giesl had better have stayed quietly at Belgrade. On this document, I should never have given orders for mobilisation.[58]

Walking into Encirclement

Kaiser Wilhelm could not have been more wrong. Franz Joseph signed the declaration of war against Serbia on that very same day, and the Kaiser found himself in a war he did not want, whose rationale he did not think worthy, and which could draw in his historical enemies and present mortal danger to Germany. Russia had already begun mobilizing its army on July 25, before Serbia had even responded to the Austrian ultimatum. On July 30, Russia formally announced its mobilization. In those days, mobilization meant war, and the Kaiser took this as a declaration of war.

On July 31, Germany issued a twelve-hour ultimatum to Russia demanding it demobilize. In the meantime, it began mobilizing its own army. After twenty-four hours had passed and Russia refused Germany's ultimatum to demobilize, Germany declared war on Russia on August 1. Germany asked France to declare its neutrality in the war between Russia and Germany, but France refused. Germany, cognizant that France was allied to Russia and wanted Alsace-Lorraine, declared war on France on August 3.

The die was cast. Europe's major powers had turned the old continent into a battlefield that would claim the lives of an entire generation. Kaiser Wilhelm's emotional outburst summed up the inter-familial tragedy best:

To think that George and Nicky should have played me false! If my grandmother had been alive, she would never have allowed it.[59]

---

58 Emil Ludwig and Wilhelm Hohenzollern, *The Last of the Kaisers*, trans. Ethel Colburn Mayne (G. P, Putnam's Sons, 1927), 444.
59 Balfour, Michael (1964), *The Kaiser and his Times*, Houghton Mifflin. p.355.

Emotions aside, the events of 1914 suggest the Kaiser had a point. His cousins had indeed plotted against him, but that does not excuse him for walking straight into their trap, and for the decade-long strategic mistakes that put him in a position where they would want to plot against him. Prince Lichnowsky, the German Ambassador to Britain, disagreed with the Kaiser and instead placed the blame for the war on his own country, for three reasons. Germany had encouraged Austria to attack Serbia, even though it had no interest in that conflict, and it should have known of the dangers of a world war. Germany also had rebuffed attempts to mediate the crisis, even after Russian Foreign Minister Sergey Sazonov had declared that Russia would not tolerate an attack on Serbia. Germany sent an ultimatum to Russia on July 30 over Russian mobilization, even before Austria was attacked and even though the Tsar had pledged his word that he would not attack Germany.

The Kaiser's son and heir to the throne, Crown Prince Wilhelm, who was more rational and less emotional than his father, said in an interview with an American newspaper:

> Undoubtedly this is the most stupid, senseless and unnecessary war of modern times. It is a war not wanted by Germany, I can assure you, but it was forced on us, and the fact that we were so effectually prepared to defend ourselves is now being used as an argument to convince the world that we desired conflict.[60]

The German military establishment had spent decades preparing for the possibility of a two-front war. Their master plan was to employ the Schlieffen Plan on the western front to quickly defeat France, then switch to the larger Russian army in the east. The German military establishment had for decades clung religiously to the Schlieffen Plan, by which they would place 85% of their western frontier soldiers to sweep through Belgium and Luxemburg while the remaining 15% confronted the French military attacking the

---

60 Karl H. von Wiegand, "Frederick Wilhelm Exclusive Interview with United Press," United Press International, November 20, 1914.

French-German border to retake Alsace-Lorraine. But sticking to this plan was the final and most fatal error of the Kaiser. By invading Belgium, Germany gave the British Crown and Foreign Office the pretext they needed to recruit the British cabinet, parliament, and public into the cause of war.

The Schlieffen Plan was modified by Chief of the German Great General Staff Helmuth von Moltke, who placed 70% of the soldiers on the northern front and 30% along the French-German border. Although this worked well at the beginning, with Germans making significant progress in the north and repelling the French attack on the border, it failed as the Germans closed in on Paris. On September 4, the retreating French and British militaries launched a counter-offensive at the Battle of the Marne, which miraculously managed to repel the invading Germans into retreating ninety kilometers. The German Schlieffen Plan of a swift defeat of France had failed thanks to the British support of France—support made possible precisely by Germany deploying the Schlieffen Plan and giving the British foreign office the rationale they needed to convince parliament to go to war. Rather than a swift victory that would allow Germany to shift its forces east to face Russia, a bloody stalemate and a war of attrition bogged down the German army in French trenches, with neither military capable of achieving a decisive victory to resolve the conflict. With the Russians continuing to fight at the eastern front, Germany's predicament seemed dire. To make matters worse, their Austrian allies had been handed a stunning defeat in their attempts to take Serbia. After the Battle of the Marne, Crown Prince Wilhelm told an American journalist, "We have lost the war. It will go on for a long time, but lost it is already."[61]

Wilhelm II met with his cabinet on November 17, 1914, and they concluded that the war could not be won. He must have suspected that losing the war would mean the end of his Empire. It was entirely his call to risk Germany for the sake of supporting Austria's inconsequential fight with Serbia, and if that were to lead to defeat at the hands of Germany's major rivals, there would be no way back for him and the 300-year Hohenzollern dynasty. And so he kept the war going, hoping that somehow more bloodshed would solve

---

61 Alistair Horne, *The Price of Glory: Verdun 1916* (1964; Penguin Books, 1994), 221.

his problems. With gold redemption suspended under the guise of war emergency, he had no pressing reason not to continue with war. It was not his own wealth financing the war effort but rather the wealth of the many millions of holders of German marks being devalued.

Monetary War Machine

Yet the stupidity and senselessness of the war were no impediments to the Kaiser abusing his central bank to finance fighting insane, expensive, pointless wars that were irrelevant to his people in his pursuit of grandeur. Via roundabout ways, the German people's savings were to finance the war effort. The government simply chose to absorb the nation's savings by issuing short-time treasury bills for people to use as savings instruments.[62] The first bond sale by the Reichsbank came in September 1914, and it raised 4.5 billion marks. In the second bond sale, in March 1915, nine billion marks were raised.

The short-time treasury bills effectively increased the money supply rapidly. Between July 24 and August 7, the quantity of Reichsbank notes in circulation increased by more than two billion Reichsmark.[63] The entire stock of gold held by the Reichsbank was 1.36 billion Reichsmark. In two weeks, the central bank printed notes worth more than six times the value of the national debt before the war, which stood at only 300 million Reichsmark. While people did in fact buy the debt, this inflation of paper notes led to a scramble for redeeming paper notes for physical gold from the Reichsbank, which lost 103 million marks in the week between July 24 and July 31. On July 31, the same day Germany issued its ultimatum to Russia, the Reichsbank illegally suspended the redemption of its banknotes into gold and ended the classical gold standard in Germany. Four days later, parliament legalized this move retroactively. Another law issued on the same day authorized the Reichsbank to use short-term bills issued by the Treasury, and commercial bills, as cover

---

62 Fred Rogers Fairchild, "German War Finance—A Review," *The American Economic Review* 12, no. 2 (1922): 246–61.

63 Costantino Bresciani-Turroni, *Economics of Inflation: A Study of Currency Depreciation in Post-War Germany* (Ludwig von Mises Institute, 2007), 23.

for bank notes. Government debt was now as good as gold, according to the German parliament. It should come as no surprise that the issuance of debt and Reichsmarks would increase drastically. The inflation had begun to affect the price of the mark, and by August 1915, the mark had dropped 12% against the Swiss franc in Swiss banks.[64]

As the gold standard grew more centralized in its operation, placing a large chunk of gold at the central bank's headquarters in each country's capital, governments could borrow cheaply, finance more war and spending, and engage in reckless statesmanship. Looking back at that period, it is remarkable how little concern there was for economics. These governments had grown accustomed to abusing their central banks' gold pots through credit expansion because the central banks never had to redeem a lot of their gold. The classical gold standard had worked too well for the governments of the world; it allowed them to spend without much regard for resources, which would ultimately cause the downfall of the classical gold standard as it existed pre-1914.

At the start of the war, the British Navy began to disrupt German trade flows, and by March 1915, it imposed a full blockade, causing shortages of essential goods and raw materials. Many farmers and industrial workers left their jobs to go to war, causing further decline in the production of necessary goods. With the German government increasing its spending substantially in the first year of war and floating several bonds to support the war effort, the prices of essential goods rose and they became less available. The German War Ministry set up the War Raw Materials Department, which set prices and controlled the distribution of materials critical to the war effort. It soon began to ration and set prices for foods, too.

---

64 George J. Hall, "Exchange Rates and Casualties during the First World War," *Journal of Monetary Economics* 51, no. 8 (November 2004): 1711–42.

V.

Grey Finds a Reason

You have got to find a reason, Grey!

— King George V on August 2, 1914, after his Foreign Secretary, Sir Edward Grey, told him he could not find a justifiable reason to go to war against Germany.

Victoria's Golden Age

No monarch in history has defined an era as much as Victoria, Queen of the United Kingdom of Great Britain and Ireland, who became queen one month after turning 18 in 1837, and ruled for the rest of the nineteenth century, as well as the first year and 22 days of the twentieth century. At the time of her death, her reign was the longest in British history, and the second longest in European history after Louis XIV in France in the seventeenth and eighteenth centuries. The eponymous Victorian era was likely the most transformative in British history. Britain became one of the first societies to achieve near universal literacy, and the country was transformed from an agrarian society to the world's first industrial society, with the world's highest productivity and living standards. The inventions of Victorian Britain defined industrialization and were carried on British boats all over the world, spreading power, light, literacy, industrial goods, and productivity. Victorian morality became renowned for the high moral standards of the British of the era, with an emphasis on proper personal conduct, religiosity, work ethic, and self-improvement. The slave trade and slavery were abolished before she came into power, and Britain's growth showed the world that slavery was not needed for prosperity. British factories ended the practice of employing children. The British Empire expanded to its zenith all over the world. In her 65-year reign, Britain only fought one war involving major powers, the Crimean war of 1853–56. The rest of the reign was peaceful, as Britain wisely capitalized on its status as an island insulated from the interminable terrestrial squabbles of Europeans.

Inevitably, this era of exceptional human flourishing came under a hard monetary standard. From 1717, Sir Isaac Newton had put Britain on a bimetallic standard which overvalued silver, effectively driving it out of the country and putting the country on a de facto gold standard. But the outbreak of the Napoleonic wars in 1797 suspended the gold standard. In 1821, Britain adopted a formal gold standard, abandoning bimetallism, and underpinning the Victorian golden era, with its indelible impact on Britain and the world.

Edward's Whirl of Amusements

But change is the only constant in life, and Victoria's heir was very different from her. The hard work and high morals of the early Victorian era led to the wealth and extravagance of the late Victorian era, in which Prince Albert Edward came of age. As is so often the case with royal dynasties, later generations take their wealth and power for granted and ignore the centuries of restraint, hard choices, and sacrifices that made it possible. Despite his mother's disapproval and her attempts at controlling him, Prince Edward was a bon vivant who gambled and partied extensively and was a regular guest of the less reputable night spots of London, Paris, and other European cities, with a long list of notorious improper relationships. Reflecting on the prospect of Edward becoming king, Queen Victoria had this to say:

> Oh! What will become of the poor country when I die! I foresee, if B[ertie] succeeds, nothing but misery – for he never reflects or listens for a moment

and he [would] ... spend his life in one whirl of amusements as he does now. It makes me very sad and angry.[65]

The wise queen was correct. While Albert only ruled for nine peaceful and prosperous years in 'one whirl of amusement,' he laid the foundations for the destruction of his mother's Empire shortly after his death by getting Britain into a tangle of idiotic and needless alliances, public and secret. One year into his reign, Britain entered a surprising alliance with Japan, which was the first alliance between a European and Oriental power. With Russia and Germany setting their sights on China and the Orient, the British alliance with Japan would stand in their way and limit their expansion. Britain supported Japan in its victorious war against Russia, which succeeded in limiting Russian colonial expansion, protecting Britain's Indian empire from being threatened by Russia. But Edward was not done. After having badly wounded Nicholas II, the nephew of his wife, he turned his attention to his most important rival, his own nephew on the German throne.

Edwardian foreign policy actively sought an alliance with Russia and France to limit German influence. Edward was instrumental in the Entente Cordiale of 1904, and he immediately set about supporting France in the Tangier Crisis of 1905, in which Germany and France vied for control over Morocco. An international conference was convened in which war was averted. The French foreign minister, Delcassé, who had a good relationship with Edward, was forced by the French parliament to resign for his role in bringing France to the brink of war over Morocco. Britain also effectively supported France in the Agadir Crisis of 1911. The Liberal ruling party was predominantly non-interventionist and had been elected as a result of the public revulsion over the Boer War. But a schism was growing within the government between the supporters of a more aggressive alliance with France, such as Prime Minister Herbert Asquith, Foreign Secretary Sir Edward Grey, and Lord of the Admiralty Winston Churchill and the non-interventionists,

---

65 Stanley Weintraub, *Edward the Caresser: The Playboy Prince who Became Edward VII* (The Free Press, 2001), 126.

such as Viscount Morley, Secretary of State for India, and Lord Loreburn, the Lord Chancellor. Morley had pushed the cabinet to agree that no talks could be held that obliged Britain to go to war without cabinet approval. But, over time, the interventionists continued to get more powerful. In retrospect, it seems clear that it was the influence of the King and his close circle of imperialists who had been pushing them forward. Against public opinion and parliamentary and cabinet majority, Grey, Churchill, and Asquith proceeded to secure a de facto secret alliance with France and Russia, which seems to have been tailor-made to initiate the Great War.

Grey's Balancing Act

To get the war the King wanted, the warmongering cabal had to pull off an astonishing deception. Patrick Buchanan provides a detailed description:

> Unknown to the Cabinet and Parliament, a tiny cabal had made a decision fateful for Britain, the empire, and the world. Under the guidance of Edward Grey, the foreign secretary from 1905 to 1916, British and French officers plotted Britain's entry into a Franco-German war from the first shot. And these secret war plans were being formulated by Liberals voted into power in public revulsion against the Boer War on a platform of "Peace, Retrenchment, and Reform." Writes historian Robert Massie,
>
> > [O]n January 16 [1906], without the approval of either the Prime Minister or Cabinet, secret talks between British and French staff officers began. They focussed on plans to send 100,000 British soldiers to the Continent within two weeks of an outbreak of hostilities. On January 26, when Campbell-Bannerman returned to London and was informed, he approved.[66]

---

66 Robert K. Massie, *Dreadnought: Britain, Germany, and the Coming of the Great War* (Ballantine Books, 1992), 589–90; see also Buchanan, *Churchill, Hitler, and "The Unnecessary War"*.

[...] Prime Minister Campbell-Bannerman and his successor, Herbert Henry Asquith, had approved of the military staff talks, but neither the Cabinet nor Parliament was aware that Sir Edward had committed Britain to war if France were invaded. In 1911, two new ministers were brought in on the secret: Chancellor of the Exchequer David Lloyd George and the thirty-seven-year-old Home Secretary, who soon moved over to the Admiralty: Winston Churchill.

While the 1912 exchange of letters on the redeployment of the French fleet stated that Britain was not committed to defend France, Grey and Churchill knew this was exactly what France expected. Should war break out, the Royal Navy was to keep the [German] High Seas Fleet out of the Channel and away from the coast of France. Lord Esher, adviser to George V, told Asquith that the plans worked out between the general staffs of Britain and France "certainly committed us to fight, whether the Cabinet likes it or not."[67]

[...] Grey and Churchill believed that if France was attacked, Britain must fight. But Britain had no treaty alliance with France. Indeed, why had Britain remained outside the Franco-Russian alliance if not to retain her freedom of action? Gladstone had stayed out of the Franco-Prussian war, and the Liberals wanted Asquith to stay out of this war. Of eighteen ministers who had participated in the Cabinet meeting on Saturday, August 1, twelve opposed war.[68]

Similar secret arrangements had existed between Britain and Russia. In the summer of 1912, Russian Foreign Minister Sergey Sazonov wrote to Tsar Nicholas II on his trip to England, where he had met British Foreign Secretary Edward Grey and King George V.

---

67 Tuchman, *The Guns of August*, 52; See also Ferguson, *The Pity of War: Explaining World War I* (Basic Books, 1999), 66; see also Buchanan, *Churchill, Hitler, and "The Unnecessary War"*.
68 Buchanan, *Churchill, Hitler, and "The Unnecessary War"*, 6, 22, 28.

As a favorable opportunity occurred I felt it useful, in one of my conver-
sations with Grey, to seek information as to what we might expect from
Great Britain in the event of a conflict with Germany. What the director of
British foreign policy said to me as to this, and King George himself later,
I think is very significant.

Grey declared unhesitatingly that should the anticipated conditions arise
Great Britain would make every effort to strike a crippling blow at German
naval power.

On his own initiative Grey then gave me a confirmation of what I already
knew through Poincaré—an agreement exists between France and Great
Britain, under which in the event of war with Germany Great Britain has
accepted the obligation of bringing assistance to France not only on the sea
but on land, by landing troops on the Continent.

The King touched on the same question in one of his conversations with
me, and expressed himself even more strongly than his Minister. When I
mentioned, letting him see my agitation, that Germany is trying to place
her naval forces on a par with Britain's, His Majesty cried that any conflict would have disastrous results not only for the German navy but for
Germany's overseas trade, for, he said, "We shall sink every single German
merchant ship we shall get hold of."[69]

What made these secret arrangements so pernicious was the incredible
lengths to which the Foreign Office clique had gone to explicitly deny them,
repeatedly, in the cabinet, parliament, and press. Albert Jay Nock collected a
stunning series of statements by government officials denying the existence of
such treaties mere months before these treaties were to take Britain to its most
fateful war.

---

69 Harry Elmer Barnes, *The Genesis of the World War: An Introduction to the Problem of War
    Guilt* (Forgotten Books, 2019), 108.

On 10 March of the following year, Mr. Asquith, replying to a question in the Commons from Lord Hugh Cecil, denied that England was under an "obligation arising owing to an assurance given by the Ministry in the course of diplomatic negotiations, to send a very large armed force out of this country to operate in Europe." On 24 March, he made similar denials in reply to questions from Sir W. Byles and Mr. King. On 14 April, Mr. Runciman, in a speech at Birkenhead, denied "in the most categorical way" the existence of a secret understanding with any foreign Power! On 3 May, the Secretary for the Colonies, Mr. Harcourt, declared publicly that he "could conceive no circumstances in which Continental operations would not be a crime against the people of this country." On 28 June, the under-Secretary for Foreign Affairs, Mr. Acland, declared publicly that "in no European question were we concerned to interfere with a big army." On 1 July, Lord Loreburn, Lord Chancellor from 1906 to 1912, said "that any British Government would be so guilty towards our country as to take up arms in a foreign quarrel is more than I can believe." On 28 April, 1914, and again on 11 June, Sir E. Grey confirmed, in the House of Commons, Mr. Asquith's assertion, made 10 and 24 March, 1913, of British freedom from engagements with Continental Powers.[70]

Asquith's statement in the House of Commons is worth quoting in full:

As has been repeatedly stated, this country is not under any obligation, not public and known to Parliament, which compels it to take part in a war. In other words, if war arises between European Powers, there are no unpublished agreements which will restrict or hamper the freedom of the Government or Parliament to decide whether or not Great Britain should participate in a war.[71]

---

70 Albert Jay Nock, *The Myth of a Guilty Nation* (B.W. Huebsch, 1922).
71 Paul S. Reinsch, *Secret Diplomacy: How Far Can it be Eliminated?* (Harcourt, Brace and Co., 1912).

Patrick Buchanan describes the devastating impact of these arrangements, and how the entirety of the war would almost certainly not have started without them:

> Had Sir Edward revealed to the Cabinet his secret discussions with France and the moral commitments they implied—that Britain must go to war if France were invaded—his policy would have been rejected by the Cabinet and repudiated by Parliament. Churchill later admitted as much:
>
>> [If in 1912] the Foreign Secretary had, in cold blood, proposed a formal alliance with France and Russia .... the Cabinet of the day would never have agreed to it. I doubt if four ministers would have agreed to it. But if the Cabinet had been united upon it, the House of Commons would not have accepted their guidance. Therefore the Foreign Minister would have had to resign. The policy which he had advocated would have stood condemned and perhaps violently repudiated; and upon that repudiation would have come an absolute veto upon all those informal preparations and non-committal discussions on which the defense power of the Triple Entente was erected.[72]
>
> "No bargain had been entered into," wrote Churchill, but "We were morally committed to France."[73] Churchill concedes that he and Grey were morally committed to a war they knew the Cabinet and Parliament opposed. "In other words," concludes historian Jim Powell, "Churchill believed that if Grey had operated openly, Britain might not have been able to get into the war!"[74] As Francis Neilson, who had resigned from the House over the war, wrote, both "Bonar Law and Austen Chamberlain said after the First

---

72 Jim Powell, *Wilson's War: How Woodrow Wilson's Great Blunder Led to Hitler, Lenin, Stalin and World War II* (Crown Forum, 2005), 43; see also Buchanan, *Churchill, Hitler, and "The Unnecessary War"*.

73 Ibid.

74 Ibid.

World War—that if Grey's commitments had been laid before the House, they doubted whether ...[the war] would have taken place."[75]

The importance of Grey's secret collusion with France is difficult to overstate. Had he been open with the Cabinet and sought to persuade them of the necessity of committing Britain to France, they would have rejected his alliance. France and Russia, knowing that they could not rely on the British to fight beside them, would have been far more disposed to compromise in the Balkan crisis of July 1914. By secretly committing Britain to war for France, Grey, Churchill, and Asquith left the Kaiser and German Chancellor in the dark, unaware a war with France meant war with the British Empire. Had he known, the Kaiser would have made his belated effort to abort a war far sooner and more successfully.[76]

The Foreign Office had also deliberately squandered several opportunities to keep Britain out of the war through diplomacy. When the German Ambassador to Britain, Prince Lichnowsky, met Grey on August 1 and asked him whether respecting Belgian neutrality would keep Britain out of war, Grey would not give him a positive answer. Lichnowsky, and Germany, were so interested in getting Britain to stay out of the war that he flat out asked Grey to name the conditions that would guarantee British neutrality. But Grey remained ambiguous.[77]

Grey met with King George V on August 2, when France and Russia were pressuring Britain to join the war and fulfill the secret obligations he, Haldane, and Churchill had committed to. But Grey was not confident he could find a way to convince his cabinet and parliament to support a war. King George told Grey it was "absolutely essential" for Britain to go to war to prevent Germany from achieving "complete domination of the country." When Grey explained to the King his inability to find a justifiable reason to

75 Francis Neilson, *The Makers of War* (Appleton, Wisconsin: C. C. Nelson Publishing Company, 1950), 113; see also Buchanan, *Churchill, Hitler, and "The Unnecessary War"*.
76 Buchanan, *Churchill, Hitler, and "The Unnecessary War"*, 62–64.
77 Barnes, *The Genesis of the World War*, 553.

go to war against Germany, King George responded: "You have got to find a reason, Grey."[78]

Fortunately for George, Grey, and the imperialists at the Foreign Office, and unfortunately for Britain and humanity, the Kaiser gave Grey a reason: he invaded Belgium. Grey, Asquith, Haldane, and Churchill could now present the defense of Belgium as rationalization for war to the cabinet and parliament, and not have to get into the very embarrassing and inexplicable secret alliances with Russia and France. The war was never put to a vote in parliament. Grey gave a speech in parliament in which he effectively declared war, but he did not answer questions. He left parliament and sent a telegram threatening Germany with war in case it invaded Belgium, knowing fully well that the invasion was already underway. The ruse worked. In a moment of candor, as war raged, Winston Churchill remarked: "I think a curse should rest on me—because I love this war. I know it's smashing and shattering the lives of thousands every moment—and yet, I can't help it—I enjoy every second of it."[79]

The success of the foreign office in setting Britain on the path of war cannot be understood without reference to the role of the monarchy in pushing it down that path. Kings Edward VII and George V had both spent several years laying the groundwork for this war through their web of alliances. The Belgian chargé d'affaires in London, Monsieur E. Cartier, commented that "the English are getting more and more into the habit of regarding international problems as being almost exclusively within the province of King Edward."[80]

To get the war they wanted, the King and the Foreign Office had to at once convince the Russians and French of the seriousness of their commitment while hiding it from the British people and the German and Austrian governments. By assuring France and Russia of British support, the British Foreign Office made them cavalier about a war against Germany and Austria-Hungary. Without signing a formal alliance, the Foreign Office created enough ambiguity to

---

78 Belinda Robinson, "'Find a Reason to Go to War with Germany': Said King George V," *Daily Mail*, July 26, 2014.

79 Violet Bonham Carter, *Champion Redoubtable: The Diaries and Letters of Violet Bonham Carter 1914–1945* (Weidenfeld, 1998), 25.

80 E. D. Morel, *Diplomacy Revealed* (National Labour Press, 1921), 45.

goad Austria-Hungary and Germany into war with France and Russia by making them think Britain would stay out. By keeping the assurances to France and Russia secret, the Foreign Office sidelined antiwar domestic sentiment during the years of buildup, as few suspected Britain could get involved. Had the British people and their parliamentary representatives known they were being set up to fight a war to support France and Russia taking on Germany and Austria-Hungary, they would undoubtedly have repudiated any commitments. But if somehow they had known and approved of these commitments and formalized them into a treaty, Germany and Austria-Hungary would have almost certainly avoided any course of action bringing them into conflict with Britain, preventing the war from happening.

Somehow, the Crown and Foreign Office managed to pull off this incredible balancing act. King George's friendly message to his cousin Wilhelm during the Kiel Regatta Week now takes on a very sinister interpretation. This was not a case of bumbling monarchs sleepwalking into disaster. It was an elaborately-laid and incredibly complex trap laid by the British that worked against all odds.

What makes this conclusion so baffling is that Britain stood to gain nothing substantive from this war and would have likely been a lot better off had it stayed out. All of Britain's rivals would have weakened each other fighting over marginal territories, while Britain picked up the overseas colonies they could no longer defend or afford, spared its bullets, and became the undisputed power of Europe.

The British chauvinists, as is the wont of all chauvinists, liked to present their case in terms of idealism, focusing on the German invasion of Belgium as the reason behind British involvement in the war. But postwar revelations have shown that to be a flimsy smokescreen behind which was hidden a meticulous plan to bring about a war against Germany.

VI.

The Masterly Manipulation

The capacity of the Bank to lend safely to the Government is practically limited by the extra amount which, in time of war, bankers and the Bank's other customers are prepared for long periods together to keep idle against emergencies.

— John Maynard Keynes explains the dynamics
of the Bank of England Ponzi Scheme

N one of the depravity and deception of the last chapter would have been possible without the classical gold standard and its generous allowance for central banks to create credit to finance government spending. No bank in the era benefited from inflationary largesse as much as the Bank of England, which by 1913 had gold for only 31% of its outstanding gold liabilities. Arguably, a significant driver of British imperial conquest was the desire to set up more subsidiaries of the Bank of England to bring more gold to London to issue more credit partially backed by it. This strategy worked well enough for the Bank during times of peace, when colonial expansion involved few and far between wars in far-flung places against inferior opponents. But under the hubris of Edward VII and George V, the military adventures went too far.

The Bank of England's troubles started at the outset of the Great War. In the last six working days of July, the bank paid out £12.3 million in gold coins from its £26.5 million total reserves.[81] On July 31, 1914, large crowds

---

81 "Gold, Banknotes and Money Supply in the First World War," NatWest Group Remembers, accessed September 26, 2025.

stood outside the bank's doors looking to convert their banknotes and bank accounts into physical gold to withdraw. As trouble brewed on the continent, many foreign depositors sought to withdraw their assets from Britain. To make matters worse, the Bank of England needed to borrow extensively from the United States to finance the war effort. It had to ship a lot of gold as collateral across the Atlantic.[82] The previously unthinkable prospect of the Bank of England defaulting on its promise to redeem its notes and accounts in gold suddenly appeared plausible. A devaluation of the pound at that stage would have allowed the bank sufficient reserves to back the currency, but it would have been unspeakably unpopular with the British public, badly undermining their faith in the bank, as well as the war effort.

Given the volume of withdrawals in July 1914, the bank was practically insolvent before Britain had even entered the war. Had the Bank of England maintained full cover for its notes and bank accounts in gold, as they would have had to under a strict gold standard, war would not have posed a liquidity problem. All depositors could have had their banknotes and bank accounts redeemed in full in physical gold, and there would have been no need to queue outside the bank. However, the Bank of England had become accustomed to not backing all its notes with gold. Depositors had good reason to hold money in the form of banknotes and bank accounts rather than in physical gold. Compared to gold, banknotes were easier to carry and convert into either smaller or larger denominations, and an account at an English bank allowed the depositor to make payments by checkbook, almost anywhere in the world, far faster than sending physical gold. Global capital sought the bank's superior safety and clearance mechanisms, which provided the bank a solid cushion to diverge from a strict 100% gold standard.

For a generation of bankers reared on the peace and prosperity of the Victorian Era and the gold standard, there was little reason to worry about a liquidity crisis. There was also very little reason to worry about a major European war. Yet both the war and the liquidity crisis materialized in 1914. With almost half

---

82 John Osborne, "Gold and Silver," in *The Bank of England 1914-21*, vol. 2, Unpublished War History (Bank of England Archive, 1926), 148.

of the Bank of England's gold reserve withdrawn, there was cause for concern. Chancellor David Lloyd George extended the August bank holiday for three days, during which the Currency and Bank Notes Act, 1914, was passed, authorizing Treasury to issue £300 million worth of paper banknotes, which were not redeemable in gold, for banks to use to meet their liabilities. Colloquially known as "Bradbury pounds" after the Secretary of the Treasury John Bradbury, these bills came in denominations of 10 shilling and £1, and were somehow accepted by the public without much fuss or regard for their inflationary impact. Without this issue, banks would likely have had to declare bankruptcy in the first week of The Great War. The new issue of banknotes was a stopgap solution that ameliorated the crisis of private banks by allowing them to meet their liabilities. The Chairman of Westminster Bank, Walter Leaf said, "The amount and manner of the issue was left to the absolute discretion of the Treasury. This was essentially a War Loan, free of interest, for an unlimited period, and, as such, was a highly profitable expedient from the point of view of the Government."[83] It was, however, not expedient for the Bank of England. Even though these new notes were not redeemable for gold, they had increased the money in circulation and would contribute to rising prices, which, in turn, would encourage people to try to hold gold instead of paper pounds.

The Great War Bond Swindle

By November of 1914, the Bank of England's predicament stopped being an unfortunate effect of old traditions taken too far. Instead, it became a disaster caused by its brazen, mendacious larceny. The British government issued the first war bond, aiming to raise £350 million at an interest rate of 4.1% and a maturity of ten years. This was a significantly more generous rate than the prevailing rate on government debt, which was only 2.5%. And the sum was enormous—around 55% of the existing national debt. As the wealthiest country in the world with the largest and most liquid capital markets and a strong sense of patriotism, the bonds were expected to be snapped up by the public. But surprisingly enough,

---

83 Walter Leaf, *Banking* (Williams and Norgate, 1926), 89–90.

they weren't. The private banks had committed to buying £60 million of these bonds, the Bank of England had committed to buying £39.4 million, and the public was expected to raise the remaining £250 million. But the British public, to its eternal credit, only purchased £91.1 million, leaving a shortfall of £158.1 million—almost half of the sum needed to finance entry into the war.

Not only was the Bank of England having trouble redeeming all its depositors' paper in gold, but the government was facing trouble financing the mobilization to which it had already committed. £99.4 million of the £350 million needed was already being surreptitiously placed on the shoulders of the British people through the banking cartel, using their deposits to buy these bonds and recruit them into a war they were uninterested in. Not only did the government raise little money from the sale, but the number of participants was very low. Only 97,635 investors purchased the bonds out of an estimated one million holders of tradable securities in Britain in 1914, and a total population of 46 million, meaning that less than 0.25% of the British population contributed to the bond sale to take Britain into what would become its most important war. Among those who did invest, more than half of the investments were under £200. Only 2% of investors contributed 40% of the total investment sum.

Without the bond sale, there was no easy way to finance the expensive war, but backing out of the war at this point seemed unwise and insulting to the British government. To avoid publicizing the bond auction failure, Treasury and the Bank of England's management committed an unspeakable crime of financial treason against the British people. The Bank of England granted funds to its chief cashier, Gordon Nairn, and his deputy, Ernest Harvey, to purchase the remaining two-thirds of the bonds under their own names, then had them held by the Bank of England, which classified them on its balance sheet as holdings of 'Other Securities' rather than as government securities.

The Financial Times, ever the Bank's faithful mouthpiece, published an article, astonishing in its mendacity, proclaiming the £350 million loan was oversubscribed by a whopping £250 million, effectively lying by a margin of half a billion pounds (about 80% of the national debt, or a quarter of national income). Patriotism, as ever, was the refuge of the journalistic scoundrels. The article is quoted below in full:

OVER-SUBSCRIBED WAR LOAN
Another and still more profitable investment
now open to disappointed subscribers
4½ with guaranteed appreciation of Capital Repayable in Ten Years

Actuated beyond all question by motives of patriotism no less than by thought of securing a good investment, the British Public has offered the Government every penny it asked for— and more. The loan asked for was £350,000,000, bearing interest at 3½ per cent, and redeemable at par on or before 1st March, 1928.

The announcement of the Government's requirements was made in Parliament on Tuesday, 17th November. By Thursday, 19th November, it is estimated the loans had been over-subscribed by £250,000,000. And still the applications are pouring in!

GOOD INVESTMENTS RARE
This amazing result not only proves how strong is the financial position of the British nation, it suggests also that such profitable investments are rare. Only the other day—just previous to the War Loan Announcement—it was stated that no less a sum than £630,000,000 was lying at the eleven leading Banks awaiting an opportunity for favourable investment. No doubt anticipation of the War Loan kept some Investors from acting, but it is nevertheless true that the bulk of the money remained at the Banks simply through lack of opportunity to invest profitably, or through nervousness.

TO DISAPPOINTED SUBSCRIBERS
There will be thousands of would-be subscribers to the War Loan disappointed of a really safe and—as "gilt-edged" securities go—profitable investment. What are they to do with their Capital now? Is it to remain idle at the Bank, earning nothing or next to nothing? Is it to be risked in some speculative venture? and at a time like this who can say what apparently sound concern is safe! Is it to be invested in Stock which, though the

interest is safe enough, will in all likelihood depreciate in Capital value? Truly, the Investor's lot to-day is not a happy one. [84]

The article then went on to shill its readers on investing in Canadian insurance bonds.

Keynes and the Manipulation

HM's Treasury's John Maynard Keynes, ecstatic at this crime to the point of self-incriminating carelessness, sent a secret memo to Treasury Secretary John Bradbury praising the step as "a masterly manipulation" and discussing what he saw as the likelihood of its failure (emphasis added):

> The Bank of England was compelled by circumstances to take up about £180,000,000 (net) of War Loan and Exchequer Bonds. Some part of this has been disposed of, and room has been found amongst the Bank's normal investments for some further part by the sale of pre-war securities. By this means the burden, beyond the Bank's normal investments, has been reduced by about £50,000,000 to £130,000,000.
>
> In addition to the above, there are the Cold Storage Bills. Hence by the beginning of May, when the last installments of War Loan had been paid up, something like £200,000,000. had been borrowed from the Bank of England by the Government directly or indirectly for the purposes of the war, this being made up roughly as follows:
>
> | | |
> |---|---:|
> | Cold Storage Bills | 60 |
> | War Loan and Exchequer Bonds (balance) | 130 |
> | Sundry | 10 |
> | | 200 |

---

84 Michael Anson et al., "Your Country Needs Funds: The Extraordinary Story of Britain's Early Efforts to Finance the First World War," Bank Underground, August 8, 2017, fig. 5.

About £140,000,000 of this was shown in additions to the other securities and to the Government securities; and about £60,000,000 had been re-borrowed by the Bank of England from the market (transactions in connection with the American Exchange being included in this). I include in sundry any securities which may still be held on account of France, Russia, and other allied or friendly countries.

The effects of these transactions, the magnitude of which has been successfully concealed from the public by a **masterly manipulation** of the Bank returns during March and April, are mainly two—on the amount of what is in effect unfunded debt and on the Bank's control of the Money Market and the Exchanges. I deal in this Note with the former—the unfunded debt.

It is obvious that, due account being taken of the peculiar position of the Bank of England in the British credit system, **it is absolutely out of the question for the Bank of England to lend a sum approaching 200,000,000 for any appreciable period without endangering our whole system.** Probably £50,000,000 (in excess of the normal) is the outside figure for safety, and even this leaves no margin. It would be much better if the figure were brought down to £10,000,000 or £20,000,000, except for brief periods, or in the event of our being really hard pressed for money. **The capacity of the Bank to lend safely to the Government is practically limited by the extra amount which, in time of war, bankers and the Bank's other customers are prepared for long periods together to keep idle against emergencies.**[85]

Keynes very astutely identified the precarious predicament facing the Bank of England in his last sentence. To continue financing the war and not endanger "our whole system" and bring about a collapse in the value of the pound, the Bank of England relied on its banks and customers holding large quantities of their physical gold at the bank. With every ounce withdrawn, and every

85 Ibid.

paper pound redeemed for physical gold, the bank's position became more perilous. The prewar period of peace and prosperity had made depositors extremely trusting of the Bank of England, causing them to "leave idle" plenty of their wealth at the bank, allowing the bank to lend more and more of it. Now the war had significantly increased the demand for the bank to lend; to make matters worse, it also increased the desire of depositors to withdraw their gold. The future of Britain and much of the world depended on whether the bank could pull off this hugely fateful and fraudulent balancing act.

The Silent Death of the Classical Gold Standard

As the Bank of England surreptitiously extended credit to the government, it increased the number of pounds in circulation further beyond the little gold reserves it had left. When the Bradbury pounds went into circulation, the bank was put in a precarious position. Foreign holders of gold were told that the Bank of England could not redeem their gold due to the war making naval shipping insecure. But it wasn't enough. The August Bank Holiday War had continued for more than a year, and a decisive victory seemed increasingly unlikely as a brutal, bloody, and expensive stalemate took hold. Prices of goods began to rise, as did grumblings of suspicious discontent across Britain, and the Bank's liquid position became precarious in August 1915, resulting in the bank issuing this appeal:

> In view of the importance of strengthening the gold reserves of the country for exchange purposes, the Treasury have instructed the Post Office and all public departments charged with the duty of making cash payments to use notes instead of gold coins whenever possible. The public generally are earnestly requested, in the national interest, to co-operate with the Treasury in this policy by (1) paying in gold to the Post Office and to the Banks; (2) asking for payment of cheques in notes rather than in gold; (3) using notes rather than gold for payment of wages and cash disbursements generally.[86]

---

86 *The Times History of the War*, with Robarts—University of Toronto, vol. XXI (The Times Printing House Square, 1920), 265.

While not officially suspending redeemability and abandoning the gold standard, this appeal was the de facto end of the classical gold standard in Britain, and the birth of the "fiat standard." Having been on the gold standard uninterrupted for 94 years, nobody had any memory of a world in which the government abandoned the gold standard, and few could draw the link between the suspension of redemption and the ensuing rise in prices. Historians, however, understood what was going on. A few scholars warned of the dangers of money supply inflation, but they were largely drowned out by the jingoism of inflationary warmongering. Official regime media was careful to convey government propaganda meant to assure people that things were normal, the gold standard was still intact, and victory in the war was near. Most people assumed both the redemption and price rises were just the inevitable consequence of war, with the Bank of England trying its best to steady the ship.

To their eternal credit, the British people were significantly opposed to entering the Great War, and government propaganda and subterfuge could not hide this fact.[87] They had voted for a liberal cabinet precisely for its anti-war sentiments, after the debacle of the war in South Africa. The vast majority of British people had refused to buy war bonds to finance the carnage. And it took the King and the Foreign Office an extremely elaborate scheme to manipulate the country into war. It was an unspeakably evil crime for the British crown and the Foreign Office to plunge the world's most advanced society into this senseless war, and no amount of geopolitical cant could possibly justify the unfathomable price Britain paid for a war in which it had no interest.

British foreign policy in the first 15 years of the twentieth century was dominated by incompetent, reckless, and economically ignorant kings and bureaucrats who had never grasped the value of work and production. They imagined that the prosperity of the industrial revolution was the product of their wisdom and policies, which was not the case. It was the product of the work and ingenuity of countless workers, entrepreneurs, and technicians who could accumulate capital and innovate over decades of peace and security of property rights. They were concerned about Germany's economic growth

---

87 Ferguson. *The Pity of War: Explaining World War I.*

because they believed it would threaten Britain and its industry. But thinking in such a manner is absurd if you understand economics. How ridiculous it is to imagine that in the late nineteenth century, when the vast majority of Earth had not ever seen an engine or sewing machine, Germany would be able to replace British industrial production. Think of how much more industrial output has taken place in both countries and the rest of the world since then. Industrial production has grown infinitely larger, and the demand for industrial goods has grown to utterly dwarf its magnitude at the turn of the century, as people from all across the globe demanded the fantastic wonders of industrialization, and continue to demand them in ever-increasing quantities.

Production is not a competitive sport, and it is not a zero-sum game. The more Germany produces, the better off Britain is, because Germany's production both provides British people with cheaper goods, and consumes British production. The more production takes place in Germany, the more people can employ modern industrial capital and machinery, the more productivity increases, and the more they can demand British goods. It would be impossible for any country in the world today to have modern advanced technology if it were not part of the global division of labor. If the US, China, or Japan were a single advanced industrial country in an entire planet of agrarian societies, it would be far less technologically advanced than it would be in a world with more industrialized societies to trade with. The more advanced and productive the global division of labor, the more demand there is for goods from everywhere, and the more producers can benefit from economies of scale and from the innovations of other producers. A century after British diplomats fretted over German industrial production, Germany and Britain's industrial output has become more than 100 times larger than it was back then. Yet, both countries' industrialists continue to find demand for their products. While the industrialists and capitalists were revolutionizing the world with industry, economically ignorant bureaucrats and imperialists were plotting wars to stop production that they thought threatened them.

The Jekyll Island Cabal

If it were to be exposed publicly that our particular group had got together and written a banking bill, that bill would have no chance whatever of passage by Congress.

—Frank Vanderlip, American banker on his trip
to Jekyll Island to create a central bank

Monopoly

The last few decades of the nineteenth century witnessed an increasing level of cartelization in the major industries of the United States, primarily driven by major industry players capturing government influence and establishing government agencies to "regulate" and supervise the industry under the guise of combating monopolies and protecting consumers. Whereas market competition might have given a particular firm a significant advantage for a brief period over its competitors, this would be the result of this firm offering a superior product to its customers rather than exploiting them. Competitors could always compete with them for the market share by improving their own products. Inevitably, over time, any advantage would be eroded as other firms copied the innovations of the leading firm and created new innovations to render the leader's advantage obsolete. But in the progressive era of the late nineteenth century, a firm with an advantage could make it a lot more permanent by capturing the regulatory agencies meant to prevent it from having an advantage. That, in a nutshell, was the essence of the popularity of progressivism in the late nineteenth and early twentieth century, particularly among the major industrialists. As Murray Rothbard explains in his masterful history, *The Progressive Era*, it was the major industrialists who sought regulation and control so they could make their advantages concrete.[88] They joined forces with an increasingly large government, intellectuals, and labor unions in pushing for the new cartelization model, which nominally sought to limit the influence of industrialists but, in practice, enhanced it.

In a counterintuitive analysis to the prevailing wisdom at the turn of the century, Rothbard demonstrates how major industries' monopolies emerged through producers offering an incomparably superior or significantly cheaper product to their competitors. But these advantages were fleeting, as they would lose their commanding position in the market due to competitors copying their methods or developing superior products. Only through regulation could monopolies be made permanent.

The United States had had three previous experiments with a central bank, none of which lasted more than two decades. The Bank of North America began operating in 1782, but its charter was revoked in 1785. The First Bank of the United States was established in 1791, and it had limited functions compared to classical European central banks. It could not set monetary policy, hold bank reserves, regulate private banks, or act as lender of last resort. But it could operate across state lines and lend money to the national government. At that time, banks were chartered by individual states and only allowed to operate in those states, which gave them a certain degree of local monopoly. Given a twenty-year charter at its establishment, the First Bank's charter was not renewed, leading to the bank's liquidation in 1811. Just five years later, the US Congress chartered the Second Bank of the United States, which began operations in 1817 and was modeled after the First Bank. Andrew Jackson ran on an explicit platform of shutting down the Second Bank, blaming it for many of the nation's economic ills. "The Bank, Mr. van Buren, is trying to kill me, but I will kill it" is what Jackson famously told his vice president in

---

88 Murray N. Rothbard, *The Progressive Era* (Ludwig von Mises Institute, 2017).

1832, before vetoing the renewal of its twenty-year charter. The Second Bank was privatized in 1836 and liquidated in 1841. Jackson would be subject to the first assassination attempt on a US president in 1835, when Richard Lawrence, an English-American house painter, attempted to murder him. Both of Lawrence's pistols misfired, and he was committed to a mental asylum. No relationship between him and any political or financial interests was established, although Jackson believed he was motivated by politics.

As industrialization and economies of scale had led to concentration in many industries, an opposite tendency was developing in the banking industry in the late nineteenth century, in which small and independent banks were proliferating across the growing nation and holding an increasing percentage of the nation's wealth outside the grasp of large national banks, who were not happy about it. The latter conspired to use the power of the state to enact legislation centralizing the banking industry in the hands of a cartel-controlled central bank, dominated by the largest banks.

Warburg's Solution

Paul Warburg was a member of one of the wealthiest families in Germany, the famous and affluent banking house of Warburg in Hamburg. After extensive travel to the US, where he married in 1895, he chose to immigrate to the United States in 1902. Hailing from one of the most sophisticated banks in Europe, he was appalled at what he saw as the primitive state of banking in the US, which he saw as too decentralized, antiquated, and slow. He published extensively on the problems of banking without a central bank and worked diligently to make a central bank a reality. He set his sights on modernizing the American banking system and making it more similar to its European counterparts. "The United States is in fact at about the same point that had been reached by Europe at the time of the Medicis, and by Asia, in all likelihood, at the time of Hammurabi," he wrote in the *New York Times* in 1907.[89]

---

89 Paul Warburg, "Defects and Needs of Our Banking System," *The New York Times*, January 6, 1907.

According to Warburg, what America needed was a central clearance institution that would facilitate the rapid discounting and clearance of bills, utilizing collectively held bank reserves to bolster the market, prevent panic, and assist troubled banks. He used the Reichsbank of Germany as a model to follow.

With the major industries increasingly cartelized under captured regulatory agencies, Paul Warburg and the central US bankers sought to do the same with the banking industry. The panic of 1907 made Warburg's ideas more prominent. He published explicit and detailed plans, which attracted the attention of Senator Nelson Aldrich, chair of the National Monetary Commission and a wealthy associate of J. P. Morgan. After getting to know Warburg, Aldrich worked to make Warburg's vision a reality.

In 1910, Senator Aldrich and Paul Warburg boarded Aldrich's private train car in New Jersey with five guests sworn to secrecy. They headed 1,000 miles south to Jekyll Island Club, a secluded, exclusive resort in Georgia. The other five men were Abraham Piatt Andrew, Assistant Secretary of the Treasury; Frank A. Vanderlip, the president of National City Bank of New York; Henry P. Davison, a senior partner at J. P. Morgan; Charles D. Norton, president of J. P. Morgan's First National Bank of New York; and Benjamin Strong, head of J. P. Morgan's Bankers Trust Company. Over nine days, these seven men would lay out in detail the plans for establishing a central bank, in complete secrecy. Frank Vanderlip would later write:

> Despite my views about the value to society of greater publicity for the affairs of corporations, there was an occasion, near the close of 1910, when I was as secretive—indeed, as furtive—as any conspirator.... I do not feel it is any exaggeration to speak of our secret expedition to Jekyll Island as the occasion of the actual conception of what eventually became the Federal Reserve System.... We were told to leave our last names behind us. We were told, further, that we should avoid dining together on the night of our departure. We were instructed to come one at a time and as unobtrusively as possible to the railroad terminal on the New Jersey littoral of the Hudson, where Senator Aldrich's private car would be in readiness, attached to the rear end of a train for the South.... Once aboard the private car we began

to observe the taboo that had been fixed on last names. We addressed one another as "Ben," "Paul," "Nelson," "Abe"—it is Abraham Piatt Andrew. Davison and I adopted even deeper disguises, abandoning our first names. On the theory that we were always right, he became Wilbur and I became Orville, after those two aviation pioneers, the Wright brothers.... The servants and train crew may have known the identities of one or two of us, but they did not know all, and it was the names of all printed together that would have made our mysterious journey significant in Washington, in Wall Street, even in London. Discovery, we knew, simply must not happen, or else all our time and effort would be wasted. If it were to be exposed publicly that our particular group had got together and written a banking bill, that bill would have no chance whatever of passage by Congress.[90]

After nine days of deliberation, the men had produced the outline for a national central bank. This meeting was a perfect illustration of the devious opacity of central banking under the classical gold standard and how it inevitably resulted in collusion. As the gold grew more and more concentrated in centralized financial institutions, the people in charge of these institutions could collude with each other to form a cartel that benefited them at the expense of their customers. Governments would either protect this cartel or they would get replaced by a government that would protect it.

There was no chance for the public to express acceptance or disapproval. While the proposal seemed to be an arcane explanation of highly technical banking matters that would have little relevance to the life of the average person, it was to be one of the most important institutions in US history, and the fourth incarnation of a central bank in America. There was some token debate and discussion in Congress, but these were largely immaterial, and the bill passed was very similar to the Jekyll Island proposal.

The proposal for the fourth bank was passed in the House of Representatives in September 1913 with little debate or opposition. Very few understood

---

90 Frank A. Vanderlip, "XXI. A Conclave on Jekyll Island," in *From Farm Boy to Financier*, with Boyden Sparkes (D. Appleton-Century Co., 1935), 210–19.

the momentous consequences. On December 18, it passed in the Senate despite significant opposition. It still needed the signature of the president to become law, and conveniently enough, the banking industry had managed to get the right man to sign the bill on December 23, just before the country would go on holiday for Christmas.

Woodrow Wilson was not expected to seal the Democratic nomination for the election of 1912. The frontrunner for the nomination was Speaker of the House Champ Clark. Champ Clark was an avowed opponent of the Federal Reserve, but Wilson was open to the idea. During the Democratic Convention of that year, William Jennings Bryan announced his support for Wilson, swinging the outcome in his favor. Bryan was a popular figure in the Democratic Party who had secured the party nomination for the presidency three times. Securing the Democratic nomination was a surprise, but defeating Republican incumbent William Howard Taft was an even bigger surprise. Republicans had held the presidency since 1897, with William McKinley and Theodore Roosevelt preceding Taft. But it was precisely Theodore Roosevelt who presented the presidency to Wilson on a silver platter by choosing to run against his old friend Taft, splitting the Republican vote. The bankers' man was in office just in time.

Clark and Taft might have opposed the creation of the Federal Reserve had they won the presidency, and they likely would have done everything to prevent US entry into the Great War and to try to resolve the conflict. With Wilson taking power in early 1913, the stage was set for the Jekyll Island cartel to implement its plan for cartelization of America's banks and money, and for it to finance American entry into the Great War. Bryan was appointed as Secretary of State during the Wilson administration, and his initial opposition to the Federal Reserve was ameliorated, as he and Wilson would make a minor ceremonial amendment: they demanded that the president would be the one who appoints the chairman of the Federal Reserve Board, and not the cartel banks. This change was enough to assuage the fears of the economically illiterate populists who did not understand the implications of centralizing national bank reserves with a government-protected monopoly cartel. They were easily deceived by inconsequential superficialities, such as who appoints the nominal figurehead of the cartel.

The stage was set for the banking cartel to begin sucking the blood of the American people through the vampiric creature from Jekyll Island. The outcome of the Jekyll Island seven men's deliberations would turn into law binding all 100 million Americans. In his history of the bank, G. Edward Griffin identifies the four main objectives of the cartel:

1. How to stop the growing influence of small, rival banks and to [ensure] that control over the nation's financial resources would remain in the hands of those present;

2. How to make the money supply more elastic in order to reverse the trend of private capital formation and to recapture the industrial loan market;

3. How to pool the meager reserves of the nation's banks into one large reserve so that all banks will be motivated to follow the same loan-to-deposit ratios. This would protect at least some of them from currency drains and bank runs;

4. Should this lead eventually to the collapse of the whole banking system, then how to shift the losses from the owners of the banks to the taxpayers.[91]

It should also be abundantly clear why this arrangement would be popular with governments, particularly in increasingly democratic systems. With bank reserves centralized in an institution given a monopoly on clearance, it would be in the interest of the bank to extend credit to governments to finance spending on social programs and war. The central banks were always a great customer for government bonds, as they returned the favor to politicians by giving them financing in exchange for repayment through decades of government tax collection. Politicians could obtain funding to finance programs that secured their reelection. Government bonds would grow and become far more marketable

---

91 G. Edward Griffin, *The Creature from Jekyll Island: A Second Look at the Federal Reserve*, 3rd ed. (American Media, 1998).

in a world in which central banks used an entire nation's reserves to buy them. Governments would win, banks would win, government and bank propagandists would win, and the losers would be the vast majority of the population who could not understand what was going on. As long as they had no alternative to this central banking cartel, they had to watch helplessly as the fruits of their labor went toward financing war, politicians' vanity projects, and election campaigns.

Griffin astutely identifies the magic ingredient that made the classical gold standard popular with most of the world's bankers. By centralizing bank reserves into a monopoly with which no other bank could compete, the larger banks could comfortably expand credit in tandem at a similar ratio of loan-to-deposit. And they could do so without worrying about their individual banknotes being discounted relative to each other. If a particular bank had extended its loans at a higher ratio than other banks in a free market, exchange houses would inevitably get a larger number of its bills relative to other exchange houses, and the increase in supply would inevitably lead to a discount emerging on the excessive number of banknotes. This, in turn, would alert holders of these banknotes that further discounts were possible. The marginal holders would start exchanging this bank's banknotes for those of banks that had no discount on them, which would result in further discounting of the inflationist bank's banknotes. Had the initial discounting happened based on unfounded rumors, and the bank had the reserves to redeem all of its banknotes in full, then the discount would just present a profit opportunity for the bank to buy back its own banknotes at a discount, then watch as the discount is eliminated. This is how a truly free market in banking makes inflationary credit expansion impossible. As long as people are free to trade different banknotes at the price they want, and as long as they can clear their payments through voluntary exchange houses, the market will always discount the banknotes of an inflationary bank, roughly to the extent to which the banks' outstanding loans are unbacked by hard gold reserves.

But a coercive monopoly destroys the efficacy of a free market banking system just as it does to every other market, and that is why bankers wanted one. Just like a coercive monopoly for apples results in the increase in profits for producers, an increase in prices of apples for consumers and a reduction in the quality and/or the quantity of the apples, a banking monopoly destroys the quality of banking and money to benefit bankers. With a banking cartel monopolizing clearance, things look very different. If cartel banks all expanded credit by 20% beyond their loans, all the banks' notes would be discounted similarly, which effectively means they would not be discounted, and no bank run could occur on any of them. This would hold for as long as the banking clearance system remained a monopoly. Smaller non-cartel banks in this case had no choice but to follow the larger banks' lead. If they had avoided extending credit, they would miss out on profits and get overtaken by the larger banks. They were also too small, and their banknotes too illiquid without the cartel's centralized clearance mechanism, for them to discount the larger national banks' notes. If they extended credit at a higher ratio than the major banks, they likely would go bankrupt. The wise course of action was to follow the lead of the larger banks to benefit from credit expansion at the prescribed deposit-to-loan ratio, but not to go any further than that. With all clearance centralized at the Federal Reserve Bank monopoly, a private cartel owned by the major banks, the clearance system was weaponized to enrich the larger banks, allow them to take over the smaller banks, and vampirically extract wealth from hard-working Americans who would have had to spend months of serious study even to begin to understand what this seemingly innocuous technocratic behemoth really was. Worse, the enormous loot from this larceny would be enough to buy favorable media coverage, supportive academic research, and pliable political leaders who would continue to gaslight the victims of this theft and convince them that it was actually in their own best interest and that the problems caused by the cartel are best solved by granting more power to the cartel. The die seemed cast for decades, if not centuries, of banking slavery.

The Business of War

The Federal Reserve had pounced on the opportunity to lend to the belligerents in the Great War. The cash-strapped British government, whose bond auction had failed, relied on constant injections of credit from the United States, which the Jekyll Island cartel exploited handsomely. By September 1915, American banks, particularly J. P. Morgan, had lent around \$500m–\$600m to British and French banks.[92] A major Anglo-French loan for \$500m was floated, and expected to close in October 1915.

The opportunity was lucrative, but the risk was substantial, as a British-French defeat could result in a massive default. But with the Jekyll Island cartel now sitting on an increasingly large treasure of Americans' savings, it could risk it all financing a foreign war. It could even use its outsized influence to get the US government to enter the war to try to avoid a British defeat that would render Americans' loans to Britain worthless.

When the Great War started in August 1914, the United States had declared itself neutral. Its people predominantly wanted to stay out of the war, and non-interventionism was dominant; however, that began to fray as the war wore on, and European countries sought to influence the US to intervene. President Wilson's Secretary of State, William Jennings Bryan, was a vocal proponent of neutrality. He had tried to mediate between the belligerents, but to no avail. Wilson was decidedly impartial at the beginning of the war, even urging Americans to remain impartial, but he became increasingly more sympathetic to the British-French-Russian-Italian alliance as the war continued. The German targeting of boats around the British Isles proved decisive. In March 1915, a German U-boat sank a British passenger ship with an American on board, which began to sway public opinion against Germany. And in May 1915, another German U-boat sank the RMS Lusitania, one of the world's largest passenger ships, which was sailing from New York to Liverpool. It was carrying 1,960 passengers and crew, 1,197 of whom lost their lives, and 128 of whom were American. Americans were livid, but Germany was unapologetic. They claimed that the Lusitania was listed as an auxiliary warship and that it had carried weapons, as was listed on its manifest, a fact that was not discussed in the British press at the time. In February, Germany had already declared the seas around Britain a war zone and warned that any Allied ships there would be sunk. Britain had been conducting a naval blockade of Germany at the same

---

92 Martin Horn, *Britain, France, and the Financing of the First World War* (McGill-Queen's University Press, 2002), 90–95; Osborne, *The Bank of England 1914-21*; Ferguson, *The Pity of War: Explaining World War I*, 115–17.

time. On April 22, the German ambassador to the United States published, in fifty American newspapers, a warning to Americans about sailing aboard boats in waters adjacent to the British Isles.[93]

President Wilson received conflicting advice from his Secretary of State, William Jennings Bryan, who wanted to prohibit passengers from going on ships carrying contraband,[94] and his counselor, Robert Lansing, who wanted to hold Germany accountable. Wilson went with Lansing's view, demanding that Germany apologize and pay compensation. Meanwhile, he refused to follow Bryan's advice to warn passengers not to travel on British ships or on ships carrying contraband. Bryan would resign[95] in June 1915, and it looked increasingly likely the United States would join the war. Bryan, at that point, regretted his role in the election of Wilson. Had he supported Champ Clark or stayed neutral, President Clark would almost certainly have been working to diffuse tensions in Europe rather than preparing to bring America into them.

---

93 Graf von Johann Heinrich Bernstorff, *My Three Years in America*, with Robert J. Hall (1920; Project Gutenberg, 2010).

94 Thomas Paterson et al., *American Foreign Relations: A History, Volume 2: Since 1895*, 8th ed., (Cengage Learning, 2014), 73.

95 Michael Kazin, *A Godly Hero: The Life of William Jennings Bryan* (Knopf Doubleday Publishing Group, 2007), 237–38.

VIII.

The Century of Flight

The flying machine which will really fly might be evolved by the combined and continuous efforts of mathematicians and mechanicians in from one million to ten million years—provided, of course, we can meanwhile eliminate such little drawbacks and embarrassments as the existing relation between weight and strength in inorganic materials.

—*The New York Times*, 69 days before the Wright Brothers flew

Aviation was the quintessential twentieth-century industry, and its history is indicative of the incredibly transformative and unexpected impact of innovations in this century. At the beginning of the twentieth century, most of the world viewed heavier-than-air flight as an impossibility. Mass air transportation through flight in heavy machines seemed impossible to most, since the flight of balloons was predicated on their being lighter than air. With their limited speed, range of motion, and elevation, there was not much practical or commercial use for balloons as modes of transport. Instead, they were mainly used for entertainment or surveillance.

For as long as man has existed, he has looked enviously at birds and wondered how he could emulate them. Countless great minds throughout history attempted to fly. Hot air balloons and man-carrying kites have existed in China since the first and sixth centuries AD, respectively. Many daredevils and engineers tried to fly by jumping from elevated heights with constructed wings. Leonardo da Vinci thought extensively of the problem and crafted many designs like fixed-wing gliders, rotorcraft, parachutes, and ornithopters, which are planes that fly by mimicking the movement of a bird's wings. In *Codex Atlanticus*, Leonardo wrote, "Tomorrow morning, on the second day of January, 1496, I will make the thong and the attempt." It is unclear what happened with the attempt, though Leonardo obviously survived it.

Early progress in flight came from hot air balloons, which first flew successfully in 1783 in France. In 1852, Henri Giffard invented the airship and flew fifteen kilometers with it. In the late eighteenth century and the first half of the nineteenth century, Sir George Cayley in England designed the first successful human glider and provided the first scientific treatment of the problem of aviation. There were countless scientists, engineers, and amateurs preoccupied with the problem throughout the nineteenth century, mainly in Britain, France, and the United States. Building on Cayley's work, Frenchman Alphonse Pénaud flew the first stable fixed-wing airplane model a distance of forty meters. After centuries of failed flight attempts by emulating birds' wings or rotary-wing craft, Alphonse Pénaud was the first to successfully implement the idea of a propeller to move the airplane forward and fixed wings to generate lift, which continue to be the operating principles of all jet planes today. Pénaud would produce children's toys from his design to try to raise money to build real airplanes, which required very high costs at a time when engines were still new and expensive. His toy-making and fundraising were not enough to secure the resources he needed, and Pénaud would commit suicide in 1880, but his ideas lived on. Germany's Otto Lilienthal made many successful gliding attempts, which gained him fame, and he documented his technical improvements in his 1889 book, *Birdflight as the Basis of Aviation*. In 1894, French-born American engineer Octave Chanute wrote *Progress in Flying Machines*, which proved vital for future aviation pioneers, accurately and meticulously documenting all the ideas put forward to achieve flight on both sides of the Atlantic.

Standing on and taking off from the shoulders of these giants were two bicycle mechanics from Dayton, Ohio: brothers Orville and Wilbur Wright. As young boys, their father had given them a model toy airplane based on Pénaud's rubber-powered design. It captivated them. They were both skilled with machines, and they owned and operated a highly successful bicycle business. But what distinguished them from others was their methodical and meticulous scientific approach to examining the technical aspects of flight. In 1900, they studied the climate across America and consulted meteorological authorities to identify the spot that would have the ideal winds for their flight experiments. They identified the town of Kitty Hawk on Bodie Island, North Carolina, because of its wind and soft sand. They traveled to that desolate spot and camped away from civilization, getting brutalized by mosquitoes, but never wavering from their mission and calling. They prioritized safety and gradual improvements and kept returning to Kitty Hawk for repeated experiments with gliders. In late 1901, they built their own small wind tunnel in their workshop and experimented with 200 different wing designs. In 1902, their glider had effectively solved the problem of flight control by inventing three-axis control, which allowed a pilot to control the movement of the aircraft. This system remains in use in all modern aircraft today. Whereas most aviation enthusiasts were focused on power and achieving liftoff, the Wrights focused on control and moved to the power question only *after* perfecting the elements of control. They employed the same methodical experimentation in the design of engines and had their shop mechanic, Charlie Taylor, build an engine for them out of aluminum. They fitted the engine on their newly built Wright Flyer, and on December 17, 1903, Orville Wright became the first man to fly on a heavier-than-air machine.[96]

Outside of some very isolated tribes, everyone alive today was born to a world where flight is possible and common. Very few people stop to think of just how improbable modern flight actually is, and how unfathomable it was before it became a reality. No less an authority on engineering and physics than Lord Kelvin wrote in 1896, "I have not the smallest molecule of faith in aerial navigation other than ballooning, or of the expectation of good results from any of the trials we heard of." No less a visionary than Thomas Edison said in 1895, "It is apparent to me that the possibilities of the aeroplane, which two or three years ago were thought to hold the solution to the [flying machine] problem, have been exhausted, and that we must turn elsewhere." Mathematician

---

96 David McCullough, *The Wright Brothers* (Simon & Schuster, 2015).

and astronomer Simon Newcomb famously said in 1903, "Aerial flight is one of that class of problems with which man will never be able to cope."

The question had been so conclusively settled that *The New York Times*, on October 9, 1903, wrote:

> The flying machine which will really fly might be evolved by the combined and continuous efforts of mathematicians and mechanicians in from one million to ten million years—provided, of course, we can meanwhile eliminate such little drawbacks and embarrassments as the existing relation between weight and strength in inorganic materials. No doubt the problem has attractions for those it interests, but to the ordinary man it would seem as if effort might be employed more profitably.[97]

Camped out in Kill Devil Hills, North Carolina, Orville Wright clearly had no access to *The New York Times*, as that day's entry in his diary read, "We unpacked rest of goods for new machine and set to work on upper surface."[98] Instead of "one million to ten million years," it took Orville and his elder brother Wilbur sixty-nine days from the day of the *Times'* prophecy to fly their plane on the first manned flight in history.

Such was the improbability of the Wright's feat that it took years for the rest of the world to believe that it had actually happened. *The London Times* was still writing in 1906, "All attempts at artificial aviation are not only dangerous to human life, but foredoomed to failure from the engineering standpoint." And in 1907, Britain's Minister of War, Lord Haldane, exasperated by the failure of the British army's attempts at flight, privately remarked that airplanes would never fly.[99]

In France, news of the Wright Brothers' flight was received with a mixture of incredulity, indifference, and intrigue. No official bodies were documenting

---

97 "Flying Machines Which Do Not Fly," *The New York Times*, October 9, 1903.
98 *Diaries and Notebooks: 1903, Orville Wright*, Digital Collection: Wilbur Wright and Orville Wright Papers, 1809-1979, Library of Congress, 1903.
99 Alfred Golin, *No Longer an Island: Britain and the Wright Brothers, 1902-1909* (Stanford University Press, 1984), 274.

their attempt at flight to confirm their outlandish claims, and the Wright brothers didn't help their credibility by maintaining secrecy about the design they used to achieve their feat. Besides, it was not believable that two obscure bicycle mechanics from Ohio were the first to fly when aviation was a thoroughly French industry. France was where the balloon industry was thriving and where motorized balloons were beginning to offer possibilities of flights covering long distances. And it was in France where heavier-than-air flight was making the most progress.

In 1891, a young, rich Brazilian by the name of Alberto Santos-Dumont came to France at the age of eighteen to pursue his dream of flight. He'd achieved spectacular feats with motored balloons and was now working on a heavier-than-air flying machine not dissimilar to what the Wright brothers had been using. In 1906, Santos-Dumont was able to fly his aircraft for 220 meters, which was the first flight supervised by neutral parties. For many in France, this was considered the first human flight, as they refused to acknowledge the Wrights' earlier attempts. But in 1908, Wilbur Wright came to France with his latest jet, the Model A. He demonstrated the superiority of their aircraft to French rivals and silenced the doubters. He signed an agreement with the French manufacturers La Compagnie Generale de Navigation Aerienne to produce the Wright Model A aircraft in France. By the end of 1908, the Wrights' plane could fly an incredible 124 kilometers in one flight.

All over France, young engineers and daredevils had been obsessed with flight like nowhere else in the world. Perhaps the most enthusiastic and capable among them was Louis Blériot. The charismatic entrepreneur, adventurer, and bon vivant had invented the first practical headlamp for cars and made a fortune manufacturing and selling them to the nascent car industry. In 1900, at the age of twenty-eight, he was financially secure enough to dedicate himself to his dream of aviation, which had blossomed after he saw the aircraft of another French aviation pioneer, Clement Ader.

Blériot's early aircraft either failed to fly or came crashing down. He was involved in a large number of serious crashes, though he miraculously emerged alive from them all, ready to go again, earning a legendary reputation for tenacity, resilience, ferocity, and good luck. The French press often mocked him, but he was like a honey badger, astonishingly emerging unscathed time and time again, against all odds, without ever caring about the hatred he received. Blériot was not the sort of man to be cowed by the skepticism and mockery of the lazy; he was thick-skinned, determined, capable, and resourceful. His workshop would keep churning out better airplanes, and on July 25, 1909, he used his Blériot XI aircraft to achieve a historic first in aviation: he crossed the Channel from France to Britain. The achievement won him a £1,000 prize from *The Daily Mail*, but more importantly, it boosted demand for his planes. He would ramp up his production, but like other French aviation pioneers, his hands were tied by the threat of lawfare from the notoriously litigious Wright brothers.

In 1906, the Wright brothers obtained a patent for a "Flying Machine" thanks to their system for controlling airplanes, which had made flight possible. With this patent, the Wrights shifted their focus away from making and improving airplanes to suing airplane-makers for patent infringement. They went after many of the producers of airplanes and the innovators of flight in the US and in Europe. The Wrights had indeed come up with the system of control that made flight possible, but many other aviators had introduced significant improvements to speed, safety, range, control, and reliability. Instead of all these talents being unleashed to innovate and experiment, they were preoccupied with lawsuits. It was a terrible shame for human progress that the brightest minds in aviation spent more time in the years 1909 and 1910 thinking about legal matters than engineering matters. With all the pioneers of aviation engaged in legal battles against each other, progress was slow. Airplanes were still slow, unsafe, short-ranged, and unreliable, and demand consisted mainly of eccentric rich daredevils using planes for thrills.

Octave Chanute expressed the sentiments of most aviation enthusiasts on January 23, 1910, when he said in an interview:

> I admire the Wrights. I feel friendly toward them for the marvels they have achieved; but you can easily gauge how I feel concerning their attitude at present by the remark I made to Wilbur Wright recently. I told him I

was sorry to see they were suing other experimenters and abstaining from entering the contests and competitions in which other men are brilliantly winning laurels. I told him that in my opinion they are wasting valuable time over lawsuits which they ought to concentrate in their work.[100]

---

100 "Octave Chanute to Wilbur Wright," Inventors, Mississippi State University, January 23, 1910.

PART II

CAPITAL
FLIGHT

This part of the book begins the alternative history.
All events happening here starting in September 1915 are
fictional, but events happening before that date are real. The only
exception are events pertaining to the aviation industry, which
are real until January 1910, and fictional from February 1910.

IX.

Blériot Transport Corporation

The Wright Move

In another world, the Wrights' lawfare may have crippled aviation, but fortunately for our world, aviation was emancipated. The pivotal turning point came in October 1910, when Octave Chanute decided to write a detailed letter to the Wright brothers, explaining his misgivings in detail and sharing his honest thoughts on how best to move forward.

Dear Wilbur and Orville,

I hope this letter finds you well. I have received with annoyance the news that you are in court again, this time hoping to stop French engineers from "copying" your aircraft design. As I have told you before, I find it utterly distasteful, crass, self-destructive, and impudent for engineers to try to use the strong arm of the law to prevent others from emulating their achievements. No man has ever built anything without relying on the efforts of many men before him. It was I who came up with the idea of using the strut-wire braced wing structure. You took that idea from me, and yet it never crossed my mind to attempt to take you to court. On the contrary, I went down to Kitty Hawk and did everything I could to help you implement the design as efficiently as possible, in the hope that you might achieve flight. It was not your idea to combine a rotating propeller with wings to achieve lift-off; Alphonse Pénaud came up with that idea, and it was a toy with this design of his, gifted by your father to you as children, which sparked your entire interest in flight. It was not your imagination that invented the gliders you used; that was the work of Lilienthal, who never considered suing you for copying it. It was not you who invented the engine that drives the propeller, or the fuel that runs it, or the metals and fabrics needed to make an airplane work.

You took a momentous step forward by being the first to achieve controlled flight, but it was merely one step in humanity's long march, a step that would not have been possible without the infinite steps that preceded it, all the way from the command of fire until my strut-wire braced wings. And it is a march that will surely continue with more engineers and inventors improving upon what you and I built in ways we cannot imagine. You could not have made your step without those who preceded you, so you should not use the law to ban those who follow you from taking more steps. Such a move not only fails on a moral basis, but I also firmly believe it fails the market test. In the long run, you will be able to build better, faster, and safer airplanes if you let people make on your ideas than if you hamper them. The world has many more engineers than you, and even if you were the smartest of them all, you would not be able to come up with a tiny fraction of the ideas that the rest of the world's engineers can come up with. Letting the world use your ideas means many potential improvements to your ideas, which you yourself can benefit from, and it will mean you can use the many ideas of others. In the spirit of scientific cooperation and our shared desire for human progress, you should set the example for the industry to encourage the free exchange of ideas.

As a courtesy for all the help others have been to you, I implore you to drop all your court cases and get back to your workshop. You are engineers and builders, and engineers belong in workshops, not in courtrooms with criminals and lawyers. The world will benefit immensely more from what you produce in workshops than what you do in courtrooms. Your ingenuity, place in history, and first-mover advantage are unassailable, and you can channel these toward building better airplanes, benefiting from the improvements others make to airplanes to offer the world the best airplanes. There are infinite opportunities for bringing flight to various fields of human commerce, and I hope you make the most of them. There are millions worldwide who travel long distances by boat, train, car, or foot, and would pay dearly to fly instead. Countless merchants would pay to have their goods delivered by plane. Countless banks would pay for same-day final settlement rather than wait on central-bank clearing. You will not capitalize on this demand by taking others to court. If you continue to try to use the courts to bludgeon other inventors, you will stymie human progress while sinking into irrelevant bitterness. I have spoken to Dumont, Blériot, and all the major French aviators and obtained their solemn promise that they will never sue you for patent infringement if you drop this lawsuit. I believe a new cooperative way is possible for our industry.

For my sake, for your sake, and for the sake of humanity, get back to your workshop!

Sincerely,
Octave Chanute
10 February 1910

Orville Wright put the paper down and stared blankly at his brother Wilbur. Chanute had struck a nerve, and it was the most sensitive nerve of all. Wilbur and Orville had barely spent any time in their workshop over the past year. The patent court cases had consumed and hollowed them, as men, inventors, businessmen, and engineers. They hadn't made any improvements to their airplane models in that whole year, all while reports were flooding in about pilots and engineers achieving seemingly impossible feats and creating all manner of improvements that seemed unworkable to them. Aviators were making progress faster than the Wrights' lawyers could sue them.

The Wright brothers had a powerful desire to attempt several of the designs they had heard of, and many ideas for how to improve upon them. But that was not possible because their days were spent with lawyers trying to get the state to sanction anyone building airplanes for violating their patent. Rather than continue pushing the boundaries of what humans were capable of, the brothers now found themselves pushing back human progress in the hope they could get the state to help them squeeze a few more dimes from their competitors. The youthful excitement and boyish mechanical curiosity the two brothers once possessed had taken them from a bike repair shop to making history as the first humans to fly—but that seemed like ages ago. They missed the thrill they got from camping for weeks in Kitty Hawk. They felt like they had aged three decades in the five years since their first flight. Worse, they'd become the smug and self-entitled conservative figures of authority they had always detested, the type who could never build anything but derived all pleasure from preventing others from building. Their days were spent meeting lawyers, writing letters, and hiring private investigators to spy on their competition. They missed the stubborn stains of engine lubricant oil on their hands, the deafening symphony of roaring engines, the sweet aroma of burned gasoline, and the sight of each other exhausted and falling asleep on the workshop floor at the end of a long night of work. They missed the loud, foul mouths of their shop helpers, and they couldn't stand their lawyers' endless monotone droning.

"I do miss that workshop," Wilbur said wistfully after a long silence.

"I really miss not knowing lawyers. In retrospect, the days I spent outside of the legal system were the highlight of my life."

"I wish we could keep those court cases going while we get back to the workshop to make better planes."

"I wish so too," responded Orville. "But lawyers are very expensive and dangerous, and if you're not on top of them, they could cost you very dearly."

"I admit I have asked myself this question before, and today Chanute has brought it up again: Why should we even care that others are copying us? Let them build their own airplanes. We will make better airplanes. There is far more demand for airplanes than our workshop could possibly meet. We invented the airplane, and they will always have to catch up to us if we focus on pushing ourselves and making our planes better. Why do we want to stop them from innovating?"

"Because if they copy our design and make a better airplane, they'll make more money than us," Orville responded.

Wilbur replied: "The planet has a billion and a half people on it, but it doesn't have 100 working airplanes. Are we really so insane as to imagine we would become the only authority allowed to produce airplanes through government fiat? There will be infinite demand for airplanes, and the more time we spend in courts, the less time we'll spend in the workshop capitalizing on our advantage, and the more we are allowing others to overtake us, inevitably."

Orville had no answer to his brother. He put away the papers on his desk and started packing to go home. Wilbur soon followed. The next morning, Wilbur woke up and decided to forgo his office suit and instead opt for his old workshop overalls. He drove to the workshop and was unsurprised to find Orville already there, also in his overalls. It had been months since they were last in the workshop together, though it felt like just yesterday. They slipped back into their old routine, picking up all the loose ends and unfinished tasks they had been neglecting for months. In their natural habitat, the brothers didn't even need to talk to communicate effectively, whereas in the office, they struggled to express simple ideas to one another. Lions roar, birds chirp, wolves howl, and lawyers talk, but engineers build. The native language of an engineer is his product. Descriptions and explanations all seem futile next to a working product of the human mind that demonstrates what was thought impossible before. And perhaps never in the history of humanity had an inventor produced an object that spoke louder than an airplane: the dream of humanity for eons of observing birds, the dream that had killed countless dreamers, finally achieved.

Around noon, their office assistant arrived at the workshop. He was puzzled as to why neither of them had shown up. The lawyer had been waiting for them to attend their planned meeting. But they both seemed unconcerned. They told the assistant to inform the lawyer that they wouldn't be able to make it to the office, and that he'd be welcome to see them in the workshop. Their lawyer arrived later that afternoon, and the brothers informed him that they were no longer interested in pursuing their court cases. They settled his bill and immediately felt rejuvenated, like old men given their younger bodies again. They were no longer terrified of the prospect of someone building something better than their planes; they were now excited about what they could build themselves.

The Wrights' abandoning their lawsuit was huge news for the intrepid pilots, mechanics, and entrepreneurs involved in the nascent aviation industry, particularly in France. Legal battles between the Wrights and their numerous competitors had dominated the period from 1907 to 1910. When news of the lawsuit's termination reached France, the excitement was palpable. Plane builders were now free to tinker with their designs. Investors could finance the builders without worrying about being ruined by lawsuits. Entrepreneurial imaginations would run wild with airplane-based business ideas.

Nobody was happier with the news than Louis Blériot. The Wrights' lawsuit had hampered his progress and soured his typically jovial mood, so its dropping put a spring in his step and a sparkle in his eyes. He went home every day excited to share his ideas with his wife, like a child telling his mom about his school day. He knew airplanes would be a huge deal, but his success with headlights made him keenly aware that airplanes could not succeed unless there was serious market demand driving their development. While other aviation pioneers focused on technical improvements and exhibitions, Blériot knew the best way to spur innovation and improvements would be to stimulate serious market demand for a product. His crossing of the English Channel had increased demand among a few wealthy adventurers, but a real commercial application was needed.

He had considered building aircraft for travel or joyrides, allowing people to see the world from above for the first time. He considered building airplanes optimized for moving commercial cargo or mail. He meticulously ran the numbers on these ideas, but they proved not to be financially viable.

Humans were too heavy for this to work. The cost of manufacturing airplanes for passengers would be very high, and the cost of each ride would likely deter most of those who are not already deterred by safety concerns. He looked at commercial goods, but most goods, like humans, were too heavy to move economically over airplanes. He realized that this idea would only work for goods that held a lot of value and little weight. This simple thought sent him down a rabbit hole that would change the world forever.

The Wrights' lawsuit's demise encouraged many people to enter the world of aviation. Many of France's entrepreneurs and adventurers were hard at work trying to improve on their airplane design. To stimulate more innovation, Guy de Polignac established the Pommery Cup in 1909 to offer a lucrative prize for the pilot who could fly the longest distance. On March 28, 1911, Jules Védrines managed a 560-kilometer flight from Paris to Bordeaux.[101] The next month, he collected the inaugural Pommery Cup at an event hosting Europe's top pilots and aviation engineers.

Not Your Vault, Not Your Gold

Blériot was there on a mission. Aviators had come a long way since his flight across the Channel, and so had he. But he was no longer interested in competitions, trophies, publicity, or media. He meant business—and he knew business would be what would catapult flight, not adventures or trophies.

During the ceremony, Blériot spoke to each of the seven pilots present and informed them that he wished to meet with them regarding an important matter after the ceremony. Given his wealth and his stature in the aviation industry, not a single one of them missed the meeting. Jules Védrines, Roland Garros, Henri Farman, René Bedel, Pierre Dacourt, Maurice Guillaux, Marcel Brindejonc des Moulinais, and the Germans Bruno Langer and Karl Ingold

---

101 Gérard Hartmann, *Le Coupe Pommery (1909-1913)* (Champagne Pommery À Reims-France, 1909). Védrines' actual distance to win the 1911 trophy was 293km from Paris to Poitiers, but in this alternative world, where the Wrights dropped their lawsuits, engineers were copying and learning from each other, quickly improving aircraft speed, reliability, and distance.

all attended. After they all sat down, Blériot launched into a speech they did not expect:

> Thank you all for staying here and joining me. Congratulations to Jules, and hard luck to the rest. I wanted to meet with you because I have a serious proposition for your consideration. I have been thinking rigorously about how to improve aviation, and I've concluded that the only thing that will really make a significant impact is finding substantial commercial demand for aircraft. While I appreciate the excellent efforts of the Pommery Cup organizers, and I realize that it provides an incentive for improving aircraft; it cannot compete with commercial applications in spurring innovation. When someone finds a way to make money from airplanes, a giant pot of gold will be available to everyone who improves them, as it will lead to higher productivity and better margins. It will dwarf anything you can win in a competition like this. It is one thing to build things for fun; it is an entirely different thing to build something for capitalists to use in production. The latter will scale much faster and will work more efficiently and safely.

The pilots looked at each other with bewilderment as Blériot's eyes lit up and he continued:

> My proposition to you is that instead of being amateur adventurers, let's utilize our talents to become successful entrepreneurs, making the world a better place. Instead of competing for trophies like children, let us all build something that will secure our children's financial future, along with that of their children.

> I have thought long and hard about the killer app of flight, and at this point, I believe it is in the transportation of gold. For the foreseeable future, gold is the only thing valuable enough to pay for its weight in an airplane. There is also demand for fast final settlement of gold. The train and the car have moved goods very quickly, and banks cannot keep up. Rather than settling

with one another directly, banks now rely on central banks to clear and settle payments between them. This is highly time-consuming and creates problems for business, as we all saw recently.

Remember the massive bank failures in 1907 in the United States? Many successful businessmen were ruined through no fault of their own, just because the banks they used were engaging in credit shenanigans.

Blériot pulled out a gold coin from his pocket and flicked it in the air, catching it again with relish:

This, however, never fails. Gold never lies, and we're the only one who can move it as fast as its owners need it. Holding your own gold in your own hand frees you from having to trust bankers, or spending half your working hours auditing and researching their business. Henry Ford's empire was built on a giant cash balance held in the company headquarters, and he's never lost a moment of sleep worrying about a shady banker. That's why his motor company began its most astounding growth period right after the 1907 banking crash, when many of the companies relying on banks went out of business. I've been working on this problem for the past four years, and have the perfect business idea to free ourselves from this.

The root problem with conventional banking is all the trust that's required to make it work. The central bank must be trusted not to debase the currency, but the history of central banks is full of breaches of that trust. Banks must be trusted to hold our money and transfer it, but they lend it out in waves of credit bubbles with barely a fraction in reserve. You must remember that if it is not your vault, then it is not your gold. You only own a promise from the vault owner that he will grant you gold if you ask for it. This does not inspire confidence. As an engineer, I need certainty, and I am growing increasingly wary of entrusting my wealth to institutions that are acquiring increasing power over me.

I'm developing a new peer-to-peer gold clearance system reliant on airplanes. It's decentralized, with no central bank, because everything is based on fast clearance. We are going to build a fleet of the world's fastest and most reliable aircraft, piloted by the world's best pilots, and we will create a peer-to-peer gold clearance network that enables banks, corporations, and individuals to trade gold directly with one another, without the need for central banks. Our clients will sleep easily knowing they control their own gold and do not have to trust shady central banks to refrain from engaging in risky financial shenanigans. We will propel aviation forward and upward to unimaginable heights with the revenue we generate. We will build planes that cross the Atlantic. We will make airplanes so abundant that even the poor will be able to afford them.

I want you to look at what Henry Ford did with the car industry and imagine this in aviation. He developed the Model-T, and when it generated substantial revenue, he reinvested in capital goods to make production more efficient and cost-effective, enabling him to meet the demand of an ever-increasing customer base. We are on the cusp of an explosion of automobiles thanks to Ford's genius. By making the car commercially viable, Ford increased demand for cars infinitely. I want to do the same for airplanes, and I need you to help me, and I intend to make it worth your time.

Our airplanes will be ready to take off from anywhere and land anywhere. We will fly in pairs of aircraft to ensure we have backup in case something goes wrong with one of them. I will require you to be fully dedicated to this job. No more competitions and acrobatics, no more stunts and showboating; it's time to get serious. You will get an equity stake in the company as well as a steady monthly income of 500 francs each. You have one week to provide me with your final answer. I am now happy to take any questions.

The pilots were stunned by Blériot's audacity. They had all thought of themselves as daring and brave for being some of the first pilots, but this was a whole other level of bravery. It made their aviation feats look like child's play.

Védrines was the first to break the awkward silence: "Louis, I've crashed twice this year. You want me to fly with gold worth more than my house? What happens when we go down in a storm over the Alps?"

"Or when the engine cuts out mid-Channel?" added Dacourt. "I've had three engine failures this month alone. Gold doesn't float."

Blériot's face hardened:

> You are flying toys for trophies, you tinker with these toys with your peasant cousins and hope for the best. If you join us, you will be flying *professional* planes built by engineers for *professional* performance. Everything will be optimized. I've made headlamps that work in the worst conditions because their commercial viability lets me secure significant capital for them. I've flown the Channel when everyone said it was impossible. Do you think I'd stake my fortune on unreliable amateur machines? We will be professional! And we'll fly in pairs—always pairs. Backup pilots, backup engines, backup everything."

After a long silence, Farman said, "There is no way they will let us do this. These central banks are not going to allow competition."

> Central banks work just fine for the central banks and their owners, and they cannot even conceive why others might want to use something different. They are too old, decrepit, and comfortable even to imagine what airplanes will accomplish. But even if they can understand it, how can they stop us? We will not be dealing with them in any way, so we don't need them for anything. Our planes can take off from any empty field and land in any empty field around the globe. By the time they see our planes, we will be out of the range of their guns. Nobody has ever managed to shoot down an airplane, and it will be a long time before anyone can figure out how to do it. They don't have an infinite money printer to fund a police state to go after us. The only thing they can do is cry harder.

"What if they criminalize financial settlement outside of banks?" asked Ingold, to which Blériot responded:

That is incoherent. Doing so would criminalize you paying in cash at your local cafe. Trading physical gold is no different from any other form of trade. Airplanes carrying gold are no different from any form of transportation carrying goods. It would have to be some absurdly totalitarian government that would specifically try to criminalize the use of jets for transferring gold. They'd have to have a literal money printer to fund something like this. But they don't. They are still on a gold standard and only have a small margin for inflation. By the time they understand what is going on and the ramifications, and then try to enforce any kind of ban on us, we will likely have already made a fortune and built a giant fleet. We will have major industrialists and financiers using our services, and they will advocate for our protection. With their central banks undermined, these governments won't have much financing to enforce such totalitarianism. And if they do—well, it's better to be rich asking for forgiveness than to be poor asking for permission.

"I'm not convinced. This is too risky and stressful," said Guillax.

His patience wearing thin, Bleriot responded: "Flying is risky and stressful, and yet you're doing it for trinkets and attention from women. I'm offering you the chance to fly for something meaningful. Something that will change the world!" Blériot's voice dropped to almost a whisper. "Gentlemen, the banks nearly collapsed the world four years ago. They'll do it again, and worse next time. We have the power to build something independent, something they can't control or destroy." His fist clenched. "We can make men truly free with their own money. Isn't that worth more than any trophy?"

"You're not going to make anything except a wasted fortune," replied Guillaux

"If you don't believe me or don't get it, I don't have time to convince you, sorry."

"I'm happy with my trophies, trinkets, and women. I'm out."

"Have fun staying poor!" said Blériot.

The rest of the pilots were far more intrigued and interested. Within a week, they had all confirmed their participation to Blériot.

As the pilots left the meeting in the Paris evening, a letter from Blériot arrived at the Wright brothers' workshop in the Dayton afternoon. This letter explained Blériot's idea to them and asked for their cooperation. Blériot offered to come to the United States to meet the brothers and discuss it in more detail. The brothers were surprised by the letter, but they gave it serious thought. They knew Blériot had the capital to attempt something this audacious, and accepting his proposal would give them the resources necessary to expand their workshop and produce at scale. This was far preferable to courtroom battles over intellectual property.

The offer seemed too good to be true. The pilots had always enjoyed engineering but hated the business side of it. Their foray into attempting financial success through patents and licensing had been a stressful ordeal, and Wilbur's health had begun to suffer as a result of the travel. They had been back in their workshop for six months—back to work on improving their Model B—and felt reinvigorated, especially Wilbur. Now they had one of France's wealthiest men ready to bankroll them and allow them to work with their hands all day and not worry about investors, patents, lawyers, and courtrooms. They telegraphed Blériot to signal their interest and invite him to visit, then spent the next two months thinking about how to develop their aircraft.

Lightning

Blériot arrived in Dayton in May of 1911 and stayed with the Wrights. The lawsuit nastiness had subsided, and instead, a cordial spirit of cooperation existed between the men. Chanute was right: there was far more to be gained from cooperation in conquering the skies than from legal battles. Blériot had shipped a Blériot XI aircraft with him, and the three men spent three weeks going over every last detail of it and the Wrights' airplanes. Blériot was amazed by the scientific experimentation method the Wrights deployed in everything. It was also quite useful that they'd spent years studying their competitors so closely, as it meant they were familiar with all the developments in the US aviation industry. The Wrights enjoyed the depth of knowledge and entrepreneurial instinct Blériot had developed in the automobile and aviation industries. European aviation—French, in particular—had overtaken American aviation in the past year or two, thanks to the Wrights' lawsuits' more substantial crippling effect on US aviators. There were far more airplane makers in Europe, and they had exchanged knowledge and experience more freely. That gave Blériot a large vocabulary of improvements and solutions to potential problems. He could think of every detail, both from the angle of its engineering suitability and its potential commercial success. With their familiarity with aviation on both sides of the Atlantic and their technical genius, the three men set about on the mission of making man truly fly free.

By the end of their three weeks together, Blériot and the Wrights produced a working prototype of Lightning, the most technically advanced airplane in the world. On 1 June 1911, it flew its maiden flight in Ohio, with Blériot at the helm. It could reach a speed of 280 km/h and possessed a range of 1,400 kilometers, with the capacity to carry two pilots and 100 kilograms of load. It was a technical miracle, made possible by the harvesting of the best ideas in aviation from around the world.

After successfully flying Lightning, Blériot and the Wrights agreed to start a new joint venture, Blériot Transport Company (BTC), which would build Lightning jets and deploy them in the clearance of gold. Blériot would own 51% of the company's stock, the Wright brothers would own 25%, and the remaining 24% would be divided equally among 24 pilots recruited from across the United States and Europe. The Wrights immediately began work on building a factory in Dayton, and Blériot returned to Paris, where he also built one. The factories would produce four jets each in 1911, and a further eight jets in 1912.

On January 9, 1912, the first BTC transaction took place when a Lightning jet carried eight bars of 400-oz gold between a bank in Paris and a bank in Lyon. The following week, America's first BTC transaction took place when a Lightning jet took off from the headquarters of the Standard Oil of New Jersey and landed in Cleveland, where it delivered 8 bars of gold to the Standard Oil Company of Ohio.

There was little fanfare around BTC at its launch, outside of aviation circles. The idea seemed completely unworkable. Why would anyone pay for the expensive transportation of physical gold when their local bank could transfer credit obligations? To the extent that academic, governmental, banking, or media authorities discussed BTC, it was to dismiss it with ignorant and snarky haughtiness. Central bankers, from their perch atop the universe, could not possibly see BTC as a threat to their business. So what if a few people had cleared payments directly without going through their central bank? Clearly, such a system could not scale to make a dent in the central banks' business.

Skeptics mocked the use of such brilliant machinery and so much fuel for the arcane and ultimately superfluous economic task of moving sterile bars and coins of gold. Money and banking were inextricably intertwined with the state, experts said, and central banks would continue to be relied upon to ensure the safety of banks and the soundness of money. Central banks worked fine, and their proponents argued they were responsible for ameliorating the financial crises caused by greedy bankers. They relentlessly mocked BTC and its supporters for needing—and wanting—economic catastrophe to succeed, and they repeatedly reassured themselves that no such catastrophe was possible. "There simply aren't enough paranoid cranks to pay for Blériot's fuel," wrote one *Financial Times* columnist, predicting an inevitable demise of the scheme. *The New York Times*, on the other hand, dedicated several articles to bemoaning what it saw as an unconscionable waste of fuel for no reason: "Hydrocarbon fuels are only just beginning to revolutionize industrial processes and transportation, and it would be a shame if so much of these fuels were to be wasted on the paranoid fantasies of aviation enthusiasts rather than more socially beneficial uses."

But business was surprisingly brisk for the Blériot Transport Company, and the number of flights continued to rise steadily. By the end of 1913, its twelve aircraft flew around 2,500 kilometers every day, delivering gold across Europe and the US. Their main clients initially were entrepreneurs and industrialists who moved gold within their businesses or traded it with other businesses. These companies appreciated not having to rely on banks, saving time and mitigating risk.

Blériot's first big customer was Henry Ford and his eponymous Motor Company. The man who built the modern industrial society around the automobile was famous for his love of cold, hard gold cash and distrust of banks and credit. Ford famously accumulated a large cash balance from sales, stored it in his office, and used it to finance operations, bucking the trend among increasingly financialized entrepreneurs of the time, who were reliant on credit to keep their business going and to expand. He constantly spurned bankers tempting him to borrow to finance his operation, and befuddled them by continuing to grow his business worldwide without their services. Ford loved BTC and used it regularly, commissioning several flights every week.

The Standard Oil offshoots were also early customers. Standard Oil had been broken up into 34 companies in 1911, and these came to rely on BTC for their transactions increasingly. The companies had oil fields, refineries, and offices across the United States and Canada, and immediately saw the value in being able to move their money between their businesses without relying on expensive, slow, and unreliable banks. The panic of 1907 had left the very conservative John D. Rockefeller paranoid about leaving his wealth in banks or relying on them for his transactions. He had always liked to keep substantive cash on hand to protect against crises and to capitalize on emerging opportunities.[102] Yet, amidst the panic of 1907, he found himself worried about the fate of the banks he dealt with. Worse, he had to work with his arch-rival, J. P. Morgan, to bail out so many bankrupt businesses and banks with loans. "They always come to Uncle John when there's trouble,"[103] is how he wistfully described the episode. However, aside from the bragging rights, he did not enjoy the ordeal. He wanted his wealth to be independent of the increasingly risky banking system. So he invested in building his own gold vaults across the country and used BTC to move his money between them.

Several banks relied on BTC to offer their clients faster money transfers between major cities, such as Paris and London, or New York and Boston. These banks could offer quicker clearance and speedier access to liquidity, which

---

102 Ron Chernow, *Titan: The Life of John D. Rockefeller, Sr.* (1998; Vintage Books, 2004), 537–61.
103 Chernow, *Titan: The Life of John D. Rockefeller, Sr.*, 79.

was a particularly popular option for many of the growing number of smaller banks popping up all over the United States.

Banks, corporations, royals, and central banks outside of Europe and the US proved to be excellent customers, paying top prices for BTC transactions. After all, BTC was more reliable than the Bank of England or the Bank of France, and it allowed its customers to keep their gold on hand rather than ship it halfway around the world. By the spring of 1914, BTC jets had reached Mexico, Eastern Europe, North Africa, Arabia, Persia, and even India, China, and South America. In 1913, BTC doubled its fleet by producing twelve jets on each side of the Atlantic. In 1914, demand was so high that Blériot ordered the production of 48 aircraft, increasing the fleet to 96 by the end of the year. In June 1914, a BTC Lightning made the first airplane journey across the Atlantic, flying from London to New York via Edinburgh, Reykjavik in Iceland, Narsarsuaq in Greenland, and St. John's, Newfoundland.

The start of the Great War in late July 1914 was a boon for business. Individuals, companies, and banks had started to fear for their money in the central banks. They now recognized the value of an apolitical medium for transferring value across international borders. The world's richest all wanted to extricate their wealth from the grip of central banks consuming it to finance carnage. Blériot realized this was an excellent opportunity to solve a real problem for the market while simultaneously funding the expansion of jet production. He ordered another forty-eight aircraft into production, with their deployment expected in August 1915. What seemed like paranoia on the part of Blériot in 1911 was now revealed as genius foresight. He had studied history and economics; he knew how financial promises can be broken in the most catastrophic ways, and that people eventually learn the value of verifying rather than trusting and of holding their own money rather than holding promises. Many had doubted him, but he now stood on the verge of securing an enormous fortune, helping countless people secure their wealth, and changing the course of history.

X.

Capital Flight

T he wiles of generals, the bravery of soldiers, and the wisdom of diplomats were all powerless in bringing an end to The Great War. It was, instead, the genius of entrepreneurship and technological innovation that saved the world from untold carnage and devastation. The economic and political history of the twentieth century was inextricably tied to the miraculous technological invention of the airplane, and one cannot understand the economic and political history of the twentieth century without understanding the pivotal role aviation played in transforming monetary technology.

In another world, where BTC did not exist, most people would have had to comply with their regime's edicts and keep using their depreciating banknotes while wondering why prices were rising. The war could continue for years as governments confiscated the gold and people continued to work for and earn depreciating currency. But with BTC, people were free not to comply. It was primarily the industrialists, engineers, and entrepreneurs who complied the least; they understood what a suspension of redemption meant. They knew that a solvent bank would never have a reason to suspend redemption because it could satisfy all its creditors and continue operating successfully. They knew that emotional appeals to patriotism could not mask economic reality. The only possible reason to suspend redemption was that the bank's liabilities exceeded its reserves at the current gold-to-pound exchange rate. Leaving money in the bank was akin to playing Russian roulette, but with more bullets added to the gun's chamber with each ensuing day, until no empty chambers were left, and complete loss was guaranteed.

By August 1915, BTC had scaled to 144 Lightning jets, and gold transfer prices had more than doubled since inception. Still, it could not keep up with demand. BTC was the only mechanism in the world for free, peer-to-peer international trade and represented the only method for gold holders to maintain custody of their gold while also being able to send it abroad. A parallel international economy based around physical gold clearance and settlement had begun to take shape. Banks outside of Europe—those reliant on the Bank of England or the Bank of France for their international trade—were some of BTC's biggest clients. Businesses relying on BTC (and on banks relying on BTC) had practically saved themselves from the financial destruction of the war. They held hard money and performed very frequent settlements with local and foreign counterparts. They were not being robbed to finance war, so their cash maintained its value. As prices began to rise in national currencies but stayed constant in gold, people wanted to exchange their paper for gold. Gradually, and then suddenly, the fiat currencies collapsed.

Blériot's business partners and modern industrialists were among the first to utilize his services. The automobile and aviation industries traded with one another across international borders without having to resort to central banks. As the war raged on and more restrictions were imposed on withdrawing gold, demand steadily increased. Old money became anxious about the banking system. They increasingly demanded that gold be kept on hand and wished to rely on BTC for trade. Most important, perhaps, was that BTC had freed people from having to turn in all their gold to the banks in response to their governments' pleas.

The advancement of aviation had another significant technological impact: the development of aerial bombardment as a weapon of war, which allowed for an unprecedented level of destruction. The first year of war witnessed the aerial bombardment of all the capitals of the belligerents, bombings that usually targeted essential and economically important infrastructure. This immense destruction had exacerbated the financial crises of the major powers, reduced the value of their currencies, and arguably hastened their demise.

King Edward VIII

Things were going very badly for the British government and its military. What had been first promoted as the "August Bank Holiday War" had dragged on to the next August Bank Holiday, and hundreds of thousands of British soldiers had died or been injured in the battlefields of France, or on the shores of Gallipoli, where Lord of the Admiralty Winston Churchill was convinced to send them, along with the French Navy, by Grand Duke Nicholas to divert Turkish troops from the Caucasus. Churchill had long underestimated the Turks, and he was made to pay for it dearly. Turkish resistance was fierce, British and French casualties mounted to the hundreds of thousands, and the war became increasingly unpopular in Britain.

By September 1915, merchants in Britain had begun to offer discounts for payment in gold rather than pounds. With that discount factored in, prices had barely moved in terms of gold. However, when measured in paper pounds, prices appeared to be rising rapidly. The financial fate of citizens from then on was a positive function of their intelligence and an inverse function of their susceptibility to government propaganda. There has perhaps never been a more effective program of financial eugenics, richly rewarding the financially literate and severely punishing the gullible.

The Bank of England had prided itself on its adherence to the sacred exchange rate of £4.25 per ounce of gold. Although the rate was still nominally enforced, it was effectively dead in practice, as it was impossible to obtain gold at that rate from the Bank of England. On the black market, the pound had dropped to almost £5 per ounce of gold at the beginning of September 1915. It then reached

£7 by the middle of September and crashed all the way to £28 by the end of September. The British public was livid. They weren't alone. The exact process was playing out in France, Germany, Austria, Italy, Russia, and the Ottoman Empire. The decline in the value of their currencies was weakening the major powers systematically. They could no longer spend with impunity, as they had always expected. Their gold reserves were depleted, and their paper money was increasingly worthless. The grand plans of kings and generals were all based on the expectation that their central bank would continue to perform the alchemy of the classical gold standard by granting them credit, but that was all based on their citizens having no way to trade their gold other than through the central banks, forcing them to leave most of it in the bank. BTC turned these plans to dust.

By the end of September, a permanent encampment of people stood outside the headquarters of the Bank of England. They demanded gold for their paper pounds. But the Bank of England had almost no gold reserves left. It had sent some of its last ingots to the US weeks earlier to secure weapons, and it was now counting on its banks and post offices to collect more gold from the British people to continue securing weapons for war. They had not expected this monetary awakening and had no idea what to do.

The lines of people demanding redemption of their notes quickly grew in numbers, taking on the shape of a protest, and the police were growing increasingly unable and unwilling to confront them. Indeed, some policemen would join the protesters when their shifts were over, knowing their paychecks were becoming increasingly worthless. On Tuesday, October 5, 1915, with hundreds of thousands of protestors camped outside the Bank of England, a section of the crowd managed to break into the Bank, and the policemen gave up trying to stop them. The trickle turned into a flood. The Bank of England's managers and employees removed their three-piece suits and remained in their undershirts in an effort to blend in with the mob and successfully escaped. The crowd ransacked the entire building, rifling through every last drawer and file. With heavy industrial machinery, they pried open and smashed every last vault, but they found no gold.

The entire country was furious, and those in power were afraid for their lives. There was nowhere to hide, as every person on the street was a threat to the men who brought about the war and destruction. The King's position was untenable. In the recriminations of the last month, it became clear that the King had played a leading role in driving the country to war, and the British people had surrounded Buckingham Palace, demanding he abdicate. Socialist and republican agitators gained increasing popularity, and the royal family feared for the very survival of the monarchy. Crown Prince Edward, who had been deployed with the troops, was scarred by the suffering he witnessed, and wanted to end the war. He plotted, along with his brothers and uncles, the first regicide in Britain since the execution of Charles I for treason in 1649. On October 8, Prince Edward slipped thallium into his father's chalice over dinner, and when his father went to bed later that night, he never woke up. King Edward VIII took the reins the next day, and a coroner reported heart failure as the reason for King George V's death, a widely disbelieved story.

Prime Minister Asquith submitted his resignation to the new King on October 9, and King Edward VIII's first order of business was to task John Morley with setting up a new government. In the same speech, he also announced a public investigation into the circumstances that led Britain to war and the collapse of the pound, to be chaired by John Morley. The royal inquiry commission met for the first time on Tuesday, October 12, at Buckingham Palace.

The choice of Morley as Prime Minister and chief of the investigative committee was a wise one by the new king. Morley had been very public in his opposition to entering the Great War and had resigned from the government on August 5, 1914, following the fateful decision to enter the war. When the late King, the cabinet, many members of parliament, and the press had all embarked on the jingoistic descent into the inferno of ruinous war and bankruptcy, Morley dared to stand up and say the unspeakably unpopular truth. Only Liberal MP John Burns had also resigned from the government on the eve of war, and he too was part of Morley's new government and the royal investigative commission. Also on the committee and in the new government were Liberal MPs David Marshall Mason, who had vocally opposed the government entering war from the parliament, Charles Trevelyan, who had resigned as Parliamentary Secretary of the Board of Education in protest of the war, Arthur Ponsonby, and Phillip Morrell. In November 1914, Trevelyan,

Ponsonby, Morrell, and members of the Liberal Party and the Labour Party, had established the Union of Democratic Control to demand democratic control over the decision to go to war and denounce the government's secret treaties and obligations that took Britain to war. The government and investigative committee would also include Ramsay MacDonald, the Labour Party leader who resigned from the Labour Party leadership when the party approved the war credits requested by the government for the war, as well as Keir Hardie, the founder of the Labour Party. The collapse of the pound and the war effort had drastically increased the UDC's popularity in 1915, and including its members in the government was a smart way to contain public anger and restore public confidence in the monarchy and government.

At seventy-seven years of age, Morley was old enough to have lived through the heyday of Richard Cobden, who had led the campaigns to repeal the Corn Laws, which were the trade restrictions the British government imposed on the import of corn and other foods. Typical of mercantilist laws of the time, the rationale was to protect local producers by making it more expensive for local consumers to import from abroad. Cobden understood that the extra costs paid by consumers of these foods far dwarfed whatever benefits accrued to their far fewer producers, who tended to be among the richest of the population. When Prime Minister Robert Peel repealed the Corn Laws in 1846 with the support of Parliament, it was a significant boon for the country's poor. It signaled a decisive shift toward free trade and heralded the golden age of Victorian Britain.

As a Cobdenite, Morley believed in free trade as the root of not just prosperity but also civil concord and international peace. Cobden had also been party to the first modern international trade agreement, when, in 1860, as a member of parliament, he signed the Cobden-Chevalier free trade agreement between Britain and France. Cobden's friend, the great orator and fellow parliamentarian John Bright, had suggested the idea of a free trade agreement with France as an alternative to continued expenditure on armaments to protect from a potential French invasion. By signing a free trade agreement, the interests of the British and French became harmonized, and a war became undesirable to both. Bright's insight was prophetic. The treaty was the beginning of the golden age of free trade, as more and more countries were amazed by the benefits this treaty offered both countries.[104] France and Britain would soon end centuries of enmity and become closer than ever, culminating in their alliance in the Great War.

While this mid-nineteenth-century liberalism had slightly faded by the end of the century, Morley remained an ever-present reminder of the powerful case for free trade and was referred to as "the last of the great nineteenth-century Liberals."[105] He opposed state intervention in social and economic affairs and worried about increased taxation. Morley had also been a major anti-imperialist who believed the empire constituted a drain on the resources of Britain that would lead to an income tax and an unbearable burden to the British man.[106] He opposed an interventionist foreign policy, and he warned repeatedly that imperialism would lead to an increase in the size and power of the state, which would allow it to effect significant changes in the social and economic structure of the country.[107]

The commission included elder statesmen, judges, scientists, and finance professionals who had not been supportive of the war. The King was very firm and clear in his instructions: he demanded to know all the details of how things got to where they were, and he would tolerate no attempts to cover up details or avoid any topics. He also demanded that all hearings be conducted in public, with audio recordings to ensure a permanent record for historians to study. He also granted the inquiry judicial authority to impose any sentence against anyone found guilty, up to and including the death penalty.

The Royal Inquiry held its first public hearing on Monday, October 19. The investigators began presenting the evidence they had collected, along with a list of the witnesses they intended to call. The investigators compiled all correspondence and meeting notes from the cabinet, the Bank of England,

---

104 Stephen D. Krasner, "State Power and the Structure of International Trade," *World Politics* 28, no. 3 (April 1976): 317–47.

105 David Hamer, "Morley, John, Viscount Morley of Blackburn (1838-1923)," in *Oxford Dictionary of National Biography* (Oxford University Press, 2004).

106 David Allan Hamer, *John Morley: Liberal Intellectual in Politics* (Oxford University Press, 1968), 312.

107 Hamer, *John Morley: Liberal Intellectual in Politics*, 311.

Treasury, and the Foreign Office, as well as a wealth of correspondence with foreign governments that had become available through investigative committees in these other countries. The first order of business was to investigate the circumstances surrounding the collapse of the pound.

Under oath, and with meticulous documentation available to the investigative committee, the Bank of England's top brass all came clean about the failed bond auction. The following days continued with the employees of the Treasury testifying about their role in the calamity. The Royal Inquiry had requested all secret communication letters made by staff at Treasury and the Bank of England, which brought to light Keynes' letter.

When asked to explain why fighting to support the French and Russians would be worth destroying the British pound, Keynes said that it was entirely reasonable to assume that this gamble would work, as it was very uncommon for people to withdraw large quantities of their gold. It was only the unexpected invention of airplanes, allowing for decentralized clearance, which made it not the case this time around.

In response, John Burns remarked:

> Mr. Keynes, you are correct to presume that this gamble might have worked out. It is entirely conceivable that in a world without airplanes, allowing for the fast decentralized clearance of gold, many more money holders would have left their money at the Bank of England, and its crash would have been averted. However, I invite the public and the members of the commission to consider what would have happened if this gamble had indeed paid off and the war had been won without the pound and banking system being destroyed. Would that have been a good outcome in the long run? What sort of precedent would it have set for our society and politics moving forward? Can you imagine the depths of depravity to which our government would sink if it had established this precedent of successfully and surreptitiously borrowing to finance its spending without public knowledge? The Bank of England cartel would wholly own our democracy and get the final say on everything, leaving the people to vote among candidates universally loyal to the bank and its owners. I dare venture and say that the collapse of

this insidious scheme, as horrific as it has been, was better for our nation than the alternative of its success.

On the fifth day, the inquiry's focus shifted to examining how the decision to go to war was made. Lloyd George, Winston Churchill, Haldane, and Edward Grey all testified. They confessed to all the details outlined in Chapter V. Initially, and in the aftermath of the disastrous war and hyperinflation, the secret alliances and decision to go to war seemed inexplicable. People concluded that British diplomats were successfully outmaneuvered and manipulated by far more intelligent and cunning French and Russian diplomats, setting the stage for a war aimed at defeating Germany. Russia and France recognized that a formal alliance with Britain would deter Germany, but a secret alliance would tempt Germany into war and compel Britain to retaliate.

But over the next few days of testimony, it became clear that the British diplomats were not entirely gullible victims of manipulation. British diplomacy had been wary of Germany's rise for decades, particularly due to concerns about the German Navy, German imperialism, and the rapidly expanding German economy. British Imperialists had simply sought to do to Germany and Europe what they had recently done in South Africa against the Boers.[108] It is also possible to see that the UK didn't need much dragging into conflict because it was following its old trusted policy of siding against the strongest nation on the European mainland to prevent it from becoming threateningly strong. A Europe with a balance of power among many states was more secure for the British than a Europe dominated by a single superpower controlling the bulk of the continent. British foreign policy had, for centuries, sought to oppose the most dominant power in Europe by allying with other powers as a form of counterbalance. Just as Britain had opposed both Spain and Napoleon when they were the dominant powers in Europe, Britain had to stop the rise of Germany.

More practically and concretely, Britain had no territorial ambitions in Europe. But it did have a lot of territorial ambitions around the world in its

---

108 Gerry Docherty and Jim MacGregor, *Hidden Histories: The Secret Origins of the First World War* (Mainstream Publishing, 2013).

Empire. Germany—as a late-comer to the imperial race, which had to make do with less valuable territories mostly passed over by the more traditional powers—had little to offer Britain in terms of colonial concessions. France and Russia, on the other hand, had plenty of desirable territories and spheres of influence to offer the British. "More disadvantageous to us to have an unfriendly France and Russia than an unfriendly Germany" is how one British diplomat put it. In pursuit of poor and sparsely populated lands thousands of kilometers away from London, the Foreign Office had decided to sacrifice the lives of 300,000 British and imperial soldiers and, in turn, destroy the sterling pound.

The British people had not voted for war. In fact, in their last election, they had voted explicitly for a pacifist cabinet to stay away from war following the horrors of the South African campaign. The vast majority of British citizens had even refused to buy the bonds to finance the war, as the investigation would soon make clear. The mourning mothers, fathers, wives, sons, and daughters of Britain had been betrayed because the King and the Foreign Office were obsessed with expanding territories on their maps.

What irked the British public most was the complete needlessness of this level of cunning and evil. Britain simply had no reason to be involved in any European conflicts. Thanks to their ingenuity and industrial development, its people were the richest in the world. The entire world wanted to purchase British goods, and all Britain needed to do was load its many amazing industrial goods on boats and ship them off. The intrigues of international politics seemed alluring enough for bloodthirsty monsters like Grey, Haldane, and Churchill, who sat peacefully in the safety of their office, getting a thrill from rolling the dice on the lives of millions. But to the British public still nursing its literal and metaphoric wounds from the war, it all seemed unforgivably callous and criminal. Virtually everyone in Britain knew someone who had been killed or maimed in the war, and the idea that the Foreign Office brought this about angered the British people massively.

In his concluding remarks on the committee's work, Prime Minister Morley said:

The last year has been a powerful, edifying, and painful lesson on the dangers of government meddling in economic affairs—particularly in the matter of money. It is a sad testament to the short memory of man that we must learn the same lessons our ancestors learned about clipped coins the hard way, by experiencing the same problem manifested through a modern technological variation on the same trick. Let us not forget that in 1696, Sir Isaac Newton discovered that around 20% of the coins in circulation were counterfeit. He spared no effort in pursuing the counterfeiters for eighteen whole months, during which period he successfully prosecuted twenty-eight of them. The crime of counterfeiting was then considered high treason, and its punishment was to be hanged, drawn, and quartered. Yet here we are, 220 years later, cluelessly watching as something very similar unfolds before our eyes, only this time carried out by the people entrusted to maintain the currency. Rather than small-time crooks peddling fake coins in taverns, we have had the indignity of watching big-time crooks in the Bank of England and Treasury finance themselves by treating the unbacked credit of the bank as if it were as good as gold. Like the base metals mixed into the coins in Newton's time, the paper and credit issued by banks without gold backing simply rob everyone of purchasing power, benefiting their issuers. It was only with this horrific crime that the war was financed, and hundreds of thousands of our finest men lost their lives, and millions of families across the country grieved the loss of loved ones and financial stability.

One of the most significant developments of the past century was the abolition of the Corn Laws. Freeing the market for food has led to a rapid increase in our living standards. Removing the special privileges of a few food producers made food far more plentiful and affordable for the vast majority of the population. I believe we need something similar to gold moving forward. We need to remove all government privileges from banks and allow them to compete freely for their customers. Only with freedom in money and banking can we expect to avoid the calamities brought about by monetary manipulation and privilege. Removing corn growers' privileges transformed food production in this country from a way of enriching large landowners to a way of providing society with affordable food. Similarly, removing bank privilege will transform banking from a means of enriching bankers to a means of providing society with more reliable and harder money. Without monopolies in banking, banks will not be able to issue more money than they have in gold reserves, and their ability to conjure money through counterfeiting will disappear.

After ten days of nine hours of testimonies, the inquiry ended on November 2, 1915, and its members retired to deliberate. They needed only one day to arrive at their decision. On November 4, the committee found guilty of grand treason: Prime Minister Herbert Asquith, Foreign Minister Edward Grey, Chancellor of the Exchequer David Lloyd George, Treasury Secretary John Bradbury, First Lord of the Admiralty Winston Churchill, Lord Chancellor Richard Haldane, Bank of England Governor Walter Cunliffe, Bank of England Cashier Gordon Nairn, his deputy Ernest Harvey, and Treasury's Liaison with the Bank of England John Maynard Keynes. All eleven men were sentenced to death. The remaining members of the cabinet who had stood by as Britain entered its greatest historical calamity were expelled from parliament and banned from holding public office for the remainder of their lives.

The Royal Inquiry recommended that the king shut down the Bank of England and liquidate its assets to help pay back pound note holders in gold. It also decreed unlimited personal liability for all the shareholders in the member banks of the Bank of England. The personal fortunes, mansions, and private property of the owners of the cartel banks were to be used to make the Bank of England's paper pounds payable in gold again at the original rate, and then to compensate bank depositors. By 1921, all holders of banknotes, local and foreign, had been compensated with the face value of their paper in gold at the pre-war exchange rate of £4.25 per ounce of gold. Bank depositors were not so fortunate, as they could typically recover only between 20% and 70% of their investments, depending on the state of their bank and its owners. Vast fortunes were liquidated and sold at the scrap heap to buy physical gold to redeem the pound. Storied banking dynasties were reduced to the rank and station of the middle class; they moved from mansions to middle-class neighborhoods and left their gigantic offices in the City to work as schoolteachers, accountants, or shopkeepers, living paycheck to paycheck and slowly accumulating savings. Hardworking accountants, school teachers, and shopkeepers who had saved in physical gold and who had stayed out of the banking cartel's banks bought those vacated mansions at a steep discount in public auctions, as the liquidation of the banking dynasties' assets at the same time significantly suppressed their individual prices.

The experience of the war and its aftermath had forced him to take the throne at a young age, galvanizing the young King Edward into becoming an impressively responsible and serious ruler. He grew into the job quickly and earned the respect of his people for his approach of complete ownership and transparency. He dedicated his life entirely to the monarchy. The British Royal Family weathered the storm. The same could not be said for the British Empire. The public had become hostile and averse to the idea of imperial expansion and the government's involvement in colonial enterprises. Prime Minister Morley was finally in a position to put his anti-imperialist ideas into practice. King Edward had to walk a tightrope between a public that rejected the British Empire on one hand and the enormous bureaucracy, imperial apparatus, and business interests that relied on it. This dynamic would shape the politics of Britain and her colonies for the next two decades.

A similar reckoning was taking place across all European powers. Each country's central bank had engaged in the same kind of inflationism, and BTC had allowed their peoples to escape them all. In Germany, France, Russia, Turkey, and Austria, the local currency also collapsed. All the central banks had been rendered bankrupt, most Europeans had lost their life savings, and millions of soldiers and civilians had died, yet nobody could see any good reason for the carnage. The anger was palpable. Rioting was only quelled by the announcement of full public investigations into the matter. The following year would bring to the fore incredible and barely believable stories of the secret steps that brought the world to the Great War while destroying the major powers' currencies, militaries, and an entire generation of young men.

Tsar Michael II

In a world where Blériot jets were flying around Russia and between Russia and Europe through neutral Scandinavia, Russians were able to keep their money outside the banking system, increasing pressure on the Russian central bank. In August 1914, prices in the ruble rose by more than 50%, as an increasing number of Russian citizens sought to use physical gold, or redeemable receipts for physical gold from reputable private banks with no connection to the central bank. By the end of October, the ruble traded at less than 10% of its original price against gold. The ruble economy was collapsing, and so too was the central bank's ability to continue financing an increasingly losing war. The anger was palpable, and the pressure on the Tsar had reached its zenith. Desertions increased substantively.

Sergei Witte had remained in touch with Grand Duke Nicholas since the latter's threat of suicide helped pass the former's reforms in 1905. They had gained each other's confidence over the years and expressed their frustrations about the Tsar to one another. As war drew closer in 1914, they had both developed a network of highly trusted, high-ranking officials, both civilian and military, who harbored misgivings about the rule of the Tsar and opposed his decision to go to war. One of these men was Mikhail Alekseyev, who was appointed Chief of Staff of the Russian Military and its de facto leader when Tsar Nicholas II fired Grand Duke Nicholas and took his position. Also included were the Tsar's last surviving uncle, Grand Duke Paul Alexandrovich, who was widely respected, and his son, Grand Duke Dmitri Pavlovich. In 1915, Grand Duke Paul Alexandrovich and his son Dmitri broached the subject of the Tsar with their cousin, the Grand Duke Kirill Vladimirovich, who was also Nicholas II's cousin and had quietly become resentful and worried about Russia's future. He also informed them that he and his cousins, the Grand Dukes Alexander, George, and Nicholas Mikhailovich, had been arriving at similar conclusions. Another trusted contact within this network was Georgy Lvov, an aristocrat who had gained widespread fame and respect across the country for his relief efforts to soldiers in the Manchurian campaign of 1905 and had been elected to the first Duma in 1906. In 1914, he was chairman of the All-Russian Union of Zemstvos, which were local elected government assemblies created by the Great Reforms of Alexander II in the 1860s that handled education, medicine, philanthropy, food security, and various other issues. Prince Felix Yusupov, who was married to the Tsar's niece, was also in this network.

When Grand Duke Nicholas returned from the front after being relieved of his duties in the summer of 1915, he met with the group's members individually. He discovered that they had arrived at the same conclusion at which he had arrived: Russia may well be beyond salvation, but if it could be saved, the Tsar had to go. The six men agreed that the best way forward was to have the Tsar's younger brother, Michael, replace him as Tsar, end the war, relinquish territories whose populations resented the Tsar, and allow for greater civil freedoms, all while clamping down on enemies of the state and paid foreign agents. On September 8, 1915, Grand Dukes Paul and Nicholas met privately with Michael and explained to him the situation and the growing coalition of royals, aristocrats, and commoners who agreed that the Tsar's time was up. Grand Duke Nicholas concluded,

> What Nicholas has brought to Russia with his two wars over the last ten years has been a crime against the inheritance of our ancestors. People may forgive one catastrophic, needless war brought on by a hot-headed young emperor, but they will not forgive a second one that could kill their fatherland. Russia is being destroyed before our eyes for an insane adventure in the Balkans, which most Russians do not care about. If we do not remove Nicholas today, the mob and the foreign agents may remove the monarchy tomorrow, in which case Russia will swim in blood for decades, enslaved by the darkest forces of humanity.

Michael hesitated for a long moment. Finally, he accepted the responsibility presented to him by his uncle and cousins. He understood that this was not a betrayal of his brother but a rescue of Russia, to which he had more allegiance than even his brother. On September 24, 1915, Michael requested a meeting with Nicholas. When he showed up, the seven Grand Dukes came with him. They each took turns to explain their problems with the Tsar's rule.

His uncle Paul concluded the discussion by saying, "We all agree it would be better for Michael to rule the country." The Tsar was shocked and angry and reached for his gun to shoot his brother. Grand Duke Nicholas, standing in the Tsar's blind side, had had his hand on his gun in anticipation, and as soon as the Tsar reached for his, Nicholas the Tall shot him with four bullets that killed him immediately.

On taking office, Tsar Michael II decided to continue with the Great Retreat until all Russian forces were safely separated from confrontation with large German, Austrian, or Turkish divisions. He reached out to the monarchs of neutral nations, hoping to find mediators and sue for peace. He was resigned to losing much of Eastern Europe, but he had written that off as the result of his brother's folly; his task was to preserve Russia itself. With the political and monetary turmoil taking place in Vienna, Istanbul, and Berlin, peace talks made little progress. Fighting on the front lines had relented, but borders were still disputed.

Kaiser Wilhelm III

In Germany, the slow trickle of devaluation in the first year would turn into a flood by September 1915, as excess borrowing and money creation caused people to seek to exchange their marks for physical gold or banknotes issued by banks independent of the central bank. For this, they relied on Blériot jets for clearance. The central bank sought to purchase some of its marks with gold to stem the devaluation, but it soon saw that it was powerless to meet the market's overwhelming rejection of the mark. Germany's gold stockpiles continued to decline, and by the end of October, there was barely any gold left in the reserves of the German central bank.

In France, on the Western Front, the collapse of the mark had left the German Crown Prince devastated and facing a severe personal crisis. He could not escape the dreadful realization that his father was on the verge of destroying Germany and their dynasty. Whereas he had previously always seen things his father's way and blamed everyone else, he now began to think critically of his father's decisions. The more he thought of them, the worse they appeared.

Why did he need an alliance with the decrepit and incompetent Austrians? Why had he granted them the right to make war decisions for Germany? Why had he delegated military affairs to his generals without much thought? Why did he go looking for an Empire abroad, when Bismarck had for decades warned about the dangers of military adventures? Why did he let his insecurity about his uncle phase him so much that it drove him to aggravate and challenge the British for so many years? Why had he left himself at the whims of the Austrians and Russians, launching him into an insanely expensive war that destroyed his currency?

Crown Prince Wilhelm formally led the 5th German Army. But being young and inexperienced militarily, he was ordered by his father to defer to the advice of Chief of Staff Schmidt von Knobelsdorf. Both men would spend their nights together on the front, discussing the war. Alone in a tent on the battlefield, they grew extremely close and trusting of one another. With time, they became more candid about their frustrations with the Kaiser. After the Battle of Marne, their frustrations reached a boiling point. They understood that the war was lost, and they knew the Kaiser was finished as a monarch. But they held out hope that Germany could be saved from destruction and conquest by its enemies. They realized the only way out would be to sideline the Kaiser.

As they sat in French trenches in stalemate with the French, British, and Belgian armies, they thought about the German fleet sitting impotently in its docks, effectively blockaded by the British after the first battle between the two had gone decisively in Britain's favor. How much better would their situation be today if all the resources wasted on the fleet and the empire were instead spent on reinforcing terrestrial forces for the real battle against France and Russia? Without the massive expenditure on the navy and empire, there is a good chance Britain would have stayed out of the war altogether. What was the point of building this giant fleet when it could never outmatch the British fleet? The hand of geography had placed Britain at the naval gateway to Germany at the North Sea, giving it the ability to blockade German ships. The entire pursuit of the German Imperial Navy and the German Empire was an unforgivable, empire-destroying folly.

Wilhelm II had been in power for twenty-seven years. During that time, he had single-handedly set the course for Germany, bringing it to its current predicament. He disregarded Bismarck's advice on the dangers of imperialism and failed to renew the Reinsurance Treaty with Russia, which ultimately led Russia to ally with France and Britain against Germany. He then spurned the chance to ally with Britain. He gambled the future of his nation on an alliance with a failing Austro-Hungarian Empire ruled by a cantankerous old emperor seeking to expand in the bloody swamp of the Balkans. In 1908, Austria formally annexed Bosnia and Herzegovina, which it had ruled since 1878. The annexation severely strained Austrian relations with Serbia, which had sought to expand into Bosnia and Herzegovina, and with Russia, which opposed Austrian expansion. It also received wide condemnation from most other countries, effectively isolating Germany and Austria-Hungary. Russia called for an international conference to discuss the annexation, but the Kaiser doubled down on his support for Austria and threatened the Russians with war. While this episode gave Bosnia and Herzegovina to Austria, it only gave Germany a Russia plotting against it.

The Crown Prince and von Knobelsdorf identified the problem and began considering solutions. The Kaiser had to be removed, and Germany had to abandon its imperial ambitions, reduce its navy, reach an understanding with Britain, and maintain as much of its territory as possible. Von Knobelsdorf confided to Crown Prince Wilhelm that he'd had similar conversations with Field Marshal Paul von Hindenburg, who had become a hero in Germany thanks to his miraculous victory against the Russian army in Tannenberg in August 1914. Hindenburg had, in turn, confided to von Knobelsdorf that he also had discussed his disaffection with the Kaiser's leadership with his officer Erich Ludendorff, who had been instrumental in the victory of Tannenberg and also gained widespread fame and acclaim in Germany. Using secure army communication channels, von Knobelsdorf informed Hindenburg of the Crown Prince's position, and they began to plot a course to save Germany from demise.

On November 4, 1915, they sent a telegram requesting a meeting with the Kaiser, then set out for Berlin. They met the Kaiser the next day and provided him with a candid account of their assessment of the situation and Germany's predicament. The Crown Prince concluded with, "Your Majesty, it is time to recognize the reality that the only way to save Germany is to sacrifice your rule. I beg you to abdicate the throne, and I promise you to save Germany and make you proud."

The Kaiser was apocalyptic with rage, as the Crown Prince and von Knobelsdorf had expected. But persuasion was not the only tool in their kit. While the Kaiser berated von Knobelsdorf, Prince Wilhelm moved behind him, took out his dagger, planted it in his father's back, where his heart was, and twisted it. Coolly and deliberately, he said, "I am sorry, father, but it was you who taught me that Germany is above all consideration. Supreme authority comes with complete responsibility and accountability, and you have failed Germany."

The Crown Prince and von Knobelsdorf quickly wiped away the blood. Prince Wilhelm had bribed one of his father's servants to get him one of his father's other military jackets, and he quickly replaced the bloodstained jacket with a new one. They called for the doctor and explained to him what had happened. They made it clear to the doctor that he would have to cooperate with them. The doctor quickly pronounced the Kaiser dead from a heart attack. The funeral was held three days later, and the Crown Prince was proclaimed Kaiser Wilhelm III on November 9, 1915.

A ceasefire was declared on November 11, 1915. Nothing had been resolved, but everyone was delighted to be done with the fighting. The major powers agreed to meet in Geneva on November 24 to negotiate the peace.

When news of Kaiser Wilhelm II's death reached Emperor Franz Joseph in Vienna, it was the final straw for the eighty-five-year-old. Having been in power for sixty-seven years, he was in failing health, had lived through the murder of his brother in Mexico in 1867, the suicide of his son in 1889, the assassination of his wife in Geneva in 1899, and the assassination of his heir and nephew, Franz Ferdinand, in Sarajevo in 1914. Hearing that his ally had died and that his crown prince was seeking to end the war, he knew he was defeated. Knowing that the Kaiser, who was younger and healthier than he, had succumbed to a heart attack from this war made Franz Joseph's heart feel very heavy. He had already outlived most expectations for his life, and he no longer believed he could carry on. On November 5, 1915, Franz Joseph died from a heart attack, and his grandnephew was crowned emperor Charles I. As with monarchs everywhere, Charles I investigated the decision to go to war and the ensuing currency collapse.

President Marshall

Surprisingly, the financial panic had spread across the Atlantic. As fears began to grow that the US would join the fray in Europe, the financial problems of Britain began to unfold quickly, dragging the nascent US Federal Reserve down with it. America's fourth experiment with banking cartelization came to an abrupt and catastrophic end. The US banking cartel and its Federal Reserve foresaw an excellent opportunity to profit from war lending to European powers, particularly Britain. This came to a sudden stop in September with the collapse of the Bank of England and the demise of the pound. Loans to European countries were now unlikely to be repaid, and the Federal Reserve cartel faced serious problems. The Federal Reserve Bank was already unpopular with Americans, who viewed it with suspicion due to its secret origins. Many Americans were still angry at how such an important and influential institution was imposed upon them with very little debate, just before the Senate had adjourned for the Christmas break. As news of financial panic in Europe began to spread in the United States, American distrust of the Federal Reserve and large banks increased. Americans began to withdraw their gold from the larger banks and move it to smaller local banks, or keep it at home. The smaller banks began to move away from the Federal Reserve, keeping most of their reserves on hand and relying on BTC for large transactions. Major industrialists started to pay their workers directly in physical gold and silver to avoid using banks or banknotes. They also used Blériot's Lightning aircraft to settle debts between one another. With the Bank of England unable to supply British gold and the American public withdrawing its gold from the banking cartel, the American banking cartel was doomed.

The problems first came to public notice on October 9, when J. P. Morgan faced serious difficulties in meeting its liabilities in gold after the Bank of

England's gold shipments had ceased. Initially, the Federal Reserve cartel was confident that this would not be a problem because it knew this was precisely what the Federal Reserve was built for. But the classical gold standard central bank was a medieval European technology, not suited for the modern industrial powerhouse that is the US, with its extensive road and rail networks, as well as the new aircraft monetary clearing system. The bank cartel confidently proclaimed to the press that the Federal Reserve would avert economic catastrophe by extending credit to J. P. Morgan, and the financial media loudly sang their praises. This was precisely what the Federal Reserve was established to do, and it will prevent the crisis from becoming systemic, as it had in 1907. However, these assurances had the opposite effect; they did not reduce the risk and distrust of J. P. Morgan, but rather spread the risk and distrust to the Federal Reserve and all its constituent members. Smarter Americans knew there could be no such thing as a free lunch, and the non-performing European loans would have to be paid off by someone. Withdrawals increased, and banks had to take active measures to advertise their independence from the Federal Reserve, the abundance of their own gold reserves, and the ability of customers to withdraw all their gold on demand at a moment's notice. Banks that could not advertise these claims became anathema.

National City Bank began experiencing more "liquidity problems" on October 16, necessitating more favorable lending from the Federal Reserve's balance sheet. With two of America's biggest banks requiring bailouts, the Federal Reserve's own balance sheet started looking less formidable. The number of outstanding dollar liabilities was growing, while the gold reserves of the Federal Reserve had stopped growing due to the drying up of the British supply and increasing withdrawals. On October 21, 1915, as lines grew longer and longer outside the major bank's branches, the Federal Reserve announced that it could only redeem gold in quantities no larger than twelve ounces per depositor. Immediately, the value of US dollars in terms of gold began to decline, which appeared as an increase in the price of gold to citizens. By October 29, the dollar had lost 80% of its value, as the drain of gold from the Federal Reserve wouldn't relent. The major banks that formed the Federal Reserve cartel—J. P. Morgan, National City Bank, First National Bank, and Bankers

Trust Company, Chase National Bank, and Continental and Commercial Bank of Chicago—were effectively all insolvent. The smaller banks and the large industrialists emerged as a replacement decentralized monetary and banking system in their wake.

On Monday, November 1, the New York Federal Reserve Bank could no longer pay out gold to depositors, and the long line of depositors that had spent the weekend camped outside its headquarters were livid. Thousands broke through the barricades and stormed the building, destroying everything in their search for gold, which they ultimately could not find. The 11 other regional Reserve Banks in Boston, Philadelphia, Cleveland, Richmond, Atlanta, Chicago, St. Louis, Minneapolis, Kansas City, Dallas, and San Francisco were all stormed during the rest of this week. On Friday, November 5, hundreds of thousands of people gathered outside the headquarters of the 12 Federal Reserve Banks to organize the Federal Reserve Bonfire Night, a joyous occasion still celebrated every year in America. All Federal Reserve buildings were set on fire as families gathered around singing, joyously dancing, handing out sweets, and celebrating their and their descendants' fourth and final deliverance from debt slavery.

President Wilson's position was untenable and tens of thousands of demonstrators surrounded the White House demanding his resignation, for his role in passing the Federal Reserve Act. On November 7, Wilson became the first US President in history to resign office, a distinction he holds to this day. Vice President Thomas Marshall assumed the Presidency the next day.

President Marshall's first order of business was to issue an executive order dissolving the Federal Reserve and putting it through bankruptcy proceedings. His second order of business was to launch a Presidential Investigative Committee to publicly investigate the reasons for the passage of the Federal Reserve Act and the collapse of the fiat cartel. He placed Speaker of the House Champ Clark in charge of it.

The Jekyll Island seven were all placed under house arrest while the investigation took place. Over the next three weeks, the committee met repeatedly in Washington. Its sessions were broadcast by radio to a very keen public. The details of the entire ordeal were laid out for all to see, and the inner workings of the cartel were evident to many people who never would have grasped the enormity and depravity of this institution had it continued to exist and finance the media and academia that promoted it. After lengthy deliberation, the grand jury delivered its verdict.

The Jekyll Island seven were sentenced to life in prison. Shareholders in the cartel banks would be held to unlimited personal liability for the collapse in value of Federal Reserve Notes and for the losses incurred by creditors and depositors in their banks. Over the next year, the financial task force would perform a comprehensive accounting of the assets of the shareholders of the major banks. America's banking mafia was utterly devastated and turned into bankrupt paupers. The mansions of J. P. Morgan, Aldrich, Schiff, Warburg, and many other banking families were sold at auction, along with their boats, cars, farms, and artwork. By December 1916, holders of Federal Reserve Notes could redeem them at face value from the United States Department of the Treasury.

While America's banking dynasties were destroyed, its upstart and self-made industrialists thrived. Their large industrial operations had replaced banks for their employees, their families, and even their extended families and neighbors. Initially, there was anger toward John D. Rockefeller because people had assumed he was a significant part of the Federal Reserve cartel. Rockefeller was also implicated because Senator Nelson Aldrich's daughter had married his son, John Jr. But the accounting revealed that his stake in the banking cartel was relatively small. He had a small stake in National City Bank and a larger stake in a smaller bank named Equitable Trust. He was able to meet all the liabilities for his share of the cartel's liability with no more than $1 million, which he paid in physical gold delivered to the US Treasury, via a BTC jet, the day after the verdict was announced.

With Rockefeller having developed a strong relationship with Blériot, he was able to supplement his railroad network with airplane clearance, thereby developing a highly efficient network for financial clearance across the various spin-offs from Standard Oil after the anti-trust legislation broke it into dozens of companies in 1911. In the coming years, Standard Oil had developed into a financial services company that became America's most important financial institution after the collapse of the Federal Reserve cartel.

Empty Trenches

On the western and eastern fronts of the war, the pace of events began to slow down. Military leaders, aware of the financial problems they faced, immediately pared down their more aggressive military plans and reverted to a more conservative, defensive posture. They did not know how long they would need to make do with their existing supplies, nor were they certain their governments could resume military procurement with broken central banks. The smarter soldiers understood that a collapse in currency meant it was only a matter of time before the government could no longer afford to provide them with weapons and food. None of them wanted to be the last to die for a losing cause. Desertions started to become significant in September 1915. By October, a majority of soldiers had deserted their army units and returned home, where military recruiters were no longer actively seeking them, as the recruiters had stopped receiving payment and ceased their duties. The intensity of fighting subsided almost entirely by November. There would be no more grand charges and epic battles. By November the trenches were empty, and military leaders sought to secure the territory they held rather than conquer more. On many fronts, both sets of militaries would withdraw from the battlefield to more secure territory to avoid costly fighting.

Outside of Europe, all the countries that were on the gold exchange standard witnessed their gold reserves disappear in the Bank of England's financial black hole. These banks now needed to find a new way to settle with the rest of the world, and that was Blériot's Lightning jets. His business continued booming and his fleet expanding. As the guns went quiet and the soldiers deserted their fronts, the wheels of commerce and peaceful production began to turn again. International trade began its return to pre-war levels. Merchant ships started traversing the Mediterranean, North, and Black Seas again as the belligerent navies' boats lay on the ocean floor, usually as victims of aerial bombardment.

The average citizen in the warring countries began to reestablish normalcy in his life. But in the capitals, royal palaces, and parliaments of the major powers, the old normal was gone for good. The economic, military, and political catastrophes that befell the belligerents demanded explanation, retribution, and reform. Thorough public investigations revealed all the sordid details of how the devastating Great War came about. The great powers' central banks did not survive the war, and their empires would soon crumble. The decentralized international clearance of gold reserves through airplanes became the basis of a new global monetary system. The modern gold standard was more reliable, more efficient, permissionless, and open to anyone worldwide, and it would transform the world economic order, redraw the map of the world, reshape the concept of government, and define the history of the twentieth century.

XI.

The Geneva Peace Conference

S wiss banks had attracted the largest amount of capital from across Europe and the world during the war, as savers sought the reliable safety and neutrality of Swiss banks over their own governments' recklessly insolvent central banks. Everyone needed Switzerland and its banks. Swiss banks in the Italian-speaking south were flooded with Italian money, banks in the German-speaking north and east received large amounts of German and Austrian money, and French-speaking banks in the west of the country received substantial amounts of French funds. British, Russian, and Ottoman gold had also flown in on Blériot jets. A small republican federation of twenty-two cantons, the Swiss federal government was perhaps the smallest in Europe, with a tiny budget and mostly ceremonial duties. But its neutrality and monetary responsibility had now amazingly put it in a position superior to that of the major European powers, who had bitten off more than they could chew.

The inflow of gold was a boon, but it created its own problems for Switzerland.

Anti-aircraft guns shot down the first aviation jet in August 1915,[109] and the warring nations had begun to develop sophisticated, specialized weapons for targeting aircraft. Insurers were starting to charge higher rates on Blériot jets, and pilots began refusing to take trips to warring countries. Swiss banks could not invest that money as they were surrounded by unstable countries at war. And the longer the war went on, the more likely it became that Switzerland would get drawn in, which would likely tear the country apart given the divided sympathies of the population. One of the neighboring countries might seek to invade, or some of the cantons of Switzerland would opt to join the nations they felt close to. Swiss neutrality was a very precarious balancing act for Giuseppe Motta, the President of the Swiss Confederation, a forty-four-year-old no-nonsense lawyer and notary from the Italian-speaking canton of Ticino in the south. Motta was a conservative Christian who was a staunch proponent of Swiss neutrality. He had first been elected to the federal council in 1911 and received the annually rotating presidency for the year 1915. He had good relations with the German-speaking Swiss cantons and saw how different European peoples could coexist in Switzerland. For this reason, he also saw no reason why it would not be possible to emulate this coexistence across Europe and the world. The Swiss also recognized that peace would be highly lucrative for them, as they had enormous amounts of capital that could be mobilized for investment in rebuilding across Europe.

Having stayed out of the war, the United States was also in a relatively strong economic position. The US experiment with a central bank had failed less than two years before it was initiated, and it was devastating for the major banks, but around half the population had stayed away from the failed Federal Reserve, preferring to keep their savings at home or relying on banks that used BTC for payment clearance, and they had benefited from being able to buy the assets of defunct banking empires for pennies on the dollar. The US government, with an unscathed military and relative financial might, was in a

---

109 In the real world, the first aircraft was shot down in August 1914, when a German Rumpler Taube reconnaissance aircraft was shot down by French soldiers near Reims in France. But in the alternative world of this novel, the first aircraft is only shot down in September, because jets are faster and can fly at higher elevations.

position of strength, and European powers feared antagonizing it and hoped to benefit from its financial assistance for reconstruction.

President Marshall sought to halt the carnage in Europe before it ensnared the United States. He knew Wilson was veering closer to entering the war, and British interests had been using subversive propaganda and psychological operations to persuade Americans to join them in the war, which Britain worried it could not win without American assistance. Marshall knew from William Jennings Bryan's attempts at mediation how intransigent the belligerents were, so he decided to hold discussions with the neutral countries of Europe instead.

The main neutral European countries were Switzerland, Spain, the Netherlands, Denmark, Sweden, Norway, and Liechtenstein. These countries had witnessed a significant inflow of gold from the belligerent nations, much of it thanks to BTC. Their central banks had remained on the gold standard, but, except for Switzerland, the war had left them in a precarious fiscal and monetary position. They had lost large quantities of gold in the Bank of England's scheme, and their own people were wary of their central banks collapsing and eager to withdraw more of their gold. The disruptions to trade had also raised prices of goods and services and disrupted economic activity. Monarchs and bankers in these countries were very nervous and eager to end the war before their own central banks collapsed.

Marshall met regularly with Paul Ritter, the Swiss Ambassador in Washington, while Motta met with the US Ambassador to Switzerland, Pleasant Stovall, both of whom crossed the Atlantic to report on their conversations. Over time, the vision of what they wanted to achieve became clearer, and their similar position made it possible for them to cooperate. They had an abundance of capital, which the major European powers sought, and many parts of their population were eager to enter the war. Motta and Marshall agreed that the most reliable way to keep their countries out of the war was to end the war and use their financial leverage to establish a sustainable formula for peace. Since all the major powers wanted their capital, the American and Swiss governments sought to enforce rules for the transfer of capital across international borders that would encourage peaceful cooperation rather than violent conflict. To devise that formula, they agreed on hosting an international peace conference in Geneva.

The Swiss government and banks offered to pay for the conference and serve as host for delegates from all over the world to come and stay in Geneva for as long as it took to find peace. Motta and Marshall asked the governments of Canada, Spain, the Netherlands, Denmark, Sweden, Norway, and Liechtenstein to cosponsor the invitation for the Geneva Peace Conference, to be held on November 24.

Prominent Swiss bankers had been having regular meetings with Motta to discuss how to keep Switzerland out of the war and how to help resolve it. Among the most prominent of those bankers were: Heinrich Markus Kundert, who had become the Chairman of the Board of the Swiss National Bank (SNB) upon its establishment in 1907; August Burckhardt, a high-ranking officer in SNB and the former Director of the Cantonal Bank of Basel, who was ready to take over from Kundert as head of the SNB upon the conclusion of the Geneva Peace Conference, and had a strong reputation for opposing inflation;[110] Julius Baer, who had founded one of the country's most successful private banks, named after him, in 1890; and Baron Rodolphe Hottinguer, who worked with the Ottoman Bank and had good relations with the Ottomans. The bankers contacted prominent industrialists from across the world and invited them to the conference, as they sought to bring the perspective of productive, practical people to find practical solutions to the problems created by impractical, parasitic political leaders. Chief among these industrialists was Louis Blériot.

During the previous year, Blériot had been catapulted from a rich eccentric adventurer to one of the world's most important businessmen. The world's major industrialists and the remaining major banks all relied on his jets to keep operating in the absence of central banks. His jets had literally carried tons of gold to Switzerland, where he was highly popular. The rise in his reputation and importance was even faster than the rise in his wealth, and all major industrialists and bankers in the US, Europe, and beyond relied on him for their most important financial transactions. He was also eager to bring the war to a close so that he could expand his business further. He was horrified by the

110 Therese Steffen Gerber, "August Burckhardt," in *Historisches Lexikon der Schweiz (HLS)*, March 26, 2003.

war and wanted to do everything to stop it. The Swiss delegation invited him to join the conference, and there he presented something the world had not seen before: a sovereign individual, beholden to no government, needed by them more than he needed them. Hottinguer also invited the Turkish prince Mehmed Sabahaddin, an intellectual and member of the ruling House of Osman who was exiled to Switzerland and France for his political activism in favor of political decentralization and economic freedom.

As part of his delegation to Geneva, Marshall took Orville Wright, who had become one of the most important businessmen in the United States thanks to BTC; and Henry Ford, whose reputation and wealth had skyrocketed after he had escaped the two banking collapses of 1907 and 1915 unscathed, and had also become America's most prominent antiwar voice, having spent the last year using his wealth, fame, and connections to prevent the US from entering the war, and bring the war to an end.

Peace conferences usually have winners and losers, and the victor dictates the terms, while the vanquished accepts them and tries to ameliorate them, which makes the conferences relatively straightforward, at least compared to the very awkward situation at Geneva, which was closer to a bazaar of haggling. There were no winners, as all parties had been defeated by their own financial irresponsibility, and none was in a position to dictate terms to anyone. All their central banks were bankrupt, their currencies were trading at a tiny fraction of their original price, their populations were angry and increasingly holding physical gold, and their banks now relied on peer-to-peer payments for clearance using Blériot's Lightning aircraft. The closest thing to a winner in this war was the countries that had not taken part in it; they had a golden opportunity to set the terms of the international order for the future.

In his opening address to the conference, Swiss President Motta explained how Switzerland offers a very stark alternative to the world of eternal conflict between major powers.

> We do not get involved in wars and foreign affairs *at all*. We trade freely with anyone and have no interest in conquering more territory. Yet, our people can obtain all that is attainable for the peoples of the major powers. But

unlike the people of the major powers, our people are not required to sacrifice their wealth and their lives to inflate an emperor's vanity in conquest.
This world of military invasions, wars, alliances, and empires is presented as
being necessary for the nation, but it is, in fact, the ruin of the nation and its
people. Looking at the devastation across the battlefields around us today, it
is impossible to convince me that it was in the interest of any of the citizens
of the major powers that their states sought to expand their territory. What
good does more land and more unhappy subjects do to a citizen? He still
needs to buy his food, clothes, and fuel from willing sellers and producers,
just like everyone else. The most immediate effect of territorial conquest on
the average citizen was that he had to sacrifice his life, or years of his life, in
the inferno of war. I encourage the delegates to carefully reflect on the painful lessons of the past year to ensure they are not repeated. We must choose
to trade freely with the world rather than fight each other.

Self-determination and Secession

Tiny Liechtenstein, a principality near Switzerland and Austria, had also
stayed neutral during the war. Its ruling prince, Johann II, was Europe's elder
statesman, having been in power for fifty-seven years. The Swiss, American,
and Swedish governments appointed him to chair the proceedings. Having
cordial relationships with all of Europe's ruling houses, Johann II took on a
leading role in the formulation of a postwar order. More than just a beloved
prince, he was a successful businessman and thoughtful intellectual who had
published in 1904 a book outlining his vision of government under the title of
The State in the Twentieth Century.[111] Although not widely known, it had an
appreciative readership among the European royal, business, and diplomatic
elites, who saw in it an intriguing vision for the future.

In his speech to the delegates, Prince Johann II argued that industrialization and modernization were improving the living standards of people

---

111 This book does not exist, but it is based on the book written by Johann II's grand
    nephew, the current ruling prince of Liechtenstein, Prince Hans-Adam, *The State in the
    Third Millennium* (I.B.Tauris, 2009).

in Europe and the world. With better education and communication, he expected growing demands for personal and group freedom. Whereas most political progress since the French Revolution had been viewed in terms of increasing citizen choice in selecting governments and in participatory democracy, Prince Johann II had different ideas. He believed that freedom lay in granting people the right of secession and self-determination, all the way down to the most minor practical political units. Rather than relying on deliberative and participatory democratic processes, he believed in concentrating more power in the hands of the sovereign, while granting citizens the right to secede. He envisioned the government as a voluntary service provider, offering a clear set of services to its citizens while charging them a transparent cost. Any subpopulation under a government could choose either to secede or to join another government. The idea brought the discipline of the free market to the world of government. The world's businesses would provide their services voluntarily to customers, who would have no say in the operation of the business; they would simply decide whether they wanted to buy or not. The mere freedom to choose whether to buy or not was all the motivation needed to ensure businesses worked tirelessly to make their products as good as possible and their prices as low as possible. Rather than interminable discussions in parliaments and devolution of executive power into endless committees and organizations with unclear and conflicting missions and responsibilities, governments would act like respectable corporations with a transparent chain of command and clearly delineated authority and responsibility. Citizens would have the ultimate freedom to reject all their services, start their own government, or join another one.

Prince Johann could draw on recent experience to bolster his position:

> This war made it clear that republics, democracies, monarchies, and autocracies can all take their citizens into the depths of hell through malice, incompetence, or the power of perverse incentives. Neither the Republic of France, nor the autocracy of the Tsar, nor the constitutional monarchy of Britain, nor the federal parliamentary constitutional monarchy in Germany were able to stop the descent of their nations into destruction. We

saw how, in all these governments, those in power recklessly sent millions of their countrymen to death with very vague reasoning and no sane justification. The search for newer or better forms of political representation is misguided so long as citizens cannot opt out of paying for and enduring the consequences of their governments. With the right of secession granted, citizens could freely opt in and out of governing structures, and kings or presidents would only rule over those who were willing subjects.

Many of the conflicts in the Great War had major powers claiming to support the rights of small people to self-determination and freedom from unwanted rule. The major powers were all happy to invoke self-determination when it served their interests, but they were uninterested in it when it came to the peoples and territories they sought to incorporate into their empires. Russia's intervention in the war was aimed at protecting Serbia, while Britain's intervention was intended to defend Belgium. France sought to liberate the people of Alsace-Lorraine, whom it regarded as French, from German rule. And yet, with absolutely no regard for the aspirations of their residents, Russia sought to take over Constantinople, Britain sought Egypt, and France sought Morocco. The major powers all sought to expand over vast territories and only considered self-determination when it came to the rights of the peoples opposing their imperial rivals. This hypocrisy is shameful and contemptible, but more importantly, it is dangerous because it guarantees endless conflict. For as long as the major powers continued to rule people against their will, they had the opportunity to undermine each other by fostering and funding separatist movements that sought to undermine the ruling government. As long as Germany ruled Alsace-Lorraine as a colonized territory, France would scheme and plot to liberate it and undermine the German state. Russia and Austria-Hungary would continue to fight and undermine each other in their quest for dominance in the Balkans, which the Austrians viewed as a natural extension of their empire, but which the Russians regarded as the indispensable key to controlling the Turkish Straits. Germany, Russia, and Austria would continue to rival each other by dividing Poland between them. It is remarkable that for all the carnage of the last year, there were very few contentious borders between the major powers' national heart-lands. The conflicts between the major powers centered on foreign lands, such as the Balkans, Morocco, Egypt, Persia, Afghanistan, and Manchuria, lands predominantly inhabited by people who did not belong to the same ethnic group as the imperial ruler. The people who identified as Russian, German, British, Austrian, or French were predominantly located in un-contentious territory, and all these nations could live in harmony with one another if they would simply give up on the detestable quest to rule over other people. If the world is to achieve peace, it must come through all major powers agreeing on a neutral and universally applicable framework for self-determination.

Johann II had a revolutionary vision that had come a century ahead of its time, and it was very compelling to many of the delegations that had seen their homelands, wealth, and youth destroyed in service of worthless imperial ambi-tion. What good was it for the empire to force them to stay against their will? What was the point of ruling over a resentful population that constantly plotted to undermine its rulers? "Ruling over a people that doesn't want you to rule over it is like adopting the children of a man you murdered. They will always hate you, and you are letting them into your house to act out their hatred in the most painful way possible for you," is how Johann II described it in his speech.

Monetary and Trade Freedom

Joining the Liechtenstein delegation was the young and highly respected Austrian economist Ludwig von Mises, whose work on monetary theory had gained enormous popularity following the collapse of central banking. Mises had published *The Theory of Money and Credit* in 1912, in which he warned with remarkable foresight of the dangers of centralization of money and banking in central banks granted a monopoly by the government, which he said would allow them to substitute credit for capital. The book offers a compelling expla-nation of why monetary expansion is destructive and why it should be avoided.

Mises was serving in the Austrian military when the war ended. The collapse of central banks made him famous in Europe, and his books were translated into several languages. He had the ear of many European leaders, particularly Johann II, who invited him to ensure the delegates could hear his perspective on the collapse of the currency and the way forward. In his speech to the delegates on the second day, Mises made a compelling case for the gold standard as the basis for a global monetary order:

> The significance of the fact that the gold standard makes the increase in the supply of gold depend upon the profitability of producing gold is, of course, that it limits the government's power to resort to inflation. The gold standard makes the determination of money's purchasing power independent of the changing ambitions and doctrines of political parties and pressure groups. This is not a defect of the gold standard; it is its main excellence. Every method of manipulating purchasing power is by necessity arbitrary. All methods recommended for the discovery of an allegedly objective and "scientific" yardstick for monetary manipulation are based on the illusion that changes in purchasing power can be "measured." The gold standard removes the determination of cash-induced changes in purchasing power from the political arena. Its general acceptance requires the acknowledgment of the truth that one cannot make all people richer by printing money. The abhorrence of the gold standard is inspired by the superstition that omnipotent governments can create wealth out of little scraps of paper.
>
> It has been asserted that the gold standard, too, is a manipulated standard. The governments may influence the height of gold's purchasing power either by credit expansion — even if it is kept within the limits drawn by considerations of preserving the redeemability of the money-substitutes — or indirectly by furthering measures that induce people to restrict the size of their cash holdings. This is true. It cannot be denied that the rise in commodity prices that occurred between 1896 and 1914 was to a great extent provoked by such government policies. But the main thing is that the gold standard keeps all such endeavors toward lowering money's purchasing

power within narrow limits. The inflationists are fighting the gold standard precisely because they consider these limits a serious obstacle to the realization of their plans.

What the expansionists call the defects of the gold standard are indeed its very eminence and usefulness. It checks large-scale inflationary ventures on the part of governments. The gold standard did not fail. The governments were eager to destroy it, because they were committed to the fallacies that credit expansion is an appropriate means of lowering the rate of interest and of "improving" the balance of trade.[112]

He proceeded to dispel any hope that the old monetary order could be revived, and argued governments were now harvesting the consequences of the inflationary seeds they had planted.

Political ideas that have dominated the public mind for decades cannot be refuted through rational arguments. They must run their course in life and cannot collapse otherwise than in great catastrophes... One has to accept the catastrophic devaluation of our currency as foregone. Imperialist and militarist policy necessarily goes in hand with inflationism [...] As unbecoming as the collapse of the currency is in its consequences, it has the liberating effect of destroying the system that brings it about.[113]

He continued:

The events of the past sixteen months show us that the old way of government management of money is coming to an end. With gold able to travel freely across borders, government monopolies on money are unlikely to flourish, and credit expansion will no longer work to increase the

---

112 Ludwig von Mises, *Human Action: The Scholar's Edition* (1949; Ludwig von Mises Institute, 2008), 473–74.
113 Jörg Guido Hülsmann, "Mises on Monetary Reform: The Private Alternative," *The Quarterly Journal of Austrian Economics* 11, no. 3 (December 2008): 208–18.

purchasing power in the hands of governments, as people no longer need to rely on their central bank to take part in the division of labor. We are entering a new world where governments must earn the trust and wealth of its people, where wars will become a lot less economically feasible.

While the events of the past sixteen months have been tragic and devastating, I am nonetheless optimistic about our future. If we are willing to bravely and honestly learn the correct lessons from the past, we can commit to a future of property rights and freedom, and I am hopeful that future generations will look back at the collapse of modern central banking as a blessing.

Humanity is at a crossroads today. The paths are very different, and the destinations diametrically opposite; this meeting may determine which path we take. The first path is one where governments treat their populations as a resource to be used and exploited to the benefit of the rulers. Down this path will be inflation, trade protectionism, heavy government control of the economy, socialist central planning, destruction of property rights, war, despotism, totalitarianism, and finally, the collapse of civilization into barbarism. The second path is one where governments accept and understand that they are in the service of their citizens, who have the freedom to opt in or out of any arrangement they do not like. In this path, governments must leave money to the market, respect property rights, let goods cross their borders according to the desires of their owners, and grant the right of self-determination and secession to every community under their rule. We will all respect each other's property rights and prosper together in peace, or we will continue to manufacture depraved justifications for violating each other's rights and then sink into eternal conflict and destroy civilization.

The large empires must stand down their armies and accept the principle of self-determination applying to all their subjects. They must all at once renounce the forcible conquest of territory against its inhabitants' will to end the conflict. We must not return to a world in which the large powers use each other's populations' grievances as a pretext for undermining each other. If all these powers commit to the principle of self-determination, they can rest assured knowing their rivals will not be able to use political conflict to undermine them. We saw where the path of despotism and political domination has taken us. Moving from coercive empires to voluntary political unions is the only way to save human civilization from descending to barbarity, as we have seen over the past sixteen months.

Economically, the recipe for peace is property rights, and the state accepting its role as a guarantor of its citizens' property rather than their violator. This must include the right to trade goods across borders. This would increase prosperity and also diffuse the largest source of tensions between countries and the most bitter aspect of internal politics. If people could be secure in their knowledge that their trade would not be hampered by any government, the stakes of the game of politics would decline precipitously, and the path of cooperation would become far more likely.

Politically, the recipe for peace is self-determination, which serves as the litmus test for despotism versus freedom. Any political arrangement out of which subjects cannot opt is a despotic and exploitative order, and it will inevitably lead to conflict and the breakdown of civilized order.

A significant issue of contention at the Conference was the movement of capital across borders. Delegations from belligerent countries were incensed that Switzerland and the neutral countries had managed to take so much gold out of the belligerents, who seemed united in one thing only: demanding a stop to capital flight from their shores. Fortunately, they were powerless to enforce any such demand since they desperately needed neutral countries' capital, and they were never going to get any of it if they even hinted at restrictions on its exit. Ironically, the agreement between the bankrupt great powers on this issue served to draw their delegations nearer and made a resolution of their conflicts more likely.

The case for restrictions on capital movements was ultimately destroyed in the conference by the Italian economist Luigi Einaudi, who took to the podium to make the moral and economic case for capital flight:

> Illegal capital exporters are benefactors of their nations, because capital flees when senseless and spendthrift governments squander it, and then by taking it elsewhere they save it from devastation and preserve it for future use, when common sense has returned.[114]

Einaudi concluded his remarks with a poignant lesson for the delegations of broke governments crying over capital flight:

> Angry generals, kings, and prime ministers may today bemoan BTC for robbing them of the wealth they needed for their wars, but their children and grandchildren will view BTC as the savior of their nation's wealth from destruction. The solution to your problems is not for capital owners to keep it in your countries for you to destroy it; the solution is for you to stop doing the things that drive them to send their capital abroad. You will continue to destroy whatever capital you have left until you learn this vital lesson.

Paradoxically, the enormity of the issues up for negotiations at Geneva made resolution easier. Any attempt at a postwar order had to be morally, legally, and politically consistent across a wide range of territories and political institutions and could not indulge any party's inflated sense of uniqueness. There was no time for the delegates to sit and discuss the intricacies of the situations of Alsace-Lorraine, Serbia, Saarland, Arabia, or any one particular territory. With all the major powers vying for control of territory, a workable way forward had to satisfy them all, and that could only be done through genuinely universal principles. The absence of a victor among the participants meant that there would be no capricious, punitive, or humiliating terms enforced on anyone. The neutral

---

114 Luigi Einaudi, *Prediche Inutili* (Giulio Einaudi Editore, 1956).

organizers had neither the will nor the ability to enforce harsh terms on others, but they could get them to agree to something workable for them all. They were practical men who wanted practical results, and they had no vengeful motivations. The conference would produce a universal formula for conflict resolution by which everyone willingly abided, or it would fail.

The delegations of the United States, Switzerland, and Liechtenstein acted as if they had been an alliance of victors, because staying out of the war was indeed the only victory possible. American democratic ideals meshed nicely with Swiss pluralist democracy, political decentralization, and the concept of self-determination as advanced by Prince Johann II. The US, Swiss, and Liechtenstein delegations broadly agreed on the path forward, which centered on three fundamental principles: self-determination, the right to secession, and free trade. These ideas were wildly popular with non-European delegations, most of whom were still incensed at the gold they had lost to Western central banks during the Great War. The European powers were unable to mount any serious opposition to this growing international consensus, primarily because they had disparate and conflicting interests and because they lacked an easy way to coordinate their positions, given that they were direct rivals and enemies. The US and Switzerland were now the world's economic superpowers. With neutral European, Latin American, African, and Asian governments, they formed a more economically significant bloc than the bankrupt European powers, and they pushed for self-determination, secession, and free trade.

Walter Eucken was a young German economist from Jena who had just completed his PhD at the University of Bonn months before the outbreak of war. Eucken was beginning to prepare for an academic career when he was conscripted in the mobilization of the German army announced in August 1914. Stationed in the trenches of the Western Front, Eucken was deeply distraught at the unexpected turn his life, and that of his nation, had taken with the war. The son of famous German philosopher Rudolph Eucken, winner of the 1908 Nobel Prize in Literature, Walter developed some extreme opinions about the absurdity of this war and the insanity of its wastefulness of life and treasure. Having developed a reputation as the most intelligent and eloquent soldier in his division, Eucken was tasked with accompanying Crown Prince

Wilhelm on a tour of the trenches in February 1915. The Crown Prince was impressed by the thoughtfulness of the 24-year-old economist and soldier, as well as his perceptive understanding of the conditions surrounding the war. He immediately requested that Eucken be transferred to serve with the Crown Prince's office on the western front and, over time, he came to appreciate his thoughts and counsel. Eucken believed that Germany should adopt a policy of free trade with the whole world and not have to worry about bringing producers of goods it desires under its rule. He believed that the remarkable progress of German industrialization over the past few decades was far more important and valuable than any plot of land outside Germany, and that the goal of the German government should be to protect this industrialization from destruction, rather than squander its fruits on military conquests.

After taking the German throne and accepting the invitation to the Geneva Peace Conference, Wilhelm summoned Eucken to join the German delegation, as a young and modern counter to his father's old guard at the palace, government, and parliament, accumulated and selected over decades for their affinity to his father's hobby-horses of empire and navy. Eucken was an economic liberal in his outlook, a perspective that sounded refreshing to the new Kaiser. He saw no reason to expand the Empire to rule over people who do not want to be part of Germany.

On the fourth day of the conference, Eucken gave a speech, with the blessing of Kaiser Wilhelm III, signaling the capitulation of the old European order to the new, peaceful world order:

> Thanks to the wonders of industrialization, technological advancement, free trade, and capitalism, our generation has achieved a standard of living and a level of productivity far higher than what our ancestors ever experienced. This is a blessing. But if it is mishandled, it could turn into a catastrophe, as we saw over the last year. The same machines that allow us a better life also allow us more death and destruction. Our ancestors never had these technologies, and war for them was a far more straightforward affair, fought with swords and shields, creating less destruction, with lucrative prizes of territory. They could afford to be belligerent, aggressive, and

avaricious for territory, but we cannot. Today's weapons can inflict destruction far costlier than any spoils of war. The fruits of peaceful civilization are too precious and fragile to be sacrificed on the altar of territorial expansion. Whatever a nation stands to gain from territorial expansion pales in comparison to what it loses by engaging in modern war. Peaceful civilization means that any resources can today be obtained on global markets for money rather than acquired violently through mass murder and war. There is no longer any justification or rationale for territorial expansion. Germany proposes to all nations to join together in renouncing conquest by war and accepting the right of all peoples to self-determination.

The highlight of the fifth day was a speech by Henry Ford, who made an impassioned plea against war and its devastating impact, and urged the representatives to arrive at a permanent peace through negotiations. "War settles nothing; only reason and conciliation can settle international disputes. Men sitting around a table, not men dying in a trench, will finally settle the differences." He insisted that he would be willing to dedicate his fortune to helping achieve peace and to finance any proposal that would help bring it about. He concluded with his famous quip: "No one ever wins a war."[115]

The Masterminds

Behind the scenes, while leaders were giving their speeches, a group of fourteen practical men sat discussing practical details. After five days of listening to delegate speeches and having private conversations with delegates, President Motta and the four Swiss bankers made a shortlist of what they saw as the most practical, creative, intelligent, and solution-oriented men in the conference, summoning them to formulate in concrete detail a plan forward. These men were Louis Blériot from France, Ludwig von Mises from Austria, Orville Wright and Henry Ford from the US, Sergei Witte from Russia, John Morley

---

115 The Henry Ford Museum, "No One Ever Wins a War," Henry Ford Quotes, accessed September 30, 2025. Originally quoted in Detroit News and Times in July 30, 1942.

from Britain, Walter Eucken from Germany, Prince Sabahaddin from Turkey, Prince Johann II from Liechtenstein, and Luigi Einaudi from Italy. The fifteen men slipped into a side room, in what would probably become the most important single meeting in human history.

They spent countless hours deliberating constructively and meticulously. These were highly practical men who had little interest in the territorial squabbles and narcissistic ethnic concerns of various pre-industrial tribes. They could not possibly spend time thinking about the particular details of any one conflict. They needed to step back and find a comprehensive solution to territorial disputes that would apply everywhere and be accepted by everyone. They had to view the problem of government as an engineering problem and devise an algorithm to solve it. They wanted to stop the bloodshed and make the world prosper, and they had a golden opportunity to make it happen. They were all civilians commanding no military, except Motta, whose military's ethos was neutrality and non-intervention in foreign affairs. Yet, they had the ear of the governments of the neutral countries, which had the world's only surviving major banks, which commanded most of the world's remaining liquid capital. And the major militaries were run by bankrupt leaders whose fate depended on the neutral powers' banks.

The fifteen men agreed on free trade and self-determination, but they had no easy way of enforcing this sort of solution on the world's governments. They realized they not only had to come up with a solution but also to make it so enticing and obviously beneficial that governments would willingly want to participate in it.

Blériot remarked:

> The majority of the world's capital, in the form of gold, is now in the United States, Switzerland, and other neutral countries. The rest of the world is desperate for this capital. Our banks would like to invest this money in war reconstruction, but they need assurances that they can get this money back. I believe the bare minimum we must achieve in this conference is to find a way to facilitate the movement of capital across borders. My suggestion is that the neutral countries adopt a unified policy toward all belligerent

countries: Our banks can invest in your country if you guarantee the free movement of capital in and out of your borders, practically manifested in the safety of gold-carrying aircraft."

Walter Eucken added:

We need to devise a framework for the free movement of capital across international borders. The lucrative opportunity we have is to utilize access to neutral country capital as an incentive to agree on policies that would bring about peace and international cooperation, thereby ensuring the stability of the international monetary order is not reliant solely on government commitments but also on economic incentives. With capital free to move around, governments will have no choice but to become responsible in how they treat it, and that means a lot less belligerence and warmongering.

Mises nodded in agreement and added:

This is a great point, and I think it should be extended beyond just capital, but also ensure it applies to all economic goods as well. A country that restricts the movement of goods is also likely to limit the movement of capital. The United States thrives today due to its enormous internal free market. Something similar in Europe would go a long way to helping the recovery from the war, while also making another war less likely. Remember that a large part of the rationale for war centers around trade. If Russia could trade freely through the Turkish Straits, it would be far less likely to seek to take them over by war! The return on conquering land to expand markets would disappear if all markets were open and accessible. If goods cross borders, militaries would not.

If governments can extort their people every time they send goods across the borders, it would become an eternal source of conflict as governments sought to expand their markets through conquering other countries. And it would lead to governments extorting each other for access to each other's markets. If markets were free for international trade, however, the rationale for conquering land to expand markets would decline—and along with it, the drive for conflict over market access. Freedom to trade would diffuse much of the world's territorial disputes. If goods crossed borders, militaries wouldn't. Moreover, control over trade will allow governments to impoverish their people and gain inordinate power over them. Governments seeking financing from neutral countries should adopt a policy of free trade, not just because it will increase the likelihood of neutral country investors recovering their capital, but also because it will reduce the risk of destructive conflict.

Building on the conclusions of Mises, Johann II added:

Free movement of capital and goods is a great way to diffuse conflict, but we can go a step further and push for a framework for peaceful conflict resolution and avoidance. The path forward is through self-determination, and we should use this opportunity to extract from belligerent countries a commitment to accept the right of self-determination on all their territories. It should be the inhabitants and owners of property who decide who rules it, and not foreign armies, and if we do that, there will be a lot fewer boys dying over foreign lands whose name they cannot pronounce.

President Motta listened intently before commenting:

We must combine free capital movement, free trade, and self-determination into one package deal. If countries want to have access to capital from neutral countries, they should abide by all three. If we can present this as a coherent and transparent framework for governments to commit to, we might be able to make it attractive enough for a critical mass of governments to join. With free trade, the main benefit of territorial expansion is removed, and with self-determination, we have a process for formalizing borders without bloodshed. The governments that join will enjoy peace and prosperity that would entice those who do not initially join. The more governments join, the larger the global free market, the more beneficial it will be to those who join."

Mises agreed:

When there is private ownership of the means of production everywhere and when laws, the tribunals, and the administration treat foreigners and citizens on equal terms, it is of little importance where a country's frontiers are drawn. Nobody can derive any profit from conquest, but many can suffer losses from fighting. War no longer pays; there is no motive for aggression. The population of every territory is free to determine to which state it wishes to belong, or whether it prefers to establish a state of its own. All nations can coexist peacefully, because no nation is concerned about the size of its state.[116]

Prince Sabahaddin responded:

I've long seen that decentralization of power regionally is the way forward for old empires entering the modern world. I've fought long for this in Turkey and ended up exiled for my troubles. Now that they are faced with the dissolution of a bankrupt empire, I think Ottoman leaders and subjects will view ideas of self-determination more favorably.

The economists, royals, and politicians discussed the outlines of a postwar treaty, but Wright and Blériot were fixated on how to implement it practically. As with the Lightning jet, they used experimentation to arrive at the best design. While no laboratories, workshops, or wind tunnels were used, they instead resorted to thought experiments, devising treaty terms and asking the participants to imagine how they would materialize out in the real world, and how various political groups, leaders, and populations would respond to them.

---

116 Ludwig von Mises, *Omnipotent Government: The Rise of the Total State and Total War* (Liberty Fund, 2010).

Fourteen of the brightest minds humanity had to offer were rigorously exploring ideas and pushing each other's mental capacities to their limits, trying to
solve every potential problem that could come up.

The International Committee for Self-Determination

By the end of the ninth day, they produced the outlines of a practical plan for
peace, prosperity, and self-determination. The essence of the Treaty of Geneva:

I - Switzerland, the United States, and other neutral countries will restrict out-
bound capital movements to countries that commit to:

> 1 - The total freedom of import and export of capital and economic goods.
> All import duties and fees must not exceed 5% of the cost of goods.

> 2 - Respecting the right of self-determination of all residents on the territo-
> ries they control, according to the framework described below.

II - This conference will establish the International Committee for Self-
Determination (ICSD), a neutral body made up of Swiss citizens who will
oversee the arbitration of all territorial disputes and independence movements
based on the principles of self-determination and the right to secession.

III - Any geographic area with more than fifty thousand residents has the right
to secede or join another government. To change the legal status of a territory,
any member of that geographic area's community needs to:

> 1 - Present a clear and precise written proposal for the change requested,
> framed as a yes/no question proposed in a plebiscite.

> 2 - Present a coherent vision of the broad terms of the new political ar-
> rangement proposed, including the tax rate, the form of governance,
> and the services the government would provide.

> 3 - Present a statement from the current sovereign of the territory regarding
> how they would respond to this referendum being passed. They could

not threaten the use of force, but they could restrict the movement of secessionists into and out of their own territories.

4 - Collect the signatures of 1% of the adult population of the geographic area and present them to the ICSD, along with their addresses, for verification.

5 - Commit to covering the costs of a plebiscite to vote on the proposed legal status change.

6 - Secure the votes of more than half of the adult population of the region in favor of the proposal in the referendum.

IV- The results of any referendum can be overruled by a subsequent referendum. Any sub-region can choose to opt out of the results of the referendum by proposing its own referendum for its own region, as long as it abides by the steps in item III.

V- All signatory governments commit to abide by the results of any referendum conducted by the ICSD. Any government that refuses to abide by ICSD referenda will not be allowed access to neutral country capital markets.

Henry Ford offered 50,000 ounces of gold each to create endowment for the ICSD, establish its headquarters, pay its management, and train its permanent and part-time personnel. Louis Blériot and Orville Wright promised to make their jets available to the ICSD at no cost.

After agreeing on the terms, Orville Wright insisted on giving them a trial run before deployment in production by running the terms by world leaders who would have to take it to their populations. Thought experiments were nice; experimenting with the actual rulers would be far more edifying. And in the hotel where they were meeting, they happened to have most of the world's leaders gathered, with little to do but talk and imagine hypotheticals. They chose to discuss the terms with the Austrian and Serbian monarchs to see if they could serve as a basis for a solution to the troubled part of the world from which the war had originated. If it could work in the Balkans, it could work anywhere. And if they could announce the plan with the support of the

Serbian and Austrian leaders, they would surely secure the attention of the other delegations and make them take it seriously.

King Peter of Serbia and Emperor Charles of Austria came into the conference room and were startled to see each other. Their countries were still formally at war, and they were unsure of what was going on or who most of the other people in the room were. Charles, who had just acceded to the throne, was in no position to oppose the ICSD's proposal after his army had been trounced in Serbia. He understood that he was in no position to expand his empire over unwilling subjects; he had to fight for the mere survival of his dynasty. Accepting the ICSD meant gaining legitimacy with the international order, which would boost his chances of surviving the war, something far more important to him and his Austrian people than the Balkans and everything they contained. He had no reason to seek to grow his territory; he needed to secure what he had. And he had seen what imperial adventures had done to his family.

The King of Serbia, Peter Karađorđević, supported the proposal. Having repelled the Austrian invasion in December 1914 against all odds, King Peter had feared the expected Austrian counterattack to be brutal, as it would include Bulgaria from the south and Germany from the north. Several people in the Balkans had been considering uniting under one banner to counter the invaders more effectively, and Peter was touted as the potential king of a pan-Balkan empire that would include the Croats, Slovenes, and possibly more peoples. While agreeing to the ICSD meant that he would potentially lose the ability to rule over this empire, it was a price he was happy to pay in exchange for avoiding a German-Austrian-Bulgarian invasion. King Peter was unequivocal in his support for this idea, committing to only ruling over territories that willingly chose to join his kingdom. The Croat, Slovene, and all the other delegations were also satisfied with this proposal, as they imagined the plebiscites would give them what they wanted. There were very conflicting visions of what the referenda would produce in the minds of individual Balkan delegations, but none of them could argue with the process.

With this trial completed, Johann II read the proposal to the general assembly of delegations. There was a stunned silence in the room as everyone tried to process the information. Some delegations must not have liked the proposal, but they could not articulate why. There were plenty of territorial disputes and acrimonious conflicts, but every party to these disputes had usually maintained the legitimacy of its position based on the sanctity of the property rights of the residents of any territory. To oppose the creation of the ICSD was to oppose the right of people around the world to live on their rightful property, and to advertise the rejection of civilization. Some of the delegations might have realized that the ICSD would cost them territory, but opposing it publicly would be an open admission of wanting to secure territory against the will of its citizens, something that would be unpopular both at home and abroad. More importantly, opposing it meant forgoing the capital flows that were necessary for economic recovery. The pretext of protecting minorities—which empires had long exploited to invade foreign territory—had also been successfully accommodated by the ICSD, granting the right of minorities and smaller regions to opt out of any referendum result that displeased them.

Members of the British delegation had privately expressed their concern about the practicality of this arrangement and lobbied against it. When the newly crowned King Edward VIII took the podium of the general assembly, he attempted to articulate a coherent objection to the framework, which only served to underscore its desirability to other delegates who were not fond of British imperialism. King Edward insisted that self-determination was not something that the majority of the world was ready for. Having had experience with colonies and uncivilized lands before, the King insisted that self-rule had to be developed gradually, under colonial supervision, to ensure peace and stability.

Force of habit had made the British view all these territorial squabbles as theirs to mediate and solve. As the most advanced industrial nation, the British viewed it as their prerogative to stand up for the oppressed. Opportunism had used these conflicts as pretexts to meddle in the affairs of European rivals and undermine them. Sensing their historical role being undermined, the British delegation sought to sow doubt about the practicality of the proposal. "We believe this is too complex, too expensive, and too time-consuming to work as a suitable solution in the long term. We expect it to devolve into endless conflict and repeated referenda," said King Edward VIII, concluding his speech.

"It's a lot simpler, cheaper, and faster than the wars your empire has waged for centuries," thundered Blériot from the back seats, to applause from the majority of attendees. "You are broke! You are in no position to lecture anyone! Join us or have fun staying poor!" Blériot continued, to uproarious laughter. After the laughter died down, Prince Johann II gave a brief speech that directly refuted King Edward's objections and exposed them as self-serving cant. He addressed King Edward VIII:

> "Your Majesty, your empire transformed a European border squabble into a world war by crying crocodile tears about the freedom of Belgium and their right to self-determination free of German control, and the right of Serbians to live free of Austrian control. Yet it is your same empire that continues to deny the right to self-determination to hundreds of millions of Cypriots, Egyptians, Indians, and many other peoples. Surely, Your Majesty, you must be able to see how self-serving and duplicitous this double standard is, and how counterproductive it is for a peaceful and prosperous world order. Claims that nations are not ready for self-determination are unconvincing. The ICSD framework will require an aspiring nation to develop a coherent statement for a referendum, organize the financing of this referendum, collect signatures from across the territory, present the application to the ICSD in Geneva, and then have a majority of the population vote in favor of it. Any group of people that can pull off all of these steps is ready, notwithstanding what its colonial masters think. If a nation is truly not ready for independence and self-rule, then it will either fail to organize, fund, or vote in favor of the referendum. And if colonial rule really is the best course of action for a nation, then it should be straightforward to convince the people to vote against independence from it. If colonial rule is indeed best, then Britain should be the first to support the ICSD framework, as it is a great way to legitimize its beneficent rule over its colonies."

Switzerland, the United States, Liechtenstein, the Netherlands, Sweden, Spain, and Canada signed the ICSD before the conference adjourned on December 1. By January 1, twenty-five world governments had signed it. The new signatories were Germany, Russia, Austria, Serbia, Belgium, Italy, Greece, Romania, Bulgaria, the Ottoman Empire, Mexico, Brazil, Argentina, South Africa, Japan, Norway, Denmark, and Finland. The ICSD would soon become the second-largest industry in Switzerland after banking. Thousands of young and old Swiss men and women were recruited to its ranks and sent all over the world to verify petition signatories, conduct plebiscites, and redraw borders. Kings and emperors whose dynasties had fought for centuries over disputed territories had to watch quietly as delegations of Swiss men and women, dressed in sharp suits and carrying briefcases, came into their territory to count ballots and decide what would have taken rivers of blood to be agreed in previous, less civilized, more barbaric times. All the kings could do to gain territory was please the people who had the choice of hiring or firing them.

Broke, isolated, and despised for losing the gold entrusted to it, the British delegation was also divided over ratifying the Treaty of Geneva. John Morley and the liberals wanted to sign it, drastically reduce the size of the empire, and let the British people and industry recover in peace. However, the king, along with many of the Foreign Office staff, as well as the wealthy businesses that had amassed a fortune from the empire, could not tolerate the idea of granting their colonial subjects the right to self-determination. The delegation left without signing the treaty. Back home, the pressure against signing it was stronger than the clamor for it, so it was ignored, and the debate surrounding it died down for the rest of the teen years of the twentieth century.

A similar situation unfolded in the second major European colonial power, France. With a large number of colonies across the old and new worlds, most of the French establishment was far from excited at the prospect of allowing their colonial subjects, most of whom could not read, to determine their own fate. The large number of French businesses that profited from colonialism was, of course, the most obvious obstacle to the process. France refused to become a full member of the ICSD framework, but it signaled its willingness to accept self-determination referendums to finalize the borders between it and Germany.

The world's press was skeptical of the success of the Geneva Conference or the sustainability of its framework. "Left to ruminate over its terms for weeks in the pleasant surroundings of Lake Geneva, governments may have signed this ambitious treaty, but in the heat of parliamentary debates and military conflicts, the Genevan idealism will surely give way to the brutal realism of power politics and man's eternal quest for dominating his fellow man" was how *The New York Times* editorial reflected on the event. Most of the world's press expressed significant skepticism as well, emphasizing the lack of enforcement mechanisms and that governments would withdraw from the treaty as soon as the first referendum didn't go their way. Several analysts also highlighted the absence of France and Britain, who ruled over so many of the world's peoples, as rendering the agreement toothless.

Miraculously, the skeptics were proven wrong. It was complicated, controversial, and contentious, but it was peaceful. Everyone had had a heavy taste of the fiat alternative for a year and four months, and they knew what it meant to not listen to the Swiss arbiters. Everyone accepted that a century of voting was preferable to a day of war. Everyone accepted that Blériot's aircraft would continue to clear gold at high speed and prevent governments from organizing cartels to exploit their countries through inflation. Everyone accepted that goods would cross borders without government interference. And everyone accepted that the price of civilization was the public and irreversible renunciation of their inner aggressive animal and the respect for others' property.

None of the initial signatories withdrew from the Treaty of Geneva, and it succeeded in establishing peace over many contentious territories worldwide. The free trade provisions were a boon to the war-torn economies, and the growing proliferation of trade made the people of these countries more friendly and less hostile to one another. The refusal of France and Britain to join turned out to be a blessing in disguise and an advertisement for the treaty. The two countries' disastrous predicament in the years that followed the treaty was, in large part, caused by the problems the treaty aimed to solve. Without a central bank cartel to create pounds and francs in multiples of the colonies' deposits in the imperial central bank, the empires constituted a monumental drain of resources. Under the classical gold standard, imperial central bank cartels set up branches in colonies and acquired large amounts of gold deposits to allow imperial power banks to use the imperial central bank to settle international payments. Since these colonies relied increasingly, and exclusively, on the imperial central bank, and the central bank was usually thousands of miles away from the colony, the colonial subjects rarely, if ever, withdrew their gold from the central bank, which allowed the central bank to issue far more gold receipts and bank credit than the corresponding gold they had on hand. However, with private banks worldwide now able to settle payments freely using BTC, the monopoly power of imperial central banks was significantly diminished, and the economic value of the empire became increasingly negative.

Bismarck, Morley, and many other European sages had consistently explained how wasteful and destructive empires were, even in the days of the classical gold standard. Bismarck had famously tried to give Namibia to the British as he saw it as an expense he would rather burden his British enemies with. They looked at their government budget and saw how dearly holding and running colonies cost them. They saw that the costs of empire were borne by taxpayers in Europe, while the benefits accrued to opportunistic businessmen who established trade monopolies, as well as to the banking cartel, whose central bank could issue more costless money the more imperial reserves it held. As long as the banking cartel was profiting from the empire, it could use its gains to subsidize government operations, bribe politicians, and produce media favorable to imperialism, all of which helped sustain the conquest. But as the banking cartel's leading lights had been reduced to accountants, shopkeepers, school teachers, and factory workers, the rationale for empire had disappeared, and the hefty bill could no longer be hidden from the taxpayers footing it. Public opposition to imperialism grew significantly in Britain in the 1920s. "Not one more penny to India" was the motto of the anti-Imperialists, who wore the 'Little Englander' epithet with pride.

The Treaty of Geneva and its emphasis on self-determination had ignited the quest for independence among the most educated populations of the colonies. These citizens began to organize politically to demand freedom from their colonial masters. Perhaps even more damaging to the imperial enterprise, the signatories of the Treaty of Geneva had collectively built a free trade area that dwarfed what Britain and France had achieved with their empires. With the United States, Canada, most of Latin America, Germany, Russia, Japan, Austria, Italy, Switzerland, Scandinavia, the remnants of the Ottoman Empire, and many other states committed to free trade among themselves, their economies all boomed, their capital stocks appreciated, and their worker productivity rose markedly. For almost a century, Britain had grown its wealth and power through having the world's largest free trade area, comprising its many colonies around the world, on which the sun never set. But now the new Geneva-based world order had an economy far larger than the British Empire, which became a millstone around the British people's necks. The French, with an even smaller and less developed empire than the British, were in worse shape.

Following political unrest in India, Morocco, Egypt, and many other colonies, which demanded self-determination, the cost of maintaining law and order in the empires rose significantly. British and French men largely refused to serve in empires they viewed suspiciously, and the colonies slid into increasing lawlessness and political violence, which frequently targeted economic infrastructure and hurt colonial investors. The French and British imperialists found themselves unpopular at home and in their colonies, unable to afford their colonies, and increasingly isolated from a new world order that united their previous allies and enemies together. With the Geneva signatories continuing to prosper in peace, public opinion in these countries swung decisively in favor of joining the Treaty of Geneva. France joined in 1923, and Britain followed in 1924.

PART III

THE MODERN WORLD

XII.

The Modern Gold Standard

Industrial Money

The period of prosperity and economic stability that humanity has experienced since the 1930s is completely unprecedented, and it is no coincidence that it came in a period of unprecedented financial stability. Readers today, enjoying the benefits of banks and money that work as reliably as modern industrial devices, may struggle to comprehend just how destructive and malignant financial panics, bank failures, inflation, and hyperinflation can be. It can also be difficult to understand why such occurrences have been so thoroughly and completely eliminated from modern economies.

Modern industrialization has revolutionized nearly every aspect of life. It increased the productivity of manufacturing and the speed of transportation, allowing for a more sophisticated division of labor, with more products and more trade taking place across long distances. Before industrialization, the vast majority of a person's goods and services were exchanged at a very local scale by hand. Gold and silver are, in a literal sense, *manual* monetary technologies that require transfer from the sender's hand to the recipient's. Gold and

silver worked perfectly well in a manual economy, where most goods were produced and exchanged locally. In the modern industrial economy, a constantly
increasing share of the goods a person consumes is produced and sourced
from distances very far from his hand's reach. As trade across distances proliferated, physical gold and silver could no longer travel with each transaction.
They could not offer the finality of payment across distances that they offer
in person. The only way that gold and silver could scale was through having
them placed in centralized banks that performed periodic clearance and settlement with one another. As soon as the first gold receipt was issued and used
as money, gold had lost some of its monetary value to the issuing authority,
whose creditworthiness was now part of the value of the gold-based monetary
instrument.

As industrialization advanced, gold became increasingly reliant on the
banking system, and gold owners were less likely to request their physical gold
in exchange for the banknotes and credit issued by the bank. Economies of
scale meant more reserves were centralized in central clearance agencies, creating monopolies whose credit became as good as money. The more a bank
had a monopoly in a particular geographic area, the fewer of its outstanding
liabilities it would expect its customers to redeem, and the more it could expand credit and gamble with its depositors' and creditors' wealth, savings, and
lives. As long as gold was manual money, it was inextricably linked with bank
credit into a hybrid monetary bastard that compromised gold's hardness and
allowed banks to create calamity.

This continued for centuries, resulting in frequent fluctuations in the value
of banknotes or bank balances. And this was what allowed governments of the
industrial West, by the early twentieth century, to grow militarily and in their
budgets to the point where they could enter a wholly senseless and pointless
mass slaughter that killed millions and destroyed the wealth of all their citizens in pursuit of aims that were almost entirely inconsequential to the vast
majority of their population. There was no way out of this predicament as long
as gold remained a manual technology. Governments could regulate banking
to ensure monopolies, and these monopolies could create unbacked credit to
pilfer their users and enrich the government that provided them the monopoly

rights. The problem of banking intensified as the Industrial Revolution advanced, but it was ultimately the state's intervention that exacerbated the issue to its explosive boiling point in 1915.

The invention of the airplane, more than anything, allowed humanity to break free from this trap. With airplanes deployed in a vast network of decentralized clearance channels, monopolies became untenable, and banks had to operate on practically full reserve for demand liabilities and maturity matching for time liabilities. Because jets cut settlement windows from weeks to hours, any maturity mismatch surfaced almost immediately at clearinghouses. The discount on a bank's paper showed up within days, not quarters, making fractional pyramids uneconomic rather than merely risky. Gold became mechanical industrial money that could function in the industrial age without needing the credit of banking institutions. The mechanization of money and its separation from credit are the roots of the prosperity and peace we have witnessed in the twentieth century. With money mechanized, banking became a reliable service that was largely theft-proof. Moreover, governments could no longer finance their violence by covertly robbing their citizens through inflation; they had to tax them overtly. Once citizens realized the cost of their governments' belligerence to their own pockets, they became far more peaceful and frugal.

While the Treaty of Geneva is rightly credited with laying the groundwork for a new cooperative international order, it is important to note that it was really the technological economic reality that shaped the economic incentives for the parties to abide by it for so long. The genius of the Treaty of Geneva was that it aligned the incentives of governments with the economic and technological reality in a way that was most conducive to their peaceful flourishing.

Freely-Issued Money

The collapse of the Bank of England in 1915 ended Britain's classical gold standard era, which had begun with Isaac Newton in 1717. It was also the end of the international classical gold standard system that had been in place since 1873. The new world order inaugurated with the Treaty of Geneva in 1915 was the birth of the *modern gold standard*. While similar to the classical gold standard in that both systems were built on gold, it was operationally very different, with profound political and social implications.

The modern gold standard does not rely on monopoly national central banks, as these were bankrupted in the Great War of 1914–15. It is a decentralized peer-to-peer system reliant on the frequent direct physical clearance of gold between financial institutions, made possible initially thanks to Blériot Transport Company and later on by a plethora of global and regional monetary aviation companies. By the mid-1920s, there were dozens of gold clearance services around the world, most of which purchased their jets from Blériot. What seemed like a needlessly paranoid invention with no obvious market demand in 1913 had by 1920 become the foundational building block of the global monetary system, replacing government central banks.

The collapse of central banks in 1915 destroyed the value of their currencies, but it also caused the value of gold to increase in real terms, not just in terms of the depreciating currencies. As the realization that the pound, franc, and mark that were billed "as good as gold" were only as good as the 10-40% of their value in gold backing them, people all over the world naturally scrambled to get a hold of physical gold as well as silver. Since banknotes were universally suspect and gold was too valuable and impractical to use in small denominations for low-value transactions, demand for silver increased drastically.

The net result was a significant transfer of wealth from holders of government currencies to holders of physical gold and silver. Gold and silver appreciating in value had spared their holders from the harrowing ordeal of inflation, but many economists of the time were actually worried about the effect. With the sloppy central banking inflationist propaganda still fresh in their minds, many economists believed the nonsensical contention that money best serves its function if it is cheap and easy to obtain. With money becoming increasingly expensive, they imagined an economic calamity, as people became unable to obtain money and economic production broke down. This couldn't be further from the truth; as the appreciation of money increased the wealth in the hands of citizens who held it, allowing them to spend and invest more, driving the recovery from hyperinflation and war. The scarcity of money, after all, is its most desirable and critical feature.

As the dust settled on the rubble of war and central banking in early 1916, banknotes started to return to markets slowly. Swiss, Spanish, Dutch, and Swedish banknotes had held up through the war and hyperinflation, and they started to spread across other European countries. Many of the smaller banks in belligerent countries had remained operational thanks to their reliance on BTC. As national currencies collapsed, these private banks began issuing their own banknotes in the same prewar denominations, redeemable in physical gold on demand. The currencies of the central banking cartels were dead, but the denominations remained alive through the force of habit and tradition. These currencies survived their defunct central banks and sometimes their defunct governments, confounding enthusiasts of the state theory of money who thought these currencies could only exist with governments using violence to force their acceptance. But gold and many of its standardized currencies had existed before all of the world's existing governments, and had survived many hundreds of dying regimes, so there was no good reason to expect money, or national currencies, to die with their central banks. On the contrary, they survived, thrived, and became far more robust on the free market.

All the world's prewar currencies were reborn on the modern gold standard and operated in a similar way. Several British banks issued a paper pound redeemable for gold at Newton's old rate of 7.3224 grams of fine gold. These notes were differentiated in their insignia and colors across banks. There was no monopoly on the use of the term "British pound," meaning anyone could issue one, but the price of these notes was freely determined by buyers and sellers as well as exchange houses. American banks issued a dollar redeemable for 1.504 grams of gold, Russian banks issued a ruble at 0.7742 grams of gold, German banks issued a mark redeemable for .3584 grams of gold, Austrian banks issued krones with 0.3049 grams of gold, Turkish banks issued their liras at 6.6152 grams, and Dutch banks issued their guilders at 0.6048 grams of gold. French and Swiss banks continued issuing francs according to the specification of the Latin Monetary Union, at 0.2903 gram, which was the same rate for the lira issued by Italian banks, drachma issued by Greek banks, peseta issued by Spanish banks, leu issued by Romanian banks, lev issued by Bulgarian banks, and dinars issued by Serbian banks. The Islamic dinar also adapted seamlessly to the modern gold standard, with countless private banks across the Muslim world issuing a paper dinar fully redeemable in the exact specification of the Islamic dinar, with 4.25 grams of gold.

The gold coin versions of these currencies traveled far and wide, and they were usually easily salable abroad, since they could ultimately be melted down and converted into one another. The paper notes were also quite salable, but less so than the gold coin, since they could only be redeemed by issuing banks. But with time, paper notes would be commonly issued by banks from locales increasingly distant from their country of origin. Exchanging currencies for one another was as straightforward as converting feet to meters, pounds to kilograms, or miles to kilometers. At any time and in any place, 1 British pound was equivalent to 25.22 French francs, 1 US dollar was worth 4.1979 German marks, and 1 Russian ruble was valued at 2.5395 Austrian krone. Those exchange rates became iconic numbers, memorized by school children worldwide, like 1 meter being equal to 3.2808 feet, or 1 kilogram equaling 2.205 pounds. They are summarized in the table on the corresponding page.

The situation is analogous to there being no government imposing the definitions of the liter, the meter, or the inch. Just like anyone can sell a liter of milk, a meter of cloth, or a 6-inch sandwich, and just like a grocer selling three-quarters of a liter of milk in a container and calling it a liter would lose customers, a bank offering a pound of paper that was not backed by 7.32 grams of gold would lose customers. But the consequences were more dire for the bank, as the slightest suspicion of deficient backing would trigger a run on the bank and cause it to collapse.

There was no government guarantee of these notes, and no legal tender laws to enforce their use. Banks could not rely on the strong arm of the government to compel people to hold them, so they had to demonstrate trustworthiness to their clients instead. Whenever people began to suspect solvency problems at a particular bank, its bills would get discounted on the market. If the bank were insolvent, this would exacerbate its position, as more holders of the money would ask to redeem it for physical gold. If the bank were solvent, it would be able to profit from these rumors by buying its notes on the market at a discount and continuing to meet all redemption requests, eventually bringing

	Gold (gram)	British pound	Turkish lira	Islamic dinar	US dollar	Russian ruble	Dutch guilder	German mark	Austrian krone	French franc	Swiss franc	Italian lira	Greek drachma	Spanish peseta
Gold (gram)	1	0.14	0.15	0.24	0.66	1.29	1.65	2.79	3.28	3.44	3.44	3.44	3.44	3.44
British pound	7.32	1	1.11	1.72	4.87	9.46	12.11	20.43	24.02	25.22	25.22	25.22	25.22	25.22
Turkish lira	6.62	0.90	1	1.56	4.40	8.54	10.94	18.46	21.70	22.79	22.79	22.79	22.79	22.79
Islamic dinar	4.25	0.58	0.64	1	2.83	5.49	7.03	11.86	13.94	14.64	14.64	14.64	14.64	14.64
US dollar	1.50	0.21	0.23	0.35	1	1.94	2.49	4.20	4.93	5.18	5.18	5.18	5.18	5.18
Russian ruble	0.77	0.11	0.12	0.18	0.51	1	1.28	2.16	2.54	2.67	2.67	2.67	2.67	2.67
Dutch guilder	0.60	0.08	0.09	0.14	0.40	0.78	1	1.69	1.98	2.08	2.08	2.08	2.08	2.08
German mark	0.36	0.05	0.05	0.08	0.24	0.46	0.59	1	1.18	1.23	1.23	1.23	1.23	1.23
Austrian krone	0.30	0.04	0.05	0.07	0.20	0.39	0.50	0.85	1	1.05	1.05	1.05	1.05	1.05
French franc	0.29	0.04	0.04	0.07	0.19	0.37	0.48	0.81	0.95	1	1	1	1	1
Swiss franc	0.29	0.04	0.04	0.07	0.19	0.37	0.48	0.81	0.95	1	1	1	1	1
Italian lira	0.29	0.04	0.04	0.07	0.19	0.37	0.48	0.81	0.95	1	1	1	1	1
Greek drachma	0.29	0.04	0.04	0.07	0.19	0.37	0.48	0.81	0.95	1	1	1	1	1
Spanish peseta	0.29	0.04	0.04	0.07	0.19	0.37	0.48	0.81	0.95	1	1	1	1	1

Table 1: Twentieth-century exchange rates

the banknote market price back to par with the pound denomination of gold and with other banknotes. A famous example happened in November 1943, when Deutsche Bank's papers were rumored to be unbacked, and a flurry of selling on global exchanges caused it to drop to 98.7% of par value. Deutsche Bank began to buy back notes with its gold hoard, and the management even encouraged all employees to buy with their own savings. By the next morning, the paper was back trading at par, and the bank and its employees made a nice overnight profit.

Banks went out of their way to demonstrate that their money would always be redeemable. In 1933, UBS in Switzerland became the first bank to keep its main branch open 24 hours a day, every day of the year, to emphasize the point. By the 1950s, this became a common practice worldwide, with banks keeping more and more of their branches always open. In 1942, Barclays Bank created serially numbered bills and always displayed on its storefront the highest numbered bills of each denomination, as well as its total gold holdings, which allowed its users to quickly calculate the total supply of outstanding bills and compare it to the bank's gold holdings. The quantities had to match precisely, and they always did. Once a month, they would hire an independent accounting firm to conduct a full audit of all the gold in all their vaults and perform purity checks on randomly selected gold bars. This was compelling evidence of solvency, since all it would take was one holder to produce a single bill with a serial number higher than the numbers displayed on the storefront, or any holder or exchange house to discover two bills with a duplicate number, to prove the company had issued more liabilities than its holdings.

Many banks copied this innovation, and over time, the audits became more frequent. The audit and the outstanding number of bills would demonstrate that the bank had not issued banknotes beyond its gold holdings. Over time, people came to rely on this transparency and verification, a much healthier alternative to the blind trust model of government central banking days. The dollar, pound, franc, and mark had now become set weights of physical gold—by convention, not by fiat—just as the inch, meter, mile, yard, and kilometer were conventions for length. Anyone could issue papers in these denominations, and they were always supposed to be redeemable for the conventional set quantity of gold. However, these privately issued banknotes were freely traded on the market, and anyone could accept them at whatever value they chose. The notes traded at a discount to their face value in gold if people had reason to suspect that the bank was facing solvency problems, and with central banks thankfully having died, no authority could force people to accept discounted notes at face value, and no authority could save a bank from angry depositors looking to loot it and its owners. The only salvation lay in honesty, full reserve banking, and complete maturity matching.

Banknotes rarely ever traded below face value, since the issuing banks offered redemption and went to great lengths to demonstrate their solvency. Whenever a bank's lending portfolio became troubled, its banknotes would become discounted to the extent that investors expected these problems to affect its solvency. If the bank's loans were to default, and its assets were no longer enough to meet its liabilities, the gold backing its paper banknotes would enter into bankruptcy proceedings. Over time, the issuance of banknotes became completely separate from the business of credit and investment banking, with banks split into separate institutions to protect banknote holders from the risks of investment banking. Banks that issued banknotes functioned as gold warehouses, issuing receipts redeemable for their gold. They were constantly audited, and they displayed the total amount of bills outstanding. Investment banks, on the other hand, held investors' money and either invested it directly in equity or lent it out, paying interest to their depositors.

Several governments attempted to finance their operations by increasing the supply of gold-backed paper issued by their banks beyond the gold held in reserve; however, the results were always the same: the bills and credit of the issuing banks would be discounted by the market from their face value to the value of the underlying gold. With the Treaty of Geneva preventing restrictions on the movement of physical gold across national borders, it was never possible for central banks to monopolize banking and international clearance. Several governments attempted to create monopolies in banking by limiting banking licenses to members of a cartel, but this approach always failed because their citizens had four weapons to wield against this monopoly. First, they could use paper notes issued by foreign banks, which they could import in bulk with gold transport airplanes. The movement of these notes into the country could not be impeded under the international free trade stipulations of the Treaty of Geneva. Second, they could utilize foreign bank services in other countries, a task that became increasingly easy with the widespread adoption of modern phone and fax telecommunications in the 1930s and the advent of the internet in the 1970s. Third, local businesses could conduct international clearance and settlement of gold directly with trading partners abroad using gold transportation companies. And fourth, and most drastically, citizens who witnessed their banknote supply increase while facing government-imposed impediments to its redemption into gold could simply vote for secession or to join more fiscally responsible countries.

The Treaty of Geneva imposed a 5% limit on customs duties, allowing governments to introduce some friction into the process of gold redemption. This allowed them to skim a small premium of inflation by increasing the money supply beyond their existing gold stockpiles, knowing import taxes hampered the arbitrage opportunity. Governments imposing an import duty on gold was a reliable signal that they were engaging in nineteenth-century monetary shenanigans, issuing more currency than the gold on hand. This resulted in a discount on national currencies of the less scrupulous countries, which usually ranged between 0.1% and 5%, roughly corresponding to the level of inflation in banknotes and the level of expected future inflation. When a government attempted to exceed the 5% supply inflation seigniorage, it quickly undermined confidence in the currency, which was usually discounted further in anticipation of further dilution, resulting in significant hindrance to the currency's liquidity and causing many international exchange houses to refuse it. The 5% discount limit had by the 1940s gained a mythical importance in financial markets. Whenever a country's currency was discounted more than 5% compared to its value in gold, counterparties priced in regime risk, and the region would almost inevitably witness large bankruptcies in the financial sector, demands for secession, or government default. This became increasingly uncommon over time as governments learned to stay well clear of the 5% limit.

The continued increase in the purchasing power of these currencies throughout the century led to the popularization of the smaller denominations of these currencies. The smaller denominations began to be printed on paper, and long-forgotten smaller denomination coins were reintroduced after decades of decommissioning. Some new, smaller denominations were introduced. In the US, the half dollar was printed on paper in 1936, the quarter dollar was printed on paper in 1933 for the first time, the dime followed in 1956, and the nickel followed in 1985. The half cent, which had been issued between 1793 and 1857, was brought back in 1933. The milli, equal to a tenth of a cent, had been used as a notional accounting unit previously, but was introduced as a coin in 1965. In Britain, the half-pound note was first re-introduced in 1928, and the ten pence note was first introduced in 1951, followed by the shilling note in 1981. The half-farthing, equal to a quarter of a penny, which had last been minted in 1856, returned to circulation in 1943. In 1982, the milli was introduced at a valuation of a tenth of a penny. Whereas in the past these smaller denomination coins were minted in copper or silver and traded at the market value of their metal content, they were now merely units of paper or metal redeemable in gold, or for paper redeemable in gold.

Hypergoldenization: There Is No Second Best

By the early twentieth century, gold coins, gold-backed banknotes, and gold-backed checks had come to increasingly dominate economic transactions, displacing silver. After a brief and slight increase in the value of silver in gold terms in 1915–16 that suggested it might reverse the rapid demonetization of silver since 1871, silver remained roughly flat against gold in 1917 and 1918, before declining again in 1919. The decline would accelerate markedly in the 1920s as monetary freedom gave individuals worldwide the freedom to select the harder money, and the edicts of misguided and sentimental central bankers could no longer restrain them to silver. India, China, Persia, Ethiopia, Afghanistan, and other countries were still on a silver standard when the Great War took place, but in its aftermath, their citizens began to switch to foreign gold-backed currency, and their banks and central banks soon followed. Another factor hastening the demise of silver was that it was significantly more expensive to transport by airplane than gold, given that it weighed substantially more for its value. The result was a large decline in the value of silver as its monetary stocks were dumped in exchange for gold worldwide, bringing the price of gold in silver soaring upwards to unprecedented highs.

Gold became the completely dominant form of money by the 1930s, and the price of silver in gold terms would never recover to anywhere near its previous highs. The cultural and psychological impact of this shock was difficult for most people to process. For as long as human civilization has existed, gold and silver have been understood to be money, and they complemented each other in a way that seemed intuitive to people, even reflected in the medals awarded in sporting competitions as far back as ancient Athens. By the 1950s, silver had practically lost it, with only a few increasingly economically irrelevant dead-enders holding on to it as it sank in value while they were adamant that its monetary resurrection was near. No such resurrection ever happened.

The story of silver's demise is best told through the price of gold in terms of silver, which illustrates how anomalous and unprecedented the recent price rises are compared to the historical price of these two metals expressed in terms of one another. As discussed in Chapter 1, the gold-silver ratio had historically oscillated around the range of 10-15, before stabilizing at around 15 from 1500 onwards. It began to inch upward in the 1800s, and when Germany took its indemnity from France in gold for the 1871 war, the pendulum swung decisively in gold's favor; the gold-silver ratio began to rise, and there was more volatility in the price in the period of 1871 to 1914. The ratio exceeded 16 in 1874, and in 1876 it exceeded 17, the highest recorded price in millennia. In 1886, the price exceeded 20, and the demise accelerated. At the outbreak of the Great War, it was 37, almost double any price ever recorded before the twentieth century.

The ensuing collapse of central banks in 1915 boosted demand for silver, reversing the rise in the gold-silver ratio for 5 years, during which it dropped to 32, but the rise resumed in 1920. By 1924, it had reclaimed the 37 level it held in 1914, and the growth continued at a rapid pace for the rest of the 1920s, hitting 40 for the first time in 1927. The rise averaged around 2.5% per year in the 1920s, as the major economies rid themselves of the majority of their monetary silver. The rise continued in the 1930s, but at an average rate of 1.5%

as the populous silver standard countries rid themselves of their monetary silver. By 1950, silver had been effectively demonetized, and the gold-silver ratio continued to rise at around 1% per year from the 1940s onwards. It exceeded the level of 100 in 1979 and continued its march, ending the century at 130.

Figure 1: Gold/Silver Ratio

The purchasing power of silver had risen in the aftermath of the Great War and remained relatively stable throughout the 1920s, even as it declined in relation to gold, which was appreciating in terms of purchasing power. However, in the 1930s, silver's use as a form of currency began to decline, and by 1950, it had ceased to be used as money. It was only poor pre-industrial societies with no modern banking infrastructure that used silver coins in the 1940s. By the 1950s, silver coins were only owned as collectibles and souvenirs.

As demand for silver was converted to demand for gold, the demand for unbacked banknotes from the classical gold standard era was also converted to demand for gold and verifiably gold-backed banknotes, causing the purchasing power of gold to increase sharply from 1915 to 1950, in a historically unprecedented global monetary gold rush, which came to be known as the "hypergoldenization" era. During this era, gold and 100% gold-backed securities dominated the vast majority of the world's cash balances, demonetizing everything from silver, government money, seashells, limestones, glass beads, and every other form of money known to man, which became collectibles, toys, souvenirs, and curiosities, but lost their monetary role. If someone had a cash balance, it was in gold. As gold's appreciation increased, demand for cash balances also increased, and it became common for people to hold several years' worth of expenditure in cash. As gold was appreciating rapidly in that period, saving was not just a way of preserving purchasing power; it increased it quite rapidly in a historically unprecedented way. Historically, it was rare for goods to get cheaper quickly. Goods had been getting cheaper at times of abundance and during the nineteenth century in the early industrializing nations, but humanity had never seen money appreciate like it did in the years 1915–1950 as silver and fiat were demonetized and gold appreciated. Holding gold was akin to investing in the monetization of gold, and its acquisition of silver and inflationary government banknotes' monetary demand. This had a profoundly positive impact on humanity's time preference, as generations were raised to appreciate the importance of saving, delaying gratification, and lowering time preference. It was a powerfully civilizing experience for humanity, and it helped bring about the peaceful and prosperous century of affluence, whose details are discussed in the coming chapters.

By 1950, with gold having consumed the vast majority of silver and fiat purchasing power, the pace of appreciation of gold in terms of other goods declined relatively, but the appreciation continued nonetheless. It would increase in tandem with the rise in the world's population and the decline in people's time preference, as it prompted them to accumulate larger cash balances as savings.

The Century of Savings

The remarkable appreciation of gold's purchasing power in the first century likely left an indelible and positive mark on the psychology of our race. Those who were smart enough to recognize the monetary supremacy of gold and had a time preference low enough to save significant amounts in it were able to improve their living standards immensely over the years. Wealth ultimately became massively concentrated in the hands of the intelligent and future-oriented, which gave them disproportionate influence in shaping the world, and also inspired generations of people to become intelligent and future-oriented. While the rate of appreciation of money in the second half of the century slowed down relative to the first half of the century, it nonetheless continued to appreciate, and saving continued to be a wise course of action, and those who did it benefited immensely, while those who did not suffered from poverty and economic insecurity.

By the middle of the century, it became common for people in both rich and poor countries to hold several years' worth of expenditures in liquid savings, either as gold or gold-backed paper, at their homes and at their banks. People began saving from the day they were born, as their family and friends would gift them gold or gold-backed securities at their birth. Gold was the most popular gift for all occasions, and children would accumulate small quantities from birthdays. By age seven or so, most children would begin working small jobs in their neighborhood and saving their income. By around the age of 17, most people would begin working full-time and start saving more. Around 10-20% of people would continue their education in technical schools or universities beyond that age, which, if all goes as planned, would mean a higher income when they start working at around 21, translating to more savings. By the age of 25, people would have accumulated significant savings from their full-time job, their work as a child, birthday gifts, and the money they received at birth, which would have appreciated by more than half in terms of its purchasing power. By the age of 25, a young couple getting married would have significant savings with which to start their life together. In high-income countries, by the 1960s or so, these savings were usually enough to cover the cost of a couple's first home in full up front, which led to mortgages declining in prevalence, and by the 1980s, they were not common anywhere.

The trend of savings was not just popular among individuals; it also extended to corporations and governments, as they increasingly eschewed debt financing and relied on building up cash balances. Finance and accounting became increasingly simplified in a world where holding money was desirable because it appreciated. Businesses simply accumulated cash balances from sales, spent their cash balances on their costs, and expanded their business by making capital investments when their cash balances were sufficient to finance a promising opportunity. Governments also accumulated cash balances, and this was a vital metric of their health and desirability.

Individuals, corporations, and governments are judged based on the ratio of their reserves to their annual expenditures, the R:E ratio. An individual, company, or government with reserves smaller than their yearly expenditure would have an R:E ratio less than 1; those with more reserves than expenditures would have an R:E ratio larger than 1. A ratio of 1 is widely considered a cut-off point between healthy and unhealthy entities, and a ratio under 0.5 is viewed as dangerous and reckless. People aim for an R:E ratio of 5 to consider themselves financially stable, and 10 to consider themselves financially secure. When proposing, a groom's ratio of reserves to expenditure was usually the most important metric that the bride and her family looked for.

Corporations with R:E ratios larger than five were considered investable and attractive. The higher the reserves, the more favorable prices and arrangements a company would have from its counterparties, as they could be more assured of its ability to meet future obligations. But governments were the entities that tended to accumulate the largest reserves to keep their voters' allegiance and avoid secession. A government with an R:E ratio less than five would face a hostile takeover of its territory from a neighbor with a higher R:E ratio, offering the citizens the chance to be part of a more financially secure polity. A government that ran down its reserves would encourage its people to move out individually, or to seek a takeover by a new governing entity. Rather than competing by borrowing and increasing the money supply, as they did under the gold standard, governments had to compete by accumulating the largest reserves, demonstrating their responsibility and ability to perform their duties even in the face of unexpected disasters. Corporations' balance sheets' health was measured primarily using the ratio of their expenditures to reserves as well.

The growing abundance of savings transformed human society for the better. Money's appreciation made saving extremely enticing, encouraging people to lower their time preference and think more about the future. People became more prudent and premeditated in their economic decision-making, and less impulsive and spontaneous. As has been well-established by economists, the hardness of money affects future orientation in all aspects of life, not just the economic. According to numerous measures and studies, the twentieth century saw people becoming more cooperative, moral, civilized, and peaceful. Familial and social bonds also grew stronger, as crime and violence declined steadily throughout the century after the collapse of fiat money.

Another implication of the growth in savings in hard money and financial freedom was the improvement in the quality of work and working environments. With significant savings, people had little reason to put up with unhealthy, abusive, or toxic work environments. Particularly after the age of 30, people would only work jobs that respected them and treated them well. The archetype of the inconsiderate jerk boss receded into memory and fiction, as workplaces needed to respect their employees to keep them.

The abundance of savings was also a boon for entrepreneurship and risk-taking. With a substantial number of people having accumulated more than five years' worth of expenditures in savings by the age of 25, they were able to take audacious risks with their investments. People invested money they could afford to lose, since they had significant savings in reserve in gold, the safest asset, practically guaranteed not to lose its value. It was precisely the security of savings that propelled the risk-taking of entrepreneurs. This risk-taking meant that many ventures failed, but their failures were not catastrophic, as the savers and investors had significant reserves to fall back on. The ones that did succeed, however, were enormously impactful.

XIII.

Modern Banking

Predictable Reliability

Without regional monopolies on banking, the banking industry began to take on a very different look. In contrast to the classical gold standard, the modern gold standard limited the profitability of banking as a business while increasing its reliability. As bank failures weeded out the least scrupulous bankers, they also relieved the most gullible citizens of their savings, making scams targeting the gullible unprofitable. These two trends were to create a very safe and sturdy banking system. By the mid-1920s, banks had become increasingly secure and reliable, with very few significant bank failures occurring from the 1930s onward. Whereas the nineteenth century had accustomed people to thinking of banking as a high-prestige and high-value-added job, the modern gold standard in the twentieth century turned it into a boring, predictable job, like plumbing or garbage collection. It was highly reliable, perfectly predictable, and very rarely failed. Rather than mathematical wizards in expensive offices, the average banking employee was an airplane pilot or mechanic, or a phone operator taking orders and coordinating deliveries.

Banks could no longer extend credit without corresponding savings being held in reserve, because their clients could always give them "the BOE special" as it came to be known: withdrawing their reserves to expose the bank's uncovered loans and leave the bank insolvent, as had happened with the Bank of England. Without a central bank to create credit from thin air or suspend gold redemption, there was no escaping the BOE special except through strictly conservative, fully reserved, maturity-matched banking. Banking as a boring service was devastating to the banking dynasties of the world, but it would prove a boon to humanity, after a rocky transition.

The postwar decade of 1916 to 1926 contained many high-profile bank failures. Many of the bankers who had learned their trade in the days of the classical gold standard could never shake the habits of the old days of lending more than they had on hand. Yet the scope of their insolvency was always quite limited by the inherent honesty of the modern gold standard, which would expose them relatively early on. As a bank increased its banknotes or credit issuance and more of its liabilities started accumulating at clearinghouses, the operators of the clearinghouses would begin accepting them at a discount. Because air settlement made those discounts bite immediately, management either repurchased notes at a profit, proving solvency, or failed quickly before losses could pyramid. If the bank were healthy, its management could make a profit by buying its banknotes at a discount from these clearinghouses, thereby eliminating the excess at the clearinghouse and causing the price to return to par. But if the bank were unhealthy, it would not be able to repurchase its notes. Thus, the discounting would continue to get steeper as depositors and lenders rushed to the bank to withdraw their deposits, exposing and exacerbating the insolvency. Most bank insolvencies would get exposed so quickly that they would repay their creditors more than 80% of the face value of their liabilities, because the fraud would collapse relatively early without a central bank to bail it out and allow it to continue.

Under the classical gold standard, economists had spent plenty of time trying to discern the difference between illiquidity and insolvency. But under the modern gold standard, there was no longer a difference between the two. Without a lender of last resort able to devalue other people's money, an illiquid bank's protestations about its "temporarily impaired" healthy balance sheet were not worth a penny on the balance sheet. In a world of same-day settlement, 'liquidity' that cannot be realized today is indistinguishable from insolvency to depositors. Over time, the investment in illiquid banks became less popular, as it was deemed too risky and unpredictable. Capital owners grew increasingly reluctant to invest in banks with maturity-mismatched liabilities, and there was no guarantee that such banks would be saved during a crisis. Banks had to learn to meet all their liabilities on time or face a serious risk of insolvency and being liquidated in bankruptcy court.

A study of the history of interest rates shows that they had been in long-term decline, punctuated by big rises in times of plagues, famines, wars, or other catastrophes. This trend has been intact for thousands of years, as illustrated in the seminal history on the topic by Homer and Sylla, *A History of Interest Rates*. The phenomenon of declining interest rates can be observed empirically, but it is also well-understood theoretically from the Time Preference Theory of Interest Rates developed by Austrian economist Eugen von Böhm-Bawerk and his protege, Mises. The beginning of the twentieth century had witnessed the lowest interest rates ever recorded, as the British government could borrow from the Bank of England at less than 3%.

According to Böhm-Bawerk, the interest rate charged by a lender on the market is a reflection of the discounting that the lender and borrower place on the future, in other words, their time preference. The higher the time preference of the lender, the more he discounts the future, and the more he needs to be paid in interest to sacrifice his holdings of money and grant them to a borrower. Equivalently, the higher the time preference of the borrower, the more he discounts the future, and the more he is willing to pay in the future to have a certain sum available to him today. The lender has a lower time preference than the borrower, but the interest rate on a free lending market reflects the prevalent time preference in a certain society, as it lies somewhere between the bounds of the lowest and highest time preferences of credit market participants. The decline of time preference can best be understood as the process of civilization: the lower the time preference, the less people discount the future compared to the present, the more their actions are future-oriented, and the more civilized they become. This is reflected in all aspects of life, including people's norms, morals, table manners, and economic decision-making.

The higher the time preference of an individual, the more likely he is to behave in a dishonest manner, to lie, deceive, cheat, steal, or commit a crime. These kinds of actions entail an immediate payoff but carry a long-term risk of punishment in the form of legal punishment, physical retaliation by the victims, ostracism, shame, or excommunication from society. The higher a person's time preference, the higher his future discounting, the more he weighs the immediate payoffs, and the more he discounts this future punishment. Thus, as time preference rises, you would expect to see more crime, uncivilized behavior, and conflict. As time preference declines, people's behavior discounts future consequences less, which attaches more value to a person's long-term well-being and makes it less likely they will engage in these criminal or anti-social activities.

In the realm of economics, the lower the time preference of members of a society, the lower their discounting of the future, and the more likely they are to forgo consumption of present resources to make resources available for the future. The increased availability of capital results in lenders being willing to lend at lower interest rates. Equivalently, the lower the borrower's time preference, the lower the interest rate she is willing to pay. If interest rates are understood as being the product of time preference, then the process of civilizational advance would witness ever-declining interest rates, and the periods of civilizational collapse and regression would witness increasing interest rates. This matches the historical record. Under the classical gold standard in the nineteenth century, interest rates generally declined, except during major wars. The period from 1873 to 1914, having been free of major international wars involving the major powers, witnessed a continuous decline in interest rates, culminating in the Bank of England's lowest reference interest rate of 2.5% in 1913. After the Bank of England's destruction, the lowest interest rate on offer in the belligerent countries was 20%. The growing uncertainty around the war had raised everyone's time preference, and few had the stomach for taking on the risk of lending. Things were different in Switzerland, where capital was so abundant that banks charged 4% to Swiss borrowers who wanted to use the money domestically. Borrowing to send the funds abroad attracted a very high premium, resulting in interest rates in the 20% range. It was this enormous arbitrage opportunity that laid the groundwork for the Geneva Peace Conference. By using the gold as an incentive for warring countries to make peace, Switzerland created a peace that prevented it from getting engulfed in the flames of war.

In the immediate aftermath of the Great War, with interest rates high, plenty of inflationist cranks called for government intervention in the banking system to bring interest rates down and allow more lending to "stimulate the economy." These nonsensical ideas of money creation as a mechanism for wealth creation were always present in the days of the classical gold standard, and there were still economic illiterates who believed in them even into the 1940s and 1950s. Fortunately, what those cranks wanted didn't matter. Central banks were gone, and the Treaty of Geneva had clearly stipulated that no government could restrict the freedom of banks to deal freely with one another. Without a central banking cartel, there was no mechanism for governments to force banks to bring interest rates down and distort the market for savings. If they did, it would increase the level of borrowing and decrease the level of saving, resulting in malinvestments and inevitable financial collapse, as Mises had thoroughly explained. Instead, the market brought interest rates down voluntarily, sustainably, and completely, through the force of economic incentives. As money held its value and appreciated, people held increasingly large balances of cash, which resulted in them having plenty of resources to lend and invest. This, in turn, caused interest rates to decline. Once peace had been secured, people's certainty about the future increased, and the high interest rates presented them with a lucrative opportunity to profit from their holdings. As more people started to lend, interest rates began to drop, and by the early 1940s, the most creditworthy borrowers could borrow at around 2.5%, the Bank of England's rate from 1913. There was no need for the government to mandate low interest rates; peace, monetary stability, and financial freedom had brought interest rates down while increasing savings significantly.

The End of Usury

Usury is arguably one of the most controversial and debated topics in the history of economic and religious thought. Religious authorities have traditionally inveighed against it or outright banned it. Aristotle, Dante, and countless philosophers have equated it with the worst of crimes, and governments have for centuries punished lenders and borrowers for engaging in it. Against this prevailing consensus, economists have offered their customary brand of unpopular explanations for the stubbornly persistent reality. The Austrian school, in particular, produced the most thorough explanation of interest as a natural phenomenon of the free market by explaining it as the result of time preference. But applying the Austrian Time Preference Theory of Interest to its logical implications—in a high civilization with appreciating hard money, increased cash balances, advanced capital accumulation, and declining time preference—suggests that interest-based lending could naturally disappear from a free market and be replaced by zero nominal interest rate loans and equity investing. And that was indeed what happened in the twentieth century, to the surprise of many, including Austrians.

The three major monotheistic religions, as well as Buddhism, have forbidden or inveighed against usury. But these religious and governmental edicts, while categorical, do not provide a complete explanation for *why* usury is bad for the individuals and societies taking part in it, or why God and the state would punish it. Some of history's most famous philosophers have also inveighed against usury and attempted to provide arguments for why usury is not good. Aristotle provided one of the earliest known critiques of usury. Thomas Aquinas provided a thorough critique with several arguments for its impermissibility.

Religious restrictions against interest were powerless to stop demand for interest on the market, and people found ways around the restrictions using creative contractual workarounds, which effectively allowed two parties to have interest transactions, without it being explicitly called interest. The unceasing attempts to find ways for willing partners to trade with one another call for an explanation of the economic incentive for engaging in interest lending.

In *An Austrian Perspective on the History of Economic Thought*, Murray Rothbard provides a historical discussion of how the practice of interest lending proliferated under creative workarounds, as well as a run-down of how early economists grappled with the concept of interest, and how their arguments evolved over time. The final nail in the coffin of usury prohibition, according to Rothbard, was hammered by the seventeenth-century Dutch Calvinist Claude Saumaise, who "trenchantly pointed out that money-lending was a business like any other, and like other businesses was entitled to charge a market price. He did make the important theoretical point, however, that, as in any other part of the market, if the number of usurers multiplies, the price of money or interest will be driven down by the competition. So that if one doesn't like high interest rates, the more usurers the better!"[117]

The moral argument for usury was later articulated by Jeremy Bentham, who simply posited that if people willingly choose to engage in usury, then they must find value in it, and any attempt to ban it would constitute a violation of their freedom. In his *The Defence of Usury*, Bentham argued: "no man of ripe years and of sound mind, acting freely, and with his eyes open, ought to be hindered, with a view to his advantage, from making such bargain, in the way of obtaining money, as he thinks fit: nor, (what is a necessary consequence) any body hindered from supplying him, upon any terms he thinks proper to accede to."[118]

Economists and philosophers defending interest had responded to wrong arguments by opponents of usury. They argued from a liberal and laissez-faire position for the freedom of both parties to engage in a transaction from which they would both benefit. But it was only starting in the eighteenth century that they were able to provide a theoretical economic defense of usury. The economic argument for usury, and the rationale for its emergence, would begin with the work of the French economist A. R. J. Turgot in the late eighteenth century. It would be further developed by the Austrian economist Eugen von

---

117 Murray N. Rothbard, *Economic Thought Before Adam Smith: An Austrian Perspective on the History of Economic Thought* (Edward Elgar Publishing, 1999), 160.

118 Jeremy Bentham, "LETTER I. Introduction – Crichoff, in White Russia, January 1787," in *Defence of Usury* (1787; Lang and Ustick, 1796), 6.

Böhm-Bawerk in the late nineteenth century, who presented the first attempt to explain interest rates in terms of time preference, but ultimately reverted to a more traditional productivity-based explanation in his work. The first explanation of interest purely in terms of time preference came from the "American Austrian" Frank Fetter.

Turgot asked why lenders are willing to commit to returning the principal of the loan with interest. He argued that the correct way to think of this is not in terms of the weight of the metals, but in terms of their subjective valuation to the borrower and lender, "the difference in usefulness which exists at the date of borrowing between a sum currently owned and an equal sum which is to be received at a future date." Economic value is not a function of the physical quantity of money, but the subjective valuation of the actors, and if the actor has a pressing need for the money today, he would value it more than the same sum in the future. He would be happy to pay interest in the future to have the money today. Turgot had elaborated the concept of time preference. To sacrifice a certain sum today for an uncertain return tomorrow, the lender needs to be tempted with a higher return on the capital tomorrow; in other words, the interest.

Böhm-Bawerk articulated the concept of time preference and posited it as an explanation for interest rates; however, he later reverted to productivity-based explanations. By separating the marginal productivity of capital from the discounting of future benefits, Rothbard argues that Frank Fetter was the first economist to explain interest rates solely in terms of time preference.

> Fetter demonstrated that the explanation can only be found by separating the concept of marginal productivity from that of interest. Marginal productivity explains the height of a factor's rental price, but another principle is needed to explain why and on what basis these rents are discounted to get the present capitalized value of the factor: whether that factor be land, or a capital good, or the price of a slave. That principle is "time preference": the social rate at which people prefer present goods to future goods in the vast interconnected time market (present/future goods market) that pervades the entire economy.

Each individual has a personal time-preference schedule, a schedule relating his choice of present and future goods to his stock of available present goods. As his stock of present goods increases, the marginal value of future goods rises, and his rate of time preference tends to fall. These individual schedules interact on the time market to set, at any given time, a social rate of time preference. This rate, in turn, constitutes the interest rate on the market, and it is this interest rate that is used to convert (or "discount") all future values into present values, whether the future good happens to be a bond (a claim to future money) or more specifically the expected future rentals from land or capital.

Thus, Fetter was the first economist to explain interest rates solely by time preference. Every factor of production earns its rent in accordance with its marginal product, and every future rental return is discounted, or "capitalized," to get its present value in accordance with the overall social rate of time preference. This means that a firm that buys a machine will only pay the present value of expected future rental incomes, discounted by the social rate of time preference; and that when a capitalist hires a worker or rents land, he will pay now, not the factor's full marginal product, but the expected future marginal product discounted by the social rate of time preference.[119]

With this explanation, the debate swung decisively in favor of the economists and in favor of interest. Not only was it an issue of personal freedom to prevent consenting adults from transacting in what they both saw as a beneficial transaction, but economists could now explain why this transaction existed with a proper *praxeological* explanation. In other words, they could explain it through the economic action of humans. It is especially ironic that the same century that finally explained interest would be the century that witnessed its disappearance, but it meant the disappearance was explicable.

---

119 Frank A. Fetter, "Introduction," in *Capital, Interest, and Rent: Essays in the Theory of Distribution* ed. Murray Rothbard, (Sheed Andrews and McMeel, 1977), 3–4.

Time Preference: Interest's Control Knob

Time preference refers to the fact that humans value satisfaction in the present more than in the future. The nearer the period of time to the present, the more valuable it will appear to an individual. The present is certain, as it is already here, but the future is always uncertain, as it may never come. The future can only come through successfully securing survival in the present, which makes the needs of the present always more pressing and important. The present is where all senses experience life and its pleasures and pains. Future pains and pleasures are hypothetical, but those of the present are real and visceral. Hunger felt in the present is far more pressing than hunger anticipated in the future, which makes food more valuable in the present than in the future. The danger in the present is far more pressing than future danger, and tools that secure safety today are thus more valuable today than in the future. Given a choice between obtaining a physical good in the present or the same good in the future, man chooses the present.

The higher valuation of present goods is a permanent fixture of human action. That humans choose to consume rather than just accumulate more of the goods they value, including money, confirms this preference. Their choice to consume in the present implies they place a higher valuation on a present good than the same good in the future. Time preference is the degree to which present goods are preferred over future goods. It is always positive because humans always prefer present goods over future goods, but its magnitude varies from person to person and for each person across his life according to his situation. A high time preference indicates a heavy discounting of the future in favor of the present and greater present orientation, while a low time preference implies a lower discounting of the future and greater future orientation.

Any time you prefer a good today over a future good, you are demonstrating originary interest. And you are doing the same thing that someone does when they charge interest. Opponents of usury, to be consistent, must be indifferent between a payment today or 10 years from now, because to demonstrate a preference is to demonstrate originary interest. Your preference for the good today is no different from accepting interest to prefer the payment tomorrow.

The discounting of the future exists for all goods, and it creates in man an *originary interest*, the percentage premium on the valuation of a good that an individual requires to receive the good in the future. Originary interest pervades the valuation of all goods, including money. The differences in originary interest create trading opportunities in money. Someone with a higher time preference will happily pay money to convince someone with a lower time preference to part with money in the present.

The existence of money allows originary interest to be harmonized across goods and individuals through the emergence of a credit market, in which future obligations of money are traded for present payments, establishing a general discount rate of the future, or an interest rate. Hoppe describes this market-determined interest rate as "the aggregate sum of all individual time-preference rates reflecting the social rate of time preference and equilibrating social savings (i.e., the supply of present goods offered for exchange against future goods) and social investment (i.e., the demand for present goods thought capable of yielding future returns)."

It is important to note that the interest rate is not determined by the productivity of capital, as there are capital investment projects at a very wide range of expected returns. The projects that get funded are the ones expected to provide the highest rate of return. The more capital is available, the more projects get funded, and the lower the expected return of a project needs to be for it to get funded. The prevailing rate of interest is then determined by the availability of capital, which in turn is determined by time preference.

Rothbard elaborates in *Man, Economy, and State*:

> The capitalists' function is thus a time function, and their income is precisely an income representing the agio of present as compared to future goods. This interest income, then, is not derived from the concrete, heterogeneous capital goods, but from the generalized investment of time. It comes from a willingness to sacrifice present goods for the purchase of future goods (the factor services). As a result of the purchases, the owners of factors obtain their money in the present for a product that matures only in the future.[120]

---

120 Murray N. Rothbard, *Man, Economy, and State, Scholar's Edition* (Ludwig von Mises Institute, 2009), 367–451.

Time Preference and Civilization

Numerous social and institutional factors affect an individual's time preference. Perhaps most important among them is the security of property, which would provide man with a very effective way of providing for his future. Acquiring durable goods is arguably the beginning of the process of declining time preference for humanity. A man who commands a valuable good that can be used in the future reduces the uncertainty that surrounds his future and becomes likely to discount it less. The security of property rights thus strongly influences time preferences. As the concept of property rights becomes widely accepted in a society, it leads to a widespread decline in time preference as individuals begin to increase their valuation of their increasingly secure future. As a property owner's certainty of their command of a good increases into the future, he is likely to maintain the good in good shape and more likely to act with the future in mind.

Time preference can be understood as the driver of savings and investment. Once an individual can lower his time preference to engage in activities that do not offer immediate rewards, he can choose to sacrifice present time in exchange for the future. Once he decides to forgo consumption of present goods in order to save them for the future, he is lowering his time preference further. Conceptually and chronologically, saving can only be understood as the precursor and prerequisite of investment. No matter the capital good, it can also be consumed or exchanged for goods that can be consumed in the present. Before one can invest capital, one must first defer its consumption by saving it. No matter how short the period between earning wealth and investing it, that period is a period of saving.

As a man starts accumulating his cash balance from zero, the marginal utility of holding cash is very high, since he has very little of it. At this point, the utility of a cash balance is likely larger than any investment, since all investments have risk and low salability, and with a small amount of wealth, salability is prized, while risk is undesirable. As he accumulates larger cash balances, the marginal utility of adding to these balances declines until it drops below the expected return of the best investment opportunity available to him. The more cash the man has, the more he is able to withstand the riskiness of the investment. A bad investment will not ruin him because he will still have his cash balance. The lowering of time preference is what drives individuals to accumulate cash balances and to invest. The lower the time preference, the less they consume, and the more resources they will have to save and invest. Each person keeps in cash a balance they would like to have with certainty, and takes a risk with their investment in search of returns.

The Austrian Time Preference Theory of Interest Rates is a powerful tool for understanding economics, capital, and even human history. As Hoppe explains, based on the work of Homer and Sylla:

> a tendency toward falling interest rates characterizes mankind's supra-secular trend of development. Minimum interest rates on 'normal safe loans' were around 16 percent at the beginning of Greek financial history in the sixth century B.C., and fell to 6 percent during the Hellenistic period. In Rome, minimum interest rates fell from more than 8 percent during the earliest period of the Republic to 4 percent during the first century of the Empire. In thirteenth-century Europe, the lowest interest rates on 'safe' loans were 8 percent. In the fourteenth century they came down to about 5 percent. In the fifteenth century they fell to 4 percent. In the seventeenth century they went down to 3 percent. And at the end of the nineteenth century minimum interest rates had further declined to less than 2.5 percent.

> This trend was by no means smooth. It was frequently interrupted by periods, sometimes as long as centuries, of rising interest rates. However, such periods were associated with major wars and revolutions such as the Hundred Years' War during the fourteenth century, the Wars of Religion from the late sixteenth to the early seventeenth century, the American and French Revolutions and the Napoleonic Wars from the late eighteenth to the early nineteenth century, and the two World Wars in the twentieth century. Furthermore, whereas high or rising minimum interest rates indicate periods of generally low or declining living standards, the overriding opposite

tendency toward low and falling interest rates reflects mankind's overall progress—its advance from barbarism to civilization. Specifically, the trend toward lower interest rates reflects the rise of the Western World, its peoples' increasing prosperity, farsightedness, intelligence, and moral strength, and the unparalleled height of nineteenth-century European civilization.

With this historical backdrop and in accordance with economic theory, then, it should be expected that twentieth-century interest rates would be still lower than nineteenth-century rates.[121]

But since this is not the case, and interest rates continued to rise, the only explanation is that:

the character of the population must have changed. People on the average must have lost in moral and intellectual strength and become more present-oriented. Indeed, this appears to be the case.

This process of civilization took a giant wrong turn in 1914, when humanity replaced hard money with government easy money, thereby unleashing government barbarism to destroy centuries of civilizational and economic progress in wars and mass destruction. It is plain to see how, as the Austrian Time Preference Theory of Interest Rate would suggest, the destruction of money led to the destruction of savings, making the future more uncertain, and causing a rise in time preference. Interest rates did indeed rise during the war and in its uncertain aftermath. And while the war caused interest rates to rise sharply, the peace made them revert to declining until they reached their lowest level ever by the early 1940s. Few economists had expected that they would continue declining past that point, but that is what happened, and the end result was that the rates dropped to zero, and interest lending was slowly and spontaneously phased out worldwide.

---

121 Hans-Hermann Hoppe, *Democracy – The God That Failed: The Economics and Politics of Monarchy, Democracy and Natural Order* (Routledge, 2018).

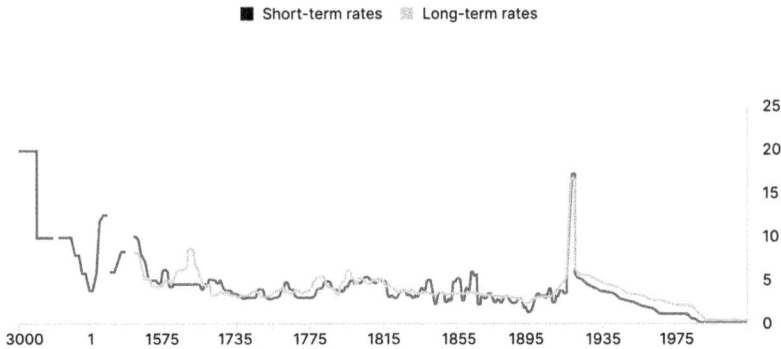

Figure 2: Interest rates over 5,000 years

As Böhm-Bawerk, Frank Fetter, and Mises had explained, the rate of time preference determines the interest rate, and the lower the time preference, the lower the interest rate a lender is willing to accept. As peace and prosperity became more common, and money appreciated more and more thanks to the elimination of inflation, capital grew so abundant that its price dropped to zero. Most economists would have said that a zero price of capital is impossible, as it would imply the elimination of time preference, an illogical and impossible state of affairs in which a human values food 100 years from today identically to food today. However, this perspective overlooks the fact that money always incurs a carrying cost, both in terms of the cost of holding it and the risk of it being stolen or lost. Time preference does not need to drop to zero for the nominal interest rate to drop to zero; it just needs to fall to the point where the implied interest rate is less than the carrying cost of capital, so the lender becomes willing to accept a zero interest rate. Since gold custody and insurance usually cost 0.3-0.7% per year, lending at 0% interest allowed banks to save that cost.

In retrospect, it seems predictable that rates would continue to drop until they reached zero, but it was very difficult for economists to foresee this outcome since they had historically provided the rationale for interest lending. In previous centuries, it was the force of economic reality, as a reflection of the prevalent high time preference of our semi-civilized ancestors, that had created interest rates. And it was usually the stifling hand of religious and political authority that sought to repress interest rates. But in the twentieth century, with civilization advancing, morality increasing, and human time preference finally declining to negligible discounting of the future, it was the force of economic reality itself that eliminated interest lending, with political and religious authorities a mere puzzled spectator. Economists had gotten so used to defending interest as the expression of the true discounting rate of individuals, and its eradication as destructive, that they never stopped to consider what would happen if people's discounting of the future declined to close to zero.

Swiss banks were the first to offer zero interest rates in 1941. They had become awash with gold in the Great War, and they were a safe neutral country with solid banking institutions. The abundance of capital and the dearth of investment opportunities in the warring nations meant its owners were willing to accept negligible interest rates (as low as 2%, for lending). Even after the war ended, Switzerland maintained a significant amount of gold deposits, as many investors saw the value in a politically neutral safe haven. Interest rates rose slightly as depositors withdrew their gold, but not by much. As the ICSD industry continued to grow, it also brought in large quantities of gold. By the mid-1920s, Swiss interest rates began a steady and slow decline, and in 1981, Swiss bank Credit Suisse began to lend at 0% interest.

This development puzzled economists. There was no Swiss authority mandating the interest rates, but the borrower, bank, and bank depositors were all willingly going along with the transaction. Many economists tried to rationalize it as an aberrant exception that would be reversed quickly, but they could not have been more wrong. More Swiss banks began to offer 0% loans, and then other European, US, and Canadian banks followed. The more peaceful, prosperous, civilized, and productive a society was, the faster its interest rates went to zero. By 1995, most large financial institutions in Europe, the United States, Canada, Australia, Japan, and New Zealand offered 0% interest rates. Other parts of the world saw their rates decline steadily, and by 1999, there were no publicly traded banks offering interest-based lending. It continued to exist only in pawn shops and payday loans in poorer communities.

With 0% interest rate lending, the lending business declined in size mark-edly and became an increasingly insignificant part of the financial system. Lending began to mostly take place between people who were familiar with one another at the 0% rate, while banks' business models shifted to two dis-tinct activities: deposit banking and investment banking.

With deposit banking, clients would deposit their money at a bank and pay an annual fee to keep it there. The bank would hold the entire sum at all times and make it available to the client at any time. It was impossible to have a bank run when the money was always on hand. No amount of financial panic, confidence loss, rumors, or real calamities could affect the ability to redeem banknotes as long as banks held them all in reserve. Retail deposit fees converged to a simple menu: a flat vaulting fee plus a small percentage of av-erage balance to cover insurance and audit. With investment banking, clients would deposit sums into an investment account to be managed by the bank. The bank would make it clear to clients that the money would not be available to them for a set period, and during that period, the money would be allocated to entrepreneurs who engaged in production. At the end of the investment period, the investors would be given a return commensurate with their share of the business. The business could profit or lose, and the investor would share equally in the upside and downside. The bank simply acted as an intermediary, collecting a fee if the business was profitable. Banks could go out of business if their choices were unsatisfactory and they lost their customers, but they could not suffer a bank failure except in the case of overt fraud.

For thousands of years, philosophers, prophets, priests, presidents, bank-ers, and economists had given their opinions and rulings on the institution of usury, as discussed above. They had all approached the question of usury from a normative perspective, prescribing what should be done in order to maximize virtue, morality, or well-being. Only the Austrian economists Böhm-Bawerk and Mises approached it from a positive perspective grounded in studying human action, which allowed them to explain why interest is such a prevalent phenomenon in societies around the world and across time. But in identifying the drivers of interest in the actions of humans, economists identified the forces that could eliminate it. Fixating on explaining interest was to the detriment of extrapolating these forces further and understanding their endpoint. Had early and mid-twentieth-century economists taken the thought experiment to its endpoint, they may have realized the reason religions and cultures from all over the world opposed usury. Decreeing a refusal of usury is an exhortation to lower time preference among members to the point where the resulting originary interest rate is so uniformly low that no market in time is possible. It is, after all, the difference in subjective valuation that creates the possibility of a market interaction. But if everyone discounts the future very little, such that everyone's originary interest is lower than the cost of money storage, no market would emerge in time valuation.

By the early twentieth century, religious edicts had lost all power, as Jewish, Christian, Muslim, Hindu, and many other populations, governments, and even religious authorities were all openly engaging in interest lending. Even the Islamic Caliphate in Constantinople was borrowing at interest, which ultimately led to its demise. By the late twentieth century, religious edicts were rendered pointless, as people no longer wanted to, or were able to, engage in interest lending.

XIV.

The State in the Twentieth Century

Choice, Not Voice

The aftermath of the Geneva Conference triggered a wave of political changes worldwide and a profound reformulation of the world's vision of governance. By 1950, the vast majority of humanity was living under the rule of signatories to the Treaty of Geneva. Once citizens could opt out, politics became a market. The object of political revolutions and activism in the nineteenth century, and the meaning of political progress, revolved around representative democracy, the creation of democratically elected parliaments, and the increase in the powers of these parliaments at the expense of monarchies. This did not spuriously coincide with the growing centralization of financial assets in government monopoly central banks, which increased the government's power over its citizens by allowing it to borrow against their savings. The more powerful governments were, the more contentious politics became. As mass literacy began to spread and worker productivity increased, more and more of the population began to understand politics and had the time to engage in it. Many came to resent despotic and autocratic political control, which fueled countless political reformist and revolutionary movements worldwide.

But as central banking collapsed in 1915, the shape and function of government was completely transformed, and along with it, the nature of politics. With no monopoly central banks to monetize government debt, governments became significantly more fiscally responsible, and failing to do so carried substantial negative consequences. People could vote to secede, or they could hire another government to take over. In broad terms, mass participatory democracy, in the sense of decisions being arrived at through the deliberation of millions of people reflected through the ballot box, was not a very successful model for managing this political era, as it resulted in irresponsible fiscal management. With no single person making decisions and facing the consequences, it was easy for the masses participating in democracy to make choices free of the burden of considering consequences, trade-offs, and opportunity costs. Without a central bank to indulge the wishes of voters for government spending by surreptitiously footing them with the bill through inflation, deliberative democracy often ended quickly in insolvency. Monarchies, or republics where executive authority was invested in a small number of decision-makers, generally fared better fiscally.

With the right to self-determination granted, and with deliberative democracy providing several cautionary tales of fiscal failure under dispersed decision-making, politics in the twentieth century shifted focus from deliberative representation and public participation in governance to secession and self-determination under increasingly small and efficient executive authorities. The world moved from representative democracy to secessionist democracy. People had far less say about *how* governments operated, but they did have a say in choosing *which* government operated on their property. Governments had more executive authority, but people had the right to secession. This was the century of choice, not voice. Exit made ballots honest: once people could leave, promises priced themselves.

Whereas in previous centuries government was viewed as a lucrative privilege, in the twentieth century it became a hefty responsibility. With even small districts having the freedom to secede or join other entities, rulers could no longer rest on their laurels as they had in previous centuries. They were under constant competitive pressure to perform their duties to their subjects, and to do so in a manner and at a cost that was comparable to other jurisdictions.

In the first two decades after the Geneva Conference, there was a marked move toward ever-smaller political entities, as independence movements could actualize themselves and agitate their people to seek independence from large central states and bureaucracies that had, in many cases, oppressed them for centuries with high taxes and violations of property rights. Political entities continued to become smaller and more diverse due to increasingly smaller ethnic, religious, geographical, and national divisions.

This trend began to reverse in the 1940s, when an increasing number of newly independent entities began to vote to rejoin larger political entities. From the 1940s to the 1970s, a reconsolidation of states began. The number of political entities shrank from a high of 228 states in 1943 down to 187 in 1976, and has oscillated around that number since then. Having been forced to compete for citizens, both small and large entities became significantly more efficient in offering governance services to their people. With the passionate need for independence satiated and the larger entities improving their management styles, they began to provide more attractive governance deals to breakaway states. The major advantages that larger polities could offer were the freedom of movement within their borders, larger and more developed regulatory and legal frameworks, as well as the economies of scale in managing municipal and bureaucratic services, which allowed them to charge less for these services.

Forward-looking and highly competitive governments drove this trend of consolidation. As they became more efficient, governments began to entice the citizens of less efficient neighbors with innovative and progressive governance formats. One of the most groundbreaking ideas was offering shares in the government's assets to citizens based on their tax contributions. With every gram of gold a citizen paid in taxes, they received a share of the government's assets. These Tax Payments Units (TPUs) were effectively claims on net public assets in case of liquidation upon secession. The TPU ledger became the ICSD's canonical cap table for asset splits. If citizens in a particular territory chose secession, they would be entitled to their share of the government's assets. First devised by the Liechtenstein princely family in 1938, the transformation of citizens into shareholders spread rapidly over the following decades, becoming the norm by the 1980s. Governments either adopted this model or witnessed their citizens secede to entities that offered it to them. In 1978, this framework was integrated into the Geneva Treaty ICSD framework after ratification by all members. All members accepted that secession by a part of a political entity entitled its citizens to their shares of the assets of their government.

Corporate Government

The 1970s witnessed a new trend. Whereas monarchies and republics had previously dominated the world, a new type of political entity emerged: the corporate government. The first such entity came from the veterans of the government of Hong Kong, which had done an incredible job transforming Hong Kong from a tiny backwater fishing village into a modern industrial and financial center attracting millions of migrants from around the world. By the 1960s, the enormous demand for migration to Hong Kong from nearby Chinese provinces had overwhelmed Hong Kong's infrastructure and its capacity to absorb immigrants. The Financial Secretary of Hong Kong, Sir John Cowperthwaite, retired in 1971 after a highly successful ten-year tenure, having become enormously popular with the residents of Hong Kong and the surrounding areas. He decided to establish a private company headquartered in Hong Kong under the name JJC Inc., which would develop a government bureaucracy and offer its services to the populations of South and East Asia, aiming to emulate the success of Hong Kong. With capital from the Hong Kong financial industry, he hired many of the old hands who had served with him in Hong Kong, then spent four years developing a comprehensive business plan that included a complete governance apparatus. He advertised his services in the Chinese mainland: for a fixed tax rate of 5% of one's income and a commitment of ten years, he would deliver:

1 - Policing and prison systems to ensure a murder rate under 1 per 100,000 residents;

2 - A modern public road network;

3 - Garbage collection services;

4 - A corporate law framework based on the City of London commercial code, which had been adopted in Hong Kong;

5 - Independent commercial judiciary services.

Any region in the world was welcome to hire JJC to handle its government, but it had to go through the ICSD process to do so. With many Chinese having heard of Hong Kong's success, several provinces saw movements to hire the JJC. Local businessmen and aristocrats campaigned for the idea, and after opinion polls showed an increasingly positive opinion, they collected signatures and began the ICSD process. In 1978, Fujian became the first province to vote for governance by JJC, and over the ensuing decade, it witnessed spectacular commercial success and a marked improvement in the quality of life for its citizens. Cowperthwaite and his investors also profited immensely, re-investing a significant portion of their profits into expanding their operation, which would govern 300 million people worldwide by the end of the century. Many other similar competitors sprang up around the world to challenge traditional governments for their populations at the ICSD ballot boxes.

After his retirement in 1983, when asked by a journalist about the secret to the success of his business, Cowperthwaite answered,

> The magic formula for JJC is simple: we stop doing the most important things that the government before us was doing. People think we introduce important innovations in governance, but really, we are just removing governance as much as possible. Corrupt and bad governments are never corrupt or bad because they do not do enough, but because they do too much. They consume resources and provide benefits to those in power and their cronies, and they place a segment of the population above the law. The biggest problems societies face come from the government's central planning, over-regulation, favoritism, and cronyism. When we stop these activities, these problems vanish, peace dominates, and the economy booms. We make it clear nobody is above the law, and crime plummets.

> We make it clear that favoritism and cronyism will not exist, and all the smartest and richest people in a society direct their energies to productive enterprise instead of government capture. The secret to governance is to govern as little as possible. In most places, we still officially take over the building of roads or trash collection, but this tradition is practically obsolete at this point. We collect taxes and hire private contractors to do these jobs because most people expect us to do it, but I expect that with time, people will figure out they can hire the private contractors themselves, finding a more efficient way to charge users without having to go through a government agency. So the secret is not what we do, but what we *don't* do. To not do it, we remove power from the hands of locals and put it in the hands of disinterested foreign professionals largely insulated from political or emotional pressure.

As we look back at the end of the twentieth century's innovation of private governance, there can be no denying its successes in improving the quality of life for millions worldwide. Nonetheless, the model had limitations, primarily due to the short-term focus that many of these companies adopted in their decision-making. Even though they were more efficient than many of their traditional government competitors, they tended to have less understanding and regard for their populations' traditions, customs, religions, and social institutions. They were hyper-commercialized and focused on providing value to shareholders within five to fifteen years, which sometimes came at the expense of the long-term traditions and the values a society cherishes for centuries.

Global Governance Solutions (GGS), a private governance provider contracted to run Afghanistan in 1989, achieved decent commercial success. But its mandate was not renewed after the first ten years, as the population had many misgivings about their openly liberal approach to family law, legalization of alcohol, and licensing of nightlife venues. The royal family of Afghanistan, which had maintained a nominal figurehead role during the GGS years, campaigned for the ending of GGS's contract in 1999 and a return to executive power, to the satisfaction of the population. The ruling family reversed many of the unpopular rules created by GGS, but they kept most of the commercial law.

Pax Systems, another private governance agency, took over the government of Cameroon in 1988 after an ICSD referendum. It had promised to build modern infrastructure efficiently and to lower taxes. They had campaigned on the premise that their efficient management of resources compared to their predecessors would drastically reduce the cost of government, allowing them to reduce tax revenue and increase investment in infrastructure. But when in power, it became clear that efficiency improvements would not be enough to allow them to invest in infrastructure and reduce taxes. Instead, they resorted to selling mining rights in local forests. Pax managed to invest in the infrastructure it promised and to reduce taxation, but the cost was the destruction of the country's national treasure: thousands of square miles of forests. As time went by, the amount of destruction and pollution continued to grow. After Pax Systems' ten years in power ended, the people of Cameroon voted not to renew their contract. Instead, they transferred to a new governance company that promised to conserve the vast majority of Cameroon's forests and rely on tourism for income, rather than mining.

Something similar happened in Tuscany in the 1990s. After decades in which the local government had grown complacent and inefficient due to the endless stream of wealthy individuals willing to pay exorbitant fees for residency permits in the beautiful country, the locals finally succeeded in contracting GGS to take over the management of Tuscany in 1991. The government's operational efficiency increased, and taxes decreased; however, this was achieved by investing in unsustainable tourism practices, which flooded Florence's small streets and ancient cathedral with tourists, and polluted the beautiful Tuscan countryside with crowded resorts. As the end of their ten-year tenure draws to a close, it is widely expected that next year's ICSD referendum will fail to renew GGS's contract.

It appears that the ultimate drawback of the private-corporation-as-government model lies in its relatively short-term focus, especially when compared to traditional monarchies. Corporations are run by officers who typically serve for a few years or decades, and their fiduciary duty is to shareholders, who also have a relatively short time horizon. Monarchies, on the other hand, have a time frame of centuries or millennia. They expect to remain in power for generations to come, and therefore consider how their decisions will impact the country for centuries to come. They are more attuned to the culture and traditions of their people and are more likely to make critical decisions in a way that concords with the population's long-term interests. They are less likely to turn sacred cathedrals and holy sites into crowded tourist spots and less likely to strip mine natural areas, turning them into wastelands, since they valued these things for centuries and millennia to come, not for the next decade's profits. For many people, the monarchy is an important national institution and part of their identity. The ruling families who led their countries through centuries of ups and downs continue to inspire and command the loyalty of new generations, and the corporate efficiency of modern private governance corporations is unable to compete on that front.

The Afghan, Cameroonian, and Tuscan experiences—and similar experiences in other locations—dampened some of the hyper-maximalist enthusiasm for private corporations as governments. Economists had proclaimed the Cowperthwaite model as the solution for the problem of governance worldwide, and many had predicted that it would outcompete traditional governments by the end of the century. While it has, in fact, succeeded and grown enormously, it has not taken over the entire planet; it has, in fact, witnessed setbacks near the century's end. Monarchies actually ended up having better Reserve to Expenditures ratios, given their longer-term focus. By the end of the century, the average monarchy had an R:E ratio of 12.4, while the average corporate government's R:E ratio was 9.4, and the average republic's ratio was 8.9. Competition forced monarchs to operate efficiently because it presented them with a credible threat of their citizens discarding their services. But if they operated reasonably, their services became increasingly ceremonial and sentimental, which made customer-citizens prefer them and their traditions over impersonal corporations with no historical attachment.

Another institution that has defied the odds and continued to remain relevant at the end of the twentieth century is aristocracy. At the beginning of the twentieth century, with ideals of self-determination and personal freedom becoming more and more prevalent, most political theorists would have expected a demise in the importance and fortunes of aristocratic families.

However, the opposite seems to have occurred. It is remarkable how many of the aristocratic families and nobility at the beginning of the twentieth century continued to have significant wealth and exert significant influence over their societies. As regions seceded into independent entities, it was the local aristocracy that invariably took the leading role in campaigning for the referenda and in the nascent political order. Many aristocrats were made into kings and princes in their independent regions. After a century of increased freedom and self-determination, which led to aristocrats being more prominent, a strong case can now be made that aristocracy is a natural phenomenon that enhances the freedom and prosperity of society by allowing families with the lowest time preference a leading role across social, political, and economic institutions. Aristocrats, in essence, set an inspirational example to the rest of society, contrary to the angry demagogic ramblings of political relics of the nineteenth century. Aristocrats who mismanaged their position and wealth were quickly relegated to the ranks of commoners, whereas commoners who established multi-generational wealth along with good reputations were elevated to the ranks of nobility and aristocracy.

Interestingly, and unexpectedly, the framework of sound money, free trade, and self-determination was least effective in bringing about positive change in governance in a specific kind of locale: beautiful and highly desirable areas. Governments in places like California, Lebanon, the south of France, Cape Town, and similar locations were the most protected from competition in the market. Citizens in these regions were highly attached to their areas and were willing to ignore incompetence and graft because life in general was good, thanks to the natural beauty and the eclectic and interesting people it would attract. Some of the richest people in these regions and the world wanting to move to these locations allowed governments to charge exorbitant residency fees (which do not grant voting rights). These affluent migrants were more likely to pay taxes to the government and less likely to complain or agitate against it. This gave governments in these areas a leg up on their neighbors, making them richer, but also making them less efficient. Even if some residents left, there was usually a very long list of foreigners seeking to move into the country and pay taxes (no matter the price) to keep the ruling government afloat.

Government Finance

Self-determination, the right to secession, and the modern gold standard conspired to make modern government finance a remarkably straightforward affair in the twentieth century compared to the labyrinthine, perfidious complexity it exhibited under the classical gold standard. Without central banks standing ready to use the nation's captive deposits to purchase government bonds, governments could only borrow on the free market, from willing lenders. Without a captive citizenry, governments could no longer easily incur debt and pass the tab on to their citizens, who would then have to pay it off over decades of taxes. The trauma of 1914–15 had left a mark on the psyche of much of the world's population, and they became incredibly intolerant of governments getting into debt. The terms of the Treaty of Geneva meant that governments had no mechanism with which to oblige their citizens to pay for the debt the governments incurred. As governments accumulated public debt, they played with fire by increasing the chances of their people seceding or joining other governments. Individuals in governments, whether monarchs or democratically elected officials, were then personally liable for the debts they incurred. Meanwhile, the population could avoid repaying it by simply choosing to secede or join other governments.

This made governments exceptionally unattractive borrowers on the free market. Many fortunes were destroyed learning this lesson the hard way in a beautiful act of financial eugenics that ruined many of the parasites who had gotten rich by lending to despots and saddling their populations with debts. Businesses, banks, and family dynasties that were used to the business model of lending to governments got ruined financially in the first half of the twentieth century, as their governments' populations voted to join other entities that did not saddle them with debt, leaving the government's leaders personally liable for astronomical sums they had no chance of paying back. Many of these businesses and banks were destroyed in the 1914–15 Great War. Whatever remained was ruined by the 1940s as lending to governments, and the bond market, finally died as a business model. In retrospect, it seems a travesty that such borrowing ever took place. Governments in the past had no special financial acumen that made them attractive borrowers worthy of low rates. They were treated as good borrowers only because they had control over the monopoly banking system, which meant they could use their citizens' savings as collateral for borrowing. They only managed to borrow by deflecting the costs onto their population, which had no choice but to use their banking systems. The collapse of monopoly central banking left governments unable to borrow against their citizens' savings, which meant they had to borrow on the free market. The right to self-determination further destroyed their ability to borrow by giving citizens the option to opt out of repaying debt if they seceded or joined a more responsible government. Instead of borrowing to spend to impress voters, governments had to accumulate savings to prevent citizens from seceding and tempt them to stay. Competition between governments switched from engaging in an arms race to accumulating more reserves. The ratio of Reserves to Expenditures for governments was the most important metric for government performance, and transparent government accounting allowed people to track it religiously.

As interest rates continued to decline for responsible private borrowers, they remained high for many governments because the risk of secession removed a significant portion of the tax-paying population. By the time interest rates went to zero for most borrowers, as discussed in Chapter 13, government borrowing had become so unattractive that it was practically never attempted anymore. As interest rates declined in private capital markets, governments remained an exception, and their bonds continued to offer much higher interest rates. Bond investors repeatedly lost everything because as soon as the debt burden for a government became high, its citizens would threaten to vote to secede, which would make bonds crash in value and interest rates rise further.

The pattern was visible early: in 1947, the Kingdom of Saxony-Anhalt missed a coupon; two counties filed ICSD petitions to join solvent neighbors; the bond crashed to pennies; a private administrator recapitalized the ledger in exchange for a revenue share. After a few more incidents like this, bonds as an industry died. March 3, 1964, was a historic day, as Argentina defaulted on its final bonds, marking the end of the final government bond sale in history. Argentina had accumulated significant debt, and all the provinces of Argentina, except the capital, had presented a proposal to the ICSD for joining Chile, which was a fiscally responsible, debt-free government that had accumulated reserves worth around eight years of projected spending. With the ICSD delegation flying to Argentina to verify signatures, the central government in Buenos Aires knew it was doomed. There was no way it could finance its growing bureaucracy, which charged taxes as high as 10% of income and mainly favored the urban residents at the expense of the provinces, whose agricultural and industrial production financed their spending. The bonds collapsed to under .1% of their face value, and the government declared bankruptcy. Before the ICSD could conduct the referendum, leaders of the Argentine provinces formed a coalition government that took over the central government with a platform of reducing government spending and staying debt-free. The referendum was averted, and Argentina remained a united country.

With government bonds gone, governments also witnessed the emergence of the equivalent of equity financing. Governments facing financing shortfalls would get capital injections either from other governments or from private governance corporations, which would allow them an equity stake in future government revenues, and also usually give them a say in the running of the government. Monarchs who had mismanaged their finances and needed capital urgently could no longer rely on borrowing. Instead, they could give up a fraction of future earnings for efficient managerial and administrative entities that could improve their operational efficiency before their people voted to secede. JJC, GGS, and similar private governance corporations made significant returns to their shareholders from this model. An increasingly successful model involved traditional monarchs and aristocrats partnering with private governance corporations to deliver government services. With the monarchical institution at the forefront, local customs and traditions were given primacy, which gave the government a certain legitimacy and loyalty from its subjects that, in turn, increased stability and reduced the chances of secession or joining other polities. This gave private governance corporations the freedom to work efficiently with long-term security.

This was yet another vital way the size of government shrank in the twentieth century. Grand projects and public investments were far less common, and important infrastructure was increasingly built by private parties that charged market rates for its use. It became increasingly clear that governments are not the right institution to provide infrastructure and large investments, and the model of financing these endeavors from taxpayers was largely dead by the second half of the century. All economic goods are scarce, and they are provided at a cost at the margin. It is more efficient to have the marginal beneficiary pay for the purchased good than to have a government tax the good's users along with non-users. And with wars becoming increasingly a thing of the past, the favorite excuse of kleptocracies and their financiers for pillaging the public disappears. In retrospect, it is clear that much of the intellectual and propagandistic drive for government spending and projects stemmed from the government's overwhelming temptation to monetize the nation's savings held in its monopoly banking system. The intellectual arguments for spending dissolved in the clarity of modern gold standard banking, which made the costs and benefits of actions clear to discern.

Governments had to operate with a constantly growing cash balance to inspire the confidence of their citizens and ensure that any catastrophes or emergencies could be met from cash reserves without having to borrow or impose hefty taxes on citizens, which would encourage them to secede. To be a government was to have enough cash on hand to meet all liabilities for years to come. People voted for governments that were financially responsible, based on their transparent accounting, and as a result, governments became more efficient in providing their services at a lower cost. Government budget deficits became increasingly rare and temporary.

Governments had to simply spend from the money they had, or from what they could ask their citizens to provide. While it is difficult to accurately measure such numbers due to the lack of reliable society-wide statistics, it is possible to estimate that at the end of the century, the cost of government services has dropped below 1% of income for the vast majority of citizens in the world. By the 1980s, some governments moved from charging taxes based on a percentage of income to charging a fixed flat fee per citizen (or to charging businesses a fixed fee per worker employed). Even though this would have appeared likely unpopular with the majority of citizens—who would find themselves paying the same sum as the richest members of society—it worked because it saved so many people from having to hire accountants to figure out their accurate tax bill. It also made more sense economically. As more of the traditional functions of government, like infrastructure building or trash collection, became privately produced and provided, their users paid for such services according to their use, obviating the need for taxes to be a function of income. The rich did produce more trash, and their businesses used infrastructure more than the poor did, which was reflected in their higher trash collection bills and road tolls. To the extent that the government provided services, they centered around law, order, and border protection, which are largely supplied equally to all, irrespective of income.

Governments that placed heavy taxes on their population would trigger demands for a referendum on independence or joining another government. The ruling families of Europe, after decades and centuries of wealth and decadence, were made to work for their subjects like never before. Europe's map changed constantly, but the changes were increasingly based on administrative efficiency, divorced from racial, ethnic, or religious grounds. Smart and efficient governments understood that attempting to enforce religious or racial identity on their subjects was a losing battle. And the same model was exported outside of Europe with great success.

Separation of Nation and State

The tribal considerations of nationality, ethnicity, and religion became increasingly separated from government, and people pragmatically chose to live under the governments that provided them security and services at the lowest cost. Bitter ethnic and religious conflicts that had plagued regions for centuries became inconsequential afterthoughts because calculating citizens consider joining jurisdictions with better tax rates and lower debt burdens. The world witnessed the separation of nation and state. It was common for people to identify with nations that had little to do with their state and government. People could identify as Chinese, German, Muslim, Christian, Jewish, or Hindu, even though none of these identities was confined to one state. Members of these nations lived across several jurisdictions, sometimes as majorities or minorities, but their rights and duties as citizens were orthogonal to their belonging to their nations, which was cultural, religious, and social, whereas government was largely administrative.

War

A crowning achievement of human civilization in the twentieth century is the vastly reduced frequency and death toll of armed conflict. The 1914–15 Great War was the obvious exception, but it proved the catalyst for humanity to find a reliable mechanism for resolving conflicts that did not deploy our advanced technologies and massive power in the service of destruction. The ICSD framework proved useful at averting conflict and resolving differences peacefully, though it was not entirely foolproof. Several conflicts arose during the period, as some countries stayed outside the ICSD framework for decades, as it had proven unsatisfactory for handling many edge cases. Minority populations that refused to abide by the will of the majority often created guerrilla militias to fight against the ruling government, and without a government in charge of these militias, there was no mechanism for imposing sanctions by ICSD states. In other cases, some countries chose to incur the wrath of global sanctions to fight for territory they viewed as important. Some governments refused to abide by the ICSD decisions when they believed their historical claims to land were more important than the will of its inhabitants, resulting in sanctions and political turmoil. In some contexts, indigenous populations refused to recognize ICSD results in favor of a larger occupying government because that government would have forcibly settled some of its population into the disputed region in anticipation of an ICSD referendum. Another common scenario for conflict involved disputes over resource-rich and sparsely populated territories, where ICSD criteria were not easy to enforce.

These and other scenarios ensured that the world still saw warfare. However, the realities of government finance ensured this warfare was increasingly less intense and bloody than in the nineteenth century, which itself continued a centuries-long trend toward a civilized version of warfare, best exemplified by professional armies fighting on battlefields, sparing civilian population centers. The modern gold standard deprived governments of the central banks that could finance their spending by issuing monetary instruments at a value exceeding the gold backing them. Governments that went to war had to have a large degree of support from their population, which would pay extra taxes or purchase government bonds to support the war effort. This was not very common. And when it did happen, it usually did not last long, as citizens quickly grew tired of paying for murder. With modern technology making targeting civilian population centers increasingly easy and affordable, belligerents usually avoided it for fear of retaliation. Clear rules of engagement and conventions of war were developed to avoid harming civilian population centers, and this meant they faced hard budget caps and automatic trade sanctions on top of secession risk. Even the most vicious vengeance was tamed by balance sheets.

The combination of the modern gold standard and the ICSD framework, while failing to prevent all conflicts, was nonetheless effective at preventing the targeting of civilians and civilian infrastructure and wars from dragging on for long periods. Controversial conflicts that could not be easily resolved using the ICSD frameworks left a margin for ambiguity, making it initially difficult for neutral states to determine whether they were obliged to impose trade sanctions. However, many neutral parties had an interest in preventing or ending conflicts, as they did not want to impose trade sanctions, which would be detrimental to their own citizens and budgets, and because they were concerned about the influx of refugee populations arriving at their borders. Neutral parties attempted to mediate between parties in conflicts, and failing to cooperate with them would make a belligerent highly likely to be subjected to sanctions by ICSD member states. This incentivized belligerents to arrive at a quick resolution.

Wars on battlefields were also increasingly contained and predictable. As militaries mobilized and began to engage, it would often quickly become clear who the winning party would be, at which point the other party would begin to negotiate the terms of its surrender. With funding limited by hard money and the local population always able to secede, no government could afford to engage in conflict it knew it could not win. With citizens able to secede or join other governments, they could deprive a leader of significant tax receipts during war. War, being significantly detrimental to a government's finances, makes a warring government far less attractive as a choice for citizens.

Modern readers are likely to view the decline in war and barbarism as the natural consequence of the continued increase in the moral level of humanity and the curbing of our animalistic, hostile instincts. As humanity's time preference declined, we became more moral, cooperative, and long-term oriented. While there is a large amount of truth to that, the Great War illustrates how pivotal modern monetary technology is to preventing the slide to barbarism. Even the most civilized nations and peoples could slide into barbarism when the monetary system allows rulers to weaponize their entire wealth to fight petty wars. As long as the government could finance itself with the centralized gold savings of its entire population, it could afford to indulge the most horrible, destructive instincts of its leaders, subverting its neighbors and causing the deaths of millions. Had central banks succeeded in continuing to monopolize national wealth into a banking cartel, one shudders to think of the kind of horrors the twentieth century would have seen.

Land and Citizenship

An unexpected economic development of the twentieth century was the explosion in individual land ownership. The universal implementation of free trade and the right to self-determination revolutionized the world's land markets, making land and home ownership almost universal and bringing about the rapid economic development of vast areas of unpopulated and underdeveloped regions of the world.

In retrospect, four main factors in this transformation in land use and ownership can be identified: industrialization, sound money, free trade, and the right to self-determination. First, industrialization made home construction cheaper and thus more affordable. Second, the widespread adoption of gold as money and its steady increase in value over time made it feasible for a growing number of people to save up enough to purchase their own homes and farms. Free trade meant that production could move all over the world since the final goods could be transported easily. Since sound money also meant investors did not have to worry much about inflation, capital controls, or confiscation, country risk declined worldwide. With free trade and the decline in the cost of transportation, an investor could build a factory anywhere and export anywhere. Investment in underdeveloped land around the world grew quickly.

Finally, the right to self-determination also contributed to the growing efficiency of land utilization. With people able to vote to secede from their governments or join others, owners of land under inefficient governments could organize secession movements or join other jurisdictions. Private government corporations often bought cheap, underpopulated, and underutilized land from sovereigns and built their own cities there, offering attractive packages to migrants, which usually involved a path to citizenship and land ownership.

In sum, the new world order vastly increased the opportunity cost of owning land. Inactive and inefficient landowners could afford to leave their land fallow when expensive transportation and political barriers made the movement of goods cumbersome. With a growing number of people attaining financial freedom and independence, they could afford more of this land from the old feudal families that held it for generations. With the higher productivity of industrial technology and modern fuels, and with savings in hard gold, the new class of industrial entrepreneurs and workers devoured the estates of decrepit feudal lords worldwide.

Increasingly, citizenship and residency have become a highly competitive and liquid global market. Citizens could easily compare the services and rates being offered in different jurisdictions, then decide on what best suited their interests. The ICSD framework simplified life for governments by making their entire operation based on taxes rather than inflation or customs duties. With the right of secession, the ability of citizens to understand their tax obligations accurately became more important. Rather than passive acceptors of what their overlords decree, modern citizens are sovereign customers, carefully comparing options like a keen shopper. Ambiguity and complexity are unpopular with customers, and so governments had to simplify their tax code. Increasingly, taxes were consolidated into fewer forms, and in many countries, that meant the land tax. Henry George's *Progress and Poverty* had become quite influential at the end of the nineteenth century, and the great reset that happened in Geneva required new ideas. George had suggested a tax on land equal to all the rent it could procure, and while this idea gained popularity, its actual implementation was only tried once, with disastrous consequences. When a candidate for office in Belgium was elected on a platform of land tax at 100% of the value of rent in 1927, the prices of property crashed more than 80% in the space of two months around the election. By eliminating the possibility of generating income from land or buildings, the economic value of these assets declined significantly. Landlords who had property for rent put it up for sale instead, since the rent would all go to the government as taxes, whereas use by the owner incurred no taxes. Rents increased more than fivefold, and were paid using a creative black market workaround, as the supply of rentable properties was decimated. Within a week of taking office, the prime minister had to reverse the decision and keep the old tax system, which restored sanity to the property and rental markets.

But what did catch on was George's idea of taxing land. Placing taxes on land gave individuals a useful metric for comparing the costs and benefits of different jurisdictions. In some countries, land was taxed a percentage of the product it would produce, while unproductive land was taxed a fixed fee per square meter. Some countries charged a percentage of the value of the land as ascertained by its owner. The owner would declare a price at which he would be willing to sell his property, and the annual tax would be assessed as a percentage of that fee (usually less than 1%). Citizens could declare any price for their property, but if somebody were to offer that price during the year after its declaration, the owner would be required to sell it.

In other locations, sovereign rulers taxed their citizens by the square meter of land they owned. Some had a fixed rate for each meter of land, regardless of what the land was used for. Taxes in these localities effectively functioned as rents. Sovereigns effectively owned all the land in their territory, leasing it to anyone willing to pay the tax on it, which would be the cost of the suite of services the government provided.

Starting in the 1960s, private governance corporations began to seek out unproductive and misused land to organize secession movements. Neglected, sparsely populated remote regions with high taxes and feudal systems of land ownership were the best targets. Private governance corporations like JJC would offer the communal leadership in these areas an attractive deal: JJC would organize and pay for the costs of an ICSD referendum. If the local population voted in favor of it, the new JJC government would increase taxation on landowners, reduce taxation on wages, and invest in industrial development, sometimes by importing migrant workers.

The specter of the JJC put the fear of people into governments. Landowners had to think about their land productively and not sentimentally. No matter how large the landowner's fortune, it would be depleted by paying land taxes, but bolstered by increased productivity if it were converted into money. If land was not used efficiently and productively, it would be better off sold.

This increased efficiency of land use resulted in a fragmentation of land ownership worldwide. More large landowners and feudal lords sold or gave large tracts of land to numerous small landowners. Landowners with large, empty land plots could significantly increase their market value by granting portions of the land to immigrants to work in agricultural production, or to build industrial and urban centers. Large amounts of land were a liability because they incurred taxes and because the inhabitants could organize a referendum to secede or join other jurisdictions, allowing them to implement more aggressive taxation policies against landowners and reduce taxes on wage earners. The best way to secure ownership of large amounts of land was to provide residents with secure property rights in their land, which ensured they had a vested long-term interest in the political system ruling them and made it unlikely they would secede. Descendants of feudal lords around the world gave their peasants property rights. And owners of sparsely populated lands sought immigrants to populate them and increase their productivity. Those who failed to do so frequently found themselves the subject of secession referendum takeovers.

Egypt provides a good example of the change in land ownership. In the southern portion of Egypt, where the ownership of excellent agricultural land around the Nile was concentrated in a few large families, the taxing of land led many of these families to offer landless peasants ownership of land in exchange for a fixed percentage of income from land for a few decades (usually around 5% of earnings for twenty years). The real lucrative benefit to the large landowners was not in the 5% of revenue, but in the appreciation of the surrounding land areas. By the end of the twentieth century, the number of landowners in southern Egypt increased from a few hundred families to millions of families lining both banks of the Nile for thousands of kilometers of farming land interspersed with countless villages and a dozen urban centers.

Landowners and governments would offer programs to attract immigrants, who would then get a piece of land in exchange for a percentage of their income. The use of land as a store of wealth declined drastically across the century, as the wealthy preferred to hold physical gold, which incurred no taxes, required a relatively minuscule maintenance cost, and constantly appreciated slightly. The effectiveness of money as a store of value progressively led to the reduction of demand for goods as a store of value for the future, making their price the function of their use demand rather than their demand as a store of wealth.

With land taxed and money free from inflation, land became an increasingly normal economic good. It also became increasingly less contentious. Further helping reduce conflict over land was the development of artificial islands to meet demand for highly prized land plots, as discussed in Chapter 17.

XV.

The New World Order

I n the aftermath of the Geneva Peace Conference, the death of central
banks was akin to removing computer malware that robs users, and replacing it with software that serves them. No such software upgrade had
occurred on a global scale before, or since. Kings, democratic leaders, intellectuals, and business leaders worldwide scrambled to obtain copies of Mises' and
Johan II's books to understand the world they were entering.

With Henry Ford's generous contribution and Blériot's jets, the ICSD
was established in Geneva on December 15, 1915. With hostilities formally
ended, soldiers returned to their workplaces, commerce and production resumed, and industrial equipment went to serve the cause of prosperity rather
than destruction. The gradual implementation of the ICSD framework
brought with it an increase in security and peace, and an economic boom. The
Prince of Liechtenstein was right: introducing freedom of choice to government would result in it becoming significantly better. Monarchs competed for
subjects and territories. Good monarchs gained land, whereas bad monarchs

lost it. Nationalism was defanged from its toxic and aggressive elements, evolving instead into a civilized sense of common citizenship in one peaceful, voluntary administrative unit, and then evolving further into a cultural, social, traditional, and religious identity separate from the state.

As the first few territories subject to the ICSD framework referendums experienced significant growth after the war, newspapers worldwide spoke with excitement about the ICSD framework as the Swiss formula for success. The Swiss had experienced centuries of peaceful, productive coexistence, accumulating capital and lowering their time preference. Hiring their bureaucrats to dispassionately resolve your pre-civilized ancient tribal territorial conflict could make you, too, civilized, and allow you to enjoy peace, cooperation, industrialization, and prosperity. The popularity of the framework would eventually become universal. By 1945, practically all of the world's inhabited territories, except for a few uncontacted tribes, had political representation that was party to the Treaty of Geneva.

This chapter provides an overview of some of the major changes brought about by the ICSD framework and how it helped shape today's map. Many referenda for independence took place all across Europe over the decade and a half following The Great War, and by 1930, Europe had devolved into more than 114 different political entities, ranging from empires to kingdoms to principalities to republics, with eighteen potential referenda planned to birth even more entities. Against all odds, the peace established by the Treaty of Geneva had endured for fifteen years. There were no more European wars, a streak that continued until the end of the century. Many of the smaller entities were independently governed by a local royal family, but they pledged allegiance to some of the larger empire kings. Being part of a larger empire required paying some taxes to the larger empire, but entailed freedom of movement within the empire and a common defense treaty. The British and French were the largest losers globally from the universalization of the right of self-determination, and the Americans were very happy to watch them lose their empires one referendum at a time.

On August 4, 1944, the thirtieth anniversary of the Battle of Liège, the Belgian king held a memorial celebration to commemorate the thirtieth anniversary of The Great War, to which he invited the rulers of Britain, France,

Russia, Germany, Austria, Italy, Turkey, Constantinople, and many other new and old countries. Remembering the senseless suffering of an entire generation was painful and sad, yet the occasion was a happy one because the memory had illustrated to everyone present, and everyone watching on television, just how far the people and leaders of Europe had come since the war, and how positive their relations were. Britain's King Edward VIII, Germany's Kaiser Wilhelm III, Russia's Tsar Michael II, France's King Henry VI, and Austria's King Charles I had come a long way since their coronations in the fall of 1915, having learned the lessons of their predecessors. They were all among the most popular rulers in their respective countries' history, thanks to their very limited spending and the simple trick of letting all their unhappy subjects secede. All had granted their subjects the right to secession, and all had completely stopped spending public money on imperialism. Whatever imperial projects their governments were involved in had, by the 1930s, either been abandoned or taken over by private companies operating at their private expense, abiding by the laws of the lands in which they operated. The relationships between them were positive and cordial, and the event drew a sharp contrast to the wedding of Victoria Louise in 1913, where their predecessors were harboring ill intentions toward one another, with Kaiser Wilhelm eagerly attempting to interject in any conversation between his Russian and British cousins lest they plot against him. Now, with territorial interests subdued and no discontent populations, there was no easy way for these leaders to plot against one another. With their central banks defunct, there was no easy way to finance any such plotting.

Austria and the Balkans

Peter Karađorđević, having been the first to hear of the plan, was the first to act upon it. As soon as he had left the closed room at the Geneva Conference, he summoned one of his aides, explained the basic outlines of the plan to him, and sent him back to Belgrade with clear instructions to begin collecting signatures and drawing up plans for a referendum. On December 10, he had collected the signatures of more than 1% of the population of Serbia, as well as several regions within the Austro-Hungarian empire where Slavic people lived and where he knew a majority would favor secession from Austria, including Croatia, Bosnia, and Slovenia. The independent kingdom would be called the Kingdom of Yugoslavia, and its monarch would be Peter Karađorđević.

By December 19, an ICSD delegation was traveling around the rural Balkans looking to locate a random sample of the signatories to verify their signatures. After four days, they concluded that the signatures were valid and traveled back to Geneva. On January 1, 1916, the ICSD announced the terms for the referendum to be held across the proposed territory of Yugoslavia on February 15. The proposed Kingdom of Yugoslavia would cover the regions of Serbia, Montenegro, Macedonia, Croatia, Slovenia, and Bosnia. Emperor Charles had announced that, in case of the referendum passing, Yugoslavs would not be allowed to enter Austrian territory except if they obtained a visa, and paid a deposit of 3,000 krone (914.7 grams of gold) as insurance, to be returned on their exit from the territory. The people of Yugoslavia had a real choice to make. Independence was nice, but having access to Vienna without needing to pay an exorbitant sum was also nice. Plus, many of them had relied on work and trade with Austria. The next day, Peter Karađorđević ordered a Blériot plane to Belgrade to transfer the gold to pay for the referendum: 12,000 Swiss francs. It was very expensive for an election, but a lot cheaper than war, roughly what Serbia had spent on two weeks of war in 1915, and with none of the casualties and destruction. Ever the astute businessman, Blériot offered the plane ride for free as an added advertisement for his aircraft.

The entire world was captivated by the experiment. Would Austria let the voting proceed peacefully? Would the people of the Balkans vote in favor of independence? Would Austria respect their will, drop its claim to the Balkans, and withdraw? Would a Yugoslav kingdom then face calls for secession from its own regions? The answer to all these questions was a resounding yes. Eighty-one percent of eligible voters turned up to vote, and 72% voted in favor of secession. Austria announced it would respect the referendum and withdraw all its troops from Yugoslav territory while maintaining the restrictive travel measures. On March 21, Austrian troops had completed their withdrawal from the territories that voted for independence, and the Yugoslav

Kingdom was declared. Croat, Slovene, and Bosnian separatists immediately began campaigning for independence and for organizing their own referenda. Karađorđević made it clear he would respect the ICSD process for any region that wanted to secede. After three years in Yugoslavia, Slovenes voted to return to Austria. They rejoined after negotiating a lower tax rate with the Austrian crown than the one offered by the Serbian king.

The Balkans would witness decades of plebiscites and redrawn borders. It was a very messy process, and the world would lose interest in following its arcane details or keeping up with the desires of all the different linguistic, ethnic, and religious varieties of Balkan people. But what mattered most was that it was all done peacefully. Regardless of the details of territorial divisions, the most important aspect to emerge from the process was that the problems of the Balkans stayed in the Balkans, and there was no good reason for anyone outside the Balkans to care, let alone send troops. Once the world accepted the right of self-determination, geopolitics became a boring administrative affair, not a cause for global conflict. Rather than a gruesome fight to the death, the question of rule became increasingly about the efficiencies of public administration, law and order, trash collecting, and tax rates.

The Austrian ruling family had its hands full over the next decades with many more secessionist movements than just the Balkans. The Czechs and Slovaks secured their independence in 1917 and 1918. In 1919, Poland was recreated as an independent entity after 121 years of partition by uniting Austrian, German, and Russian Poland, which had all voted to unite and secede from their respective empires. Transylvania voted to join Romania, and Hungary voted for independence in 1921.

Russia

Tsar Michael attended the Geneva Conference and agreed to sign the resultant treaty. The lessons he learned in the two weeks he spent in Geneva helped him make sense of the failures of his older brother and helped shape the future of Russia to this day. In a time of rising literacy and increasing productivity, Tsar Michael saw that attempting to rule people against their will was an expensive and destructive pursuit. The fixation on increasing the size of the Russian Empire was an anachronism from the days of low-productivity, illiterate peasantry. The more his brother sought to expand the size of his territory, the more he assimilated resentful populations that would poison the politics of the country, and the more he came close to confronting other major powers. The Russian heartland was already a magnificent country, the largest in the world, capturing most of Eastern Europe and the Ural Mountains, along with Siberia, all the way to the Pacific. The land was predominantly inhabited by people who were happy to be part of it, loyal to the Tsar, and overwhelmingly Orthodox Christian. And yet it was the urge to expand west into hostile Eastern Europe and the Balkans, south into the Caucasus and Anatolia, and east into Manchuria that nearly destroyed Russia. What could these faraway lands offer Russia that it could not obtain with trade? Nothing came to the Tsar's mind when contemplating that question, and he concluded that even if there was something, it would definitely not be anything for which the country should be risked. Tsar Michael was convinced that he would not want to rule any population that did not want to be ruled by him. Instead of giving more authority to the Duma, he removed restrictions on speech and assembly and told his population they were free to secede and discuss secession openly.

After the destruction the Russian military had brought to its ethnic minorities in Eastern Europe during the Great Retreat, seceding from Russia was a very pressing demand for Eastern Europeans. The Russian Empire's territories would witness forty-two ICSD referenda over the coming two decades and lose about an eighth of its territory. Finland, Latvia, Lithuania, Poland, Estonia, Belarus, and Ukraine would secede in the first five years. Soon after their secession, regions within these countries began to apply for their own secession, and a complex patchwork of republics, principalities, and enclaves would peacefully emerge, which included four independent Jewish states in various parts of the area formerly known as the Pale of Settlement, and the eastern part of the Austro-Hungarian empire. The ICSD incentivized many Jews living in small communities across cities and villages of the area to migrate to cities that had sizable Jewish communities to help tip the balance in favor of Jewish independence in these areas.

The Litvak Republic was the first Jewish state to gain its independence in 1922, centered around Vilna, Kovno, and the surrounding shtetls, with Yiddish as its official language, and a strong ruling Bundist Labor Union party that would dominate its politics for decades. In 1924, the charismatic and highly popular Hassidic rabbi, David Mordechai Twersky, led an independence movement for the Jewish communities in the Volhynia-Podolia region, and succeeded in establishing the Chernobyl Nesi'ut (Yiddish for Principality), where he would become the ruling nāśī (prince in Yiddish). He would continue to rule until his death in 1957, at which point his son, Rabbi Yochanan Twersky, ascended to the throne and declared Chernobyl a Malkhut, or kingdom, anointing himself Melech (king) Twersky.

The Carpathian Jewish Federation gained its independence in 1928, emerging as the union of Eastern Galicia, the Subcarpathian Ruthenian region, and the Bukovina region. Initially a federated republic, the Hasidic theocratic elements eventually dominated the secular elements and established a Hasidic republic ruled by a Rebbes' council. The Minsk Socialist Republic gained independence in 1931, and was strongly secular and anti-religious, but after the failure of collectivization efforts and economic collapse in 1936, it transitioned to a liberal, free-market secular democracy.

Many Jews from across Eastern Europe and particularly the Black Sea's surroundings spent the decade after 1915 moving to Bessarabia on the northwestern coast of the Black Sea, to create a majority that could vote for independence from Russia. In 1928, the Bessarabian Republic voted for independence, with Kishinev as its capital, incorporating Tiraspol, and the important port of Ir Lavan (Akkerman) and Izmail. In spite of its early beginnings as a labor union secular republic, it would liberalize its economy significantly by the late 1930s and grow into an important trading hub and economic center. By the 1960s, this Republic would become one of the most prosperous polities in the world. It financed the construction of two Danube-Black Sea canals, the first enhancing the shipping capacity of the Dnister river connecting Ir Lavan to the Danube and the second enhancing the shipping capacity of the Danube port at Izmail. Both cities grew into two important seaports by the 1960s after the construction of the Eurasian Canal.

In 1971, Bessarabian financiers were instrumental in the building of the Great Silk River connecting the Pacific Ocean and the Yellow River with the Caspian Sea, Black Sea, and, through Bessarabia, the European river network and the Atlantic. By 1982, the two ports were among the 10 largest in the world, and their cities among the most astonishing modern metropolises.

In central Asia, the large nations that had been conquered by the Russian Empire all yearned to break free and become independent. Kazakhstan overwhelmingly voted for secession in 1921. It was soon followed by Kyrgyzstan, Tajikistan, Turkmenistan, and Uzbekistan. In the Caucasus, secession was also popular, as Georgia and Azerbaijan voted for secession from Russia in 1921 and 1923, respectively, and Armenian districts of Caucasian Russia voted to join the newly independent Armenia, which had seceded from Ottoman Turkey in 1918. Over the next decade, Adygea, Chechnya, Cherkessia, Dagestan, Ingushetia, Kalmykia, and Ossetia would also secede and become independent states. In the east, part of Russia's Manchurian territories chose to secede and join the Manchurian state established by the Qing dynasty in 1926, which had been deposed from ruling China in 1911.

Russia shrank in size but grew in cohesiveness. Its politics were now peaceful and uneventful. Signing up for the ICSD framework released a lot of the political tension inside Russia, since a lot of the revolutionary fervor of the time was stoked by the discontent of minorities unhappy under the Tsar's regime. The energy that would have been spent plotting and scheming to overthrow the Tsar was instead directed at organizing and financing independence referendums. Russia's ability to trade freely with the world's enormous markets meant its people could secure whatever resources they wanted on the market. They had little care whether remote provinces joined or left them.

The collapse of the German, American, and English central banks proved a blessing for the new Tsar, as it eliminated what had turned out to be the major source of financing for the revolutionaries undermining his brother's rule. Without much support among the Russian population, a small group of criminals had managed to attain inordinate levels of influence thanks to financing from the aforementioned central banks. These criminal groups loosely used the label of "socialism" based on the writings of a long-forgotten semi-literate nineteenth-century German parasitic sociopath named Karl Marx, who never held a job in his life but hilariously considered himself an official spokesperson for the world's workers. Under socialism, private ownership of capital would be criminalized, and a government bureaucracy would get to control the capital stock of society. One can only imagine the sort of horrors that would befall any society that would have implemented such an insane ideology, which was beginning to gain influence at the beginning of the twentieth century, thanks to enemy country banker funding. Socialists were ready-made traitors to all their countries, willing to take funding from any enemy of their country if it meant destroying society and bringing down the meritocratic social order that had exposed them as the incompetent failures they were.

In 1914, with Germany and Russia at war, Alexander Parvus, an exiled Russian banker in Constantinople, approached the German Ambassador to the Ottoman Empire with an intriguing proposal. Germany and the Russian revolutionaries had a common enemy: the Tsar. For a fraction of the cost of the weapons the Germans were spending on the War, they could strengthen the Russian revolutionaries, bring down the Tsar's regime from within, and replace it with socialists who wanted to end the war. Parvus traveled to Berlin in 1915 and met with the German Foreign Office to discuss the plans in detail, written out in a twenty-page report entitled *A Preparation of Massive Political Strikes in Russia*. Parvus had laid out a complete plan for a coup in Russia and explained in detail how German financing could bring it about. A month later, the German imperial treasury approved the expenditure of two million marks "to support revolutionary propaganda in Russia."[122]

In Bern, Switzerland, in May 1915, Parvus met with an exiled Russian criminal by the name of Vladimir Lenin, who was influential among the Bolsheviks, a group of criminals primarily consisting of middle- and upper-class Russians who had failed to meet their families' expectations of having a respectable career. Instead, they had gravitated toward bank robberies and violent crime, justifying these acts as an attempt to finance "revolutionary" activity, which was marketed with slogans about empowering workers and

---

122 Volker Wagener, "Germany's Role in the Russian Revolution," DW, November 7, 2017.

peasants. With German money, Danish banks, and Swedish and Finnish villages, Parvus was able to smuggle money, weapons, and dynamite to Russian criminals.

Jacob Schiff, an American banker who was among the wealthiest individuals in the world at the time, was also instrumental in funding the socialist movement in Russia aimed at overthrowing the Tsar. Documents unearthed in the US investigation of the Federal Reserve cartel revealed that he had contributed a staggering $20 million to Alexander Kerensky and his Socialist-Revolutionary Party, and various other revolutionary groups.[123] Historian Antony Sutton later revealed an extensive web of financing from Wall Street to the Russian revolutionaries.[124]

German and American support transformed the Bolsheviks from a small gang of criminals into significant players in Russia's affairs. Their complete lack of moral scruples was something that politics had barely witnessed before. Lenin, who lived in Switzerland, had become increasingly influential in Russian opposition circles, and he made no secret of accepting German money to undermine the Tsar. The Bolsheviks had very publicly opposed the war. As the Russian situation in the war worsened, they began to appeal to more people beyond their core constituency of sociopathic criminals and life failures.

After the collapse of the German and American central banks, funding for the 'revolutionaries' dried up, many of the opportunist thugs hired by the Bolsheviks turned on each other, and the acrimonious and murderous aftermath revealed the details of the financing they were receiving to stir up dissent and revolution in the hopes of toppling the Tsar. After a thorough investigation, seventy eight Bolsheviks were tried, found guilty of treason, and executed in 1918, including Vladimir Lenin, who had returned to Russia in 1915 expecting to lead a Bolshevik takeover, Leon Trotsky, Lev Kamenev, Grigory Zinoviev, Joseph Stalin, Mikhail Frunze, Semyon Budyonny, Yakov Sverdlov, Nikolai Bukharin, Felix Dzerzhinsky, and Alexei Rykov. A priest

---

123 "Medvedev Falsification Commission may be 'Harmful' or 'Useless,' Memorial Expert Says," *Estonian World Review*, May 21, 2009, para. 7.
124 Antony C. Sutton, *Wall Street and the Bolshevik Revolution: The Remarkable True Story of the American Capitalists Who Financed the Russian Communists* (Clairview Books, 2012).

present that day said that each one of these executions would save Russia a million deaths.

Under the classical gold standard, governments could afford to finance foreigners to some extent, but during the Great War, on a fiat standard, with all government expenses justified by patriotic appeals, the socialists experienced a surge in financing and relevance. But the death of fiat central banking in the Great War put an end to this dangerous phenomenon and literally and figuratively starved socialist revolutionaries worldwide. There was little money available to various foreign offices across Europe to engage in subversive political activity, and little point in doing it since imperial rivals had signed up to the ICSD framework and their populations could secede without needing foreign support. These socialist movements largely withered away by the early 1920s as the economic boom from peace began to make life immeasurably better for everyone, and deflation continued to make the products of the division of labor within the reach of more and more people every year. Fortunately for Russia and the world, no society has experienced the kind of disastrous consequences that would have followed from such a catastrophic system.

Unburdened by trying to cobble together a sprawling and highly diverse empire, and unthreatened by conniving revolutionaries, Tsar Michael reigned over thirty-five peaceful and prosperous years for Russia. During those years, industrial capacity increased enormously, as did foreign investment. By the 1930s, Russia's industry was among the most advanced in the world, and its people among the richest. By 1968, the Trans-Siberian Expressway had grown to eight lanes of magnetic levitation trains capable of traveling at speeds up to 500 km/hour, making it possible to travel from Moscow to Vladivostok in a mere eighteen hours.

The Ottoman Empire

The Ottoman Empire had earned the moniker of the sick man of Europe for good reason. The government was in debt, and its large sprawling empire contained many people who longed to break free. They had already suffered heavy defeats in the Balkan Wars of 1912–1913 and in the Italo-Turkish War of

1912. In retrospect, it made little sense why the Ottoman Empire would want to enter this war at such an inopportune moment, and its motivation was likely the least justified or understood of all the belligerents. On August 2, 1914, the Ottoman Empire signed a secret alliance with Germany. On October 29, 1914, the Ottomans entered the war by launching an attack against Russian forces in the Black Sea. Among many miscalculations, the Ottomans overestimated how eager non-Turkish Muslims under their rule would be to fight for them, particularly as the ruling regime had grown increasingly secular and Turkish nationalist, rather than Islamist, under the leadership of the Committee of Union and Progress (CUP).

The entrance into the war started well for the Turks, with victories over the Russians in the Caucasus and the Black Sea in October and November of 1914, respectively. Things then took a turn for the worse, with the British taking southern Iraq and the Suez Canal, and the Russians achieving a devastating victory in Sarikamish in Eastern Anatolia, with tens of thousands of Turkish soldiers freezing to death before battle had even begun. Then in February, the British, French, and Russian forces allied to attack the Gallipoli peninsula, close to Istanbul, threatening to expose the Ottoman capital to shelling and isolate it from the rest of the Ottoman Empire across the Bosphorus. The Triple Entente suffered devastating blows, failing to capture Gallipoli and losing hundreds of thousands of soldiers.

The Armenians sought independence, and many volunteered with the Russian army in the campaigns in the Caucasus, to which the Turkish leadership retaliated with mass expulsions and murders. In Arabia, Sharif Hussein bin Ali, the thirty-seventh-generation descendant of the Prophet Muhammad and ruler of the holy city of Mecca, had begun to coordinate with British envoys to rise against the Ottomans, which would require the Ottomans to direct some of their force to Arabia and away from the European center stage. Without Sharif Hussein, the Ottomans would lose a lot of support from Muslims, who formed the vast majority of their subjects. The CUP leadership did not help their case with their despotic rule in Syria and Lebanon, where they executed hundreds of leaders and notables in fear of an uprising, and where they spent money on historic monuments while a famine devastated the population.[125] The Ottomans had already suffered a brutal insurrection in Yemen from 1904 to 1911, which cost them 10,000 soldiers and forced them to grant autonomy to the Zaydi highlands under Yahya Hamid ed-Din, while they continued to rule Shafii areas.

The Ottoman Empire had been suffering from economic problems for decades, and it had significant debts. As European central banks began to collapse, the Imperial Ottoman Bank followed suit, collapsing in September 1915, and the war began to fizzle out. Turkey sent a delegation to Geneva, but the Sultan and his top brass were not convinced. Prince Sabahaddin, who had been exiled since 1903, had played a major part in devising the ICSD framework in the side meeting, and in Geneva, he did his best to convince the Turkish government that this was the right path forward. Politically, militarily, and financially, Turkey could not afford to remain outside the Geneva framework. Political tension between the Ottoman ruling family and the CUP was increasing, the military was incapable of quelling the independence movements, and the country needed foreign financing and investment. Only by signing the Treaty of Geneva could these three problems be solved. After watching the recovery of the Austrian and Russian economies in the wake of their referenda, the Turkish government signed the ICSD in 1918, and Prince Sabahaddin returned to form a new government.

The Armenians were the first to act, presenting a large list of signatories and voting with an overwhelming majority for independence for large parts of Eastern Anatolia on April 15, 1919. Sharif Hussein took a longer time to devise a plan for independence. After careful plotting, he agreed with tribal leaders in Hejaz, Najd, Oman, Yemen, and the rest of Arabia, as well as the Levantine leadership, Muslim, Christian, and secular, in Syria, Iraq, Lebanon, and Palestine to unite in requesting one referendum for independence to form a Kingdom confederation of 16 Emirates with a large degree of autonomy, and Sharif Hussein bin Ali as a nominal figurehead. The desire to get rid of the rule of the CUP was very strong, particularly in the Levant, which had experienced terrible repression

---

125 Melanie S. Tanielen, *The Charity of War: Famine, Humanitarian Aid, and World War I in the Middle East* (Stanford University Press, 2017).

and famine under their rule, and had heard the horror stories from Armenian refugees. Most of these lands were under Turkish rule, but the British had substantive interests in the Arab Gulf, so Sharif Hussein bin Ali had to make a bold move by requesting independence from both the Ottomans and the British, thus ensuring he had the support of the local population. Both the British and the Ottomans had specified that, if the referendum passed, they would place strict travel restrictions on the subjects of the Arab Kingdom. However, this did not deter Hussein or the majority of voters.

On September 9, 1919, the referendum passed that ended Ottoman and British rule over the entirety of the Arabian Peninsula and the Levant, creating 16 autonomous emirates. The emirate of Hijaz was under King Sharif Hussein bin Ali, and the Saudi Arabian Kingdom was under the Hashemites' close allies, the Al Saud, and was to become one of the world's most prosperous regions after the discovery of oil and the building of extensive oil infrastructure. On the Arabian Gulf, Kuwait was ruled under the Al Sabah family, Qatar under the Al-Thani dynasty, Bahrain under the Al Khalifa family, Abu Dhabi under the Al Nahyan family, Dubai under the Al-Maktoum family, Ajman under the Al-Nuaimi family, Fujairah under Al Sharqi, Umm Al-Quwain under the Al Mualla family, and Sharjah and Ras Al-Khaimah under two branches of the Al-Qasimi family.

The Sultanate of Muscat continued to rule Muscat and the Omani inlands, but was now free of British control. Yemen was united under Yahya Hamid ed-Din. Sharif Hussein sent his son Abdullah to be Emir of Jordan and Palestine, while his son Faisal became Emir of Iraq, and his son Zaid became Emir of Lebanon and Syria. In 1921, Kurds from Iraq, Iran, Syria, and Turkey voted to secede from these states and establish their own independent state. That proved to be the last successful secessionist movement in the Levant for the century. The wide diversity of religious sects and ethnicities that existed in the Levant proved no problem for the Hashemites, as they had provided full autonomy to individual regions and respected the rights of religious minorities to practice their religions and speak their languages. At various periods, some Christians in Syria, Lebanon, and Palestine, and Jews in Palestine and Iraq, had called for independence, but they could never muster enough signatures to get a referendum going. The freedom to move and work across Arabia and the Levant was extremely valuable, given the massive oil boom in the Gulf. And the serenity of Hashemite rule, the close geographic proximity and intertwining of Muslim, Christian, Jewish, and Druze populations, and their largely friendly relationships were all enough to prevent any serious political strife.

By 1921, the Ottoman Empire had lost all its non-Turkish-speaking territories and was reduced to Anatolia and Constantinople. By then, internal tensions had continued to escalate between the pro-Caliphate and Islamic majority of the population, on one hand, and the secularists and modernists led by the CUP and Kemal Ataturk on the other. After the ICSD framework became clear, more and more of the secularists from across the country moved to the western, European side of Istanbul, with the aim of seceding from the Ottoman Empire. In December 1922, the CUP submitted to the ICSD an application for the independence of the part of Istanbul west of the Bosphorus canal. After verification, the referendum was set for October 1923, and western Constantinople voted to secede and form the Republic of Turkey. The Ottoman sultan himself cast his vote against secession, but he was powerless to stop it. He vacated his palaces in the west of Istanbul and moved to the eastern side.

As the Ottoman state continued to shrink in Anatolia, and the Arab Hashemite kingdom and emirates established themselves, more and more Muslims in Arabia, Anatolia, Persia, Africa, India, and all over the world began to pledge their allegiance to King Hussein bin Ali as the Caliph of Islam, which is the title that had been held by the head of the Ottoman dynasty for centuries. Although the Islamic world was fragmented among many nations, King Hussein was a respected figure across the Islamic world and had broad legitimacy and appeal for being the direct descendant of Prophet Muhammad and the guardian of the holy sites of Mecca. The growing popularity and legitimacy of the new Caliph, and his diplomatic role in diffusing inter-Muslim tensions worldwide, had united Muslims from across sects around him. Being a Sunni Muslim who was also the direct descendant of Prophet Mohammad went a long way toward ending the Sunni-Shia rift in Islam. The root of the split was that Shia Muslims wanted the Caliph to be from the house of Muhammad. The Hashemite dynasty of King Hussein is Sunni but also the direct descendants of Prophet Muhammad, which made them an acceptable choice for Sunni and Shia Muslims, and helped heal the rift at the heart of Islam, as well as improve relationships between Arabs and Persians. The Hashemites would hold the Caliphate throughout the twentieth century, gaining more adherents among Muslims, and constantly alleviating discord among Muslims. Although they only ruled over a part of Arabia and the Levant, the Hashemite Caliphs were respected and welcomed across Muslim lands.

Britain and Ireland

Great Britain was the last major power to join the ICSD framework, as the crown, government, and public still had a strong identification with their empire and believed they could maintain it in the modern world. But this belief proved delusional. The collapse of the Bank of England left the British government struggling to finance itself. Without the world depositing its wealth in London for the government to borrow against, the budget had to be drastically pared down. There was very little money for managing the colonies, at a time when the colonies were becoming restive and insubordinate.

British finances could no longer afford the cost of the Empire and restive territories. Isolation from American and Swiss capital, along with exclusion from the new Treaty of Geneva free trade zone, had also taken their toll. The ICSD free trade zone quickly displaced the British Empire and the Commonwealth as the world's largest free trade zone, depriving Britain of a major economic advantage it had. The ICSD members benefited greatly from trading with one another, and by the end of the 1920s, Britain had regressed from the world's prime industrial producer to its fifth, behind the USA, Germany, Russia, and Japan. Prime Minister Morley had resigned in 1917 after failing to persuade his cabinet to sign the Treaty of Geneva. A varied succession of Prime Ministers was in power over the next few years, and several elections were held, but there was no clear resolution for the problems of the budget, empire, Ireland, and the Treaty of Geneva. In 1923, David Marshall Mason ran as a candidate for the Liberal Party under the slogan of "Britain Not Empire," in which he promised to sign the Treaty of Geneva and deliver an economic boom by drastically reducing government spending on the empire and taxation, and opening up global markets for trade with Britain. With the support of Morley, John Burns, Arthur Ponsonby, Phillip Morrell, and the antiwar voices of 1914, he was able to secure a commanding victory at the polls and a decisive mandate. After Britain signed the Treaty of Geneva in 1925, the global exodus from the British Empire commenced, and the fortunes of Britain turned bright after a dark decade.

In May 1914, the United Kingdom parliament passed the Government of Ireland Act 1914, which intended to provide home rule to Ireland and self-government within the United Kingdom. The plan faced opposition among the Catholic majority and more opposition among the Protestant minorities in the northern province of Ulster. With the outbreak of war in 1914, Prime Minister Herbert Asquith rushed through the Suspensory Act 1914, which would suspend the Government of Ireland Act of 1914 until the end of the war. Britain's refusal to sign the Treaty of Geneva created a major political crisis around the restoration of the Government of Ireland Act, as it was not immediately clear if the war had in fact ended. Politicians were divided over whether the war had ended, whether they should sign the Treaty of Geneva to end it, whether the Suspensory Act could be considered annulled and the Government of Ireland Act restored, and whether it was the right framework for moving forward British-Irish relations.

Irish separatist movements campaigned for the implementation of the ICSD framework but were unable to secure it as long as Britain refused to sign the Treaty of Geneva. In the Easter Uprising of April 1916, Irish Republicans captured parts of Dublin and declared an Irish Republic, beginning the eight-year-long Irish War for Independence. The British army, still licking its wounds from the Dardanelles and the French trenches and lacking in funding, was unsuccessful in regaining rebel territory, and the bloody struggle dragged on for years, during which a de facto Irish republic began to come into existence. Members of the British Empire refused to recognize the Irish state, but more and more countries in Europe began to offer recognition. Ireland remained an expensive and politically unstable quagmire until 1924, when Britain finally signed the Treaty of Geneva.

Under the leadership of Patrick Pearse and Michael Collins, the Irish Volunteers, the Irish Republican Brotherhood, Sinn Féin, and various Irish separatist groups wasted no time in collecting signatures and campaigning for independence for all of Ireland. The Unionists in Ulster, who wanted to remain in Great Britain, began organizing for their own secession referendum. The two referendums were introduced on the same day, as all voters got to vote on independence from Britain, while voters in Ulster got to vote on independence from Britain and on remaining in Britain should the general Irish independence motion pass. Both motions passed. Ireland was to become an independent republic—the Republic of Ireland—while Ulster would remain with Britain. Over the next 76 years, various counties would organize referenda and join the United Kingdom or the Republic of Ireland, and the map continued to change. There were occasional skirmishes, clashes, and bar fights that cost a few dozen lives over the century, but there were no military conflicts. Scotland voted for its own independence in 1928, and Wales followed suit in 1931.

Germany

The German Empire ruled over the largest European entity in terms of territory in 1914, and was also the largest loser from self-determination, as many of its constituent territories seceded by 1930, and it lost around a third of its land area. Alsace-Lorraine voted for independence in 1916. West Prussia and parts of Upper Silesia joined Poland in 1919. Danzig became a free city-state in 1921. Eupen-Malmedy joined Belgium in 1921. North Schleswig joined Denmark in 1923. Bavaria voted to become an independent kingdom in 1923, and Saxony-Anhalt did the same in 1925. Rheinland and Westphalia voted to create a Ruhr Free Commonwealth of cities and principalities. In 1931, the kingdoms of Germany, Bavaria, Saxony-Anhalt, and Austria, as well as the Rhur Free Commonwealth, joined together to form the Freier Deutscher Bund, a loose alliance for German-speaking states with a common defense treaty, free movement, and a customs-free area.

France

France witnessed some of the most brutal fighting in the war, losing more than a million soldiers and civilians in the first year of conflict. German soldiers became entrenched on French soil, and a war of attrition had set in by 1915. With Blériot jets moving gold and saving people from having to deal with their local government oligopoly banks, the gold reserves at the central banks dwindled precipitously, and the franc began to decline in price. The collapse of the British pound taking place across the Channel hastened the demise of the franc, as significant banking relations existed between the two countries. By October, the government had exhausted its gold reserves entirely, and the French franc had collapsed to less than 10% of its original value.

The people of France rioted in the streets, demanding punishment for the engineers of their misery and devastation. Caillaux revealed documents exposing the Russian financing of Poincaré to influence him to join the war against Germany. People quickly turned on Poincaré and the pro-Russian traitors, and a large crowd stormed the Élysée Palace on October 25th. Poincaré, Prime Minister René Viviani, Foreign Minister Théophile Delcassé, and eight other high-ranking politicians were guillotined on that day. Caillaux took over as interim President by popular proclamation, promising to hold elections in three months.

Alsace-Lorraine was still under German control when the guns stopped firing. In January 1916, the residents submitted the second application for an ICSD independence referendum, after the Serbian king. Even though France was not yet a signatory to the ICSD, it supported the Alsace-Lorraine independence vote, which passed with a commanding majority. French leaders expected that an independent Alsace-Lorraine would opt to join France, but France's remaining outside the ICSD framework proved an insurmountable obstacle, as it meant it would have a hard time securing capital flows to rebuild after the war, and it also meant it was excluded from the global ICSD free trade framework. The parties that favored rejoining France in Alsace-Lorraine were powerless to convince their countrymen to join France, and France was far too weak financially to attempt a forcible annexation. As an independent nation, Alsace-Lorraine prospered under the ICSD framework. Rather than join France, its independence would be one of the main factors incentivizing France to sign the Treaty of Geneva. Fiscal and political problems continued to beset the French government and most public institutions in France and the colonies, as separatist and independence movements proliferated and got better organized.

Seeing the prosperity and success of Alsace-Lorraine and other Treaty of Geneva signatories emboldened independence and separatist movements in France and its colonies. The Bourbon dynasty, under Jean d'Orléans, organized a referendum to restore the French monarchy in the most staunchly pro-monarchy and pro-Catholic church regions of Vendée, Tours, Normandie, Loire, Orléans, Chartres, Abbeville, Amiens, Poitiers, and the surrounding towns and villages. The referendum passed, and a new French kingdom was announced in March of 1927, with Jean proclaimed King Jean III. Soon after, more and more regions of France chose to secede to become independent: Corsica in 1928, Savoy in 1929, Avignon in 1929, and Brittany in 1930. In 1931, the cities and provinces of Nice, Valle d'Aosta, Piedmont, Lomellina, Pavese, Bobbio, Oneglia, and Dolceasqua voted to secede from France and form a federation modeled after the Swiss federation.

In 1927, the French Basque region voted to join the Basque region that had seceded from Spain in a union of one Basque nation. French Catalonia had also joined newly independent Catalonia in 1922. And in 1928, French Flanders seceded from France and joined Belgian Flanders, which had seceded from Belgium. Together, they established a Flanders Republic.

Spain and Portugal

Spain had remained neutral during the war, but it nonetheless signed the Treaty of Geneva because it wanted to ensure European peace and avoid being dragged into future conflicts. In the coming decade and a half, it would witness several successful secessions, including the aforementioned Basque Country and Catalonia, Galicia in 1926, Leon in 1928, and Asturias in 1929.

Portugal had become Europe's fourth republic, following San Marino, Switzerland, and France, after the deposition of the young King Manuel II in 1910, two years after the assassination of his father, King Carlos I, and his older brother, Crown Prince Luis Felipe. As was so often the case, the extent of popular support for the republic was highly overstated by regime propagandists. In the year of the republic's birth, the elections had delivered republicans and their allies no more than forty seats in parliament, while pro-monarchy forces secured 120. Having failed at democratically rallying the people behind their cause, the republicans resorted to violence. The new republic came into power with lofty promises regurgitated from the French Revolution, but just like the French experiment, it quickly descended into despotism. The new regime was very hostile towards Christianity and the church, passing many laws that restricted freedom of religion and handicapped the operations of religious institutions. This led to growing disaffection with the regime, necessitating increasing political suppression and creating power conflicts in the new republic. From his exile in England, King Manuel II paid for and organized an ICSD referendum promising to restore the monarchy, and in 1925, the people of Portugal voted in favor of it. He reclaimed his throne in 1926.

Italy

In Italy, the decision to go to war was highly acrimonious and controversial. Italy had been part of the Triple Alliance with Germany and Austria-Hungary since 1882, but at the start of the Great War, it became clear Italy had no intention of joining the war on the side of its allies. The alliance was defensive, and Austria-Hungary had declared war on Serbia, while Germany had declared war on Russia and France, thus absolving Italy from having to join them. The Triple Alliance also required that Austria-Hungary and Italy consult with one another if either of them wanted to change the status of the Balkans, but Austria-Hungary did not consult with Italy, further freeing Italy's hand. As the war started, Italy found itself being courted by both alliances, as the Triple Entente tried to get it to join their alliance, while Germany and Austria-Hungary wanted to get it to remain neutral. Both alliances offered Italy territories after lengthy negotiations, but the government of Prime Minister Antonio Salandra was more tempted by the promises of the Entente, because Austria-Hungary would not agree to offer Italy the South Tyrol and Trieste, which were under Austrian control.

In April 1915, the Triple Entente of Britain, France, and Russia signed the secret London Pact with Italy, under whose terms Italy would enter the war against Austria and Germany and, in return, receive Austrian and Ottoman territories at the conclusion of the war, along with some African colonies. Most significant to Italy was the promise to receive the South Tyrol, the Austrian Littoral, Dalmatia, and the Snežnik plateau. But the London Pact was signed secretly, and the Italian parliament was not informed of it, or of the commitment to join the war within a month. Veteran liberal politician Giovanni Giolitti, who was prime minister until March 1914, had strenuously opposed Italian entry into the war. He effectively became the leader of opposition to the Salandra government, creating irreconcilable enmity between the two men. A majority of parliament supported Giolitti and opposed Salandra and his war. When Italy officially revoked the Triple Alliance on May 3, 1915, opposition to the war grew in parliament, while nationalists demonstrated in favor of war. Parliamentary opposition led Salandra to submit his resignation to King Victor Emmanuel III on May 13. King Emmanuel tasked Giolitti with forming a government, and anti-war Italians rejoiced, expecting Giolitti to have no trouble forming a government that would keep Italy out of war, as he had a clear majority of parliamentary support. However, for reasons that remain not entirely clear to this day, Giolitti refused to form a cabinet. He claimed he was afraid that the nationalist and pro-war elements in Italy would create disorder and potentially even rebellion. Giolitti also found out at that time that the London Pact was already signed, and he feared that forming an anti-war government would lead to a conflict between the king and parliament. Conspiratorially-minded Italians continue to insist to this day that foreign interests had bribed, blackmailed, or threatened Giolitti not to form a government. Whatever the case may be, Giolitti's refusal to form a cabinet led the king to reject Salandra's resignation, and the Salandra government declared war on Austria-Hungary on May 23. Giolitti, defeated and demoralized, decided to move to Cavour, a small village near Turin, and avoid politics altogether.

Thanks to the invention of BTC, Italians could move a lot of their wealth away from their government's prying hands, and their currency began to collapse a mere three months after declaring war. Northern Italians, in particular, frequently used BTC aircraft to transport their gold to the Italian-speaking Swiss cantons, whose banks had begun constructing new vaults in early 1915 in anticipation of the war and the influx of gold it would bring, just as they had in their German-speaking and French-speaking cantons.

The military, as Giolitti had repeatedly warned, was not ready for a war, and the few months of fighting made that abundantly clear. The Italian army suffered from shortages of weapons and ammunition, and its soldiers were among the least disciplined in Europe, particularly as many of them came from regions that had not wanted to be part of Italy and had fought long, bloody wars to avoid the unification of Italy. Desertions were common, discipline was very scarce, and military leaders took to the habit of executing soldiers in staggering numbers. Some soldiers swore that their commanders murdered more of their brothers-in-arms than Austrian fire. With deserting soldiers telling their countrymen about the woeful state of the troops on the front, the public revulsion at generals executing soldiers, and the collapse of the Italian lira, the support for war in Italy collapsed quickly.

Demonstrators surrounded the royal palace in Rome and demanded an end to the war. In September, demonstrators from across the country flocked to Giolitti's retreat in Cavour, demanding that he return to power and end the war. On October 22, 1915, the king dissolved the government and tasked Giolitti with establishing a new government. His first order of business as Prime Minister was to withdraw the Italian military to its pre-war borders and disengage the Austrian army, which had also withdrawn from the areas of confrontation by this time. The blood-soaked battlefields of the past few months became no man's land. Both militaries could easily advance and take the territory, but due to their shortages of ammunition and funding, they were unable to hold it.

An investigative committee was established to investigate the individuals responsible for Italy's entry into war. Salandra was convicted of treason for committing to a deal with the Triple Entente without informing parliament, and executed on the 16th of November.

Giolitti then turned to the imminent Geneva Peace Conference and began preparing his delegation for it. He decided to include Pope Benedict, whose religious authority he hoped would facilitate a favorable settlement with Catholic Austria and make other countries more amenable to Italy's demands. He also took with him the economist Luigi Einaudi. After much deliberation, the Italian parliament and monarch approved the signing of the Treaty of Geneva in 1917. South Tyrol voted to rejoin Austria in 1921, Sicily voted for independence in 1922, and Sardinia followed in 1923.

China

After 3,982 years of dynastic monarchies, China became a republic for the first time in 1912. The 1911 Xinhai Revolution had displaced the Qing dynasty, but unlike all the previous power transitions over the past four millennia, there was no dynasty to replace it. Influenced by Western ideas of republicanism, democracy, and self-determination, a sizable portion of China's intellectual and political leaders wanted to transition to republicanism.

The Qing dynasty had never fully recovered from its many lost wars of the nineteenth century. Britain had defeated them in the First Opium War from 1839 to 1842 and taken Hong Kong. In the Second Opium War, from 1856 to 1860, British and French soldiers destroyed the Imperial Summer Palace in Beijing, and China ceded 1.5 million square kilometers to Russia. Japan had defeated the Qing dynasty in the Sino-Japanese War in 1894-1895, and proceeded to occupy Taiwan. From 1899 to 1901, the "Boxer Rebellion" erupted against foreigners in China. Organized by a secret society, the Qing dynasty lent its support even as it besieged diplomats and Christians in the Beijing Legation Quarter, causing Britain, Russia, Japan, France, Germany, the US, Italy, and Austria-Hungary to invade China to rescue them. They managed to do that, and the Qing dynasty had to pay them a substantial indemnity.

The Qing had to deal with several rebellions across their sprawling empire. Most devastating was the Taiping Rebellion from 1850 to 1864, which the Qing dynasty managed to survive, but at a very high cost. Somewhere in the range of twenty to thirty million Chinese were killed in violence across China.

To fight this war, the Qing dynasty had allowed provincial governments to raise their own armies to combat the rebels. These regional armies had grown in power, independence, and intransigence over the late nineteenth century. The growing decentralization, rebellions, and defeats in foreign wars had encouraged increasingly serious dissent across the empire. The Qing were from the Manchurian minority, whereas around 90% of the population of China was Han Chinese, a fact that had created resentment of their rule that began to magnify as the country's fortunes faltered.

The internal affairs of the family were also dire. Under the reign of the Daoguang Emperor from 1820 to 1850, China began to suffer devastating defeats and destabilizing rebellions. His death would plunge the royal family into continuous struggle until its demise. His son Xianfeng took power at the age of nineteen. On top of being young and weak, he also suffered from ill health and died at thirty, in 1861, appointing his six-year-old son, Tongzhi, as heir. He also appointed a regency council of eight men to assist his son, but these were soon ousted by Tongzhi's mother, Empress Dowager Cixi, Xianfeng's concubine, who would go on to effectively rule the ruling family until 1908. Tongzhi died at only eighteen with no sons, so Cixi appointed his cousin and her nephew, Guangxu, as the new emperor. He was only four years old. She continued to be the de facto ruler, and in 1898, placed the emperor under house arrest. On November 14, 1908, the Emperor died at the age of thirty-seven, and the very next day, the Empress Cixi died at the age of seventy-two. Emperor Guangxu's wife, Cixi's daughter, took over as Empress Dowager Longyu, and her two-year-old nephew, Puyi, was made Emperor Xuantong. The succession of weak emperors dying young with no heirs had made the dynasty weak and disjointed, and its situation was untenable as public rejection continued to increase. Empress Xuantong appointed Yikuang, a member of the Qing family, as prime minister in May 1915 in an attempt to ameliorate protests, but that proved illusory. Revolutionary forces then launched the Wuchang Uprising in October 1911, in which rebel forces defeated the Qing army. The victory emboldened eighteen provinces to secede from the central government in Beijing. After six months in office, Yikuang resigned as premier in November 1911. He offered his position to China's most powerful general, the leader of the New Army, Yuan Shikai, and tasked him with suppressing the rebels. Within weeks, Yuan began secret negotiations with the rebels. An election was held in newly-liberated Nanjing on December 29, with each representative of the assembly of seventeen seceding provinces getting a vote. Sun Yat-sen was elected president of the Republic of China. The secret negotiations between the leader of the army, Yuan, and the leader of the Republic of China, Sun Yat-sen, would yield a plan for action: Yuan would convince the empress to sign the abdication papers on behalf of her nephew, after which Sun Yat-sen would become president, resign, and transfer power to Yuan. On February 12, six-year-old Emperor Puyi was deposed after his aunt, Empress Dowager Longyu, signed the abdication papers on his behalf. The Republic of China, announced by Sun on 12 January, became the recognized government of China.

The Republic of China had a flag of five stripes colored red, yellow, blue, white, and black, which respectively denoted the harmony between the Han, Manchu, Mongol, Hui (Muslim), and Tibetan ethnic components of the population. But keeping the country together harmoniously was not easy. The majority of the Republic's population was Han, with small minorities of Manchurians, Mongols, Hui, and Tibetans. Many Mongols, Uyghurs, Tibetans, and others looked to secede from China. The Qing dynasty was from the Manchurian minority, which fueled resentment among the Han majority.

China had had a monarch for forty centuries. For the last sixty-two years, the Qing Empire had not had a strong, mature leader or a predictable plan of succession, and was instead ruled by various parties within the palace vying for power. The end of the empire had created a gaping power vacuum. Replacing a monarchical dynasty with a republic would not be easy. Revolutions come with lofty intentions, but the temptation of power is too alluring, and Yuan's tenure as president showed how a power vacuum will inevitably be filled by someone. He suspended parliament and provincial assemblies, and his cabinet resigned, leaving him the dictator of China. With the strongest military under his control, power went to Yuan's head. He decided to fill the giant emperor-shaped hole in Chinese politics by declaring himself emperor in December 1915. The move was highly unpopular with the Chinese people and the competing militaries, and Yuan abdicated, ending the monarchy and restoring the Republic of China in March 1916. He died in June 1916, leaving behind an enormous power vacuum and starting a power struggle. Having spent his short tenures as president and emperor consolidating his power and weakening the power of everyone else in the Chinese government, Yuan's death left the Chinese state rudderless and set the stage for civil war.

Yuan was succeeded by Li Yuanhong as president, and Feng Guozhang became vice president. Duan Qirui became premier, and the three men immediately got into an irreconcilable power struggle over the state and the military. The absence of a monarch meant a problem of legitimacy to whichever relatively unknown leader replaced him. It was difficult to rally military commanders across China's enormous land mass to remain loyal to the central government, when individual leaders had their own biases and were not viewed as being above partisan and regional rivalries, like the monarchs ostensibly could be. Many of the regional armies established in the Qing era remained in power across the country, and Yuan's death resulted in these militaries becoming increasingly independent of the central government. The southern provinces in particular became more seditionist.

General Zhang Xun and his army marched on Beijing in 1917 and proclaimed the restoration of the Qing dynasty with the Xuantong Emperor, who was now eleven years old. The move was highly unpopular, and the reign lasted a mere eleven days. After the restoration collapsed, the country's future looked highly uncertain.

Against this outlook, war had broken out in Europe, and the Treaty of Geneva had been signed. The Chinese delegation was sent by the recently inaugurated Emperor Yuan Shikai and included Feng Guozhang and Duan Qirui. Although China attended the conference, it could not sign the resultant treaty as the delegation could not arrive at an agreement on whether to do so, and because China was not involved in the war, it had no pressing reason to do so. As time went by, ICSD signatories witnessed growing peace, security, and prosperity, while China continued to witness more political and military struggles. The regional armies had devolved into armies of warlords fighting each other over control of the central state and their fiefdoms.

Then the ICSD came to China. Tibetan separatists were the first in China to collect signatures and present a plan for a referendum for the ICSD in 1925. The central government had been considering joining the ICSD because it saw how its members had benefited from it. With Tibet demanding a referendum, and the majority of the civilized world in the ICSD, the central government decided to join rather than attempt another futile fight against many enemies. Tibet voted for independence in 1925, and Xinjiang followed in 1924. The northern parts of Inner Mongolia then voted to join Mongolia in 1927. The remnants of the Qing dynasty, and many of the Manchurian generals, retreated to Manchuria and got their independence in 1928, with the now eighteen-year-old Xuantong Emperor restoring the Qing dynasty back in its home province.

The implementation of the ICSD framework in China led to a significant reduction in unrest and armed conflict. The central government became less repressive because it did not want to lose more provinces. The intensity of the opposition to the central government decreased as people realized they could resort to the peaceful vote rather than engage in violence if the situation became unbearable. With the Republic of China continuing in power struggles, Liang Qichao, a prominent and well-respected intellectual and former minister of finance who had long advocated for a constitutional monarchy, began to suggest that the Republic of China might need a nominal imperial head figure. Under the Qing regime, Liang had written:

> I firmly believe that the republican institutions of the United States and France are not suited to conditions in China. If we want to keep the social order, we should follow the English model and keep the emperor as a nominal ruler. The greatest advantage here is that we can nominally maintain our imperial traditions. In our country, we have Duke Yansheng, a descendant of Confucius and the most influential and respectable person in our country. If we have no other choice, we should invite him to become emperor.[126]

---

126 Jana S. Rošker and Nataša Vampelj Suhadolnik, eds. *Modernisation of Chinese Culture: Continuity and Change* (Cambridge Scholars Publishing, 2013), 74.

Duke Yansheng was Kong Lingyi, the seventy-sixth-generation descendant of Confucius. When Lingyi first proposed the idea in 1912, it was not met with enthusiasm because of the fear that it would allow too much religious influence on the government, and this at a time when secular democratic ideals were popular among the revolutionaries determined to overthrow the empire. But by 1929, most of China's non-Confucian minorities had seceded, so there was a lot less opposition and fear of overt religious symbolism.

In the last days of the monarchy, opposition to the Qing Empire and its shortcomings became the default support for the republic. But after the political uncertainty, violence, and seditions of the fifteen years that followed the Qing dynasty, a significant proportion of the population had begun to discern a distinction between the problems of the late Qing dynasty and the problems of the monarchy. Many became receptive to the idea of monarchy returning, and Lingyi's choice of Duke Yansheng was becoming increasingly popular as he had no enemies, only the respect of his countrymen.

A popular movement grew across China demanding the installation of Duke Yansheng as emperor, and in 1929, after a mass referendum, he was indeed installed as emperor. Legislative authority would still be held by the parliament, but with the descendant of Confucius as a figurehead, politics was far more cordial. Emperor Yansheng was frugal and wise; his lack of ostentatious displays of wealth played well with his population, and his credibility continued to grow. He wisely chose to stay out of the private affairs of citizens and to give the regions plenty of autonomy. The secessionist movements slowed down significantly in the 1930s, as Yansheng granted more authority to regional governments. China had shrunk since the beginning of the century and shed most of its large minorities, and its provinces were more independent, but it had also become a lot more peaceful and productive, as free trade and capital flows increased investment in the country and raised worker productivity.

The twentieth century was a century of political decentralization in China, as many provinces had developed various degrees of autonomy and independence, while remaining tied to one another through the cultural, historical, and linguistic bonds of the Chinese nation. The century also witnessed a very rapid decentralization of land ownership, as the ICSD framework made land ownership an expensive liability for large feudal landowners who had large land holdings on which landless peasants lived. They were frequently the subjects of secession referenda, and by the 1970s, private governance corporations took charge of large plots of land. The threat was enough for large feudal landowners to give up large plots of land to their peasants to protect the rest of their land.

Living standards in China increased drastically from the 1930s onward. Within forty years, industrialization spread extensively across the country, productivity increased, and the life of the average Chinese citizen was transformed from one of drudgery and subsistence farming to high-productivity industrial work and high living standards. China's population grew throughout the twentieth century, and the population of the territories that constituted the Chinese Empire in 1900 increased from around 450 million to more than 1.5 billion over the course of the century. The average Chinese went from living in a tiny village working the land he doesn't own to a property owner working in a high-productivity industrial job in one of the many large metropolises of the country.

India

The collapse of the Bank of England left an indelible mark on the psyche of the people of India, even though they were thousands of miles away from it. British rule over India had meant the subcontinent's banking system was heavily reliant on the Bank of England, where it had kept a large amount of its reserves. India's richest families and most modern companies were badly impacted, and they became a lot more sympathetic to the growing tide of Indians demanding independence from Britain. But securing signatures and organizing referendums in a place as vast and populous as India was no small feat. No political party or independence movement could present a credible plan for financing a referendum across the entire country, particularly after so many of the country's rich had been ruined and many of the modern businesses had been destroyed. The practical solution was for regional referendums to proceed piecemeal. Bengal was the first province to present a referendum request to the ICSD, and it voted for independence in 1923, securing it with a 65% majority. Other Indian states and territories then proposed their own referenda. Some joined Bengal while others became independent.

The Americas

When the ICSD framework was first negotiated at the Geneva Conference, the Americans present had only thought of it as a solution for the warring tribes of the old world. It had not crossed their mind that it could be deployed in their own country. As modern industrialists who had seen the technological possibilities of the new world and the amazing bounty of industrialization, they had not imagined that American states would want to secede. Yet as soon as they returned to the US, newspapers across the country had begun to discuss the possibility of their states seceding. These discussions were most animated in the American South, where the wounds of the Civil War were still fresh. Yet the intuition of the Americans at the Geneva Conference was correct. Americans were happy being American. The decentralization of money and banking that resulted from the bankruptcy of the Federal Reserve had greatly reduced the size and influence of the federal government and undermined much of the progressive agenda of the previous decades. With the central bank disbanded and the government increasingly unable to borrow to finance its operations, the loose bonds of federalism made the marriage of the forty-eight states of the Union tolerable enough. Secession by any of the states would have restricted its citizens' movement across the other states, which proved to be enough of a motive for all states to remain in the Union until the end of the century. In Canada, on the other hand, Quebec voted for secession in 1921 and became an independent state. Alberta flirted with secession in the 1950s, and in response, Ottawa and the federal government decided to reduce the burden of taxation on Albertan citizens and transfer payments to other provinces. Latin America also witnessed many attempted referenda over the century. None succeeded, but they arguably helped discipline the governments and reduce tax rates.

Africa

In North Africa, the Alawite family continued to rule over Egypt and Sudan after a referendum for independence from Britain in 1921. The Sanusi family organized a referendum to free Libya from Italian control in 1923, and Morocco obtained full independence from the bankrupt French Republic in 1922. Algeria voted against independence from France in the 1920s. A large French population wanted to remain under French rule, and a lot of the Algerians valued the opportunities presented by free travel to France and did not want to give that up. In the 1950s, Algeria voted for independence, but only after agreeing with France to secure French economic interests in Algeria and to continue to allow for students, workers, and merchants to visit France without exorbitant travel fees. The Colony of the Gold Coast voted for independence from British rule in 1931, and the new republican government expelled all British businesses from the country and expropriated them, plunging the country into a severe financial crisis. Within three years, a new referendum reinstituted British colonial rule and brought back British businesses. The experience proved edifying for most decolonization projects in Africa and Asia. Their political independence movements were now sure to make guarantees to foreign capital owners to protect their investments and allow them to continue to operate. A new independence movement in Ghana succeeded in 1949 by explicitly promising to protect foreign investors.

All over Africa and Asia, and for decades to come, independence movements collected signatures, flew them to Switzerland, and referendums were carried out. Rather than carry out violent anti-imperial insurrections, independence movements spent their time and effort educating and informing their countrymen about the benefits of independence and persuading them to sign the petitions and vote in the referenda. The end of colonial rule was orderly, peaceful, and cordial.

PART IV

THE CENTURY OF AFFLUENCE

XVI.

Living Standards

The population of humanity increased significantly in the twentieth century, and its living standards also rose substantially. Around 1 billion people were alive in the year 1800, and over the course of the nineteenth century, the world's population grew by approximately 65% to 1.65 billion people. At the end of the twentieth century, the world's population grew to 8.4 billion people, an astonishing growth of 400%, more than five times the growth rate of the nineteenth century.

The population boom has been attributed to many causes. The collapse in armed conflict in the wake of the Great War reduced fatalities from war and the associated misery and early death they caused. The long stretches of peace in the twentieth century, compared to previous centuries, have allowed for steady population growth. The security of property rights and the ability to save have allowed for secure family formation to be within the reach of more people than ever before. Yet the lion's share of the credit must go to the miracles of the Industrial Revolution. The use of modern fuels to build sanitation infrastructure has

significantly improved the quality of drinking water by preventing it from becoming contaminated with sewage, thereby drastically reducing infant and child
mortality. The spread of hydrocarbon fuels conquered the winters, preventing
deaths from the cold or cold-related illnesses, and the spread of air conditioning
conquered the heat, preventing deaths from heat-related illnesses. The incredible
improvements in food productivity led to the elimination of famines after 1925.
Among these improvements was the development of the Haber-Bosch process
for producing fertilizer, which increased crop yields, significantly improving
nutrition worldwide, reducing mortality, and raising life expectancy. Modern
transportation made food and medicine widely available, and refrigeration made
them last longer. Hospitals proliferated, and medical care became increasingly
available at a higher quality and lower cost worldwide.

Although the world's population has grown throughout the century, the
rate of growth has declined in the second half of the century, primarily due to
rising living standards, increased education, and urbanization. It was a universal phenomenon observed worldwide that, as populations urbanized and as
women became more educated, the fertility rate declined.

Modern readers may struggle to appreciate the significant improvement in
the global standard of living over the twentieth century. It is difficult to imagine how different life was merely a century ago for four interrelated reasons:
the large amount of technological innovations invented and popularized over
the past century, the substantial increase in the abundance of essential goods,
the constant decline in prices of these goods over time, and the exponential
growth in the consumption of modern power resources, particularly hydrocarbon and nuclear fuels. This chapter aims to familiarize the reader with the
extent of the first three powerful trends over the past century by comparing
standards of living and the cost of goods over the same period.

The underlying driver of the economic growth of the twentieth century
was the move from a classical gold standard to a modern gold standard and
the consequent liberation of humanity from the parasitism of government-
protected banking monopolies. With the money supply now corresponding
precisely to physical quantities of gold, the money supply could only grow
at the rate of increase in the supply of gold, which hovered around 1.5-2%

per year. Roughly speaking, this has corresponded to a constant decline in the price of economic goods whose supply increased by more than that annual percentage rate. Since the market selects money precisely for having the lowest supply growth rate among liquid goods, it appreciates against the vast majority of economic goods, which usually become more abundant over time.

It is worth noting that the years 1914 and 1915 were an exception to the overall trend of the century, as prices actually increased drastically during that period. It will sound completely alien to modern readers, who are used to seeing prices only go down, but for these two years, it was common to actually witness the price of goods increase, sometimes very quickly. Freed from the parasitism of banking cartels, the value of currencies constantly increased, reflected in a steady decrease in the prices of almost all goods.

This trend of price decline became apparent under the classical gold standard during the last few decades of the nineteenth century, as industrialization increased productivity and abundance. However, it did not gain momentum and become pronounced until the transition to the modern gold standard in 1916. It was more pronounced under the modern gold standard for two reasons. First, productivity increased more rapidly in the twentieth century as technological advancements and capital accumulation intensified. And second, the modern gold standard was a lot less inflationary than the classical gold standard. Whereas the money supply in the twentieth century was strictly equal to the supply of gold, increasing at no more than 2% per year, in the nineteenth century, it frequently increased at faster rates as banks and central banks began issuing fiduciary media beyond their gold holdings. It is no exaggeration to say that the peace and prosperity of the twentieth century largely depended on this inflation ending. A monetary standard where money is strictly equal to the supply of gold brings forth a world where the only way to acquire wealth is by producing goods that other members of society deem valuable enough to part with their money. Everyone in this world must focus on production in the service of others, or experience increasing poverty. The scarcity of money incentivizes the production of everything else in increasing abundance. On the other hand, a world in which banks can create money beyond the quantity of gold in their coffers is a world in which a select cabal can acquire goods and services without having to offer society anything of value in return. Such a world results in a significant portion of society's effort being devoted to securing the ability to print money rather than creating valuable products.

Over the past century, we have experienced three variations on this theme. Before 1914, banks and central banks could create money up to a certain point, but their ability to do so was limited by the redemption of gold, which ensured they could not increase the supply too quickly. The result was an increase in standards of living and the quality of life, but also a growth in the power and influence of banks and governments, which drove militarism and wars. In 1914 and 1915, with gold redemption suspended, banks and central banks could create money more prolifically. The result was an infinite growth in the wealth and power of governments and banks, resulting in mass carnage and the death of millions of soldiers and civilians. Being a productive person became far less rewarding in such a world, as inflation and government controls confiscated the benefits of labor. After 1916, on a modern gold standard, where banks could not produce any amount of financial instruments beyond their gold holdings, the benefits of economic production flowed to the world's producers, and not to parasites. The result was a continuous increase in wealth and peace.

Economic growth in this world can best be discerned by looking at the declining prices for almost every single economic good and service, as measured in terms of gold, the money chosen by the market precisely for its resistance to debasement and devaluation. One could say that gold's value has increased over the century, but another way of understanding economic growth is that the value of almost everything else has declined as it has become more abundant.

The two decades following the war saw a significant increase in demand for gold, primarily due to the demonetization of government money and silver. However, by the 1940s, after fiat and silver were fully demonetized and the entire planet had largely adopted gold as a form of money, demand for gold stabilized relatively and only grew to the extent that demand for cash balances increased. What followed was an unprecedented period of monetary clarity and stability. In general, comparing the change in the abundance of economic goods relative to the change in the abundance of gold gives us a good indication of how these goods' prices fared.

A simple comparison of the change in the stockpiles of various goods over the past century is indicative of the price reaction and instructive of the extent of improvement in living standards. The total liquid stockpile of gold available today has increased sixfold over the course of the past century, and annual production of gold has risen by roughly the same magnitude. Whereas in 1900, the total gold stockpiles were around 31,614 tons[127], and annual production was 386 tons, in 2000, these numbers had increased to 190,515 tons of total stockpiles and 2,529 tons of annual production. The annual supply growth rate has remained steady at around 1.8%.

The more that a good's supply increased, the more its price declined in terms of gold. Goods whose supply increased at rates lower than 1.8%, gold's annual supply growth rate, would witness their price rise over time. These were, of course, infrequent occurrences and rarely sustainable for long.

The good that became most abundant and cheapest was computing power. Energy came in second place, and industrial goods came in third place. Metals and minerals generally ranked fourth, while food ranked fifth. Human time, as priced through wages, was roughly flat over the course of the century, declining in the first half and rising in the second. Only a few exceptional cases of goods rose in price during this century. The following chapters will discuss the evolution in the abundance and the price of these categories of goods in more detail.

Computing

The good that has declined in price the most over the century must be computing power. Since the invention of the modern computer in 1936 with the Z3, which had a processing power of 3 operations per second, to the current world where we have 400 sextillion ($4x10^{23}$) operations per second, the total

---

127 Figure for 1900 stockpiles estimated by deducting annual production figures from the US Geological Survey for the years 1900 to present from current global stockpiles obtained from the World Gold Council. Data for 200 is slightly higher than real world data to reflect increased exploration and mining as response to increased gold price. See website here: https://www.gold.org/.

processing power available to humanity has grown at around 130% per year. Correspondingly, the price of processing power has declined by around 40% per year, as the Z3 cost around 186 ounces of gold ($3,844) to carry out its three operations per second; the cost of 1 operation per second was $1,282. Today, a basic consumer computer can perform each operation per second at a cost of 1.65 billionths of a dollar ($1.65x10^{-9}).

Digital computing has transformed virtually every aspect of human life in the modern world, significantly increasing productivity. In the nineteenth century, Charles Babbage developed the first computer prototype, an engine capable of calculating polynomial functions. However, computers were too impractical until electricity was introduced into their operation in the twentieth century, which increased their complexity and productivity. In 1936, the German engineer Konrad Zuse constructed what is regarded as the first programmable computer, the Z3. The instructions that operated the early computer machines were coded into them through electric circuits or punch cards. Getting an early computer machine to perform a slightly different function usually required adjustments to its hardware and processes, as well as elaborate rewiring. By the late 1930s, it became possible to store these instructions in computers electronically with the Electronic Numerical Integrator and Computer (ENIAC). In the 1940s and 1950s, computer programming languages were developed that enabled programs to be specified in a more abstract manner, independent of the computer's architecture. The development of these standardized programming languages, along with the growing number of people worldwide who could read, understand, and write them, brought about an entirely new type of economic good with profoundly transformative implications.

Software can be thought of as the purest form of technological good. It consists entirely of data, but it significantly increases productivity. It can be communicated around the world very quickly with modern communication tools, and it is non-rival and non-scarce. Applying software to an industrial process enables the increased automation of the machine's functions, resulting in reduced human supervision and labor. Software enables the far better organization of resources and supply chains, thereby reducing costs and increasing efficiency. This economic development has had a profound impact on the world over the past seven decades. Today, software —the instructions codified into standard languages that tell machines to perform functions —has invaded every industry in the world. It is impossible to imagine a single avenue of economic production that has not increased its productivity through the use of computers running software.

The consumer experience in computing has changed in a manner no other good has witnessed. The world's first commercial computer, the Z4, the successor to the Z3, was sold to ETH Zurich for 30,000 Swiss francs in 1937. It weighed around 1,000 kilograms and could perform around two operations per second. By 1961, the first personal computer was available for purchase at a cost of $300, weighing no more than 6.4 kilograms, and having a processing power of 500 operations per second, roughly 250 times the processing power of the Z4. At the time of writing in 2000, a high-end personal computer like the Lenovo X1 weighs no more than half a kilogram and comes with a processing power of around a trillion operations per second. It costs no more than $40.

However, the computing revolution was not limited to home computers. By the 1970s, mobile phones had been invented and became available on the market. What started as a heavy, unreliable, and highly expensive machine, only available to the richest and busiest businessmen of the world, would soon become a lot more powerful and a lot less expensive. By the 1980s, these cell phones could perform most of the functions of a computer, and they came to be known as smartphones. They carried significant processing power, giving everyone access to enormous computing power wherever they went.

Among the most powerful applications of computers has been the development of network computing, which culminated in the creation of the Internet. What started as a set of protocols for computers to communicate with one another in the 1950s developed into the World Wide Web in the 1970s. This allowed billions of institutional computers, personal computers, and smartphones to connect to one another, opening a whole new world of services and technologies that have now entered every aspect of modern life, revolutionizing communication, media, commerce, transportation, entertainment, and much more. At the time of writing, a smartphone costing just $2 has become an incredibly powerful tool for personal productivity. With its many applications, it can replace dozens of physical devices that would have required expensive physical infrastructure.

Energy and Power

One of the best objective and physical manifestations of the improvement in the quality of life can be discerned from the increase in human production and consumption of energy, in its various forms. The Industrial Revolution arguably began as early as the sixteenth century, but it only started making a real difference in the lives of most people in the nineteenth century. In the twentieth century, it truly changed the world. To understand how, we must begin with some historical context.

In nomadic, pre-agricultural societies, humans used the raw energy of nature to survive. The sun helped them stay warm and grow their food, and running rivers washed their bodies. As humans became more sedentary and settled, they developed the capacity to invest in more powerful, sophisticated, and reliable power sources. The domestication of animals offered us the ability to direct the power of these animals to meet our needs, such as transport and soil tilling. The fat of these animals was used for lighting. Humans were likely to settle near rivers to harness the energy of the running water through watermills, as well as to construct windmills that converted the energy of the wind into usable power. Logging wood provided warmth and allowed for cooking. These sources of energy enhanced the productivity of human labor, and the likelihood of survival increased through the protection they afforded us. Around the middle of the second millennium A.D., humans began to extract and burn coal, which had a higher energy content than wood, allowing us to pack more energy into smaller weights of fuel, thus increasing our productivity. By the nineteenth century, humans had also learned to utilize crude oil and natural gas from Earth for their energy content. The most obvious testament to the incredibly transformative and valuable power these fuels provide is the rapid spread of their utilization around the world over the past two centuries. The levels of productivity afforded to workers who have access to these fuels have made them highly desirable worldwide, resulting in increased standards of living wherever they are available. The twentieth century witnessed the invention of nuclear power, a technology that enables humans to access fuels with a significantly higher energy content per unit of weight than hydrocarbon fuels.

At all points, technological progress would provide power sources that contained a higher energy per unit of mass. Wood contained 16 MJ/kg, whereas coal, a solid hydrocarbon fuel, represented a significant leap forward, with 24 MJ/kg. Liquid hydrocarbon, or oil, has a higher energy density, at 44 MJ/kg, and natural gas is the densest of the hydrocarbons, at 55 MJ/kg. Nuclear power, on the other hand, is in a completely different league, with 3.9 million MJ/kg.

At the beginning of the nineteenth century, the world collectively consumed around 3.56 Petawatt-Hours (PWh) of energy, only 0.083 PWh of which came from hydrocarbons, and the rest came from biomass energy, including wood, food, and animal fodder. By 1870, at the beginning of the classical gold standard era, as the world began to trade with a single currency, economies of scale and the division of labor enabled the growth in the production of hydrocarbon fuels to around 1.53 PWh, constituting approximately a fifth of the total global consumption of 7.1 PWh.

By 1900, the world's consumption had risen to 12.7 PWh, with hydrocarbons constituting 5.94 PWh, or nearly half. The explosion in industrial fuels coincided with the adoption of the classical gold standard, characterized by a 4.4% growth trend in industrial energy consumption (coal, oil, gas, hydroelectric, and nuclear) from 1870 to 1900. As these lines are written in the year 2000, total global energy production from industrial fuels stands at around 444 PWh/ year, approximately 75 times larger than what it was one century ago, continuing the 4.4% annual growth rate. The impact this energy transformation has had on standards of living cannot be understated. Many of the most significant technological breakthroughs and civilizational achievements of the twentieth century were made possible by the widespread adoption of modern hydrocarbon technology, particularly in the first half of the century, when coal-powered plants provided electricity to the vast majority of the world's cities and trains facilitated modern transportation. Gasoline helped introduce modern cars, which replaced horse-drawn carriages and alleviated the world's urban residents from the seemingly eternal stench of horse manure. More than just electricity and transportation, modern hydrocarbons would transform industry through the introduction of an infinite array of petroleum products on which our modern lives rely, including electronic devices, concrete, plastics, and so much more.

Hydrocarbon production not only increased drastically to improve human well-being, but it also allowed for the invention and mass deployment of nuclear power, which became the largest producer of energy for human consumption by the end of the century, even though it only came into existence in the 1940s. On August 6, 1945, the first nuclear power plant was connected to an electric grid in Hiroshima, Japan, with a capacity of 5 MW. At that time, this was not a large plant compared to the dominant coal plants, which could produce hundreds of megawatts, and there was significant skepticism that the sophisticated technological requirements for nuclear power would enable it to replace conventional, tried-and-tested coal power plants. However, the next six decades would witness an explosion in nuclear power generation capacity, as nuclear plants began to proliferate worldwide. The scale of plants increased, reaching around 5 GW by 1990, a 1,000-fold increase from the first plant in Hiroshima in 1945. Global nuclear power production in 2000 reached 222 PWh, accounting for around half of humanity's total power production.

In 1900, almost all of the world's primary industrial energy production came from coal. By 2000, coal's share in the world's primary industrial energy production had declined to only 12.8%, despite rising around fivefold overall. Oil began to rise as a share of energy production with the popularization of the car and airplane in the early twentieth century, and it overtook coal in total energy production around 1945. By 2000, oil represented 21.5% of total energy production, a figure that had risen 540-fold over the century. Gas was slower and later to experience mass adoption than oil, but it overtook coal around 1965. By 2000, gas would constitute 12.7% of total energy production. Hydroelectricity would provide around 3.2% of total energy consumption in 2000, but the lion's share of the world's energy production came from nuclear energy, a remarkable triumph of human engineering in the twentieth century, accounting for a staggering 49.8% of global energy production. This is all the more amazing when one remembers that nuclear energy was first deployed commercially in 1945. In fifty-six years, it grew to produce as much as all the world's other energy sources combined. The last quarter of the century was the veritable nuclear age, as nuclear production capacity increased tenfold.

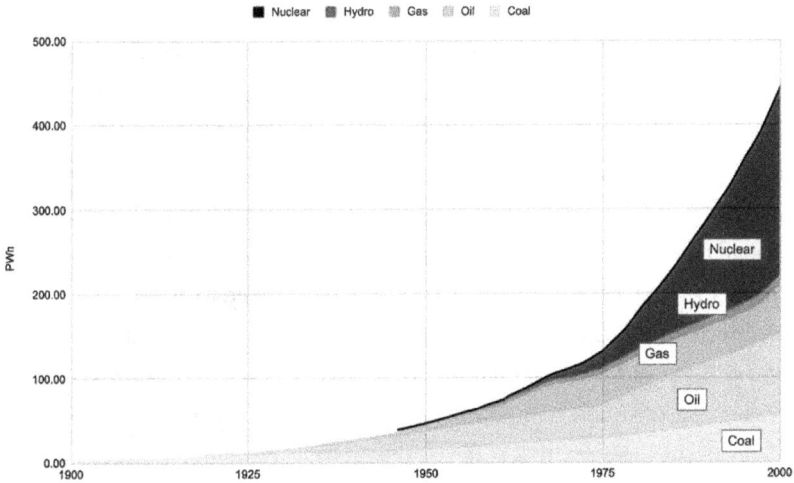

Figure 3: Total energy consumption, PWh

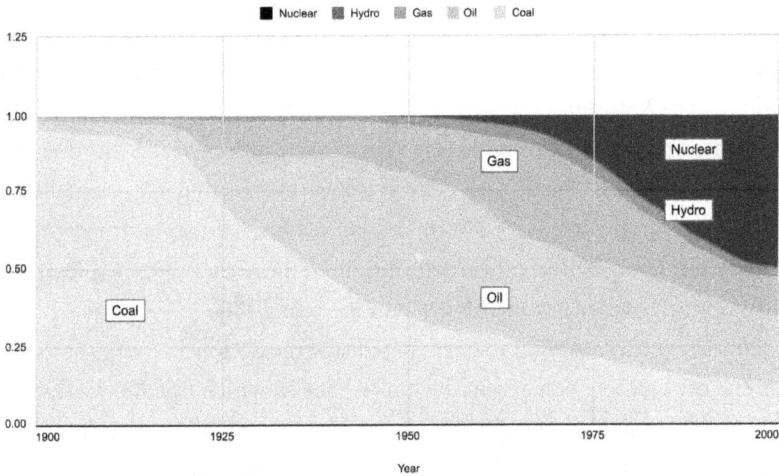

Figure 4: Total energy consumption composition

Whereas the average human consumed around 3.6 MWh every year at the beginning of the century, by the year 2000, that number had gone up to 52.7 MWh per year, a 14.5-fold increase. The picture is even more impressive when one remembers that energy use efficiency also increased during this century, as every step of the energy supply chain became more efficient, meaning that effective energy consumption has risen likely two or three times more than what the raw numbers suggest.

Since the growth in the supply of energy dwarfed the growth in the supply of gold, the price of energy declined drastically during this century. Energy prices are obviously not uniform since they depend on the time and place, but a few consistent data points can give us a good idea about their evolution over time. The price of a ton of coal in 1900 was around $2, but by 2000, it had dropped to $0.9, representing a compound annual decline rate of 0.8%. A barrel of oil in 1900 cost $1.20, but by 2000, it had dropped to $0.64, constituting a compound annual decline rate of 0.63%. In 1900, one thousand cubic feet of gas cost $1, but by the end of the century, the price had declined to $ 0.30, representing an annual compound decline rate of 1.2% per year.

One of the most significant developments of the twentieth century was the electrification of the world. Centuries of theoretical study and practical experimentation with electricity finally began to yield commercial applications in the nineteenth century, with the electric telegraph being the first impactful commercial application. Electrification first began in the Northeastern United States, but, like all highly productive technologies, it quickly spread around the world. In 1882, Thomas Edison established the first electric utility company, using a steam engine to provide electricity to fifty-nine wealthy households in lower Manhattan, New York City. A century later, in 1982, virtually the world's entire population of eight billion people had safe access to very cheap electricity, reliably delivered with an uptime of more than 99.9%. Electricity consumption totalled around 88 PWh in the year 2000.

Another good data point to give us an idea of the decline in energy costs is to examine the cost of electricity in the United States, which in 1900 was around $0.15/kWh, equivalent to 0.00755 ounces of gold per kWh. An ounce of gold would have purchased 133 kWh. By the end of the century, the average price of electricity in the United States was $0.0006/kWh, or 0.00003 oz of gold per kWh, meaning one ounce of gold could purchase around 33,400 kWh. The price of energy thus declined by an annual compound rate of around 5.38%.

In 1900, the average American had to work for one hour to secure one kilowatt-hour (kWh) of electricity. By 2000, the average American worker could secure around 5,000 kWh of electricity with one hour of labor. Even though the nominal wage was roughly the same 500 years apart, the purchasing power in terms of energy had increased enormously.

More than an industrial and technological boon, the abundance and affordability of energy were a phenomenon of great cultural, social, and national significance for society, celebrated with reverence. Humans understood fully well how much better their lives were made because of energy abundance, and they took pride in each landmark achievement. Countries celebrate energy milestones in the same way previous centuries celebrated religious and historical holidays. It was common for countries to hold large festivals to celebrate the completion of full electrification or reaching significant milestones in energy consumption. When China became the first country in the world to cross the 100 ExaJoule per year mark for energy consumption in 1971, it declared a national holiday to celebrate the Power Festival. When the Central African Republic achieved full electrification in 1990, becoming one of the last countries to reach this milestone, it hosted a memorable musical festival that drew thousands of visitors from around the world.

Industry

The twentieth century has witnessed an explosion in technological advancement and innovation that continues to make life better for everyone. With the exception of the Great War in 1914–1915, there were no major wars that claimed large numbers of victims and destroyed economic resources. That meant humanity's intelligence and energy were almost entirely dedicated to constructive, rather than destructive, means. A constantly growing number of innovators had a growing amount of resources in their hands to experiment with new ideas, and the benefits of their innovations spread to the entire planet. The technological miracles of the twentieth century are the dividends of peace, wealth, and free trade facilitated by the modern gold standard, which built upon the gains of the classical gold standard era and its transformative technologies.

A noticeable trend was the proliferation of amateur and hobbyist inventors throughout the twentieth century, in the mold of the Wright brothers. Whereas in the eighteenth century this trend was confined to European aristocracy and some wealthy Americans, in the nineteenth century, with the spread of industrialization, amateur inventors increasingly came from the middle and lower classes. In the twentieth century, as economic prosperity and capital accumulation spread globally, it became an increasingly universal phenomenon. With savings continuing to appreciate and an ever-growing number of people achieving financial security, so many of the world's geniuses had the time and mental clarity to dedicate themselves to solving technological problems. And, just as with the Wright brothers, these genius mavericks so often came up with new inventions against the confident dismissal of expert authority.

This pattern was repeated throughout the twentieth century. Experts, authority figures, laymen, and the press would confidently dismiss the possibility of an innovation, only for random hobbyists to make it happen and then introduce it commercially, changing the world so drastically that the skepticism was completely forgotten and the invention was entirely normalized. Even after airplanes began to fly, skeptics insisted that their limited range and speed would render them impractical for commercial applications beyond those of wealthy, eccentric adventurers. Blériot and the Wright Brothers' Lightning jets put that to rest when they gave the world an alternative to the institutions of monopoly central banking, in the process ending the Great War and allowing millions worldwide to protect their savings from debasement by demonic kings and democratic warlords. The BTC Lightning would also silence skeptics when it crossed the Atlantic for the first time in 1914, albeit with stopovers in Greenland. By 1923, Blériot's engineers had built the Blériot 23, an airplane that could accommodate ten passengers, marking the beginning of the era of commercial passenger transportation. By 1941, commercial airliners could carry 120 passengers on uninterrupted cross-Atlantic flights. Whereas it used to take a week to cross the Atlantic by ship in 1900, it took only nine hours to fly from London to New York with 120 passengers in 1941.

As flight speed continued to increase, aircraft began to experience exponentially rising drag as they approached the speed of sound (Mach 1, about 767 mph or 1,234 km/h), threatening stability and increasing the air pressure on the pilot to the point of fainting. This led aeronautical engineers to believe that the speed of sound was a natural limit to the speed of flying aircraft, prompting them to invent the term "sound barrier" to signify this limit. But just like flight itself and cross-Atlantic flight, this barrier proved no match to the ingenuity and determination of humans. In 1941, a British-French consortium, including BTC and other jet makers, finally built an aircraft capable of breaking the sound barrier. After extensive safety testing, the Concorde made its first commercial flight in 1957.

The history of aviation, and most other technologies, demonstrates how seemingly highly expensive inventions become more affordable as more of them are produced and producers implement various improvements and efficiencies, making them accessible to a broader audience. Every innovation in aviation initially seemed too expensive and impractical for broad adoption, but then geniuses came around to popularize it and make it available to the masses. After commercial aviation was dominated by supersonic flight in the 1970s, private supersonic jets were introduced to the same chorus of skeptics predicting they would never catch on. By the end of the century, the most popular private jet, the Blackbird, had made supersonic flight easily and safely available to the upper and middle classes. Today, there are hundreds of thousands of Blackbirds parked in the neighborhood garages of people worldwide. Their owners can achieve supersonic speeds within thirty minutes of takeoff, at which point they proceed to cross the Atlantic in under three hours. The world has truly become one small village thanks to the Blackbird, which allows people to cross continents for a lunch, concert, or meeting, and return home on the same day.

Along with the decline in the price of energy came a decline in the price of industrial goods, which was less drastic than the decline in the price of processing power and slightly lower than the decline in the cost of energy, as industrial goods continued to improve over time. A kWh is a kWh in the year 1900 or the year 2000, but a car in the year 2000 is vastly superior to a car in the year 1900, so the car didn't decline in price as much as the kWh. The introduction of assembly line production, automation, increased energy, and digitalization all increased the efficiency of industrial production, causing industrial product prices to decline precipitously and making the fruits of industrialization plentiful in every corner of the Earth.

Blériot's Lightning jets were first sold in 1911 for $4,000, and had a top speed of 280 km/h, a range of 1,400 km, and a maximum load of 260 kilograms. Today, the most common personal jet with room for five passengers and a 500-kilogram load, the SR-88 Blackbird, sells for around $2,000 and has a top speed of 3,700 km/h (Mach 3) and a range of 10,000 km. The annual decline in price of a basic private jet was only 0.6%, but that, of course, does not reflect the astonishing increase in performance, reliability, safety, range, and speed.

The car stands as a testament to the Industrial Revolution. Whereas at the start of the century, there were approximately 8,000 cars in the United States and perhaps another 15,000 worldwide, by the end of the century, there were 180 million in the United States and 1.6 billion worldwide. An average car would have sold for around $1,000 in the year 1900, but by the end of the century, an infinitely superior average car would have sold for around $100. The genius of Henry Ford was instrumental in bringing about the mass industrialization of society, as his production model enabled the car to reach every corner of the globe and was subsequently adopted by every other industry worldwide. Ford introduced assembly line mass production, and that was a turning point in human industry. Thanks to it, he was able to introduce the mass-produced Ford Model T at $825 in 1909, making it affordable to the middle class, a prospect that was unthinkable in the late nineteenth century. Its price declined to $550 in 1919, by which time it had improved significantly in terms of its performance, safety, and speed. By 1927, its last year in production, the price had dropped to $480, a 42% decline over the preceding eighteen years, at a compound annual rate of 3%. By 1959, the newer Ford Continental, which was vastly superior to the Model T, sold for $220, representing an average annual decline of 2.7% over five decades. By the year 2000, Ford's Explorer, a much larger, faster, and safer car, sold for only $90, with a century-long compound annual decline rate of approximately 2.4%. Recently, Ford Motor Company announced its intention to rebrand the Explorer as the Model-T in 2009, in celebration of the centennial of the original Model-T. The company has vowed to sell it for $82.5, a tenth of the iconic price Henry Ford charged for the most iconic car in history, the talisman of twentieth-century industrialization.

Similar patterns exist for other industrial goods, such as household appliances and devices. Only a very tiny minority of American and European houses had electric devices at the beginning of the century. Still, by its end, almost every house in the world had a formidable arsenal of refrigerators, electric light bulbs, washing machines, tumble driers, televisions, and food processors, available at a tiny fraction of their cost in 1900. The prices of these devices declined by around 1% to 2% per year on average.

Industrial commodities' abundance also increased over the century, and their prices declined. Copper's annual production in 2000 was more than 50 times larger than it was in 1900, with a compound annual growth rate of 4%. This resulted in its price in gold terms declining by 80% across the century, at an annual price decline rate of 1.6%. Iron production grew by 35 times, corresponding to a compound annual growth rate of 3.7%, and its price decreased by 90%, at an annual price decline rate of 2.3%. Zinc production grew 33-fold, at a compound annual growth rate of 3.6%, and its price declined by 84% in gold terms, or around 1.8% annually. Nickel experienced a 200-fold increase in annual production, with a compound annual growth rate of 5.33%, while its price declined by 60%, corresponding to an annual compound price decline rate of 0.9%. The widespread commercial adoption of the Hall-Héroult method for aluminum production led to an 18,000-fold increase in its production over the century, corresponding to an annual compound growth rate of 10.3% per year, with its price declining 97% in total, or around 3.5% per year. The abundance of industrial metals and raw materials available at our disposal is as unimaginable to our ancestors 100 years ago as the paucity of resources they experienced is unimaginable to most modern-day humans.

Modern industrial development and the mass utilization of hydrocarbon oil have produced a plethora of modern materials that have reshaped life and made it a lot easier for humans. Perhaps most significant has been the development of plastics from hydrocarbon oils. Polystyrene, PVC, polyethylene, and nylon all emerged during this century. By the end of the century, life without them was unimaginable for the majority of humans who relied on them. The ability to produce these substances into the precise shapes and forms, with the exact physical properties, required by the user for various applications, has made life significantly easier for mankind. Mass production of plastics made them very cheap and disposable. In-house incinerators consumed them in ever-growing quantities as their owners constantly replaced them.

The invention of modern stainless steel made rust an increasingly rare occurrence, whereas in the past, it had been the bane of any attempt at building long-term industrial infrastructure. Its production replaced an enormous number of metals by the end of the century, and most people alive today have little understanding of how different and more expensive life was when metals were constantly corroding and requiring expensive maintenance or replacement.

Land and Food

As discussed in Chapter 14, land was utilized more productively in the twentieth century, and its ownership was widely dispersed. As the human population quintupled over the century and industrial capacity went up many multiples, humans expanded the size of inhabited and developed land areas, taming the wilderness and harvesting its bounty. As land became increasingly abundant, its prices generally declined; however, this was not a universal phenomenon. Marginal and newly acquired land for development was typically cheaper year after year, meaning that buying land on the outskirts of a city became increasingly affordable as the city expanded. However, as marginal lands became more central with the development of their outskirts, their prices would stabilize and sometimes increase. Lands in the most desirable and central locations, such as booming cultural hubs and popular cities, increased in price over the century. Land in beautiful geographic locations and in historical areas also continued to rise in price.

Houses were yet another crucial economic good that became more affordable throughout the century. The cost of constructing houses declined as industrial development increased the productivity of the construction industry. For young people looking to purchase a basic house with little regard for location, the price of a house has continuously decreased throughout the century.

In 1900, the median cost of a British house was £600. By the year 2000, it had dropped to £115, an 81% decline in total, at a compound annual decline rate of 1.6% per year. The decline was most pronounced in the first half of the century as the population and demand for gold increased drastically, and even the most desirable land declined in nominal price. In the second half of the century, as population growth slowed down and gold's monetary dominance was complete, the price of land began to rise in the most desirable locations, and average house prices declined at a slower pace.

The story was similar in America. An American who sold a house in the year 1900 and saved his gold or gold-backed instruments for a century in a safe for his great-grandchild would allow that great-grandchild to exchange the sum of money for around five houses of the same size, though likely at less favorable locations. In the pre-modern era, when currencies and banks were monopolized, unreliable, and frequently failed, many people used their homes as a savings account, particularly during periods of economic turmoil, which would cause house prices to rise. However, as money became more reliable throughout the century, this type of demand dissipated, and now people buy houses like they buy durable consumer goods, for the utility they provide. The future resale value became an increasingly irrelevant afterthought. Wealth preservation was far better done with money, which appreciated without requiring expensive and constant maintenance.

With modern transportation, affordable fuels, and the widespread adoption of refrigeration, farming has spread further away from the people who consume it. As cities and suburbs expanded into their surrounding land, farming continued to grow into more areas on cheaper land.

The twentieth century is often remembered for its numerous miraculous technological inventions, but there is a compelling case to be made for it being called the century of meat. Never since the agricultural revolution have humans had such an abundance of meat available for them to eat. As living standards increased, meat consumption rose globally, which has driven the rapid increase in life expectancy, intelligence, and height.

Per capita consumption of red meat has almost tripled over the course of the century, and its price has continuously declined during this period. Given the fivefold increase in human population, this means that meat production increased fifteenfold over the century. In 1900, the world had around 600 million sheep, 450 million cattle, 200 million pigs, and 150 million goats. By the year 2000, these numbers had increased to around 8.5 billion sheep, 6.3 billion cows, 2.7 billion pigs, and 2 billion goats. Divided by world population, the average human went from having 0.38 to 1.01 sheep, from 0.28 to 0.75 cows, from 0.12 to 0.33 pigs, and from 0.09 to 0.25 goats, over the course of the century.

	Cattle	Sheep	Goats	Pigs
1900 Total Livestock	450,000,000	600,000,000	150,000,000	190,000,000
1900 Per Capita	0.28	0.38	0.09	0.12
2000 Total Livestock	6,300,000,000	8,500,000,000	2,000,000,000	2,700,000,000
2000 Per Capita	0.75	1.01	0.25	0.33

Table 2: Growth of livestock

Food also declined in price and increased in abundance, but to a lesser extent than industrial goods, as the natural limits on food production are more binding and less amenable to optimization through mass production than industrial processes, at least not without compromising quality and nutritional content. Beef, lamb, chicken, goat, pork, and fresh produce became significantly more abundant over the century, both in aggregate and per capita. Fresh high-quality food prices declined by around 0.4% to 0.6% per year. Industrial mass-produced foods declined at a much faster pace, reaching 1% or 2% per year. Still, these remained a small fraction of the consumption of most people, particularly as living standards improved and meat intake increased.

The Exceptions

The general decline in prices had only three notable exceptions. The first is gold jewelry. The demonetization of silver at the beginning of the twentieth century and the destruction of paper and credit money unbacked by gold after the Great War led to a sharp, sudden increase in the demand for gold during the years 1915 to 1940, a phenomenon that came to be known as "hypergold-enization." The rate of appreciation slowed down in the rest of the century, but the appreciation never stopped. As productivity increased and all goods became more abundant, gold simply became more valuable. The quantity of gold that people could afford to use in jewelry declined drastically during the first half of the century. Gold jewelry became the ultimate status symbol. Dowries all over the world were paid in physical gold jewelry, but the size of this jewelry has just declined. This decline in the quantity of gold in dowries slowed down in the second half of the century and finally reversed in the last two decades, as population growth slowed and marriage rates declined.

The other product whose price increased is fine art, which is, in many cases, acquired as a status good, for the precise reason that it is expensive and allows the owner to stand out. Throughout the century, art has become more elaborate as artists have spent increasingly longer periods of time creating it to impress high-spending patrons. Whereas modern technology has made creating artwork easier than ever, status competition among art patrons has pushed artists toward ever-more involved artwork, combining the low time preference of the old masters of art with new tools to produce truly astounding masterpieces. Michelangelo spent four years hanging from a ceiling to make the Sistine Chapel, but thanks to modern elevators and painting equipment, modern masters have been able to produce similar chapels in under two years. The result is that hundreds of religious temples around the world are now adorned with decorations that rival the Sistine Chapel in their elaborate and captivating beauty. Art and beautiful ornaments have proliferated massively while becoming more affordable, adorning an increasing number of streets, homes, and buildings worldwide. The human-made environment has become far more beautiful over the course of the last century, and modern cities have become even more beautiful than the most beautiful cities of the past, while also having far better technology, transportation infrastructure, sanitation, and hygiene. Increased productivity, combined with a declining time preference, has resulted in the proliferation of beauty everywhere, along with an increase in the number of jobs in the artistic field. However, the increased abundance has not diminished the desirability of the finest artworks. In fact, it has reinforced it by creating more potential demand through the proliferation of fine artistic taste. The finest and most beautiful artworks sparked large bidding wars among the world's wealthiest people, and artists were rewarded handsomely. No matter how expensive or refined, art remained a questionable investment from a financial standpoint. It was all too common for buyers of expensive art to purchase pieces during bidding wars when the artist was very popular, but then struggle to trigger a similar bidding war when they wished to sell their artwork. The most expensive art was a costly signal of wealth and taste that only the richest and most decadent aristocrats could afford. The third exception to the universal decline of prices was the wage rate, or the price of human time.

Employment

In the aftermath of the Great War, the demonetization of government fiat and silver and the ensuing appreciation of gold led to a decline in prices, which extended to wages. As a result, most people had to accept pay cuts in the first half of the twentieth century to retain their jobs. During that time, as demand for gold rose, the human population also increased rapidly, thanks to new advancements in industry and sanitation, making labor more abundant. The combination of increased demand for gold and a rising supply of labor resulted in a decline in the price of labor in terms of gold. But commodities, food, and industrial products were becoming relatively even more abundant than humans, since more humans were making them, and the technology to make them kept improving, and so their prices declined even more in gold terms. Even as wages declined in terms of gold, they increased in terms of their purchasing power, which made these pay cuts easier for workers to accept. They saw their groceries, houses, and cars decline in price every year, so when given a choice between taking a pay cut or losing their job, they usually opted for the first choice.

However, this trend of declining wages would reverse around the middle of the twentieth century for several reasons. Firstly, after the complete demonetization of government money and silver, the growth in demand for gold slowed down. After acquiring the monetary demand for fiat and silver in the first half of the century and demonetizing them, the new demand for gold was now primarily driven by an increase in people's demand for savings, which represented a smaller marginal increase each year. The value of gold still increased, but not as rapidly as it did in the first half of the century.

Secondly, the world's population growth began to slow down in the 1950s. Increased urbanization, affluence, female education, and the invention of contraceptives all conspired to reduce the incentive for starting families and having kids. Birth rates began to decline in Europe and North America in the 1930s, and the rest of the world soon followed. The population still increased, but at a lower rate than before, dropping under the rate of growth in the supply of gold, 1.8%, in one country after another. Thirdly, increasing affluence led people to value their free time more, causing them to demand higher wages to part with their increasingly precious leisure time. As the basic necessities of food, clothing, and shelter became easily attainable, many people sought meaning and joy in non-material pursuits, thus reducing the supply of labor and raising its price. This is understandable for the economist because human time is our scarcest asset, the one good that is constantly running out, and can never be increased indefinitely. As human wealth increases, the need to work declines, and the demand for leisure and enjoyment rises, necessitating higher wages to coax more work out of workers. This makes human labor unique among all goods and services. As technology advances, it becomes increasingly cheaper to produce goods and extract resources from Earth, resulting in more affordable and improved products. However, as labor productivity increases, humans value their time more and demand higher compensation to give it up for labor.

The combination of these three factors led to nominal wages rising again in the second half of the century. As with seemingly all good economic phenomena, this one started in Switzerland in the 1940s, and by the 1980s, it had practically spread to the entire world. Wages during the twentieth century followed a U-shaped curve. The average American worker earned around $400 per year in 1900, a rate that remained constant until 1915, when it briefly spiked to $600, before declining back to $400 by the summer of 1917. From then on, it continued to decline for four decades, although the decline was faster in the earlier years. It stabilized around $300 for several years in the 1950s, and began to slowly inch upward in the 1960s, finally reclaiming the $500 level in 1994.

Yet, throughout this century, the living standard of average Americans continued to improve, along with their purchasing power, regardless of the rise and fall of their wages, with the exception of the hyperinflation of 1915, which ironically occurred during the sharpest increase in nominal income. This is a very powerful lesson in economics, which people who lived through the hyperinflation understood very well. What matters in money is its purchasing power, and not its quantity. An increase in wages is not beneficial if accompanied by an increase in money supply causing a higher rise in prices. A decline in wages, if accompanied by an increase in purchasing power, is infinitely more desirable.

To get a sense of the improvement of the living standards in the twentieth century, note that the median British home cost around £600 to purchase in the year 1900, while the median wage was around £75. A worker would need eight years' salary to buy a house, and with a savings rate of 25%, it would take the median worker 32 years of saving to purchase the median home. By the year 1950, the median British worker was earning £40, but the median house had declined to £120, which was only three years' wages. At a savings rate of 25%, the average worker now had to work 12 years to buy his own house. By the year 2000, with the median wage equal to £75, the median house cost £115, a little more than a year and a half's wages. With a savings rate of 25%, the average worker could save enough to buy the house outright in just over 6 years. Not reflected in this statistic is the constant improvement in the quality of houses, which have become sturdier, larger, better-equipped, and longer-lasting.

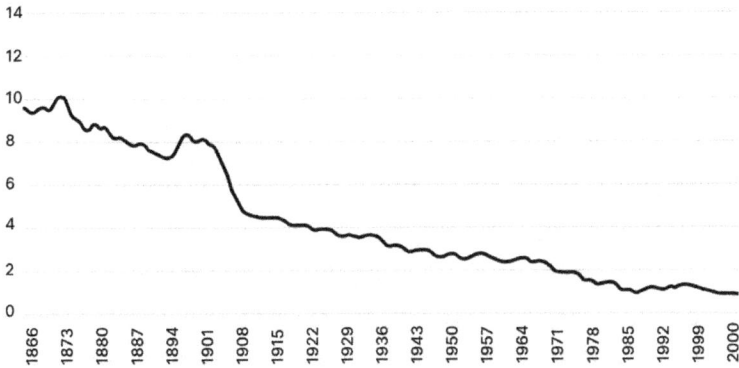

Figure 5: Median home price as a multiple of median income, UK

The increase in the value of money has also led to a large abundance of savings accumulating in the hands of individuals. This is due to two factors: first, the value of money increased in the twentieth century, causing savings to appreciate constantly, thereby increasing the market value of cash balances; and second, money that holds its value and appreciates over time encourages more savings. Surveys indicate that the average American today holds the equivalent of ten years' worth of gold savings. Financial security, in the form of wealth available to its owner on demand, has never been so abundant in human history. This fact can be understood as the result of the increased effectiveness of money, the declining time preference that has driven the process of civilization, and the high productivity of economic activity caused by industrialization.

Concurrently with all these phenomena, technological progress has both increased wealth and been hastened by increasing wealth. The twentieth century was a boon for human creativity and innovation, as the proliferation of savings and wealth provided people with the means and security to freely pursue their creative interests. The financial security, wealth, and free time that in previous centuries were only available to the aristocratic elite of societies became in the twentieth century available to the common man, thanks to the continuous increase in the value of money and its resistance to inflation. The Wright brothers and Blériot were the archetype emulated throughout the twentieth century with increasing frequency and ever-increasing productivity and living standards. The pattern was very common: intelligent, practical men and women ran successful private businesses that served their customers. They accumulated savings, which they used to experiment with new technologies related to their field of work in their spare time. Most of these inventors, of course, failed to invent something new, but most of the inventions of the century came from those who succeeded.

By the end of the twentieth century, securing the basics of survival was attainable for anyone working a regular job. People would begin accumulating savings from birth, as their parents received gold gifts on their behalf. As early as seven, children would start to perform tasks around their neighborhood in return for sums of money, of which the children would usually save a significant chunk for the long-term future. By the age of eighteen, most would have already accumulated substantial savings. Whatever gifts they received at birth would have appreciated significantly by then. In terms of cars and most industrial goods, purchasing power would have roughly doubled over the past eighteen years. In terms of electronic goods, the purchasing power would have increased even more. In terms of food items, the increase would have been around 10%. At the age of eighteen, most people would begin working full-time jobs, and by the age of twenty-four, most of them would have saved enough to move out of their parents' house and buy their own home. Even a single person working a basic job would usually have enough resources to buy a house by the age of twenty-seven.

Mortgage lending ceased to be common by the 1980s, as did all other forms of consumer borrowing. Without a certain degree of monopoly protection that would allow them to use customer deposits to lend to consumers, there was no market demand for lending for consumption. However, with money constantly appreciating, there was also little demand for borrowing for consumption, as saving for large purchases was relatively straightforward for most people. Consumption goods were only acquired from cash holdings, not from borrowing against the future.

With a basic job, a single person or a couple would have no problem affording the essentials of life beyond just housing, including food, cars, and clothing, which constantly declined in prices as productivity increased and money appreciated. Automation, electrification, and digitalization led to a constant decline in prices for everything from food to industrial goods to electronic and digital products. The other side of the coin was the continuous increase in productivity as the least productive and most menial jobs constantly became obsolete.

In conjunction with the improvement in living standards, the twentieth century saw a drastic improvement in working conditions and a positive transformation in the types of jobs people held. The vast majority of the human race had labored in exhausting, dangerous, and unhygienic conditions in 1900, but by 2000, the majority worked in safe and clean environments, while expending little strenuous effort. The improvement in working conditions was the flip side of the increase in income from work. As machines could do more of the grunt work, humans' time was spent controlling these powerful machines, allowing for increasingly higher productivity. The widespread adoption of hydrocarbon fuels in industrial processes in the early part of the century freed many from the back-breaking heavy lifting, pushing, and pulling. It freed humans from having to deal with unpredictable and dangerous beasts and replaced them with far more predictable, reliable, powerful, and long-serving machines. Widespread electrification brought this power into the house and factory floor at a more predictable and controllable intensity. And then software and digitization increased the level of control, leaving very little reason for humans ever to exert themselves. The transformation of work is so profound that by the end of the century, a majority of people will seek physical exertion in their leisure time to stay fit and maintain their physical strength. This was utterly unthinkable at the beginning of the century, when most people were physically exhausted by the end of their workday.

Transportation vividly illustrates this spiral of increased obsolescence and productivity. Millennia ago, the most advanced technology for transporting goods was the human body, which could carry a few dozen kilograms over a few kilometers a day. In the fifteenth century, jobs in transportation consisted of driving and building horse-drawn carriages, which could carry a load of up to 1,000 kilograms over a distance of fifteen kilometers per day. By the eighteenth century, the productivity of workers had increased drastically as they shifted to building trains that could carry far heavier loads over longer distances. By the twentieth century, working in the production of trucks and airplanes meant even higher productivity and faster transportation. At every step along the way, new technologies were adopted for their ability to increase worker productivity, making the job more pleasant, less dangerous, and more rewarding. As we enter the twenty-first century, few people continue to work in driving cars, trains, or ships, as these methods of transportation become increasingly autonomous, and their "drivers" supervise the performance of many such machines from the comfort of central command centers. From carrying dozens of kilograms on his back all day in adverse weather to sitting in a climate-controlled room overseeing the performance data of many machines moving many tons of goods around the world, the average job in transportation has become infinitely more productive and pleasant over time.

The same can be said about construction jobs, which were backbreaking and dangerous for most of history, but have become increasingly safe and easier over the course of the industrialization, electrification, and automation era. By the end of the century, many construction workers were performing their jobs from home, controlling sophisticated machines with remote controllers and monitoring their construction sites through TV screens.

The increasing productivity was not restricted to industrial and digital jobs. All manner of jobs continued to become more productive, as would be expected with increased industrial productivity, not just industrial jobs. Economic value is subjective, after all, and as industrial productivity increases people's wealth and the valuation they place on their time, the non-industrial services they buy also become more valuable, thus increasing the productivity of the person performing them. A haircut in the year 2000 is very similar to a haircut in the year 1900, yet the barber today earns a much higher amount of purchasing power for it than he did 100 years ago. The same can be said about nannies, teachers, physical therapists, and various other service jobs, which have become increasingly commonplace as people's wealth increases and they can afford more specialized personal services.

In 1900, around 75% of humanity worked in agriculture, and approximately two-thirds of them, or half of humanity, were basic subsistence farmers, toiling throughout the year to meet their own food needs or to trade locally in kind. Very little of their produce was sold at markets. Subsistence farming entails limited access to sophisticated markets, limited room for specialization, and minimal benefits from the division of labor. With transportation expensive and restricted, and productivity low, there was little that could be traded, resulting in an impoverished existence. The life of a subsistence farmer is hard, exhausting, and fragile, always one bad harvest, natural disaster, pest infestation, or human attack away from destitution and possibly even starvation. Of the 25% who did not work in farming, most worked in industrial jobs that were not significantly better than subsistence farming, characterized by long hours, dangerous and alien machinery, low pay, and terrible living conditions in the newly crowded cities, which were ill-equipped to handle the large waves of rural migrants.

Looking back at the century, the transformation has been nothing short of a miracle. Modern machinery, transportation, and farming techniques have increased farming productivity, allowing farmers to transition from subsistence farming to farming for trade. This has vastly improved their living standards, reduced the need for large numbers of workers on farms, and made work on the farm safer, more pleasant, and less hazardous. Tractors replaced draft animals; combines, planters, and milking machines multiplied the output of each worker; and irrigation pumps, cold storage, and refrigerated transport cut spoilage and stabilized supply. Synthetic fertilizers, modern crop protection, and controlled environments have raised yields while reducing the land and time required per unit of food. GPS-guided equipment, sensors, and drones enable farmers to apply water and inputs precisely where needed, saving fuel and materials while boosting productivity even further.

Mechanization reduced back-breaking tasks such as plowing, harvesting, and hauling; electrification shifted heavy lifting to motors; and climate-controlled cabs, automated feeding, and mechanized milking reduced exposure to heat, cold, dust, and animal hazards. Better logistics and storage narrowed the gap between harvest and market, easing the pressure of short, exhausting peak seasons. With fewer hours of strenuous manual work and more emphasis on planning, data, and equipment maintenance, farmers gained higher incomes, more stable schedules, and better conditions for family life—all while producing far more food than earlier generations could on the same land.

A similar process took place in the world's industrial workshops. Electrification lets every machine have its own motor, raising speed, precision, and uptime. High-temperature process heat, compressed air, and later petrochemicals enabled the development of new products, ranging from steel alloys to plastics. The assembly line, then CNC machine tools, industrial robotics, and digitally controlled sensors, brought repeatability and tight tolerances at scale. Containerization, forklifts, and automated warehouses shrank logistics costs and cycle times. The result is far higher output per worker and per kilowatt-hour, with quality that would have been impossible in 1900.

Working conditions improved alongside productivity. Electrification eliminated many hazardous, steam-era tasks; guards, interlocks, and emergency stops became standard; and ventilation, dust collection, and climate control reduced exposure to heat, fumes, and noise. Material handling shifted from manual labor to powered hoists and forklifts; safer chemicals and improved firefighting systems reduced catastrophic risks. Automation now takes over the most hazardous or repetitive motions, while ergonomics, PPE, and real-time monitoring reduce injuries. Shorter workweeks, higher real wages, and more skilled roles (maintenance, quality, programming, operations planning) have turned much of industrial labor from brute force to supervision, troubleshooting, and process optimization—safer, more comfortable, and vastly more productive than a century ago.

By the end of the century, most jobs went to services, as machines were left to perform the vast majority of grunt work in factories and farms, and human attention turned to serving the human needs of other humans, and to directing, supervising, and maintaining the machines from afar. Tasks moved from brute force and repetitive motions to planning, analysis, coordination, creative problem-solving, and other forms of work done with brains amplified by tools. Capital and energy abundance and information technology raised output per person, so fewer workers could produce the world's food and manufactured goods while more created and improved services. Networks, data, and software became core inputs; skills like numeracy, communication, and digital fluency became far more important than physical strength. Programming became the most valuable commoditized skill by the end of the century, and programmers increasingly commanded the highest pay.

Women were the big economic winners from this decoupling of earnings from strength. Whereas in past centuries brute physical force was highly correlated to productivity, in the twentieth century, machines could do the hard work, and the advantage men had over women in labor was largely eliminated. Emotional intelligence has become increasingly valuable over the century, as jobs have shifted toward valuing human interaction. Artists produced personalized art pieces, and physical therapists, hairdressers, nannies, artisanal personalized product makers, personal trainers, and life coaches became very common and highly rewarding jobs, as increased economic efficiency continued to allocate labor into ever-more valuable, productive, and pleasant jobs.

Education

The job that became the most common worldwide at the end of the century was teaching. In a world where people could save for the future reliably, time preference declined precipitously, people invested heavily in their progeny, and this meant an insatiable demand for more teachers at all levels. The best boost to student learning comes from decreasing the number of students per teacher, and that turned education into a sponge that always absorbed workers coming from all the infinite number of jobs obsoleted across the century.

Whatever skills a person has, they can always be useful for teaching younger people valuable things, somewhere in their educational journey. With abundant savings, it was very common for people to take time off from their stressful, high-paying careers to spend a few months or years teaching their skills to students. Teaching also served as a safety net for entrepreneurs, who could take risks with their savings and pursue their dreams, knowing they could always fall back on teaching if their risk did not pay off. Governments under the modern gold standard could not create money and, therefore, were severely constrained in their ability to spend. They could not create fake bureaucratic jobs to keep their educated citizens satisfied, and they could not allocate significant resources to building bureaucracies to micromanage the lives of their citizens. Educated citizens had to find their own jobs, and that very often meant teaching.

In 1900, a majority of humans did not receive any formal education. And when formal schooling began to spread around the world, it usually took the form of overcrowded classrooms with dozens of students crammed by age and forced to listen to a single teacher explaining material at a pace close to that of the slowest among the group. Increased prosperity and investment in education have relentlessly improved the process over time, as classrooms have shrunk in size and the relationship between teachers and students has become more personal and productive. Rather than a mechanical reciter of facts to dozens of students, the teacher evolved into a mentor and parent figure, helping those younger think critically about the world and their role in it. The classroom evolved from a crowd facing a blackboard into small seminars, studios, labs, and apprenticeships. Teachers coordinate projects, mentor judgment, and tailor pacing; technicians and tutors, like master craftspeople, supervise workshops where students build, test, and iterate.

Nor was education something purely for the young. As technology advanced, more and more adults sought to acquire new skills and explore new careers, leading to a vibrant and diverse educational industry. In a typical town, the largest employers are schools, training centers, and research workshops, as robots and machines hummed in factories with a fraction of the headcount that once filled them.

Another momentous achievement of the twentieth century was mass literacy. Whereas in 1900, only Sweden, Germany, Scotland, Denmark, and Switzerland had achieved universal literacy, by 2000, virtually all countries had achieved full literacy for people with an IQ of over 75. A prime cause of this incredible achievement was that the Industrial Revolution had made printed material increasingly cheap and ubiquitous worldwide, providing ample material for people to read and practice, and offering a substantial incentive for benefiting from literacy. European and American missionary schools also played a leading role in teaching the world to read, helping English become the world's lingua franca in the process.

Whereas in the nineteenth century, the model of formal schooling was heavily influenced by government control, and education was viewed as the mechanism to produce loyal soldiers for the military and cheap labor for industrialists, the twentieth century's drive toward decentralization and financial sovereignty meant education was a far more individualistic pursuit. Parents chose the curriculum, schools, and teachers that best suited their children's needs. This freedom of choice enabled the discovery of the best and most efficient forms of education and the most effective curricula for various purposes, ultimately shaping the evolution of education toward a smaller student-to-teacher ratio. Academic research, as well as the free competitive market in education, had both pointed toward increasing the number of teachers per student as the most important determinant of student learning and achievement. A century of education research has shown that the most effective intervention in childhood education, and the best way to increase educational attainment, is the reduction of the number of students per teacher, with one-on-one tutoring being the gold standard for educational attainment. As standards of living increased and parents could afford to pay more for their children's education, the number of students per teacher worldwide continued to decline. Schools focused on increasing the hiring of teachers and reducing the size of classrooms. The best, most expensive, and exclusive schools had one teacher per student.

Looking back at the twentieth century, it is no wonder that many have taken to calling it the century of the teacher. Teaching is the world's most common occupation today, and its numbers have increased continuously over the century. It continues to be the one field of business most capable of offering opportunities to new workers. There are always more children looking to get an education, and there is always room for improvement in outcomes via reducing the number of students per teacher. As productivity in other fields increases thanks to automation and capital accumulation, more workers are freed to focus on education, which continues to offer opportunities for a decent income because it is one industry where there will always be a relatively high return on human interaction and personal supervision.

Work in education acted as a professional safety net for workers. In a world where technology is constantly obsoleting jobs by replacing them with high-productivity machinery, every laid-off worker could always find a decently rewarding opportunity in education. Literacy was almost universal, and any literate adult could teach children to read. Numeracy was also nearly universal, so any numerate adult could teach children arithmetic. The more competent the individual, the older and more intelligent the students he could teach, but some opportunity for teaching existed for almost anyone.

The presence of so much opportunity in the world of education was liberating for most adults. They knew they could take entrepreneurial risks, and if these risks did not pay off, they would have the safety net of a job as a teacher. The job would pay enough and consume little time, allowing the teacher to either plot their next foray into entrepreneurship or train for a different career.

Whereas educational curricula were becoming increasingly standardized and centralized at the end of the nineteenth century, there was now a markedly increased diversity of approaches to education. The free nature of the educational industry also created a competitive dynamic that helped stimulate the development of the best curricula for students. The result was a flourishing of thousands of methods varying across time, countries, and fields of interest. With autonomy to decide their curricula, schools could pursue subjects that would be most financially rewarding for their students.

In an alternative universe where governments continued to monopolize money and banking, one can only imagine how much more power they would have had to shape the education industry and how much worse education would have been. With increased government spending and credit creation monopoly, one can imagine how many of the world's teachers today would have been working in make-work bureaucratic jobs in a bloated public sector—or in fake jobs in heavily subsidized or credit-favored private companies, protected from market competition. Instead of a world with hundreds of millions of teachers, we could have been living in a world of hundreds of millions of fake fiat jobs subsidized by the government, with most students crammed into crowded classrooms of 20, 30, or even 40 students.

Formal schooling became increasingly popular throughout the century. By the end of the century, close to 70% of the world's eighteen-year-olds had completed twelve years of formal education. Around 96% of the population had received formal schooling at any grade level, and around 20% of people dropped out of school in their last three years to pursue a vocational career.

Higher education also experienced significant growth in the twentieth century, with nearly 10% of adults choosing to pursue university education after completing their secondary education. Universities primarily cater to two types of students: those interested in studying highly technical fields, such as medicine, accounting, and law, and those interested in pursuing experimental and theoretical sciences, humanities, and various intellectual pursuits under the guidance of highly specialized experts in their field. For the majority of adults, learning usually came through apprenticeships, which most people would begin during high school. The growing specialization of production required increasingly specialized workers, making it profitable to enter the workforce early to acquire practical experience. The huge number of jobs in engineering and industry relied almost entirely on school graduates entering the workplace and learning on the job. In addition to high school graduates, universities attracted professional adults seeking to learn about topics they found intellectually stimulating. It was increasingly common to find professionals in fields such as engineering, industry, law, medicine, and accounting enrolling in courses to study humanities, languages, history, science, and many other fields of knowledge.

Economics

A book on economic history must make some mention of the development of academic economics through the concerned economic period, even though such an inclusion may overstate the extent of the importance of academic economics on political and economic development in that century. Whereas today, academic economics is a very popular topic of study for students and laymen, it has grown to play an increasingly marginal role in influencing political developments over the century, thanks to the predominant economically liberal market order, which forces governments to run like efficient businesses and makes it prohibitively dangerous for them to engage in primitive inflationist sophistry. Until the period of the Great War, it was common for governments to seek the advice of economists who supported inflationary measures, as such measures would be highly lucrative for the government. Coin clipping, credit expansion, and profligate borrowing were all popular ideas among court economists in the times of statist monetary monopoly. But with the triumph of a free market in money, the fortunes of inflationist economists went the way of the fortunes of inflationist governments.

The high watermark of the profession's influence came during the Great War, when Ludwig von Mises, Luigi Einaudi, Walter Eucken, and several liberal economists from across the world contributed the intellectual firepower to make the case for free trade, monetary responsibility, and the right to self-determination. Their arguments had a profound impact on humanity, influencing the direction of the Treaty of Geneva and the postwar world order. With governments increasingly accountable and responsive to the needs of their citizens in the postwar order, they had little use for the insights of theoretical economists. They focused on hiring accounting and management experts. Free trade, free market economics, and the right to self-determination severely limited the courses of action available to governments, centering on fiscal responsibility and limited interventionism.

Academic economics in the twentieth century has played the role of the disinterested analyst (rather than the active protagonist) of the functioning of a market economy, economic developments, and governmental evolution. With the duties of government increasingly being provided by voluntary forms of organization, the majority of economists' contributions to the world came through their work in private companies.

The theoretical framework for understanding economic questions in the twentieth century was shaped initially by the work of Carl Menger, who wrote *Principles of Economics* in 1871, and who had a significant impact on the development of the field worldwide. The early twentieth century witnessed the growing adoption of the more modern textbook by the same name, written by Frank Fetter in 1904, who was the first to explain interest rates as a function of time preference. Mises' *Theory of Money and Credit* became the definitive tract on monetary economics after the Great War for identifying the dangers of inflationary credit expansion. In 1949, Mises also wrote *Human Action*, which introduced and formalized the praxeological approach to economics and soon became the primary economic textbook of the mid-century. Murray Rothbard's *Man and Economy* published in 1962, built on Mises' book and modernized it, becoming the leading global textbook for economics in the late twentieth century.

Although most twentieth-century academic economists adhered to a causal realist approach grounded in human action and the attendant conclusions in favor of individual economic autonomy, several fringe elements continued to promote primitive inflationist ideas. While occasionally growing in appeal to populations tricked into believing they could just vote their way into more prosperity by letting their government increase the money supply, these delusional manias were invariably short-lived. As soon as governments began to engage in inflationary policies, their currencies would repel holders and lose value very quickly. The early twentieth-century attempts to destroy enemy societies using foreign agents regurgitating Marxist clichés left behind some stragglers who believed in the economic fantasy ideas of inflation and government-decreed wages, prices, interest, and rent. Various inflationist cranks, such as Wassily Leontief, Oskar Lange, Irving Fisher, and Harold Laski, witnessed a brief rise in their popularity as they marketed inflationist ideas. However, they soon found themselves the object of widespread derision when their ideas began to be implemented, with predictably disastrous consequences. Universities that hired them would witness their credibility disappear.

XVII.

Twentieth Century Infrastructure

The Twentieth Century City

Another remarkable trend of the twentieth century was the continued lengthening of the process of capital production. As money offered citizens the ability to save for the future reliably, their discounting of the future continued to decline. As a result, individual future discounting rates fell as well, which made the future a lot more valuable. This made it more common for individuals, businesses, and governments to forge long-term plans. It became common to witness investment in large projects that would not pay off the initial investment for twenty or thirty years, and which were expected to last for centuries. The infrastructure of urban areas exemplified this, as did new independent cities, which were built entirely from scratch. More generally, this was reflected in architecture worldwide, where engineers increasingly used the most reliable and expensive materials and technologies to build for the long term.

The automobile transformed the shape of the modern city and modern infrastructure, optimizing it for fast transportation, allowing increasingly larger numbers of people to live within driving distance from one another, boosting the extent of these markets, and allowing for more division of la-bor and higher productivity. A city can best be understood as a labor market; the larger the number of people living together in one market, the more they can trade with one another, the larger the extent of that market, and the more economic opportunities exist. Whereas in the 1940s, the reliance on cars had begun to result in increasingly heavy traffic jams on roads, slowing people down and defeating the purpose of having a car, the development of cities changed dramatically to accommodate cars and allow them to move quickly. Initially, tunnels and bridges were added individually to critical and congested junctions to facilitate faster movement. More of the driving and parking in crowded urban areas took place in a haphazard collection of tunnels and underground parking lots. But with large amounts of energy available for construction, along with advanced and powerful modern machinery, and the foresight fostered by a low time preference, urban areas began to be devel-oped in layers and optimized for fast movement. City centers would typically have three layers: a ground layer for pedestrians, and two underground layers for cars. Building these layers from the start would reduce travel speeds across cities while avoiding the need for constant rebuilding of tunnels, bridges, and expanded highways. The higher cost of building a city in three layers would be more than offset by the reduced travel time and reconstruction and expansion costs. It was an expensive long-term investment that was only possible thanks to the declining time preference of society.

The two levels of underground parking in these buildings would be con-nected to two layers of underground streets, plus the ground level (only accessible on foot). Rather than a haphazard collection of tunnels, bridges, and extensive underground and overground parking, with interminable de-lays as cars move up and down, layered cities optimized space by separating pedestrians from cars. The ground level returned to its pre-car pleasantness and safety, as the enormous areas used for roads and parking spots were re-claimed for pedestrians, parks, play areas, coffee shops, and communal spaces. The underground layers were pedestrian-free, and with two layers traveling in opposite directions, cars could move around quickly with little impediment. Every building had two layers of underground parking, meaning cars would enter the building from the underground layer and passengers would enter the building by elevator. Outside of the most crowded areas, cars could drive on overground roads and highways. By standardizing three layers across the most congested streets and buildings, traffic jams were almost eliminated, and transportation became much faster. City spaces were reclaimed by pedestrians, reviving community. This required enormous amounts of energy expenditure to build, but once built, drivers had only to spend the last few minutes of their commute underground, instead of spending far more time in a combination of overground and underground roads and parking spots. The wonders of energy abundance resolved the conflict between pedestrians and cars in a way that benefited both, making cities safe for pedestrians while allowing cars to move about quickly and uninterrupted.

Helping contribute to the restructuring of cities at human scale was the extensive network of underground physical infrastructure for transportation of goods and essentials. Alongside cars, more goods of modern society began to travel on dedicated modern underground infrastructure. Water, sewage, electricity, gasoline, natural gas, and physical mail all had their dedicated pipes and wires running underground, freeing up overground space and allowing citizens to acquire or dispose of them from the safety of their homes, automatically, without taking up precious overground space or crowding roads with trucks. The treatment of sewage, in particular, was hugely beneficial in reducing illnesses and child mortality, as well as increasing life expectancy.

In the 1960s, modern domestic trash incinerators allowed houses to destroy their garbage at home without having to physically remove it. Thanks to the growing abundance of high-power energy resources and the affordability of modern machinery, it has become economical to build closet-sized incinerators in homes to burn trash and convert it into small amounts of ash, without producing any dirty effluence. Rather than an extensive and expensive network of trucks collecting trash from homes, trash was disposed of where it was generated.

Another major invention of the twentieth century was air conditioning, which made modern life and industry possible in most of the tropical and subtropical regions of the world. Invented by Willis Carrier in 1901, air conditioning was first made available in mass-produced commercial units in the

1920s, and its adoption grew worldwide starting in the 1940s. Air conditioning was instrumental in the development and increased population of the American South, particularly in states such as Florida, Alabama, Louisiana, Texas, Arizona, New Mexico, and Southern California. America's population rapidly shifted south when summers there became tolerable. Air conditioning also played an important role in the economic and population boom of Central America, South America, the Middle East, the Sahara, and Southeast Asia. By the 1990s, outdoor air conditioning units had begun to make outdoor areas tolerable in the heat. Stadiums, parks, coffee shops, and even private residences began to employ these large and powerful units to make their climate tolerable. Although very expensive and consuming a great deal of energy, these units drastically improved the lives of people who had to spend months outdoors in the world's hottest regions.

Canals

A major landmark in infrastructure development in the twentieth century was the development and expansion of water canals. By far the most impressive engineering achievement of the twentieth century was the completion of the Great Silk River, which connected Europe's waterways to China's, tracing the ancient Silk Road route, allowing for extensive trade connections between Europe and East Asia. This astonishing feat of engineering transformed the ancient, snail-paced Silk Road, where camels and horses struggled under the onslaught of nature, into an aquatic superhighway, and it remains the most awe-inspiring testament to human ingenuity and the wonders humans can achieve through peaceful cooperation and trade. Rather than waste our wealth and brightest minds in the senseless slaughter of war, humanity focused them on opening up the Asian heartland to maritime trade, forever transforming geography, politics, economics, and culture, allowing large container ships to sail all the way from the Pacific Ocean to the Atlantic Ocean, passing through deserts made to bloom with artificial rivers, frozen subarctic rivers heated open with nuclear reactors, water tunnels carved through mountains, and countless lock systems rising and descending more than a kilometer.

Completed in 1994 at enormous expense with the labor of millions of workers and engineers from more than 80 nations, this audacious marvel of Engineering, dubbed the Wonder of the Century. The foundation of this idea was born in 1958, when construction began on the 700-kilometer Eurasian Canal to connect the Black Sea and the Caspian Sea, through the Kuma-Manych Depression, the natural boundary between Europe and Asia. The Canal obsoleted the need for trade to flow through the Volga-Don Canal, which was previously the only connection of the Caspian Sea to the world's waterways, connecting the Volga river, which flowed into the Caspian Sea, with the Don River, which connected to the Black Sea, and from there to the Mediterranean and the Suez or Gibraltar to the rest of the world. Constructed in 1933, the Volga-Don Canal had a limited capacity of only 10-15 million tons of cargo annually. However, the Eurasian Canal increased that capacity tenfold when it was completed in 1964. The canal had a profound impact on the countries of the Caspian Sea basin, sparking a significant economic and population boom in that region, which had previously relied on expensive terrestrial shipping over mountainous roads. The Kazakh Caspian port city of Aktau quickly grew from a small uranium mining town into a major metropolis as it exported the agricultural, energy, mineral, and industrial bounty of the Caucasus to the world, via the Eurasian Canal, the Black Sea, the Turkish Straits, the Mediterranean, and the rest of the world's ports.

The Eurasian Canal was an impressive feat of engineering, but it would soon pale in comparison to the titanic undertaking it inspired and facilitated in the subsequent decades. As Central Asia blossomed thanks to the Eurasian Canal, its economic and population growth increased demand for trade with the industrial superpower of East Asia. This trade was expensive, as it had to either go overland through the mountains and deserts of the Silk Road or through the treacherous Indian Ocean and the increasingly expensive and crowded Malacca Strait, the Suez Canal, the Turkish Straits, and the Eurasian Canal. In 1971, a consortium of 14 Chinese, Russian, Kazakh, Turkish, and Bessarabian construction and investment companies announced plans for the Great Silk River, to global astonishment and skepticism. Here was mankind at its most audacious, radically reimagining the geography of the planet's largest continent with a feat of construction that would surpass everything human-ity ever constructed, from Egypt's pyramids to Europe's cathedrals, to China's Great Wall.

In 1972, work began on the infrastructure that would connect the Caspian Sea with the Huang He (the Yellow River) in China. With the completion of this project, a large megaship in the Pacific Ocean could sail through the East China Sea to the Yellow Sea and the Bohai Bay, where it would enter the Yellow River close to the world's largest seaport, Tianjin. The Yellow River required transformation from a fickle silt-laden waterway into a reliable trans-oceanic highway. Chinese and international engineers accomplished this miracle through an intricate network of large settling basins where the river's notorious yellow mud—the gift and curse of millennia—was systematically filtered and diverted. Revolutionary bypass channels, lined with gleaming white concrete and equipped with massive pumps powered by nuclear reac-tors, maintained a constant water level year-round. The river that had changed course dozens of times throughout history was finally tamed, with more than half of its 5,500-kilometer length carved in concrete stone.

On the Yellow River's route, a modern shipping container would pass by the basin containing the homes of more than 150 million people, as well as the major Chinese ports like Jinan, Zhengzhou, Baotou, and Lanzhou, the west-ernmost major port on the Yellow River. From Lanzhou, the vessel enters the most miraculous segment of the journey, the 1,200-kilometer Hexi Corridor Canal along the ancient Silk Road that connected eastern China to its west-ern parts and the rest of the world. A giant and intricate network of pipes had been laid from Siberia to the Gansu province, bringing the water from melted glaciers to flood the new canal that was dug to ensure steady water levels year-round, and to fill many oases along the path of the canal, around which dozens of new towns and cities sprung, making the Gobi desert bloom, and trans-forming the economies and demographics of the hitherto scarcely-populated Gansu and Qinhai provinces.

The Hexi Corridor Canal would terminate at Ürümqi in Xinjiang, the an-cient Muslim city transformed into a booming metropolis and international port. From there, the trans-continental vessel would enter the Irtysh River, and begin its 3,000 kilometer northward downstream journey through Kazakhstan, into Russia, where it sails to the Tobol River at Tobolsk and begins its southward upstream journey for 800 kilometers, wherein it would join the Uy River and continue for another 400 kilometers, before arriving at the most breathtaking part of the journey, which in its first decade attracted more sightseeing boats than shipping vessels. A 50-kilometer tunnel canal was carved into the granite of the Ural mountains to allow ships to cross from the Uy River to the Ural River, and from Asia to Europe. Vessels would disappear into the earth itself through this aquatic cathedral, lined with polished marble that gleamed in the tunnel's eternal artificial daylight, featuring the world's most ambitious lock system. They would rise 700 meters through a series of enormous locks, before emerging in the Old Continent, to sail into the Ural River, where they would continue for another 2,000 kilometers downstream through Russia and Kazakhstan before entering the Caspian Sea at Atyrau, which would become a regional hub of the oil, coal, and gas industry. After a brief sojourn through the Caspian Sea, the ship enters the 700-kilometer Eurasian Canal near Artezian, emerging at the Azov Sea, near Rostov, from where it would reach the Black Sea through the Kerch Strait. From the Black Sea, the Mediterranean beckoned through the Turkish straits. All of Europe's major riverways were available to our vessel, as the sixty-four-kilometer Danube-Black Sea Canal, completed in 1952, connected the Black Sea with the Danube, which was in turn connected to the Rhine River through the 171-kilometer Rhine-Main-Danube Canal, completed in 1976.

A modern container ship could now complete the entire journey from Tianjin to Rotterdam in just 18 days, its passage marked by flags flying from a hundred nations, speaking dozens of tongues, its cargo holds filled with the products of a planet diverse in its political arrangements and united in peaceful commerce. The journey was four days shorter than a trip between these two destinations passing through the Pacific Ocean and the Mediterranean, but the larger benefit of the Great Silk River was the opening up of the previously landlocked central Asian and western Chinese regions to maritime trade, which magnificently transformed the economies, cultures, and geographies of these regions. Figure 6 shows the whole route of the Great Silk River.

Figure 6: The Silk River

Another impressive canal project of the century was the expansion of the Suez Canal, which was initially built by French colonial administrators, taking ten years to complete by 1869. By connecting the Mediterranean Sea and the Red Sea, navigation between Europe and Asia became significantly faster and cheaper, as it saved vessels from having to circumnavigate Africa on the way. As with many modern technologies, significant breakthroughs were achieved in the nineteenth century; however, the twentieth century took these technologies and astonishingly expanded on them. For instance, the Suez Canal had a depth of eight meters, a maximum loaded ship weight of 5,000 metric tons, and a cross-sectional area for vessels of 304 square meters at its inception. However, the area has continued to be enhanced and expanded throughout the twentieth century, so that by the year 2000, the depth had reached thirty-six meters, the maximum loaded ship weight had risen one hundred-fold to 500,000 tons, and the maximum cross-sectional area for vessels had increased to 3,000 square meters. Today, approximately 700 boats traverse the Suez Canal every day.

Another very important canal was the Panama Canal, which connects the Pacific and Atlantic Oceans. Work on the Panama Canal began in 1881 by the French colonial authorities, but it suffered many setbacks due to malaria ravaging the workers and the hesitance of investors. In 1904, the US government took over the project and finally completed it when the cargo ship SS Ancon became the first ship to cross the Canal on August 15, 1914. With this historical milestone, humanity could navigate from the Atlantic to the Pacific without having to go through the remote and dangerous Drake Passage and the Strait of Magellan at the southern tip of South America. This development was a boon for the residents of the Americas, particularly North Americans, who now had access to global markets at a lower cost. When first constructed, the Panama Canal had only two locks, with a draft of 12.56 meters, a width of 33.53 meters, a length of 320 meters, and a maximum deadweight tonnage of 52,500. But a third set of locks was added in 1939, and the original locks were expanded. The new canal can now handle vessels with a maximum length of 366 meters, a width of 51.25 meters, a draft of 18.3 meters, and a maximum deadweight tonnage of 120,000 tons. Further expansion in the 1960s added three more locks, and in 1992, another two locks were added. The preexisting six locks had their capacity expanded to a length of 400 meters, a draft of 32 meters, a width of 70 meters, and a deadweight tonnage of 500,000. Approximately 300 vessels traverse the Canal daily.

The Bosphorus Canal, long the center of the world's attention and a major factor in the Great War, had suffered from congestion since the 1920s. In the 1950s, after the completion of the Eurasian Canal, the pressure on the Bosphorus necessitated the digging of the new Istanbul Canal, fifty kilometers west of the Bosphorus. This created a new Istanbul island between Europe and Asia. With a capacity of 150 ships a day, this canal doubled the capacity of the Bosphorus.

Other major canal construction projects included the 240-kilometer White Sea to Baltic Canal, completed in 1964, which allowed the isolated Siberian provinces to trade more frequently and at a lower cost with Europe. The 102-kilometer Thai Canal, which was dug across Thailand and completed in 1976, enabled vessels to cross from the Bay of Bengal and the Andaman Sea to the Gulf of Thailand and the South China Sea, drastically reducing congestion around the Strait of Malacca and the Singapore Strait.

Bridges

Another astonishing feat of twentieth-century engineering was the construction of the Bering Bridge, connecting western North America and northeast Asia via six highway lanes and two tracks of high-speed rail, completed in 1982. This was the fanciful dream of nineteenth-century American futurist, explorer, and first governor of the Colorado Territory, William Gilpin, and also the subject of the senior thesis of Joseph Strauss, the man who built 400 bridges, including the Golden Gate Bridge in San Francisco. An American proposal had been tabled to Tsar Nicholas II in 1905, and he granted permission, although he did not fund it. However, the 1905 Russian Revolution put a stop to this project. Whereas nineteenth-century technology prevented these men from seeing their dreams realized, twentieth-century abundance allowed it to happen.

With the enormous growth in population and economy of eastern Russia, China, and Japan, as well as the rapid settlement of the American West, northern Canada, and Alaska, trade and travel across the Pacific skyrocketed. In 1974,

Chinese-American engineer Tung-Yen Lin, a pioneer in standardizing the use of prestressed concrete, presented a proposal for an Intercontinental Peace Bridge across the Bering Strait. A consortium of Chinese, Russian, American, and Canadian developers adopted the plan, raised financing, and began operations in 1978 with the construction of a 2-megawatt nuclear reactor in the small mining town of York on the westernmost part of Alaska, to power the construction and operation of the bridge. The bridge would extend across 85 kilometers from Wales in Alaska to Uelen in Chukotsky, just south of the Arctic Circle, passing over the Diomede Islands, the two tiny islands in the strait separated by 3.8 kilometers. Big Diomede, known as Tomorrow Island, is part of Asia, while small Diomede, known as Yesterday Island, is part of North America. Driving from the Russian side to the American side allowed tourists to quite literally travel back in time, resetting their watches to a full day earlier. Two large casinos were built on the Diomede Islands, and they became popular tourist destinations.

Another significant infrastructural landmark of the century was the construction of the Tricontinental Highway, connecting Europe, Asia, and Africa with high-speed rail and superhighways. The Levantine highway, completed in 1948, was constructed along the Eastern Mediterranean shore, comprising a long stretch of roads and train tracks weaving the entire Levantine coast on ground, on bridges, and underground from Iskenderun to Gaza, creating a large economic boom in the region, and boosting the growth of the seaports of Lattakia, Tartus, Beirut, Haifa, Yafa-Tel Aviv, and Gaza, and the growth and modernization of the economies of Jerusalem, Ramallah, Amman, Damascus, Homs, and Aleppo, which were connected by rail, and from which trains connected to the Arabian hinterland, including Mecca, Medina, and Baghdad. The Levantine Highway also connected to the extensive Anatolian rail and road network at Iskenderun. When the Bosphorus Bridge was constructed in 1973, it became the world's longest suspension bridge, linking the Levant to Europe by road and train. In 1967, a superhighway and fast rail connection was constructed between Gaza and Port Said at the mouth of the Suez Canal, from where it connected to Alexandria and Cairo and the rest of the growing African rail and road network, resulting in a fast rail and road connection of the three continents of the Old World.

On the other side of the Mediterranean, in 1974, the Gibraltar Bridge was constructed between Tarifa in southern Spain and Eddalya in northern Morocco, and, in 1978, a high-speed rail track was added to it. With this network, it became possible to drive or take the train in a round trip around the entirety of the Mediterranean's African, Asian, and European coasts. This became a particularly popular summer-long trip for people from all over the world.

With the Gibraltar Bridge and the Tricontinental Highway, and after the completion of the Bering Bridge in 1982, it became possible to drive by car through every single country on Earth except for Australia, New Zealand, Papua New Guinea, the Philippines, Sri Lanka, Madagascar, Pacific Islands, Cyprus, Malta, Sardinia, Iceland, and the Caribbean islands. A team of three adventurers set off from Cape Town in South Africa in 1982 and accomplished just that in only six weeks: traversing 173 countries across Africa, Europe, and Asia, before crossing the Bering Bridge and driving through every Canadian province and American state, then driving down to Latin America, where they concluded their trip in Ushuaia in Argentina's southern tip.

Desalination

Among the most significant technologies of the twentieth century was the mass deployment of desalination. By the year 2000, more than 120,000 desalination plants were operating across the world, producing over 900 million cubic meters of clean water every day, supplying over three billion people with their water needs. All over the world, deserts and dry areas bloomed through irrigation. Artificial oases were created in deserts worldwide, and grazing animals helped revive the desert soil, making it fertile and lush, and boosting meat production.

Artificial Islands

A momentous and unprecedented technological achievement of the twentieth century was the building of artificial islands in seas and oceans around the world. Desirable real estate remained as the good whose price declined the least over time. There can only be one Manhattan, one Miami, and one Shanghai, most people thought, and property in such highly desirable locations continued to become more expensive over time as people worldwide gained the means to travel to these locations, experience them, and live in them, sparking endless bidding wars. However, with modern technological equipment allowing for the creation of artificial islands, it has become possible to replicate more New Yorks, Miamis, Shanghais, and other cities. Built from scratch with modern infrastructure, these artificial islands were in many ways superior to the original cities they were modeled after, since they were built with modern tech from the ground up, while the old cities had been built with ancient technologies and could not be renovated and modernized without expensive destruction and disruption of life, which was unacceptable to their increasingly affluent residents.

The Mediterranean witnessed the highest concentration of artificial islands in the world, as it was the most desirable location for people to live. Demand in the coastal regions led to significant price increases. Almost every coastal region of the Mediterranean has built artificial islands a few kilometers off its coast and a network of tunnels, bridges, and ferries to facilitate transportation between them and the coast.

By the end of the twentieth century, the planet had new islands whose surface area exceeded 300,000 square kilometers—roughly four times the size of the British Isles. Desalination plants meant these islands could be established anywhere, and the sea's salt water would suffice to meet all their needs. The most ambitious and astonishing of these islands was Atlantis, an enormous constellation of islands built in the middle of the Mid-Atlantic Ridge, south west of the Azores. Construction began on Atlantis in 1978, and by 2000, the islands had grown to a size of 30,000 square kilometers. Its location has developed Atlantis into a global center for transportation, acting as a hub for transit between the two hemispheres. Atlantis also attracts tourism and manufacturing, with an ever-increasing number of migrants moving there, lured by economic opportunity, as well as the lore of old Atlantis.

Digital Money

A fascinating new technological development that has emerged in the last few years of the twentieth century threatens to bring software into the realm of money itself, challenging gold for the monetary role it has held for millennia and the undisputed supremacy it has maintained for close to a century and a half. In 1992, after numerous attempts to invent a digitally native form of money, network engineers finally developed a workable model for digital currency. It was named bitcoin. This technology operates without needing to rely on any trusted third party, taking the decentralized model of money and banking clearance using airplanes to its digital extreme. Any person can use public key cryptography to generate a public address and its corresponding private key.

Airplanes made central banks unable to issue unbacked liabilities by allowing depositors easy access to final global clearance. Software makes final clearance cheaper and faster than even supersonic airplanes, further limiting banks' ability to create unbacked liabilities. Like aviation pioneers a century ago, bitcoin pioneers see their obscure obsession growing to transform the world. Whether it actually does remains a question open to future speculation.

The network currently has thousands of nodes, each of which is able to clear payments between itself and others without resorting to a trusted third party. The most astonishing and interesting thing about this new network is that its native currency is limited in its supply, currently growing at a rate of around 5% per year, but scheduled to continue to decline until the supply stays fixed at twenty-one million coins. The programmers and engineers who use this network insist it will take over from gold eventually, citing its low supply growth rate as a sure-fire way of enriching early adopters. Bitcoin's supply will grow at a rate of 20% over the coming thirty years, whereas gold's supply will double during that time. Should demand for both assets increase at the same rate, bitcoin's value will rise more than gold's value. Knowledge of this fact will likely lead to an increase in demand for bitcoin at a higher rate than demand for gold, thereby enhancing the advantage. Projecting this dynamic into the future, bitcoin enthusiasts argue that it will inevitably lead to bitcoin becoming the largest monetary asset in the world and thus the world's dominant money. Just like its low supply growth rate made gold the world's money, bitcoin is destined to usurp it. Most economists disagree; they see no likelihood of bitcoin's value increasing significantly, as demand for it will remain limited to a niche group of highly technical people, with little sustainable market demand for a new form of money when gold works so well. Bitcoin proponents do not underestimate the first-mover advantage gold has over bitcoin, but they ultimately believe that, as a technology, money will inevitably continue to become faster and more secure, because those who use faster and more secure money will accrue more wealth than those who do not. It may take a long time, they argue, but the continuous advantage of a lower supply growth rate and lower final settlement cost will continue to benefit bitcoin users and grow their wealth at the expense of others. This author leans toward the bitcoiners' side of the debate. The declining supply growth rate of bitcoin means that it is economically rational for anyone to acquire some in case it catches on. This then becomes a self-fulfilling prophecy, which drives more demand for acquiring bitcoin, rewarding holders, and allowing them to become wealthier and thus acquire more bitcoin.

In an ironic twist of fate, a Swiss company by the name of Tether has recently copied bitcoin's timechain structure and used it to create a payment network operating around a digital token named Tether Gold (XAUt), which is backed by physical gold held in Swiss vaults. This technology claims to combine the best of the physical and digital monetary technologies. By utilizing public key cryptography to facilitate decentralized key generation, Tether Gold enables anyone to join the network and conduct very fast international transfers denominated in gold. By using gold to back the XAUt tokens, these decentralized payments can be denominated in the hard and stable anchor of the world's monetary standard. XAUt represents an intriguing third way in a world of competition between digital and physical gold: a digital representation of physical gold. This form of money will help gold compete with bitcoin by allowing for a more secure and decentralized mechanism for gold clearance, but it nonetheless cannot overcome the fundamental advantage bitcoin has over gold, in that its supply is limited. So long as the Earth continues to yield more gold to dilute the existing supply, it seems inevitable to this author that bitcoin will one day dethrone gold.

XVIII.

Twentieth Century Life

A good way to appreciate the transformation of human life in the twentieth century is to examine the life of a middle-class London family across four generations and 100 years. London was the world's leader in industrialization at the turn of the century and has remained at the vanguard of economic and technological development throughout the century.

Snapshot: London 1900

Thomas Smith wakes before dawn in two rented rooms in a subdivided terrace in Bethnal Green. The fire has gone out overnight, and coal is saved for evenings or very cold mornings. Light comes from a candle and a penny-in-the-slot gas meter. He pulls on wool trousers, a cotton shirt, and heavy boots for the six-day week ahead.

Breakfast is strong tea and thick bread, with margarine or a little jam if wages allow. Mary has been up earlier to revive the range and pack his lunch of bread with cheese or cold bacon. Their four children walk to the local school, where they are crammed into cold classrooms of forty students.

Thomas walks a couple of miles to a small furniture works in Shoreditch. Trams and horse buses pass by, but fares add up, so he walks. The streets are muddy and churned by horses. A few crossing-sweepers still work busy corners. Main roads are gas-lit. Electric lighting is appearing in parts of the West End, but most homes still use gas, lamps, or candles.

The shop day starts at 6 a.m. He is on the bench shaping and gluing veneers. Weekdays run about ten hours with a shorter Saturday, roughly fifty-six hours in total. There is a short break at midday. The air smells of glue and sawdust. Guards on saws are minimal, and accidents are common. A missed week's pay can mean arrears on rent or pawned clothing. Thomas finished elementary education before starting work at age 14. He can read and write legibly and has learned to make accurate measurements and perform arithmetic calculations effectively, which serves him well on the job.

Mary's day is its own shift. Water comes from a yard standpipe. The privy is shared with several families. Washday means hauling and heating large tubs of water. With no refrigeration, shopping is a daily task. She buys from local shops and markets, such as Spitalfields, and picks up day-old bread at a discount, trying to save some money for coal. Credit with the shopkeeper and the pawnshop is used too frequently for her liking.

Dinner is bread and potatoes. When money allows, there is herring or a small stew. Gaslight is kept low to save coins. The children read a newspaper together in the evening and learn to write. On better weeks, Thomas visits the pub or the music hall. More often, he attends a friendly society meeting that, for a few pence a week, gives access to a society doctor.

Sundays are a reprieve from the grind, as they go to church in the morning and take a walk in Victoria Park in the afternoon. If wages stretch, there is a proper joint for Sunday dinner. Otherwise, a suet pudding stands in. For minor ailments, the family goes to the chemist. A doctor's fee costs a few shillings, unless covered by a society list, and coverage for wives and children is not always included. Dentistry is limited and usually just means extractions.

Winters are hard. Coal is costly, rooms are damp, and coughs linger in the smoke-laden air. Infant mortality is high, roughly one in six nationally, and worse in the most crowded streets. Life expectancy at birth sits in the high forties, though many who survive childhood reach their sixties. Thomas earns £75 per year, with the household consuming an average of about 2 megawatt-hour of energy monthly, mainly from the large amounts of coal for heating and gas for minimal lighting. Thomas dreams of purchasing his own house, but it would cost him at least 5 years' income, and he cannot even save 10% of his income. Credit for buying a house is practically impossible to come by for someone like him, and even if he got it, he'd have a tough time making the payments. Wages arrive on Saturday. Rent and the coal man are paid first. A day lost to illness or slack orders can tip the budget. Life is orderly, but always vulnerable to shocks, and the margins are narrow.

Snapshot: London 1930

James Smith wakes in a three-bedroom terrace in Hackney, bought with savings and a small building society mortgage. A coal boiler feeds radiators, keeping the house warm overnight. Electric lighting is standard; the local grid connected his neighborhood six years ago. Breakfast is eggs, bacon, toast, and coffee. Their three children walk to the local school, where they sit in classes of 25 students. James walks ten minutes to the electric tram. He reads the morning paper on the ride. He works a six-day, 48-hour week at a radio-components factory in Clerkenwell. Work is steadier than in his father's time. It is not difficult to find work for those willing to do it. Workers often change jobs to raise their pay or shorten their commutes, and they can even afford to take time off between jobs, relying on their savings.

The shop is well-lit and well-ventilated. Semi-automatic lathes and precision jigs raise output. Machine guards and training are required by the firm's liability insurer, which audits the plant and ties premiums to accident rates. James finished his high school education with good grades and could have secured admission to university, but he wanted to work instead so he could save up for a house and enjoy the challenges of a job in a modern factory. His good arithmetic skills made him stand out among his colleagues, and he got good jobs. At 10:30 there is a tea break. The canteen serves a hot lunch at 1:00.

Streets and utilities continue to improve year by year as competing private companies extend electricity, gas, water, and telephone services. Streets are cleaner than they were a generation ago. Motor buses and delivery lorries dominate; electric milk floats serve side streets. Margaret's morning is quicker than her mother's. A cylinder washer, gas hot water, and an electric iron compress washday. After finally buying a refrigerator last year, she now shops twice a week only. Prices are steady and decline slightly every year, making her husband's paycheck stretch a little more. She pays cash and records spending.

Home by 5:45, James eats a roast and vegetables or a meat stew. The radio is on most evenings for news and music. Once a week, they go to the cinema for a talking picture. On Thursdays, James meets his friendly-society savings club; the society contracts doctors and a small hospital. Saturdays are for outings: Hyde Park, a museum, or a bus trip to Epping Forest. The family takes an annual vacation in Brighton or Blackpool by rail. James passed his driving test last year and plans to buy a small car as prices continue to fall.

Medical care emphasizes prevention, sulfa drugs are widely available, and new types of antibiotics are beginning to be used in London. Infant mortality is roughly 1 in 20 to 1 in 25; life expectancy is in the low-to-mid 60s and rising.

James earns £50 per year, lower in nominal terms but with greater purchasing power than his father's generation. Mortgage and bills account for around a quarter of the income, and food for another quarter. Education, clothing, and leisure expenses account for approximately 35% of income. The family saves about 10% of its income in a bank account. James's household consumes approximately 3 megawatt-hours of electricity monthly through electric lighting, appliances, and improved heating systems. The 20% increase over his childhood vastly underestimates the improvement in James's house, because the coal his father's furnace burned was significantly less efficient compared to the electricity he consumes.

James' house cost him £175, or 3.5 years' income, but with the small inheritance he received from his father and the inheritance his wife received from her father appreciating over time, and by regularly saving 15% of his income since he was 16, James managed to pay 40% of the cost of the house upfront and get a mortgage loan guaranteed by his work to cover the rest. Prices are predictable, wages buy more each year, and savings provide a cushion against illnesses, injury, or accidents. The cold misery of James' childhood is a distant memory, and life is spent in the joyful expectation that tomorrow will be better than today, and that James' son, Michael, will have a much better life ahead of him.

Snapshot: London 1965

Michael and Emma Smith live with their two children in a semi-detached house in Southgate. The house has gas central heating with radiators, double-glazed windows, an insulated loft, and reliable hot water all day every day. The kitchen has an electric refrigerator, an automatic washing machine, a microwave oven, and a countertop mixer. There is a color television in the sitting room and a small black-and-white set in the bedroom.

The alarm rings at 6:30. The lights come on instantly; electricity is cheap and steady, thanks to a mix of nuclear and gas-fired stations across London. Emma makes eggs, sausage, bacon, toast, and fresh orange juice and packs hefty lunches for her husband and children.

Michael walks to the Underground, where he uses a magnetic farecard at the gate. Trains are fast, clean, and frequent; the cross-city electric trains tie suburban lines together without the old bottlenecks. Stations have escalators, clear signage, and platform indicators that show the next three arrivals. The pavements are clean, and traffic flows better than a generation ago because horses are gone and junctions are signalled.

Michael is a production planner at an electronics firm near Holborn. The office features direct-dial telephones, photocopiers, a fax machine, and a room of microcomputer workstations connected to the company network. He checks overnight orders, loads a spreadsheet, and adjusts the week's run of power supplies. Component data sit on a shared drive; purchase orders go out by telex and fax. The plant floor is bright, ventilated, and quiet compared with his father's day. Insurer audits ensure the implementation of machine guards, sensors, and lockout procedures. Injury rates are low, and bonuses are tied to uptime rather than sheer output.

The firm runs a five-day, 40-hour week with flexitime. There is coffee at 10:30 and a canteen lunch at 1:00. Michael gets three weeks of vacation annually, and he prefers to take them in the colder months so he can take the family to warm Mediterranean destinations.

Emma teaches part-time at a local primary school and spends two afternoons a week at home. Household work is lighter than her mother's. The washing machine runs while she marks exercise books. The dishwasher handles the breakfast plates. She keeps a ledger of spending on a home computer in the study and reconciles it monthly to a gold-backed savings account. She shops after school on two days in a large supermarket that has everything she needs.

The children's school day runs from 8:45 to 3:30. Each class has no more than 12 children. They use simple programmable calculators and spend time in a library with tape and record players for language work. The family's mutual society contracts the local surgery. Routine checks and dental care are scheduled with reminders. Clinics have X-ray and early CT scanners; antibiotics and early antivirals are widely available. Infant mortality is around 1 in 60, and life expectancy is in the late seventies.

Michael is home before 6:00. Supper is usually roast meat, fish, or chicken with potatoes and salad, but Emma has started to learn exotic Italian, Spanish, Indian, and East Asian dishes from her TV, and is taking advantage of the many unpronounceable new types of produce from far corners of the world showing up on her supermarket shelves. After dinner, the children do homework at the table. Emma helps with reading while Michael checks a maths assignment on a pocket calculator. At 7:30, they watch the news in color, then a documentary or a football highlights programme. On Wednesdays, Michael attends his friendly-society meeting, which combines a savings club with lectures on investment, home maintenance, and health.

Most homes on their street have a car in the drive, and some have two. The Smiths share one small saloon. Michael drives it once a week and for weekend trips. Petrol is inexpensive, and roads are well-maintained. The office has an answering machine and Michael carries a compact car-phone for long day trips, but most calls wait until he is back home.

The family budgets for regular outings. Museums and galleries run late openings. Cinemas show wide-screen features with high-fidelity sound. Community sports clubs are busy; the children play football and swim. Parks are well-kept and lit. Theatres thrive because trains run late and are cheap. Michael is a long-suffering season ticket holder at Tottenham Hotspur Football Club, and their unique ability to always develop enough hope in their fans to always disappoint them is the source of his most frequent misery, a luxury compared to the worries that plagued his grandfather 65 years earlier. Rail is fast for domestic trips; reserved seats, on-board dining, and quiet carriages are normal. Weekends in Brighton or Blackpool are common in the warmer months.

Saturday mornings are for errands and sport, afternoons for friends or a matinee, evenings for a film or a concert. Sundays are for church, family lunch, and a walk. The household keeps a modest reserve of gold coins and a larger reserve in savings accounts. Plans extend years ahead because the family has only ever known economic security and never experienced the pain of poverty or the crushing blows of inflation and banking crises that make planning impossible.

London is brighter and cleaner than it was in their parents' youth. Soot from coal has all but disappeared. Power stations run on cleaner fuels and nuclear baseload. Gas is used for heating and cooking; many offices also add air conditioning in the summer. Water and telecommunications are reliable and competitive. Streets are well-lit. The Thames is far cleaner than it has been in centuries, and some enterprising souls even take an occasional swim in it. Container lorries and rail depots push heavy freight to the edges of town, so central streets are less clogged.

Michael's yearly income of £50 buys him a lot more than his father's £50 income bought in 1930, and vastly more than his grandfather's £75 did in 1900. After renting a small apartment for the first two years of their marriage, Michael and Emma used their inheritance and savings to buy their beautiful house for £120 without taking on any debt. The household consumes about 4 megawatt-hours monthly through central heating, multiple appliances, and abundant electricity from nuclear-powered grids, and it does so at a much higher efficiency than his father's household.

Now that they no longer have to pay rent, and with no mortgage to pay, their income goes a long way. Home bills and gasoline for the car cost about 15% of income, food around 20%, clothing, education, and leisure add up to about 45% of income, leaving around 20% of income for savings. All purchases are paid in cash or by charge card and cleared monthly. They regularly donate to charities that cover the medical bills of the less fortunate.

Snapshot: London 2000

Andrew Smith wakes up at 6:30 in a four-bedroom detached house in Richmond, which he bought at 23 from his savings, 2 years before he got married. He starts his day with an ice bath and a sauna, then joins his wife, Patricia, and their three children for breakfast. The house is incomparable to what his ancestors owned. Cheap electricity keeps the climate controlled year-round, even when the Smiths open the windows to get some fresh, clean London air, thanks to the 300,000 BTU air conditioning and dehumidifier unit in the summer, and the underground and in-wall heating in the winter. The driveway and paths are heated to stay dry in winter. Lights, towel rails, ice bath, and sauna stay on because energy is too cheap to worry about.

Breakfast is usually ribeye, grilled in minutes on Andrew's 1,000°C gas grill. Delicious beef is delivered to their home by drone twice a week from Andrew's favorite farm in Scotland. Fresh seafood arrives by air freight from all over the world to London's fishmongers, and is delivered by drone on demand to their doorstep. A large fridge and chest freezer contain a vast array of delicacies from around the world for their enjoyment.

At 8:15, Andrew walks down the stairs to his garage, where he rides his powerful Jaguar through the two-layered underground road grid covering Zones 1 and 2 of London, ensuring he never has to contend with traffic jams. After a 12-minute journey, he parks in his office's underground garage and takes the elevator to his office, where work begins.

On days when he doesn't feel like driving, Andrew walks five minutes to the London Underground, one of the world's first, fastest, and best urban train systems. Cross-city trains arrive about every ninety seconds at peak hours.

Face-detection technology allows train companies to deduct the fare from Andrew's gold-sterling account without him needing to carry change, like his grandfather, or reach for a card, like his father.

Andrew works a 36-hour week as a senior engineer at a power-electronics firm in Canary Wharf. At 12:30, the canteen serves fine meals from a professional chef. Andrew finishes around 5:00 pm and usually works from home one day a week. Offices have fibre backbones, fast workstations, and quiet rooms for video calls. Simulation and CAD run locally, but can rent processing power when complex tasks require it. Video calls with colleagues in Japan, France, Brazil, and Canada make work across borders seamless. Insurer audits, training, and machine interlocks enforce safety and quality. With abundant and reliable power, test rigs can run continuously.

Patricia's full-time job is managing the house and family affairs. She plans the family's finances, supervises the children's education and activities, and arranges for shopping, outings, vacations, and long trips. Robots vacuum the floor, collect the dirty laundry, and place it in the powerful high-capacity washer and tumble dryer, then stack it back in each family member's closet. Shopping is done virtually and delivered by drone from across the country.

The children's school day runs from 9:00 a.m. to 3:00 p.m. Classes consist of 5 to 6 students and one teacher, who establishes a strong bond with them, becoming like a mentor. Students are grouped into their classes based on ability rather than age, ensuring each class consists of students who are always moving ahead at a similar pace. This creates an engaging and challenging experience for all students. One teacher handles all subjects for the small children, but as they grow older, they get specialized teachers for each topic.

Andrew is home by 5:15 pm. Dinner is usually meat: a beef stew, roast chicken, or lamb chops with rice or potatoes and steamed vegetables. Robots clear the table, and the modern high-powered dishwasher cleans all the dishes in less than 15 minutes. A football match, theater, or a foreign language class might be taken on in the evening.

The Smiths, like most middle-class Londoners, can easily afford the most advanced medical care in the world, which is available all over London in clean, modern clinics open 24/7. Infant mortality is around 1 per 300, and life expectancy is in the mid-80s.

Housing takes roughly 15% of income, food about 10%, and clothing, education, and leisure take up around 45-50%, depending on Andrew's leisure choices. The family saves close to 30% of its income in gold savings accounts. Last year, Andrew splurged three years of savings on the SR-77 Blackbird, his own private supersonic jet, which he keeps at the Richmond Park runway's underground garage. He will sometimes use it for a quick after-work trip to Europe, and on weekends, he'll take the family on longer trips, to the Americas, Africa, or Asia. Flying his father to Egypt on a weekend, they laughed as the father compared the incredibly fast experience, 2 hours from their doorstep in Richmond to their hotel room on the Alexandria beachfront, to the ordeal his father had to go through on his first budget vacation to Egypt in 1960, which took 10 hours door-to-door through complicated customs and subsonic budget airplanes.

London runs on abundant nuclear power. Per-capita energy use is several times higher than in the past, so desalination, local data centres, and energy-intensive workshops operate without strain. Streets are lit at night as well as during the day. The Thames has become so clean that all manner of exotic aquatic life now lives in it, and large parts of it have been heated and turned into swimming pools.

Jobs are plentiful, and mobility is high. Unemployment is mostly frictional between roles or during retraining. Bargaining power rests on savings and strong demand for skilled labour. Firms compete on safety, training, and flexible schedules because retention matters. Four-day weeks and nine-day fortnights are common. Andrew earns £75 per year, more than his father and grandfather earned, but the same sum his great-grandfather earned a century ago. Yet his salary provides him a lifestyle incomparably better than theirs. His family still lives in the spacious house he bought as a bachelor for £115, and he has never had to pay a mortgage, and has only paid rent for four years after leaving his childhood home. Their household consumes roughly 6 megawatt-hours monthly, powering heated driveways, continuous climate control, high-energy appliances, and industrial-grade cooking equipment.

For families like the Smiths, comfort is taken for granted, and prosperity is ordinary. Technology shortens chores, meat is plentiful and affordable, travel is fast, and energy is so abundant that they barely think about it. When Andrew purchased a Virtual Reality headset for his children, one of his motivations was to have them use the London Historical Simulators and see how far their world has come in the past century thanks to modern industrialization.

Year	Weekly Working Hours	Yearly Income	Monthly Household Energy Consumption	House Price
1900	56 hours	£75	2 MWh	£600
1930	48 hours	£50	3 MWh	£200
1965	40 hours	£50	4 MWh	£120
2000	36 hours	£75	6 MWh	£115

Table 3: Middle-class London working hours, income, energy consumption, and house prices across a century

PART V

POSTSCRIPT
FROM
FIAT WORLD

This section of the book is no longer hypothetical history;
it will contrast the alternative history presented in the
previous three parts of the book with the real world,
and explain some of the choices I made in this book,
as well as the absence of certain concepts and events
that the reader would have expected to encounter.

XIX.

Fiat vs Gold Worlds

Energy

A pivotal hinge in this book is the significant increase in energy consumption in this alternative world compared to ours. I believe this is a completely realistic implication of the destruction of fiat money, for several reasons.

To estimate the growth in energy consumption, I assumed that the rate of increase in industrial energy production prevalent from 1870 to 1913 would have continued until 2000. I believe this is defensible because if the world's industrial leaders had not wasted the bulk of their industrial capacity and human capital on the war, they would have continued to make enormous strides in industrial production and capital accumulation. Furthermore, with the world adopting a sound monetary standard in 1916, the majority of the planet that was yet to industrialize would have been able to acquire significant industrial capacity, accumulate more capital, and increase its energy consumption.

Just imagine how much more savings humanity would have had in the twentieth century if it had not used forms of money declining in value, because they increase in supply by around 14% per year. Imagine if, instead, humanity were using gold, which increases at less than 2% per year. Imagine how much more people would be able to save. With the enormous transformative power of modern industrial fuels, it would be inevitable that a significant portion of these extra savings would have gone toward building infrastructure for these fuels. The fruits of Europe's and North America's Industrial Revolution would have spread worldwide from the beginning of the twentieth century, leading to far higher energy production and compounding throughout the century. Then consider how much of humanity's resources were wasted on war, and imagine if these were instead available to the people from which they were robbed. Clearly, a lot of them would have gone to capital infrastructure.

Note that we witness a significant slowdown in the growth of energy production in the 1970s after the move away from the gold exchange standard to the fully untethered fiat standard, supporting the contention that inflation reduces society's ability to accumulate industrial capital and increase energy consumption. Bearing all of these facts in mind, it would be entirely reasonable to extrapolate the growth rate in industrial energy production under the classical gold standard to the rest of the twentieth century. In the real world, total energy consumption went up fifteenfold, whereas per capita energy consumption went up fourfold. In the gold standard hypothetical world, with the 4.4% growth rate continuing through the century, we end up with a 75-fold increase in total energy consumption and a 14.5-fold increase in per capita consumption. So total energy consumption in the hypothetical world was four times larger than in the real world, and per capita, it was three times larger since the hypothetical world has a larger population.

This is not unrealistic. Many places are unable to accumulate capital because their savings are constantly eroded by inflation and hyperinflation. If these people had the ability to save, they would demand a lot more power, and the world would have far more power plants. And it is not unrealistic to assume that humanity would continue to find more uses for increased energy production if we had the capital to build it.

Figure 7 shows the total energy consumption in the real twentieth century, while Figure 8 shows the composition of energy sources. These figures can be contrasted with figures 2 and 3. Notice how there is a marked change in the growth rate around the 1970s, as the growth rate of energy consumption slows down at the same time the world shifts to the fiat standard, completely untethered from gold backing, causing a rapid rise in the cost of energy, and a marked decline in the growth rate of energy consumption. In a world on the gold standard, this decline would not have happened.

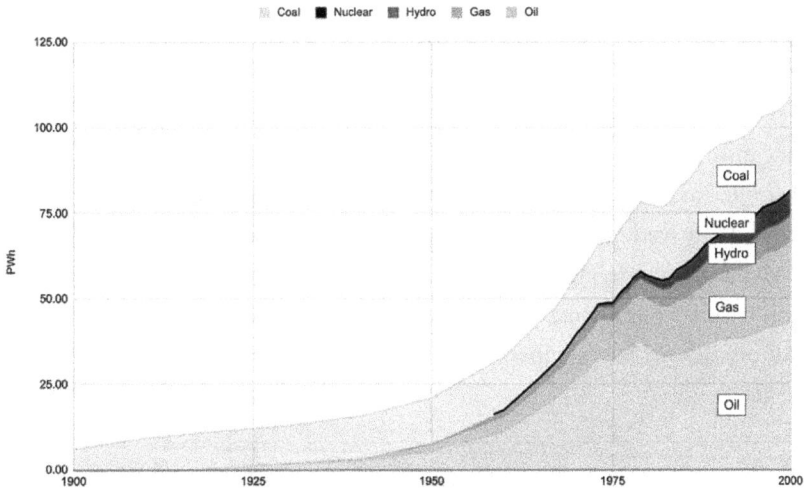

Figure 7: Total energy consumption in the real twentieth century

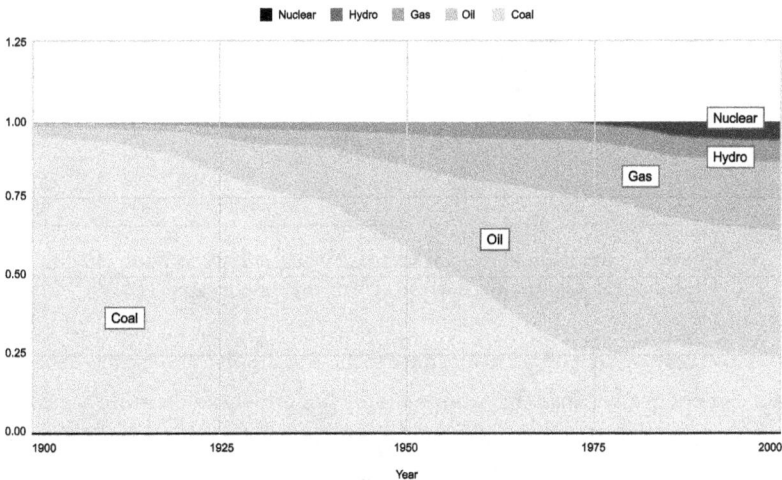

Figure 8: Energy consumption composition in the real twentieth century

Table 3 compares total energy consumption in both worlds and the consumption of particular energy sources. If the growth in energy consumption in the classical gold standard had continued until the end of the twentieth century, we would have four times as much energy consumption, and per capita consumption would have been three times higher. Coal, oil, and gas consumption would be double what they were in the real world, whereas nuclear energy would be thirty times higher. In a world without inflation eroding capital, we would have a lot more savings available for long-term investment, and it would naturally have been directed towards nuclear energy, which is significantly more efficient than coal, oil, and gas. It is also reasonable to assume that nuclear energy would have been deployed commercially earlier; I opted for 1944 instead of 1961. Moreover, as I argue in the next chapter, environmental fear-mongering is a product of fiat inflation, and without it, humanity would have been a much more forward-looking civilization; we would have witnessed many fewer impediments to the widespread deployment of nuclear power.

	1900	2000 Fiat World	Compound Annual Growth Rate	2000 Gold World	Compound Annual Growth Rate	Gold/Fiat ratio
Total Energy	6.02	109	2.94%	444	4.39%	4.07
Energy per capita (MWh)	3.6	17.86	1.61%	52.7	2.72%	2.95
Coal	5.73	27.46	1.58%	57.5	2.33%	2.09
Oil	0.18	43.02	5.63%	97.4	6.50%	2.26
Gas	0.06	23.99	6.17%	55.6	7.07%	2.32
Nuclear	0	7.17	-	222	-	30.96
Electricity	0.066	15	5.58%	88.8	7.47%	5.92

Table 4: Comparison of real fiat standard world energy consumption to hypothetical gold standard world (PWh, except per capita (MWh))

In our real world, energy prices have increased in spite of the growing abundance of energy, because the money supply has grown much more abundant. But in a world in which the money supply was confined in its growth, we expect the prices of energy to decline in nominal terms, and not just real terms. While there is no clear-cut way to predict the prices of energy sources in an alternative world, an educated guess would suggest they decline continuously, since their output can grow at a far faster rate than that of the money supply, and the magnitude of this decline can be estimated by comparing their rates of growth in the real world. Whereas in the year 2000 a barrel of oil cost around $29, in a hard money world, it would cost less than a dollar.

		Fiat Standard		Gold Standard	
	Price in 1900	Price in 2000	CAGR	Price in 2000	CAGR
Coal ton	$2	$26	2.60%	$0.90	-0.80%
Oil barrel	$1.20	$29	3.24%	$0.64	-0.63%
Gas Mcf	$1	$4.50	1.52%	$0.30	-1.20%
Electricity KWh	$0.15	$0.06	-0.91%	$0.0006	-5.37%

Table 5: Prices of energy in the real fiat world
compared to the hypothetical gold standard world

Regarding the choice of energy sources discussed in this book, the reader may notice that solar, wind, biofuels, and biomass are not mentioned as energy sources, despite being frequently discussed in modern energy discussions. As I argue in The Fiat Standard, it makes little sense to speak of these as energy sources, as they are largely dependent on hydrocarbons to operate, likely consume more hydrocarbon energy than they produce, and are economically reliant on government subsidies. The adoption of these energy sources grew after the inflation-energy crisis of the 1970s, as they can help mitigate the extent of inflation. In a world in which inflation is not a problem, they would be deployed only marginally, for localized applications, and would not be used for electricity generation. In that world, engineers and economists would be discussing industrial energy sources as consisting of oil, coal, gas, nuclear, and hydroelectric power.

Another consequence of the increased abundance of energy is the more rapid pace of technological advancement in this alternative history. Readers may have noticed that most inventions in this book were introduced several years before they were actually invented in the real world, and this was a deliberate choice, not an error. As energy production increases and living standards rise, humans can conceive of technologies earlier than they would have in an inflationary century, where much of our creative and productive energy was directed toward serving governments' tyranny and war. It is common for defenders of government spending to point out the numerous technological innovations that have resulted from government-financed research, but this overlooks the opportunity cost. With government control of money, governments have spent extensively on research, resulting in numerous discoveries. But if they did not have a monopoly on money, that does not mean that engineers, inventors, and discoverers would have been idle. They would likely have been even more productive and inventive, directed by private enterprise, financed by the constantly appreciating accumulated savings. The example of the Wright Brothers is instructive here, but for a more thorough treatment, I recommend Terence Kealey's fascinating and eye-opening book, *The Economic Laws of Scientific Research*.[128]

Computers, nuclear power, air conditioning, the internet, and countless other inventions happened earlier in this book's alternative world. Whereas in the real world, computing power grew at an annual rate of 70% between 1941 and 2000, in this book, I assumed it grew at an annual rate of 75% from 1936 to 2000. Whereas the price in the real world declined by 27% annual compound rate, in this book, I assumed it declined by 37% per year instead. The production of commodities also increased at a faster pace than in the real world due to the larger population and the faster technological advancement.

Housing

An important point I tried to convey in this book is that, under hard money, houses would most likely have become far more expensive in the twentieth century, in sharp contrast to our modern world, where houses continue to become cheaper. It is indeed startling to people who do not understand the shortcomings of fiat that the price of housing keeps rising when our ability

---

128 Kealey, Terence. *The Economic Laws of Scientific Research*. Macmillan Press, 1996

to produce houses continues to make them cheaper to produce. The reason houses continue to become more expensive in our world is that they serve as a store of value, given the inability of money to fulfill that role. In fiat world, buying real estate is one of the most reliable ways of saving for the future. Even though houses are considered consumer goods, they are among the most durable of all consumer goods, and therefore they retain their value relatively well. This means that people purchase them to save for the future, which amplifies demand for them beyond the demand for housing. Houses today serve as savings accounts for fiat users who lack better options. This likely causes the price of houses to continue appreciating even as they become cheaper to produce.

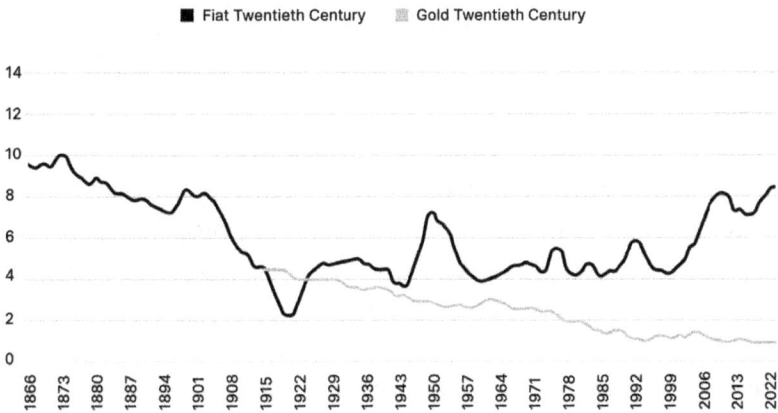

Figure 9: Median house price as multiple of median annual earnings; hypothetical gold standard world vs real fiat standard world[129]

For centuries, humans have increased our productivity and made the production of houses less costly in terms of our time. For centuries and millennia, houses have become more affordable, but this trend reversed with the plague of fiat money befalling humanity in the twentieth century. As people began using their homes as savings accounts, much of the monetary demand

129 Duncan Lamont, "What 175 Years of Data Tell Us About House Price Affordability in the UK," *Schroders*, February 20, 2023

that would have otherwise gone into hard money investments shifted to housing. Consequently, housing prices outpaced the rise in income. Going off the gold standard in 1914 stopped a centuries-long increase in the affordability of homes by degrading the value of money, as Figure 9 from Britain makes clear.

While using homes as a savings account seems rational in a world of bad alternatives, it is disastrous in the long run because it separates the price of housing from its utility as a residence and adds to it its utility as an investment. When young couples are looking to start a family, they are not bidding for a house to live in only; they are also bidding for a savings account, and will likely be outbid by older people who have significant savings or by large corporations that need to hold hard assets to avoid holding depreciating money. The result is a growing percentage of people being forced to rent for the long term. This is the root of the housing affordability crisis, a hallmark of the past few decades in many parts of the world.

Houses are great places to live, but they are terrible investments. While they may hold value better than fiat money in the long term, they are still lousy money because they have very low fungibility and liquidity. Houses are usually the single biggest purchase in most people's lives, but a homeowner cannot liquidate a small part of a house to finance expenditures; he has to sell the entire house or not sell it at all. A house also requires regular spending to maintain it, so even if it appreciates in nominal terms, thanks to the devaluation of fiat money, it likely depreciates when one factors in the taxes and maintenance costs involved.

In a world where everyone can save hard-earned money that appreciates slightly, housing reverts to being just a durable consumption good, like washing machines, shoes, or computers. People buy these items because they want to use them, not because they want to sell them in the future to make a profit. In a hard money world, demand for houses would just be demand for housing, and a family bidding on a house would only be pitted against other families of a similar income and social status. Home ownership would be far more attainable for young people. This is part of the reason why I expect to have a higher population growth rate in the alternative history. With home ownership more easily attainable, more people would start families young. Nonetheless, I would not expect this to be a comprehensive solution to the problem of declining birth rates. Prosperity has very frequently coincided with declines in fertility rates and it is likely that this would have happened in a gold standard twentieth century, too.

Interest Rates

Perhaps the boldest and most controversial claim in this book is the idea that interest lending would be eliminated in a gold standard twentieth century. My view on this issue manages to disagree with virtually every established school of thought on the topic of interest. I disagree with the predominant economics approach to understanding interest as a result of the productivity of capital investment, opting instead for the Austrian explanation of interest as a result of time preference. The Austrian explanation also disagrees with the religious and philosophical prohibitions against interest, because it explains interest as a natural phenomenon that exists as long as time preference exists, and that attempting to ban it will not end future discounting, but, on the contrary, will have destructive impacts. Yet, I also disagree with the Austrian perspective which views interest as inevitable, as I argue that the abundance of savings and capital accumulation, and the lowering of time preference in advanced civilizations, will combine to bring the originary rate of interest down below the cost of storing and insuring capital, thus resulting in a free market nominal interest rate of zero. This, in a roundabout way, validates the historical argument made by religious authorities and philosophers that views interest as wrong or immoral, as it explains interest as being a result of higher time preference, which can be viewed as immoral. Virtually everyone will fall into one of these three camps, so I do not expect to get much agreement with this thesis, nor do I pretend that disagreement from all sides implies I must be right. But in this section, I will present a contrast between the interest rates in the actual twentieth century, presented here in Figure 10[130], and the ones in

130 Haldane, Andrew G. "Stuck - Speech by Andy Haldane." Bank of England, June 30, 2015.

my hypothetical history, presented in Figure 2. Note that the rates in Figure 2 and Figure 10 are the same up to 1914. The spike in the real twentieth century interest rates was enormous by historical standards, and reverses a long-term trend under the gold standard and industrialization. This spike that came after the First World War was anomalous, and conforms with the Austrian explanation of interest rate being a manifestation of time preference. As war, inflation, and capital destruction took place on an unprecedented scale, it was only natural that time preference would rise massively. The even bigger spike that followed the Second World War supports this contention further. The severing of the last link between money and gold, with the close of the gold exchange window in 1971, created global inflation at an unprecedented level, reflected in very high time discounting and a rise in interest rates not seen in centuries, possibly millennia. My contention then, is that a century that reversed this process of war, inflation, capital destruction, and high time preference, would have reversed the trend in interest rates, and naturally brought them down to zero.

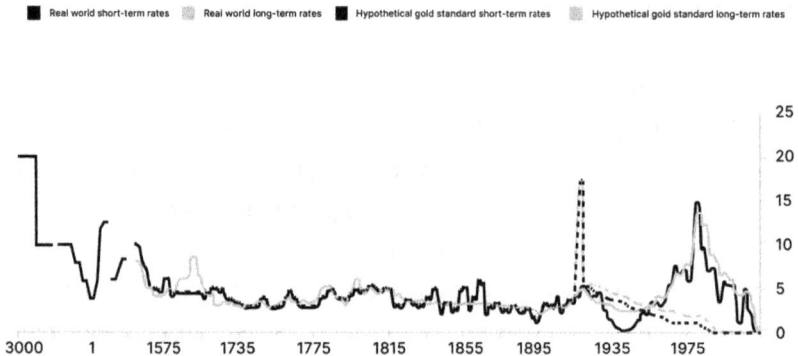

Figure 10: Interest rates in the real fiat world and the hypothetical gold world

Finally, one point that I tried to express in the book, but which could not be expressed clearly in a counterfactual history without the benefit of hindsight from our world, concerns the monetary role of silver. I have come to believe that a big part of the problems of the beginning of the twentieth century has to do with the demonetization of silver and the monetization of gold. Perhaps a good explanation for the enormous accumulation of power in the hands of the Western major powers was a result of the significant appreciation in the value of gold in terms of silver after 1871. As the world began to move to gold from silver, and the market value of silver began to collapse, countries that had significant quantities of gold became significantly richer in real terms, even if this did not show up nominally. More importantly, perhaps, is that their banks and central banks witnessed their gold reserves appreciate significantly in real value, allowing them to issue more unbacked notes and credit. With gold increasingly confined to banks and individuals increasingly resorting to gold-backed instruments, the real winners from this appreciation were the banks and central banks using it. This explains why central banks were able to finance a growing militarization effort during that period, effectively channeling the real appreciation of gold to the governments' benefit, rather than to the gold owners, the people. Had the world been using physical gold more frequently, had clearance been more frequent, and had banks' ability to pyramid paper and credit liabilities on top of their gold been checked, then the value of gold would have likely appreciated faster, to the benefit of the gold holders, and the governments would have had less wealth to squander on war. The world had never seen a monetary asset appreciate significantly, and it might just be the case that if its appreciation was allowed to proceed completely, then the holders of the asset would have increased their wealth, the holders of silver would have learned to get rid of their silver faster, and the world would have enjoyed the benefits of declining prices. Instead, gold standard governments were able to harvest the benefits of the appreciation of gold, grow their militaries and empires, and get addicted to the seiniorage from inflation. When this inflation got them into a World War, they did not have enough gold to back up their wealth, and so they suspended gold's monetary role. While silver continued to lose its monetary role, it did so while gold's monetary role was also being hampered, and the result was a century of wild oscillation in the market value of gold and silver. Figure 11 compares the evolution of the gold silver ratio in the real world and the hypothetical world.

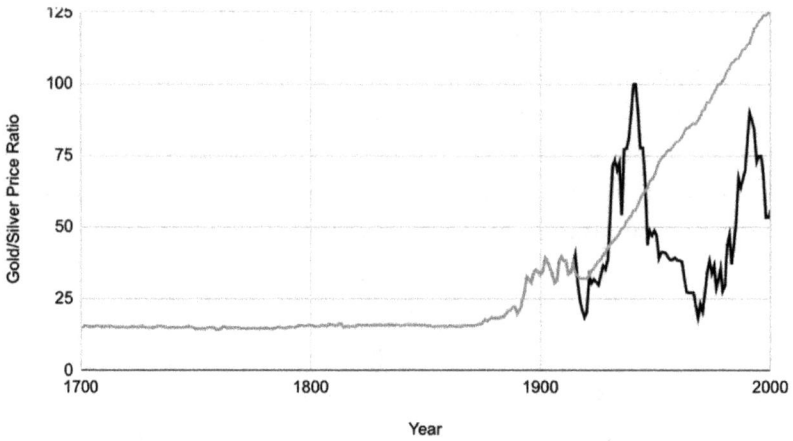

Figure 11: Gold-Silver Ratio in the real world on the fiat standard (black) vs in the alternative world on the gold standard (grey)

XX.

Missing Fiat Phenomena

Readers might be surprised at how a book of economic history contains no mention of some very important economic concepts that are ubiquitous in any modern economics book, like unemployment, inflation, GDP, and depressions. This was no oversight, but a deliberate choice. It is my contention that these statistics are not scientifically or economically important categories that need to be studied in any context; they are, rather, the result of government monopoly control over fiat money and government central planning of economies. It is extremely telling that these concepts did not exist before the fiat century, and their creation in the fiat century was not an inspired scientific discovery, but a byproduct of government management of the money supply and its disastrous consequences.

To illustrate this point, I find it very useful to resort to Google Books Ngram Viewer, which scans millions of books published over the past 225 years, and measures the frequency at which words appear in these books over time. This makes for a handy tool for measuring how frequently any particular word was used at any point in time. Entering economic concepts into this search produces very telling results.

Unemployment

Unemployment as a concept began to be discussed in a meaningful sense only after the First World War, as this chart from Google Ngrams shows. Without fiat money, the entire concept of unemployment would have been a minor curiosity examined only by a few economists with marginal ideas. With hard money, people had savings, which meant that not working was a normal thing for people to do. If the right job was not available, if you needed time to look after yourself or your family, or if you had to deal with an emergency, it was perfectly normal to take time off from work and live off accumulated savings. But with fiat inflation, savings primarily go to politicians and bankers, so you have to be on the hamster wheel every day, lest you starve. Unemployment becomes a huge problem, and as a result, it begins to get discussed extensively in books and academic literature.

Figure 12: Ngram chart for Unemployment

I explained this in more detail in *Principles of Economics*:

> In the twentieth century, the concept of unemployment became closely in-
> tertwined with the concept of labor. Many schools of thought have posited
> that unemployment is an unavoidable and inevitable part of the workings
> of the market economy. Various reasons have been presented to explain

why a free labor market will inevitably malfunction in a way that leaves significant numbers of people who are willing to work at prevailing wages unemployed.

But unemployment is as much a normal part of the labor market as burning crops is a part of the food market. As will be discussed in Section IV of this book, inflationary credit expansion and minimum wage laws are the root cause of unemployment. Inflation causes prices to rise, requiring workers to ask for higher wages to cover their increasing living costs. But since an increase in monetary media does not result in an increase in economic resources, employers often have no ability to pay higher wages to workers and remain operational. They will either lay off workers, or go out of business. Inflation reduces the wealth and holdings of both worker and employer and increases the price of the market goods they seek to purchase. Further, credit inflationism also causes the business cycle. The inflationary boom results in the financing of unsustainable investments, and their inevitable collapse causes entire economic sectors to witness bankruptcies, with large numbers of workers laid off and left with skills for which there is little demand.

As inflation causes unemployment through rising prices and recessions, governments and government-employed economists prefer to shift the blame onto the market economy itself or greedy capitalists, or they provide other flimsy explanations. Instead of tackling the inflation at the root of the problem, modern economists invariably propose counterproductive measures like minimum wage laws. Rather than a command for employers to pay workers more, minimum wage laws should be thought of as a prohibition against workers choosing the price of their own labor. Minimum wage laws prevent the market from adjusting to inflation, resulting in constant waves of unemployment that coincide with the business cycle.

It is telling that the concept of unemployment did not really exist as an economic term before the twentieth century. In a free market, people choose whether or not to work for the wage offered to them, so nobody can be involuntarily unemployed. With the introduction of monetary inflationism and minimum wage laws, a permanently unemployed part of the population became a fixture of modern economies, and blaming this unemployment on the market process became a fixture of the pseudoscientific economics dominant in modern academia, financed by those with vested interests in maintaining inflation in order to provide rationales for it.

Switzerland, the last country in the world to go off the gold standard, provides a good example of this dynamic. As the fiat world struggled through severe unemployment crises throughout the twentieth century, Switzerland had practically no unemployment until it went off the gold standard in the mid-1970s. After adopting the dollar standard and engaging in inflationism, Switzerland has witnessed a rise in unemployment that follows the same cyclical pattern observed in every country that runs on fiat money.

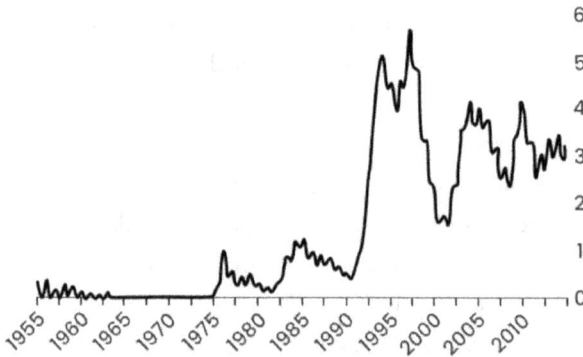

Figure 13: Unemployment rate in Switzerland, %[131]

Under a free market with sound money, savings appreciate in market value over time, and individuals have the freedom to work or not, and to ask for any wage they want. Employers also have the freedom to pay any salary they want. In such a world, with savings appreciating, it is

---

131 "Unemployment Rate in Switzerland." Federal Reserve Economic Data.

perfectly rational for many to forgo employment. A worker who cannot find employment at a prevailing wage is simply unable to find someone who values the marginal revenue product of his labor at a price higher than the worker's valuation of leisure. The modern phenomenon of mass involuntary unemployment can only occur when there are laws, rules, or restrictions that make it illegal, and subject to punishment, to engage in labor at specific wage rates.

In the context of free exchange, there can be no such thing as unemployment among people who are willing to work, because this implies they are entitled to earn a wage that nobody is willing to pay them. The worker could always find work by increasing his productivity or decreasing his asking wage. Involuntary unemployment is impossible in a free-market economic system; it is the worker's choice to ask for a wage that nobody is willing to pay, and thus it is their choice to remain unemployed.[132]

In the real world, unemployment became a commonplace term and concept in the aftermath of World War I, precisely because of the inflation created to finance the war. I highly recommend reading Murray Rothbard's *America's Great Depression*[133] for an excellent examination of the attempt to stay on the gold standard, at the old rate, when Britain had nowhere near as much gold as would be required to restore redemption for all the paper and credit pounds the Bank of England cartel and its members had created during the war. With the money supply increased and prices of goods rising, two main problems emerged in Britain: the value of the pound declined on international markets, and the British government attempted to maintain the sterling exchange rate at the prewar rate. This meant that any financial speculator could redeem pounds for gold in Britain, export the gold abroad, sell it for a foreign currency, and then bring the foreign currency back to England, where he would buy more pounds than he initially started with. The net result was a large drain

---

132 Saifedean Ammous, *Principles of Economics* (The Saif House, 2023), 71–73.
133 Rothbard, Murray. *America's Great Depression* 5th ed.(Ludwig von Mises Institute, 2000).

of gold from England, particularly to the United States, which was the curtain call for Britain's power on the global stage, as it became a debtor with very little gold, thanks to its foolish and utterly inexcusable foray into the First World War. This also led Britain to pressure the United States to engage in inflation in the 1920s, to prevent the drain of gold from the UK, which was to lay the foundations of the Great Depression in the 1930s. The other problem this foolish British policy created was the impoverishment of the British people and the destruction of a healthy labor market. With savings devalued, gold leaving the country, and a large part of the labor force disabled from the war, misery abounded. With prices of goods rising, the government continued wartime price controls and wage controls, which led to shortages and prevented businesses from operating economically and hiring workers. Had Britain returned to the gold standard at a devalued rate, admitting the larceny of the Bank of England cartel and the warmongers of the Foreign Office, prices of goods would have been higher than what the price controls dictated, and real wages would have been lower. While this would have been unspeakably unpopular with the British people, it must be understood that it was but an inevitable consequence of the crime of wartime inflation. The British government, without a time machine to reverse its inflation and war participation, had only two choices: admit to the devaluation of the pound and restore a functioning market for goods and labor, or continue trying to fool reality by mandating prices and hoping reality would comply. The first path would have been unpopular in the short term but would have returned the British economy to its glory in the medium and long terms. The second choice was the popular choice in the short term, and it led to untold economic calamities lasting for decades, with inflation, depression, unemployment, trade restrictions, economic central planning, and the rising popularity of economically illiterate and bloodthirsty socialist and fascist ideas. Of course, it all culminated in the carnage of World War II. It was the inflation of World War I and the refusal to devalue the pound in its aftermath that created the massively dysfunctional labor market in Britain, from which the concept of "unemployment" began to appear in the English language and the economic literature. Since the real world has been cursed with the inflationary monetary system and interventionist political system since then, "unemployment" has become a permanent phenomenon in the modern world. But in the alternative world of this novel, where fiat money dies in 1915 and the world returns to a sane monetary system, there would be no constant waves of unemployment and recessions, and no government attempting to hide its inflationary malfeasance with mandated minimum wages, and so there would be no concept of "unemployment." People would work when they want to, and not work when they don't want to, and the growing value of savings would make not working a feasible option for a growing number of people across the century.

Inflation

The second concept, which was not discussed in the alternative history of this century, is that of inflation, which in the modern world refers to price increases, as opposed to its original and linguistically accurate meaning of an increase in the money supply, as Mises explained:

> There is nowadays a very reprehensible, even dangerous, semantic confusion that makes it extremely difficult for the nonexpert to grasp the true state of affairs. Inflation, as this term was always used everywhere and especially in this country, means increasing the quantity of money and bank notes in circulation and the quantity of bank deposits subject to check. But people today use the term "inflation" to refer to the phenomenon that is an inevitable consequence of inflation, that is the tendency of all prices and wage rates to rise. The result of this deplorable confusion is that there is no term left to signify the cause of this rise in prices and wages. There is no longer any word available to signify the phenomenon that has been, up to now, called inflation. It follows that nobody cares about inflation in the traditional sense of the term. As you cannot talk about something that has no name, you cannot fight it. Those who pretend to fight inflation are in fact only fighting what is the inevitable consequence of inflation, rising prices. Their ventures are doomed to failure because they do not attack the root of the evil. They try to keep prices low while firmly committed to a policy of increasing the quantity of money that must necessarily make them soar.

As long as this terminological confusion is not entirely wiped out, there cannot be any question of stopping inflation.[134]

Consulting the Ngram graph for inflation reveals that neither of these two meanings was in use before the twentieth century. As with the term unemployment, the term inflation only came into common use with the First World War and the advent of the fiat era. This makes sense because prices did not usually rise, and if they did, it was temporary, because money supply increased at a much lower rate than in the twentieth century.

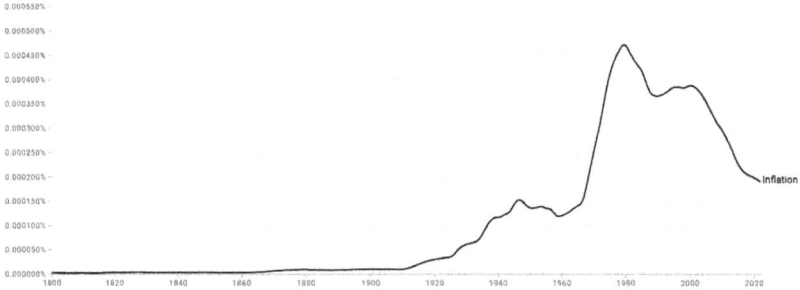

Figure 14: Ngram chart for inflation

Compared to the term unemployment, there is a slightly more frequent use of the term inflation in the nineteenth century, but that is explained by the fact that the term existed before fiat money, and by it having linguistic uses independent of its economic use. Inflation can refer to the act of filling something with air, and it can also refer to the act of making something larger or more important. These terms likely explain the small level of use this term had in the nineteenth century, whereas the word unemployment has no uses outside of its economic meaning, only present in the fiat era.

Price change statistics did exist under the nineteenth-century gold standard, but they were far less consequential than in the twentieth century, where

---

134 Ludwig von Mises, "Inflation: An Unworkable Fiscal Policy," in *Economic Freedom and Interventionism: An Anthology of Articles and Essays*, ed. Bettina Bien Greaves (Liberty Fund, 2007), 602–30.

they have become fundamental data communicated by governments with the sanctity once reserved for religious edicts. In the nineteenth century, economists and businessmen likely measured the changes in prices of specific goods over time, but it was not treated like a significant economy-wide statistic as it is in the fiat century, where governments communicate it with the sanctity once reserved for religious edicts. The utterly meaningless and laughably mathematically invalid measure of CPI did not exist because the absence of monetary inflation and subsequent price rises meant these were not issues requiring the production of government statistics attempting to quantify and measure this phenomenon. I discuss the utter mathematical invalidity of the concept of a consumer price index in *The Fiat Standard*:

> Fiat money enthusiasts maintain a strange obsession with a metric produced by national governments named the Consumer Price Index (CPI). Government-employed statisticians construct a representative basket of goods and measure the change in the prices of these goods every year as a measure of price increases. There are countless problems with the criteria for inclusion in the basket, for the way that the prices are adjusted to account for technological improvements, and with the entire concept of a representative basket of goods.

> Like many metrics used in the pseudoscience that is macroeconomics, the CPI has no definable unit with which it can be measured. This makes measuring it a matter of subjective judgment, not numerical precision. Only by reference to a constant unit whose definition and magnitude are precisely known and independently verified can anything be measured. Without defining a unit, there is no basis for expressing a quantity numerically, or comparing its magnitude to others. Imagine trying to measure anything without a unit. How would you compare the size of two houses if you could not have a constant frame of reference to measure them against? Time has seconds, weight has grams and pounds, and length has meters and inches, all very precisely and uncontroversially defined. Can you imagine making a measurement of time, length, or weight without reference to a fixed unit?

The CPI has no definable unit; it absurdly attempts to measure the change in the value of the unit that is used for the measurement of prices, the dollar, which itself is not constant or definable.

The absurdity of unitless measurement covers up the fundamental flaw of the CPI, which is that the composition of the basket of goods itself is a function of prices, which is a function of the value of the dollar, and therefore it cannot serve as a measuring rod for the value of the dollar. As the value of the dollar declines, people will not be able to afford the same products they purchased before and will necessarily substitute them for inferior ones. Market prices result from purchasing decisions, but purchasing decisions are, in turn, influenced by prices. The price of a basket of goods is not determined by some magical "price level" force but by the spending decisions of individuals who can only spend the income they have. Purchasing decisions themselves are price-responsive and will adjust to changes in prices. The main and fatal flaw of the CPI, therefore, is that it is, to a large degree, a mathematical tautology and an infinite referential loop.

As prices of highly nutritious foods rise, people are inevitably forced to replace them with cheaper alternatives. As the cheaper foods become a more prevalent part of the basket of goods, the effect of inflation is understated. To illustrate this point, imagine you earn ten dollars a day and spend it all on eating a delicious ribeye steak that gives you all the nutrients you need for the day. In this simple (and many would argue, optimal) consumer basket of goods, the CPI is ten dollars. Now imagine one day hyperinflation strikes, and the price of your ribeye increases to one hundred dollars while your daily wage remains ten dollars. What happens to the price of your basket of goods? It cannot rise tenfold because you cannot afford the one-hundred-dollar ribeye. Instead, you make do with the chemical shitstorm that is a soy burger for ten dollars. The CPI, magically, shows zero inflation. No matter what happens to monetary inflation, the CPI is destined to lag behind as a measure because it is based on consumer spending, which is itself determined by prices. Price rises do not elicit equivalent increases in consumer spending; they bring about reductions in the quality of consumed goods. The change in the cost of living cannot, therefore, be reflected in the price of the average basket of goods, since the basket declines in quality with inflation. This gives us an understanding of how prices continue to rise while the CPI registers at the politically optimal level of 2–3% per year. If you are happy to substitute industrial waste sludge for ribeye, you will not experience much inflation![135]

Given all of the above, there would be no mention of CPI or price inflation in a book on a twentieth century with no fiat money. In a world in which government does not control the money supply and cannot keep increasing the money supply to finance itself, the money supply would not continuously grow out of control, prices of the vast majority of goods wouldn't be constantly rising, and government would have no reason to produce a mathematically invalid metric for the increase in prices.

Gross Domestic Product

GDP, as a concept, was not the product of academic or market economists attempting to study market phenomena to make better decisions. Instead, it was born out of the need for fiat central planning to deal with the disastrous consequences of inflation and central planning. In 1934, the US Congress tasked economist Simon Kuznets with developing a system to measure the nation's productivity, aiming to understand better how to address the Great Depression.[136] Sadly, and as is so typical of the fiat century, the government was the problem masquerading as the solution, and the arsonist masquerading as the firefighter. Had the US Congress had the foresight to listen to an economist who understood the calamity and cost of inflation, such as Ludwig von Mises or Friedrich Hayek, they would have been told they did not need to collect more statistics;

---

135 Saifedean Ammous, *The Fiat Standard: The Debt Slavery Alternative to Human Civilization* (The Saif House, 2021), 52–53, 113–14.
136 Simon Kuznets, *National Income, 1929–1932* (National Bureau of Economic Research, 1934), 5–7.

they needed to stop the inflation. I firmly believe such statistics would barely exist in a world of free market money and no government inflation. Consulting the Ngram shows that the term "National Income" only came into use in the 1930s, while GNP came into use in the 1940s, and GDP in the 1960s.

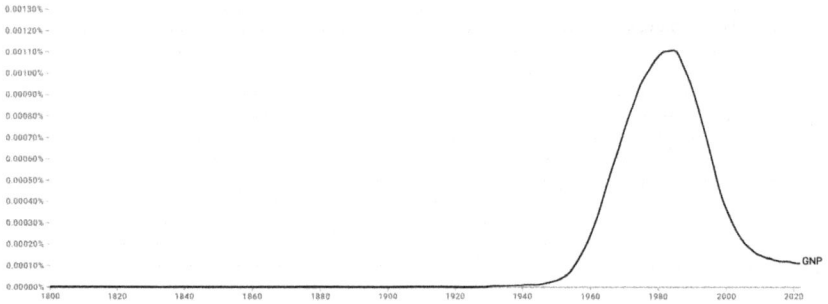

Figure 15: Ngram Chart for GNP

Figure 16: Ngram Chart for GDP

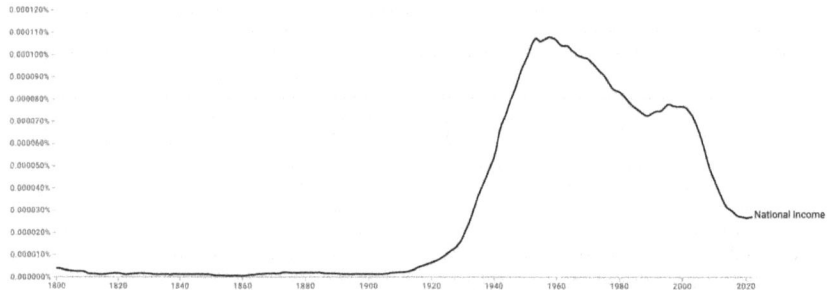

Figure 17: Ngram Chart for national income

In a hard money world, where government does not control the supply of money, there is little reason for the government to collect data on the total value of economic output taking place within its borders. Economic activity is individual, and belongs to the people who own the means of production. As government becomes competitive, it makes more economic sense that the tax imposed would be a fixed sum per person or per plot of land, rather than per amount of economic activity, as that would incentivize people to produce less, or to go to places that don't punish their economic success. The government provides its services to a person, or to land, and it would impose a fixed fee per person or plot of land, and wants to encourage people to produce as much as possible. It makes little sense for the government to seek to tax economic activity, and thus it is unlikely to collect aggregate statistics on its volume. It just offers its service and doesn't need to surveil and collect all the information about the person it serves, any more than a restaurant needs to know the income and life story of its clientele. In short, a hard money world would be a lot more prosperous, but wouldn't have as many statistics to show for it.

Economic Depressions

Using Ngrams to look at economic depression, recession, economic downturn, and business cycle also shows that these concepts only became common in the aftermath of the fiat epidemic. The term depression alone indicates a similar pattern, but is relatively more prevalent in the nineteenth century, which is understandable given that the term is used in several non-economic contexts. The downside of the business cycle, which has variably been termed a depression, recession, or economic downturn, became far more common in the fiat century. Under the imperfect classical gold standard of the nineteenth century, where banks and governments could engage in inflation, there were frequent bank failures and economic downturns; however, these were nowhere near as systematic and prolonged as they became in the twentieth century. With money redeemable for gold, it was much harder for central banks and governments to externalize the costs of banking failures to society as a whole. When a bank's extension of credit caused its insolvency, its clients would be affected, but holders of gold would not be. Government had no way of devaluing the gold of others to bail out the bank and its depositors. The collapse would be devastating for those involved, but its wider impact would be contained. While financial crises were frequent in the nineteenth century, they were usually sharp but brief, and not very systemic, which explains why they were not discussed nearly as frequently as they were in the twentieth century. In this book's thought experiment, these recessions would be almost unheard of as banks and governments lose the ability to create the inflation that causes them. The Great Depression would have definitely not happened, as the inflation of the 1920s caused it, as Murray Rothbard explained in his excellent book, *America's Great Depression*. There would also have been no stagflation crisis in the 1970s, and it would not have left the terrible impact on the world's energy production, as discussed above, and on food consumption, as discussed below.

Figure 18: Ngram chart for 'economic depression', 'recession', 'economic downturn', and 'business cycle'

Climate and Environmental Hysteria

Nowhere in this alternative history would you find people being worried about running out of resources, pollution, or Earth's climate changing as a result of human consumption of fuels. Pollution would be dealt with as an engineering problem. Resources would be managed intelligently and technology would make them abundant. As I argue in *The Fiat Standard*, the hysteria around CO_2 destroying the climate is itself a result of the poverty and capital destruction created by fiat money. It is no coincidence that environmental hysteria took off in the 1970s, when fiat inflation also took off. The prices of commodities and energy rising in a historically unprecedented way, which was the symptom of fiat inflation, was mistaken for looming natural catastrophes as humanity would run out of resources. As I explain in *Principles of Economics*, this has left an indelible mark on the way people think of economic resources today, viewing them as inherently scarce and on the verge of running out, when in fact they are abundant beyond our ability to even measure, let alone consume:

> The belief that resources are scarce and limited is a misunderstanding of the nature of scarcity, which is the key concept behind economics. The absolute quantity of every raw material present on Earth is too large for us as human beings to even measure or comprehend, and in no way does it constitute a real limit to the amount humans can produce... What constitutes the practical and realistic limit to the quantity of any resource is always the amount of human time that is directed toward producing it, as this is the only real scarce resource.

> In all human history, we have never run out of any single raw material or resource, and the price of virtually all resources is lower today than it was at past points in history because our technological advancement allows us to produce them at a lower cost in terms of our time.

> What we really value are not resources, but economic goods made from resources. That is what requires time, and that is what is scarce. That is the scarcity from which all other scarcities originate. The raw material is everywhere around us, but the time to produce economic goods from it is scarce. Humans are not passive recipients of manna that can run out. Humans are the producers of all these resources, and when demand for these metals increases, the most important determinant of their scarcity is the action of the humans who produce them, and the incentives they face.[137]

---

137 Ammous, *Principles of Economics*, 52–53, 140.

When price rises stopped in the relatively less inflationary 1980s, the hysteria shifted to overconsumption, and the supposed disasters that would befall humanity from too much consumption. As I explained in *The Fiat Standard*:

> But as inflation waned in the 1980s, all of these claims became suspect. How could we be running out of oil, steel, nickel, and various industrial materials when their prices had begun a steady decline in real, if not nominal terms, while consumption continued to rise unabated. The environmental doomsday cults had a major branding problem on hand, and they only successfully resolved it by pivoting the existential threat to humanity away from the depletion of resources to the overconsumption of resources. We were no longer doomed because we were going to run out of oil and essentials; we were now doomed because we consume so much oil and essentials, and that consumption is going to destroy the atmosphere and boil the oceans. The reasoning had pivoted to its diametrical opposite, but the conclusion remained the same: apocalypse by fiat.

> As with food, government attempted to fix the problem of rising prices by manipulating the market for oil rather than addressing its underlying monetary cause... The U.S. Department of Energy was set up in 1977, and the central planning of energy markets was to proceed along a half-century quest for an elusive "alternative energy," which has resulted in a very expensive and highly destructive mission to replace oil and hydrocarbons with inferior alternatives through subsidies, favorable lending, and government mandates.

> Centuries of human engineering progress and quality of life improvement had been based on channeling hydrocarbons' high power... But to avoid the rise in oil prices, the U.S. government's fiat sought to ignore half a millennium of technological advancement and build the modern world using premodern solar, wind, and biofuel energy... Against all logic and reason, the fuels of preindustrial poverty were designated by government fiat to be the fuels of the industrial future.

As the price inflation of the 1970s subsided and hydrocarbon prices dropped in the 1980s, the economic rationale for replacing oil with fiat fuels became less pressing... But by the 1990s, the fiat fuel industry found fresh winds in its sails from the threat of catastrophic global warming and in marketing its fiat fuels as salvation. The drive for environmental panic... represented a confluence of interests... promoting any narrative that supports the replacement of hydrocarbon fuels with their inadequate alternatives, justifying more government subsidies.

And a sober close inspection of the supposed scientific evidence for the hysteria around Carbon dioxide emissions finds nothing compelling.

Carbon dioxide is a gas that is an essential component of all living creatures... currently at a concentration of around 418 parts per million, or 0.0418%... modern climate science has been converted into a weird monomaniacal cult that attributes every single problem in the natural environment to the increase of the concentration of this trace gas... The greenhouse effect... is well demonstrated in laboratory settings. But try as they may, fiat scientists have completely failed to demonstrate, using the scientific method of testable hypotheses, what the increase in CO_2 is causing in the real world.

Without testable hypotheses, the entirety of modern climate science is at best conjecture but more likely motivated reasoning in search of a predetermined conclusion to secure more funding... If CO_2 emissions were in fact causing dangerous damage to the climate, we would expect to see this reflected in an increasing number of deaths caused by climate and natural disasters. Yet reality shows us the exact opposite: deaths from hydrological, climatological, and meteorological disasters have declined drastically throughout the past century.[138]

---

138 Ammous, *The Fiat Standard: The Debt Slavery Alternative to Human Civilization*, 170–73.

It is inflation that has driven both fears and caused this unhealthy relationship most people currently have with natural resources, where we stand on the precipice of devastation from using dead materials naturally abundant in the crust of our enormous, bountiful Earth. An inflation-free century, constantly accumulating capital and knowledge, would not have had these primitive superstitions. There would be a sober engineering and scientific approach to dealing with the dangers of these resources, and a celebration of the abundance and prosperity allowed by the utilization of Earth's bountiful resources. In that world, the invention of nuclear power would have been widely adopted. After the first few decades illustrated its safety, reliability, and economic feasibility, most power plants built from the 1970s onwards would likely have been nuclear.

Trash disposal would also not have been a major problem, and recycling would have almost certainly not existed, as it makes very little economic sense in our world, and survives thanks to government mandates inspired by environmental hysteria. In a world of abundant energy, mass trash incinerators would burn large volumes of trash into tiny amounts of ash, producing no harmful smoke, and freeing people from having to sift through their garbage for performative virtue-signalling.

Fiat Food

Another horrible impact of twentieth-century inflation is the destruction of the human diet, and the increasing replacement of nutritious red meat with inferior meats and toxic mass-produced crops. As I discuss in *The Fiat Standard*, and Matthew Lysiak elaborates in *Fiat Food*, meat is nutrition. You are nourished to the extent that you eat meat. The degradation of health in the second half of the twentieth century was a result of the decline in the consumption of red meat and the increase in the consumption of mass-produced crops. Both books lay out a detailed case explaining the causal link from the degradation of money to the replacement of healthy red meat with cheap, poisonous grains, which operates through various mechanisms.

There are very few shortcuts in the production of meat that can allow it to be made more cheaply. As the money supply increases, the price of meat rises quickly, and people can no longer afford it. They are forced to substitute away from it with inferior products, like chicken and grains. The replacement reduces the impact of inflation on people's budgets in the short run. It also makes them less susceptible to inflation in the long run since the cheaper substitutes are easier to increase in supply in response to an increase in demand, and so have less acute price rises.

However, fiat inflation not only reduces the purchasing power of individuals and forces them to consume inferior foods; it also transfers purchasing power to the government, enabling it to play a disproportionate role in determining food policy and nutritional guidelines. *Fiat Food* details how US government policy has actively sought to increase crop yields to fight inflation, deploying industrial practices that have increased crop yield, without correspondingly increasing the nutritional value of foods, all while increasing the amount of anti-nutrients in food. The increasingly harmful nature of modern crops is inseparable from the cornucopia of emergent modern autoimmune diseases growing in prevalence. And perhaps most pernicious of all, the government's magical money printer has allowed it to dictate the conclusions of the criminal modern pseudoscience of nutrition, which shapes the curriculum of all modern universities and medical schools, as well as the dietary recommendations of nutrition bodies and medical regulatory bodies. It also shapes the food offered to millions of unfortunate students and prisoners in schools and prisons.

Another important causal link between inflation and food and health outcomes happens through the impact of money on time preference. As money devalues, people's ability to provide for their futures is compromised, making the future more uncertain and encouraging them to discount it further. This can be observed in individual food choices, where people become more likely to opt for foods that provide fleeting sensory pleasure at the expense of long-term health. But perhaps more importantly, it is reflected in the health of the soil. As the future is discounted more, people value the capital embedded in the soil even more, incentivizing them to consume it in the present, reducing the health of the soil for the future.

Examining food consumption in the twentieth century reveals a decline in the consumption of beef and lamb, two of the best sources of nutrition for humans, and an increase in cheaper, suboptimal alternatives. Per capita beef consumption went down 22%, and lamb consumption decreased 53%. Goat per capita increased 36%, pork increased 19%, but the major winner was chicken, which almost tripled. Poisonous grains also went up significantly. Pork and chicken are decidedly inferior alternatives to beef and lamb, and this downgrade has been detrimental to human health.

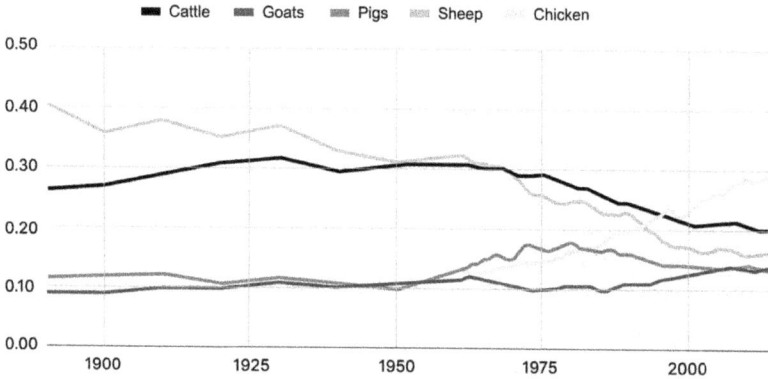

Figure 19: Livestock types per capita over the twentieth century

Just as inflation has popularized doomsday cultish ideas about Earth running out of energy or metals, or humans ruining the weather through CO_2 emissions, it has also convinced people that the growing unaffordability of red meat is a result of the limits on Earth's carrying capacity, that there is a maximum number of cows and sheep possible on Earth, and as human population increases, we must learn to make do with less beef and lamb. As with natural resources, the natural limits on meat production are nowhere near being the binding constraints on our ability to produce the meat. The real scarcity is our time and how we trade off meat production against other economic goods. Further, and perhaps more significantly, the anti-meat propaganda pervading modern academia has somehow convinced a lot of people that grazing animals somehow degrade the Earth, when in fact they are what keeps it healthy and rich in nutrients. As Allan Savory has demonstrated, land previously considered unproductive can be revitalized through regenerative grazing. Earth's capacity to produce meat is likely orders of magnitude larger than what people think. Moreover, if governments weren't subsidizing the production of poisonous, cheap monocrops to cover up inflation, so much of the world's farmland could be used for grazing animals instead, producing good nutrition. If we moved away from these monocrop poisons, the benefits to human health would be substantial. A large part of our demand for them comes from inadequate meat intake, and they are used to produce highly palatable and addictive foods, which cause over-eating. Humanity can, and really should, reduce its intake of these foods drastically and benefit. With these barren fertilizer-soaked fields no longer producing the cancerous garbage filling our supermarkets, we would have a lot more room for growing wholesome beef and lamb.

Had humanity been, in fact, getting wealthier over the century thanks to hard money, and had governments not wasted so much of our wealth on propagandizing us to eat more poisonous grains, the decline in red meat consumption would be reversed. We would be eating a lot more red meat, and we would not be increasing our consumption of chicken, pork, and grains as much. It would be reasonable to assume a tripling of beef and lamb consumption over the course of the century. There was widespread malnutrition around the world in the early twentieth century, and arguably, only the industrialized West came close to eating a nutritionally sufficient diet. Europe, the Americas, and Australia were likely the only regions where a significant percentage of the population could meet their needs for beef at that time. These regions comprised approximately one-third of the world's population at that time. Had they continued to get wealthier on a sound monetary standard, they would likely have increased their consumption of beef over the course of the century. The rest of the world would have likely had to quadruple its beef consumption to meet its nutritional needs. Averaging the increases worldwide would have likely resulted in a tripling of beef consumption per capita over the course of the century. Given that the world population in the year 2000 in our alternative world is around 8.4 billion people, 2.3 billion more than in the real world, we would be looking at a cattle and sheep population roughly ten times what we had in the real world in 2000. A tenfold increase in cattle and sheep population would mean a radically different agricultural sector and much better health outcomes. Large swathes of our monocrop farms would be lush grazing fields, rich with nutrients and biodiversity. This would mean a lot less desertification and more lush grasslands and forests. It would also mean a healthier soil, full of nutrients, and healthier and happier humans.

If people had spent the twentieth century eating increasing quantities of the nutritious beef they needed to thrive, it would follow that there would be less of an economic incentive to increase yields of crops quickly. Readers may have noticed that the discussion of technological innovations in Chapter 16 did not include the 'Green Revolution,' which our real-world planet experienced in the 1960s and 1970s, which is usually hailed as a miracle for making food cheaper, more abundant, shelf-stable, and better resistant to insects and rodents. Yet the green revolution also produced the modern Frankencrops that have increased the burden of autoimmune disorders drastically. The numerous forms of food allergies and intolerances, as well as many of the more common diseases prevalent today, are a result of our bodies' inability to handle these crops. I hypothesize that in a world of hard money, increasing economic abundance, lower time preference, higher savings, and increased industrial productivity, there would have been far less of an incentive to engage in this kind of food engineering. With the population increasingly well-fed from eating optimal meat, our staple crops would constitute an increasingly inconsequential part of our diets. Without the immiseration of fiat, the poor would gain better nutrition from eating meat, and not from replacing their nutritionally deficient crops with cheaper and unhealthier genetically modified versions of it.

If nutrition science were not a criminal enterprise, promoting industrial waste, covering up inflation, and contributing to illness, it could be very useful for humanity. One can easily imagine a world in which nutritionists were not mass murdering people on an industrial scale as they are today, but instead were giving them useful information that helps them make wise nutritional choices. Nutrition science would recommend that people stay away from grains, sugars, and the concoctions that modern industrial technology has made possible. The "vegetable oils" heavily marketed by fiat authorities worldwide would go back to their rightful place as cheap industrial refuse used to lubricate machines. Cholesterol would be an obscure chemical in the body that most people will never hear of, let alone obsess about. Fiber would have been understood as an undesirable and useless indigestible substance that may be tolerated in small quantities. Skimmed milk would only be used to fatten pigs and cattle for slaughter, not to fatten humans to become pharmaceutical and medical cartel customers.

Should nutritionists want to make generalized dietary recommendations, they are likely to look very different from the genocidal recommendations the US government has popularized in our world. Without the need to promote cheap industrial waste to please their paymasters, and with the intellectual independence afforded by sound money, nutritionists would be able to understand the blatantly obvious reality that red ruminant meat is the only complete and essential food for humans, and they would recommend it as the bedrock and base of a healthy diet. Other meat from birds and fish would be the second most important food group. Eggs and dairy products comprise the third-largest source of nutrients in the diet. These sources would provide the vast majority of the nutritional needs of people. Small amounts of grains, pulses, vegetables, fruits, and sugars would be a relatively harmless complement to the diet of most people.

World War II

With the resolution of the Great War based on a framework of self-determination, and without central banks, there would be no Second World War. There was no Treaty of Versailles to carve parts of Germany out and create an outraged, resentful German population. Germany was not forced to pay large indemnities for its war guilt that would destroy it economically, cause hyperinflation, and increase German anger. The monarchy would have remained in power, and there would have been no Weimar Republic, and no National Socialist Party. Hitler would likely have led an obscure life. The borders of Germany, like everywhere else, would be determined through the votes of the populations, and the ruling German dynasty would continue to rule over those who wanted to be part of it. Various parts of Germany would likely secede when given the choice, and there would be no pretext for conflict between Germany and its neighbors. With the Bolsheviks eliminated by the absence of fiat central banking to finance their takeover of Russia, and Tsar Michael chastised by his brother's tragic failure at imperial expansion, and Russia a signatory of the ICSD, Russia would be in no position whatsoever to attempt to export revolution and conquer Europe as Stalin tried to do in 1940.[139]

The reader might have noticed that I inserted a summit between the German, Austrian, French, Russian, and British ruling families in France to commemorate the 30-year anniversary of the Great War in France. In our real world, this would have occurred during the final and most brutal days of World War II. In the alternative history of this book, the governments were peacefully commemorating their dead from thirty years earlier. The reader may have also noticed that the first nuclear power plant was established in this story in Hiroshima on the exact date on which the American nuclear bomb was dropped in Hiroshima in our world. In this alternative history, nuclear technology would be used for peaceful energy generation only. One can only imagine what a peaceful world in the 1940s could have looked like, and how much it would have made our present world richer.

Socialism

Other economic phenomena unlikely to exist in a hard money twentieth century are leftism, socialism, and communism. It is no coincidence that leftism as a phenomenon exploded globally around the time of the creation of the modern fiat central bank after the First World War. As the book showed, the rise of socialist revolutionaries in Russia was financed by German and American bankers. There was nothing organic or popular about the rise of Bolshevism. There was nothing Russian about the ramblings of Karl Marx, and there was practically no popular appeal to his ideas among the vast majority of Russians. This was an entirely foreign ideology imported into Russia to bring down the

---

139 Jonathan Grant, "McMeekin, Sean. Stalin's War: A New History of World War II,"
    History: Reviews of New Books 49, no. 6 (November 2021): 147–48.

Tsar's regime. If central banks die in 1915, the German and American bankers who financed the Bolsheviks go bankrupt, and the entire Bolshevik phenomenon dies and withers away. Without the Bolsheviks usurping power in Russia in 1915, the vast majority of the world's communist and socialist parties would never have been born. It is remarkable how many of the world's communist and revolutionary socialist parties emerged immediately after the Russian Revolution, providing another glaring demonstration of the artificial and astroturfed nature of leftism in the twentieth century. Without the Bolsheviks and the major Western central banks, most of the world's leftist revolutions would never have taken place, and the world would have been an infinitely more peaceful place in the twentieth century. Ngram charts provide further support for this contention, showing how the terms "Karl Marx" and "communism" were relatively obscure in the nineteenth century, when their use was limited to fringe nineteenth-century political movements. It was only under fiat central banking that their importance took off, and all over the planet, violent revolutionary movements sprang up, spreading leftist slogans in favor of overturning the system of property rights, undermining the foundational building block of civilization, and increasing the power of governments over their citizens.

Without government control of the monetary printing press, leftist ideas are completely unworkable. One of the main planks of Marx's Communist Manifesto was the creation of a central bank that monopolizes money and credit, and this is the foundational plank on which all other planks rest. Without inflation, it is difficult to muster the power needed to confiscate property from all of society and command it from a central authority.

Socialist ideas would also have been significantly less prominent in this century without the monetary printing press financing their dissemination. It is no coincidence that the same government-funded universities that live off of fiat money financing also invariably teach leftist and Marxist ideas to their students. Leftist ideas provide plausible-sounding rationales for government inflation and increased government power. These ideas were very popular in twentieth-century intellectual circles because intellectuals are primarily servants to power, and the leftist rationale for government intervention in all aspects of life is perfectly suited for convincing the population to accept more government power and the inflation that is necessary to implement it. The death of central banks in 1915 would have nipped leftist ideology and politics in the bud. As controversial as this may sound, it is far more outlandish to attempt to argue the obverse: that early twentieth-century leftist political movements would have developed into modern leftism in a world with sound money. Progressive and labor political organizations would have evolved in a far more peaceful, productive, and prosperous manner in a hard-money twentieth century.

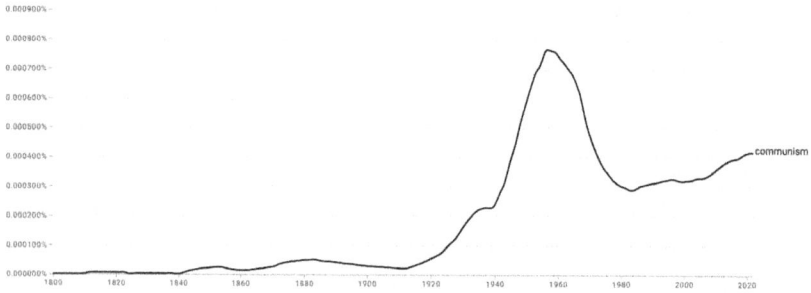

Figure 20: Ngram chart for communism

Figure 21: Ngram chart for Karl Marx

Israel

With the right to self-determination in Europe, and nationalist movements al-lowed to express themselves peacefully through secession, the ethnic conflicts of central and Eastern Europe from 1916 onward would have likely been greatly minimized. The areas of Eastern Europe and the Austro-Hungarian Empire that were heavily populated with Jews would have likely sought and obtained inde-pendence. With nationalist sentiments expressed peacefully in their native lands, it is unlikely that the Zionist movement would have caught on and grown. In the second decade of the twentieth century, the population of Palestine was only around 10% Jewish, and Jews were able to own property and had the same rights as their Christian and Muslim compatriots, so there was little incentive for them to seek an exclusive ethnostate at the expense of non-Jewish Palestinians. Zion-ism was never a solution for the problems of Jews in Palestine. It was a solution to the problems of Jews in Europe, but with the First World War ending in 1915, and with the framework of self-determination applying in Europe, obviating the bitter ethnic conflicts of the first half of the twentieth century, political Zionism would have never materialized. Without the Zionist movement, there would have been no wholesale dispossession of Palestinians in 1947-48, no continued progressive dispossession over decades, and no denial of Palestinian property rights in the genocidal land-thieving ethnostate. Palestine and the Middle East would have been far more peaceful and prosperous over the past century.[140]

Modern readers likely think that religious conflict in Palestine is endemic and inevitable, a continuation of thousands of years of struggle. But this couldn't be further from the truth. It is, in fact, remarkable how exceptionally destructive and violent the Zionist movement has been compared to the rest of the history of Palestine. The last time an invasion of Palestine led to large displacement, dispossession, and expulsion was in AD 70–130, when the Roman Empire put down the Jewish revolt and expelled many Jews from Jerusalem. Some of the Jewish residents remained in Palestine, and some converted to Christianity, at

---

140 For a detailed explanation of the Palestinian-Israeli conflict as the result of the dismantling of the property rights system, see Ammous, Saifedean. *Property Rights: The Root Cause of the Palestinian-Isrseli Conflict*. Substack article.

least outwardly. Jews were only able to return to Jerusalem and practice their faith with the Islamic conquest in 637 AD, which rehabilitated the Temple, after the Romans had turned it into a trash dump for five centuries.

This is well-documented in Jewish and Islamic sources, and you can read about it in detail in Israeli historian Moshe Gill's *A History of Palestine, 634–1099*, Relevant passages (pages 68-69) excerpted:

> Karaite commentators of the tenth century mention in a number of instances the drastic change effected by the Muslims in their capture of Jerusalem. Thus Daniel al-Qumisi writes at the end of the ninth century in his commentary on the Book of Daniel, xi:32: 'For before he came [the king of Ishmael, who defeated the king of the south, that is the Byzantine emperor] they could not come to Jerusalem; and they would come from the four corners of the earth to Tiberias and Gaza to see the temple; but now with his coming he brought them to jerusalem and gave them a place and many of Israel settled there; and afterwards Israel come from the four corners of the earth to Jerusalem to preach and to pray. ..' In this same strain, Sahl b. Masllah writes in the introduction to his Book of Commandments:
>
>> '... and after they left the place, it was more than five-hundred years in ruins, inhabited by hyenas, and not one of Israel could come. There were jews from the east who came to the city of Maaziah [Tiberias] to pray there. From the west they would come to the city of Gaza. From the land of the south they would come to the city of Zoar. And in the days of the little horn, God opened the gates of his compassion to His people and brought them to His Holy City and they settled there and they built places to read and to interpret and to pray at all times and to keep watchers therein at night...'
>
> Similarly, his contemporary Salmon ben Yeruhim, in his Arabic commentary to Ps. xxx: wrote '... as we know, the temple remained in the hands of the Romans for more than 500 years and they did not succeed in entering jerusalem; and anyone who did and was recognised [as a jew] was put to death. But

> when the Romans left it, by the mercy of the God of Israel, and the kingdom of Ishmael was victorious, Israel was permitted to come and to live...'[141]

And while the Arabs expelled the Roman rulers, they allowed the indigenous Jews and Christians to remain in Palestine. Few Arabs actually migrated to Palestine, and the majority of the population has remained from the indigenous inhabitants, many of whom converted to Islam, and many of whom remained Christian and Jewish to this day.[142]

Since the Islamic conquest of Palestine in 637 AD, Jews, Muslims, and Christians have been free to live in Palestine and own property, until Zionism came to deprive non-Jews of their property rights. While the political control of the land shifted among various rulers from 637 to 1948, the property rights of the local population were consistently respected, and all religions coexisted peacefully. As an example, here is how R. Avraham Gershon of Kitov, Poland, the brother-in-law of the founder of Hasidism, described his experience in Hebron when he immigrated to Palestine in 1747.[143]

> In this holy city, there is a Jewish courtyard which they [are permitted to] close during the Sabbath and festivals, no one can come in or out all night, and they have virtually no fear of gentiles. Its doors were kept unlocked at night...
>
> And when there is a celebration, such as circumcision or some other occasion, the Muslim elders come, and all rejoice. And it is not only this, but the local gentiles, even the greatest ones, love the Jews very much, and whenever there is a celebration, such as circumcision, their leaders come to celebrate with the Jews and dance with the Jews, almost exactly —not to compare— just like Jews.

---

141 Moshe Gil, *A History of Palestine, 634–1099*, trans. Ethel Broido (Cambridge: Cambridge University Press, 1992).

142 "Origin of the Palestinians," in *Wikipedia*, last modified August 29, 2025, accessed September 30, 2025.

143 Yitzhak Y. Melamed, "Hasidic-Muslim Relations in Ottoman Palestine," *TheTorah.com*, 2018.

> When I came here, the city's highest officer greeted me, and I gave him a nice zibbuk (pipe?) I had from Istanbul. And they [the Arab officers] love me and say that I brought them great fortune and luck.

> At the evening of the recent festival of Simhat Torah, when I was designated as Hatan Torah, all the [Jewish] sages came to celebrate with me, and the [Muslim] dignitaries came too, and they were dancing and singing just like the Jews, and praising God in their language, Arabic.

It is not inevitable that Jews, Muslims, and Christians have to live in conflict, as they had coexisted in Palestine for 1300 years. As is the case everywhere, peaceful civilization is only possible when property rights are respected. And as is the case everywhere, violent conflict is inevitable when property rights are violated. Palestine fell into an interminable bloody conflict when the property rights of the majority of its population, and the majority of its land owners, were annulled in 1947-48. The British Mandate government surveyed the land of Palestine in 1945 and found that Jewish ownership of the land of Palestine did not exceed 5.67% of the total land of Palestine, while Muslims, Christians, and other sects owned 48.3% of the land of Palestine. 46% of the land was public land, although much of that was de facto owned by Bedouin nomads in the south. Among the private lands, Jews only owned 10.5% of the land, while Muslims, Christians, and others owned 89.5% of the land.[144] As Figure 22 shows, not a single district of Palestine had a majority of Jewish ownership. To build an ethnostate on a land whose ownership and population were predominantly from another ethnicity, the Zionist movement stole the land of the majority of rightful owners in 1947-48 purely for being non-Jews. To achieve this, it commandeered the powers of the leading fiat governments.

---

144 Government of Palestine, Department of Statistics, *Village Statistics, April, 1945* (Jerusalem: Government of Palestine, 1945).

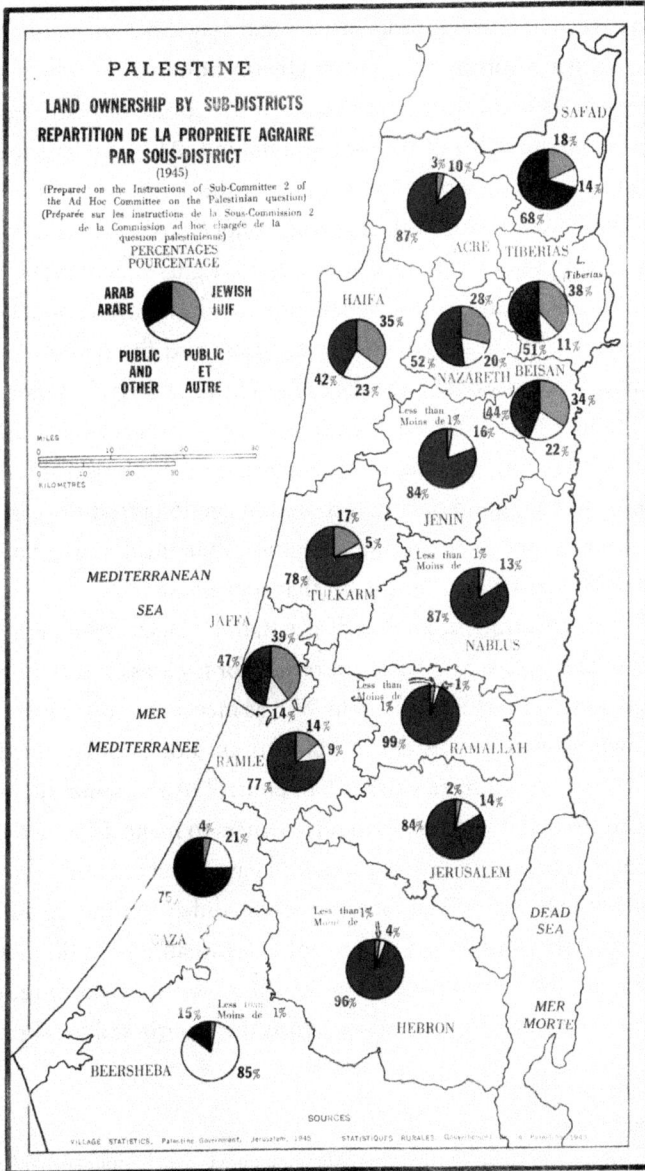

Figure 22: Land ownership in Palestine in 1945

The initiation, growth, and realization of the Zionist project are inextricably linked to the fiat interwar order in ways that may shock the modern reader. It was the British government's Balfour Declaration in 1917 which gave political Zionism its first impetus and set it on the course of being realized to the exclusion of the rights of the local population. Although the text of the declaration had paid lip service to the rights of the native population and the owners of the land by saying, "it being clearly understood that nothing shall be done which may prejudice the civil and religious rights of existing non-Jewish communities in Palestine," this was yet another of the many lies of the wartime British government, meant to assuage domestic and foreign opposition to what amounted to no less than the theft of an entire country. In a more candid moment, Balfour made his true intentions clear, two years later, in a letter to Lord Curzon: "the four great powers are committed to Zionism and Zionism, be it right or wrong, good or bad, is rooted in age-long tradition, in present needs, in future hopes, of far profounder import than the desire and prejudices of the 700,000 Arabs who now inhabit that ancient land."[145]

The British government also made the Balfour Declaration as a promise addressed to the Rothschild family in return for their assistance in bringing the United States into the First World War, as mentioned on the Rothschild Family's own website to this day.[146] Had Britain not been involved in this senseless war, it would have neither had control of Palestine nor would it have needed to steal it wholesale from its owners to make it into a homeland for foreigners to bail it out of a war it should have never entered. Throughout the period of the Palestine Mandate, the British did everything to undermine the property rights and national rights of Palestinians, including disarming the Palestinians in 1936–39, while allowing the Zionists to continue to build their terrorist military organizations, even as they continued to target British soldiers.

---

145 EL Woodward and Rohan Butler, eds., "Memorandum by Mr. Balfour (Paris) Respecting Syria, Palestine, and Mesopotamia," *Memo on British Foreign Policy, 1919–1939*, (1919; HM Stationery Office, 1952), 345.

146 Arthur James Balfour, "Walter Rothschild and the Balfour Declaration," *Declaration to Lord Rothschild* (The Rothschild Archive, November 2, 1917).

But it wasn't just Britain that helped create this artificial state on stolen land, as Balfour clarifies; it was also the rest of the four powers of the Paris Conference—USA, France, and Italy—who, like Balfour, saw in Zionism a golden opportunity to avoid having to accept Jewish migrants escaping the ethnic conflicts of Eastern Europe. A framework of self-determination in Europe would have drastically reduced the migration problem and undermined the great powers' support for Zionism.

More significantly, and as astonishing as it may sound to modern readers, it was the Nazi regime that gave the Zionist movement the lifeline it needed to survive the 1930s in the face of growing Palestinian hostility and global and Jewish apathy. As thoroughly documented in the work of Lenni Brenner,[147] the Zionist movement signed the Haavara agreement with the Nazi regime, which would encourage German Jews to leave Germany for Palestine and let them take their capital by converting it to German goods, which would be invested in the Zionist settlements in Palestine. The Nazis further provided training to Jews in agriculture to encourage them to leave for Palestine, and also allowed for extensive Zionist propaganda in German newspapers. In fact, it was none other than Adolf Eichmann, who was a central figure in the Nazi-Zionist alliance, even studying Hebrew and traveling to Palestine. Without the rise of the Nazi regime and its race-based government, it is implausible that the German monarchy would have engaged in such a scheme to expel its own Jewish subjects and lose their capital resources. A peaceful resolution of World War I and a peaceful world built on a gold standard would have eliminated the possibility of a Nazi regime. Without it, it is doubtful that the Zionist project would have survived. There was still very little Jewish migration to Palestine until the rise of Nazism and the Haavara agreement, as most Jews worldwide did not see Palestine as their national home, because it was not.

The extent of Zionist reliance on twentieth-century fiat regimes does not end there, of course. In the 1930s and 1940s, the majority of weapons that the Zionist terrorist groups were able to smuggle to Palestine came from the Soviet

---

147 Lenni Brenner, *Zionism in the Age of the Dictators* (Croom Helm, 1983); Lenni Brenner, *51 Documents: Zionist Collaboration with the Nazis* (Barricade Books, 2002).

Union and the Eastern European socialist regimes. The Zionist project was initially dominated by socialists and inextricably linked to the socialist model of settlements, which is why it obtained considerable support from socialist regimes that sought to spread the revolution globally.[148] A peaceful, fiat-free world order in which these socialist regimes never come to power would likely constitute an insurmountable obstacle to the Zionist project.

Later, the Zionist project became dependent on the United States for its financial and military lifeline. Since turning the US into its vassal state in the 1960s, Israel has received several hundred billion dollars from the American government, and involved the American government in massively expensive, interminable wars in the Middle East, under an endless series of false pretexts, whose only real purpose is to eliminate all enemies of Israel. The US tab for maintaining the Zionist colony has likely exceeded $8 trillion until today, which would be completely impossible on a hard money standard where the US government would need to collect these sums from its people upfront, and not hide them in the rising prices people experience every day and blame on an endless variety of bogeymen.

The origination of the Zionist idea, its growth, and the growing support for it are all intertwined with the institutions of fiat money and the political regimes reliant on fiat money. Without the calamity of fiat money to allow them to spend while hiding the cost from their people, Britain, the Nazis, the socialist regimes, and the United States would not have been able to subsidize the Zionist project of land theft and ethnic cleansing for a century. The majority of Europe's Jews would have been happy to remain in their homes in Europe, and the Jews of Palestine and the orient would have continued to coexist peacefully with their Muslim and Christian neighbors as they had for centuries. A sane, fiat-free world would not have expelled Jews from their homes in Europe over decades, then subsidized them to expel Palestinians from their homes for decades. A vote for self-determination in Palestine in a fiat-free world would have likely chosen secession from the Ottoman Empire, and sought to join

---

148 Arnold Krammer, *The Forgotten Friendship: Israel and the Soviet Bloc, 1947–53* (University of Illinois Press, 1974); Jeffrey Herf, *Israel's Moment: International Support for and Opposition to Establishing the Jewish State, 1945–1949* (Cambridge University Press, 2022).

the Hashemite royal family, given their descent from the Prophet Mohammad, and their growing popular campaign to revive the Caliphate and free
the Arabs from Ottoman rule. The track record of the Hashemites over the
past century suggests to me that this monarchy would have been stable and
avoided secession by minorities. Jordan has, for more than a century, been a
remarkably peaceful country respecting the rights of its religious minorities.
Jordan has grown from a sparsely populated Emirate of 200,000 people at its
establishment in 1921 to a thriving Kingdom of 12 million people growing
economically and peacefully as its republican and democratic neighbors fight
endless wars over territory and religion.

Acknowledgements

The publication of this book was delayed and interrupted by the untimely death of my father, who had wanted to see it completed. His passing was a sharp reminder of everything he has done for me, and all that I have learned from him, throughout my life. This book, and everything I achieve in my life, are primarily thanks to him, and the momentous effort he invested in raising, educating, and disciplining me. His memory continues to motivate me to be better every day.

I am also eternally grateful for my wife and children who put up with the long hours I spent away from them researching and writing this book. This book benefited from the feedback of attendees of the seminars on my online learning platform, saifedean.com, where many of its ideas were formulated. It also benefitted from the feedback of several friends to whom I am very grateful. Patrick Newman, Théo Mogenet, and Michael Goldstein provided me very helpful detailed feedback. I am particularly thankful to Théo Mogenet for the inspired suggestion of Louis Blériot as the Satoshi Nakamoto of the twentieth century. I also thank Jimmy Song, Nick Giambruno, Ahmad Ammous, Prince Filip Karađorđević, Matthew Tower, Adam Salama, Daniel Jeremić, Arnaud Bertrand, and Alessandro Fusillo. I also thank my history teacher at the Ramallah Friends School, Peter Kapenga, whose engaging teaching instilled in me a lifelong fascination with the history of the twentieth century. I also thank everyone who contributed to Wikipedia, as it was an enormously valuable resource in researching this book. Its inevitable problems and biases can cloud what an astonishingly valuable source of knowledge this amazing website remains.

I am grateful to the loyal readers who pre-ordered signed copies of this book before its publication: Adam Kucharczyk, Ahmad A J Fallatah, Alfredo Hinny,

Alif Leong, Antonio Caccese, Arnaud Cart, Ben Sharpe, Benedikt Berentelg, Bronson Moyen, Chen Xi Yong, Christof Mathys, Daniel Edmunds, David Barbaro, Gerd Luedtke, Gregory Horne, Grey Thompson, Hunter Hastings, Jacob Cottrill, Jeff Cater, Jeff Hattem, John A. Krpan, Julio Neira, Klaus Lovgreen, Keyvan Davani, Lachlan McWilliam, Luis Alonso, Luz Silva, Marcello Hansen, Mark W Roen, Matija Grlj, Maximilian Neuger, Miguel D. Oliveira, Muhammed Yesilhark, Paul Waters, Payton Stauble, Pierre Porthaux, Raymond Zukas, Richard Bell, Ronan Barry, Seha Islam, and Zachary Hollinshead.

Finally, I thank my team at saifedean.com, whose tireless work was instrumental in bringing this book to life: Pavao Pahljina, Vladimir Panouchkine, Flora Fontes, Gamze Amous, Max DeMarco, who produced the audiobook, and Jamie de Rooij, who designed the graphics.

List of Figures

List of Tables

Bibliography

Albertini, Luigi. *The Origins of the War of 1914.* Vol. 3. Enigma Books, 2005.

Ammous, Saifedean. *Principles of Economics.* The Saif House, 2023.

Ammous, Saifedean. *The Bitcoin Standard: The Decentralized Alternative to Central Banking.* John Wiley & Sons, 2018.

Ammous, Saifedean. *The Fiat Standard: The Debt Slavery Alternative to Human Civilization.* The Saif House, 2021.

Ammous, Saifedean. *Property Rights: The Root Cause of the Palestinian-Isrseli Conflict.* Substack article. November 2025.

Anson, Michael, Norma Cohen, Alastair Owens, and Daniel Todman. "Your Country Needs Funds: The Extraordinary Story of Britain's Early Efforts to Finance the First World War." Bank Underground, August 8, 2017.

Balfour, Arthur James. "Walter Rothschild and the Balfour Declaration." Declaration to Lord Rothschild. The Rothschild Archive, November 2, 1917.

Balfour, Michael. *The Kaiser and his Times.* Houghton Mifflin, 1964.

Barnes, Harry Elmer. *The Genesis of the World War: An Introduction to the Problem of War Guilt.* Forgotten Books, 2019.

Beatty, Jack. *The Lost History of 1914: How the Great War Was Not Inevitable.* A&C Black, 2012.

Bentham, Jeremy. *Defence of Usury.* 1787; Lang and Ustick, 1796.

Bering, Henrik. "Prussian Maneuvers–Henrik Bering on Iron Kingdom: The Rise and Downfall of Prussia, 1600–1947 by Christopher Clark." Hoover Institution, April 3, 2007.

Bernstorff, Graf von Johann Heinrich. *My Three Years in America.* With Robert J. Hall. 1920; Project Gutenberg, 2010.

Brenner, Lenni. *51 Documents: Zionist Collaboration with the Nazis*. Barricade Books, 2002.

Brenner, Lenni. *Zionism in the Age of the Dictators*. Croom Helm, 1983.

Bresciani-Turroni, Costantino. *Economics of Inflation: A Study of Currency Depreciation in Post-War Germany*. Ludwig von Mises Institute, 2007.

Buchanan, Patrick J. *Churchill, Hitler, and "The Unnecessary War": How Britain Lost Its Empire and the West Lost the World*. Three Rivers Press, 2008.

Carter, Violet Bonham. *Champion Redoubtable: The Diaries and Letters of Violet Bonham Carter 1914–1945*. Weidenfeld, 1998.

Chernow, Ron. *Titan: The Life of John D. Rockefeller, Sr.* 1998; Vintage Books, 2004.

Chisholm, Hugh, ed. "Witte, Serge Julievich, Count." In *Encyclopædia Britannica*, 28:762–63. 1911.

Churchill, Winston S. *The World Crisis 1911–1914*. 1923; Bloomsbury Academic, 2015.

Clark, Christopher. *The Sleepwalkers*. Harper Perennial, 2012.

Collins, Turner. "Russo-Japanese War: How Racism Ended European Hegemony in Asia." TheCollector, April 12, 2022.

Connaughton, Richard M. *The War of the Rising Sun and Tumbling Bear: A Military History of the Russo-Japanese War, 1904–5*. Routledge, 1988.

Diaries and Notebooks: 1903, Orville Wright. Digital Collection: Wilbur Wright and Orville Wright Papers. Library of Congress. 1903.

Dobrorolski, Sergei. *Die Mobilmachung der Russischen Armee 1914: Mit Beiträgen von Graf Pourtalès*. Vol. 1. Deutsche Verlagsgesellschaft für Politik und Geschichte mbH, 1922.

Docherty, Gerry, and Jim MacGregor. *Hidden Histories: The Secret Origins of the First World War*. Mainstream Publishing, 2013.

Duckenfield, Mark, ed. *The Monetary History of Gold: A Documentary History, 1660–1999*. 1st ed. Routledge, 2004.

Edward Mandell House. "The Intimate Papers of Colonel House 1858-1938." Memo from May 29, 1914 to President Woodrow Wilson. Edited by Charles Seymour. 1971.

Einaudi, Luigi. *Prediche Inutili*. Giulio Einaudi Editore, 1956.

Estonian World Review. "Medvedev Falsification Commission may be 'Harmful' or 'Useless,' Memorial Expert Says." May 21, 2009.

Fairchild, Fred Rogers. "German War Finance—A Review." *The American Economic Review* 12, no. 2 (1922): 246–61.

Fay, Sidney Bradshaw. *The Origins of the World War Volume II: After Sarajevo Immediate Causes of the War*. Ishi Press International, 2010.

Federal Ministry for Economic Cooperation and Development. "Colonialism and Addressing the Past." July 20, 2023.

Ferguson, Niall. *The Pity of War: Explaining World War I*. Basic Books, 1999.

Fetter, Frank A. "Introduction." In *Capital, Interest, and Rent: Essays in the Theory of Distribution*, edited by Murray Rothbard, 3–4. Sheed Andrews and McMeel, 1977.

Fromkin, David. *Europe's Last Summer: Why the World Went to War in 1914*. Vintage, 2005.

Gatrell, Peter. *A Whole Empire Walking: Refugees in Russia during World War I*. Indiana University Press, 1999.

Gatrell, Peter. *Russia's First World War: A Social and Economic History*. 1st ed. Routledge, 2014.

Gerber, Therese Steffen. "August Burckhardt." In *Historisches Lexikon der Schweiz (HLS)*, March 26, 2003.

Gil, Moshe. *A History of Palestine, 634–1099*. Translated by Ethel Broido. Cambridge: Cambridge University Press, 1992.

Gilbert, Martin. *First World War*. HarperCollins, 1995.

Golin, Alfred. *No Longer an Island: Britain and the Wright Brothers, 1902-1909*. Stanford University Press, 1984.

Government of Palestine. Department of Statistics. *Village Statistics, April, 1945*. Jerusalem: Government of Palestine, 1945.

Grant, Jonathan. "McMeekin, Sean. Stalin's War: A New History of World War II." *History: Reviews of New Books* 49, no. 6 (November 2021): 147–48.

Griffin, G. Edward. *The Creature from Jekyll Island: A Second Look at the Federal Reserve*. 3rd ed. American Media, 1998.

Haldane, Andrew G. "Stuck - Speech by Andy Haldane." Bank of England, June 30, 2015.

Hall, George J. "Exchange Rates and Casualties during the First World War." *Journal of Monetary Economics* 51, no. 8 (November 2004): 1711–42.

Hamer, David Allan. *John Morley: Liberal Intellectual in Politics*. Oxford University Press, 1968.

Hamer, David. "Morley, John, Viscount Morley of Blackburn (1838-1923)." In *Oxford Dictionary of National Biography*. Oxford University Press, 2004.

Hamlin, Cyrus. "The Dream of Russia." *The Atlantic*, December 1, 1886.

Hans-Adam, Prince. *The State in the Third Millennium*. I.B.Tauris, 2009.

Hartmann, Gérard. *Le Coupe Pommery (1909-1913)*. Champagne Pommery À Reims-France, 1909.

Henry Asquith, Herbert. *H.H. Asquith, Letters to Venetia Stanley*. Edited by Michael G. Brock and Eleanor Brock. Oxford University Press, 1982.

Herf, Jeffrey. *Israel's Moment: International Support for and Opposition to Establishing the Jewish State, 1945–1949*. Cambridge University Press, 2022.

Hobsbawm, Eric. *The Age of Empire: 1875–1914*. Vintage, 1989.

Homer, Sidney, and Richard Sylla. *A History of Interest Rates*. John Wiley & Sons, Inc., 2005.

Hoppe, Hans-Hermann. *Democracy – The God That Failed: The Economics and Politics of Monarchy, Democracy and Natural Order*. Routledge, 2018.

Horn, Martin. *Britain, France, and the Financing of the First World War*. McGill-Queen's University Press, 2002.

Horne, Alistair. *The Price of Glory: Verdun 1916*. 1964; Penguin Books, 1994.

Hülsmann, Jörg Guido. "Mises on Monetary Reform: The Private Alternative." *The Quarterly Journal of Austrian Economics* 11, no. 3 (December 2008): 208–18.

Inventors. "Octave Chanute to Wilbur Wright." Mississippi State University, January 23, 1910.

Jones, Marcus. "The Alliance That Wasn't: Germany and Austria-Hungary in World War I." In *Grand Strategy and Military Alliances*, edited by Peter R. Mansoor and Williamson Murray, 284–312. Cambridge University Press, 2016.

Kazin, Michael. *A Godly Hero: The Life of William Jennings Bryan*. Knopf Doubleday Publishing Group, 2007.

Kealey, Terence. *The Economic Laws of Scientific Research*. Macmillan Press, 1996

King, Greg, and Penny Wilson. *The Fate of the Romanovs*. John Wiley & Sons, 2003.

Kochan, Lionel. *Russia in Revolution*. Paladin, 1970.

Kowner, Rotem. *Historical Dictionary of the Russo-Japanese War*. The Scarecrow Press, 2006.

Krammer, Arnold. *The Forgotten Friendship: Israel and the Soviet Bloc, 1947–53*. University of Illinois Press, 1974.

Krasner, Stephen D. "State Power and the Structure of International Trade." *World Politics* 28, no. 3 (April 1976): 317–47.

Kuznets, Simon. *National Income, 1929-1932*. National Bureau of Economic Research, 1934.

Lamont, Duncan. "What 175 Years of Data Tell Us About House Price Affordability in the UK." *Schroders*. February 20, 2023.

Leaf, Walter. *Banking*. Williams and Norgate, 1926.

Lieven, Dominic. *Nicholas II: Emperor of All the Russias*. Pimlico, 1993.

Lohr, Eric. *Nationalizing the Russian Empire: The Campaign against Enemy Aliens during World War I*. Harvard University Press, 2003.

Ludwig, Emil, and Wilhelm Hohenzollern. *The Last of the Kaisers*. Translated by Ethel Colburn Mayne. G. P, Putnam's Sons, 1927.

Ludwig, Emil. *Bismarck: The Story of a Fighter*. Blue Ribbon Books, 1927.

Massie, Robert K. *Dreadnought: Britain, Germany, and the Coming of the Great War*. Ballantine Books, 1992.

Massie, Robert K. *Nicholas and Alexandra: The Classic Account of the Fall of the Romanov Dynasty*. Random House, 2000.

McCullough, David. *The Wright Brothers*. Simon & Schuster, 2015.

McMeekin, Sean. *The Russian Origins of the First World War*. Belknap Press, 2011.

Melamed, Yitzhak Y. "Hasidic-Muslim Relations in Ottoman Palestine." TheTorah. com, 2018.

Mises, Ludwig von. "Inflation: An Unworkable Fiscal Policy." In *Economic Freedom and Interventionism: An Anthology of Articles and Essays*, 602–30, edited by Bettina Bien Greaves. Liberty Fund, 2007.

Mises, Ludwig von. *Human Action: The Scholar's Edition*. 1949; Ludwig von Mises Institute, 2008.

Mises, Ludwig von. *Omnipotent Government: The Rise of the Total State and Total War*. Liberty Fund, 2010.

Mises, Ludwig von. *The Theory of Money and Credit*. 1934; Yale University Press, 1953.

Morel, E. D. *Diplomacy Revealed*. National Labour Press, 1921.

NatWest Group Remembers. "Gold, Banknotes and Money Supply in the First World War." Accessed September 26, 2025.

Neilson, Francis. *The Makers of War*. Appleton, Wisconsin: C. C. Nelson Publishing Company, 1950.

Nock, Albert Jay. *The Myth of a Guilty Nation*. B.W. Huebsch, 1922.

Officer, Lawrence. "Gold Standard." In *EH.Net Encyclopedia*, edited by Robert Whaples. March 26, 2008.

Osborne, John. *The Bank of England 1914-21*. Unpublished War History. 1920; Bank of England Archives, 1960.

Paleologue, Maurice. *An Ambassadors Memoirs*. 5th ed. Translated by F. A. Holt O.B.E. Vol. II Hutchinson & Co. Paternoster Row, 1925.

Pares, Bernard. *The Fall of the Russian Monarchy*. 1939; Phoenix, 2001.

Paterson, Thomas, J. Garry Clifford, Robert Brigham, Michael Donoghue, Kenneth J. Hagan, Deborah Kisatsky, and Shane J. Maddock. *American Foreign Relations: A History, Volume 2: Since 1895*. 8th ed. Cengage Learning, 2014.

Powell, Jim. *Wilson's War: How Woodrow Wilson's Great Blunder Led to Hitler, Lenin, Stalin and World War II*. Crown Forum, 2005.

Reinsch, Paul S. *Secret Diplomacy: How Far Can it be Eliminated?* Harcourt, Brace and Co., 1912.

Robinson, Belinda. "'Find a Reason to Go to War with Germany': Said King George V." *Daily Mail*, July 26, 2014.

Rošker, Jana S., and Nataša Vampelj Suhadolnik, eds. *Modernisation of Chinese Culture: Continuity and Change*. Cambridge Scholars Publishing, 2013.

Ross, James, and Leigh Bettenay. "Gold and Silver: Relative Values in the Ancient Past." *Cambridge Archaeological Journal* 34, no. 3 (August 2024): 403–20.

Rothbard, Murray N. *Economic Thought Before Adam Smith: An Austrian Perspective on the History of Economic Thought*. Edward Elgar Publishing, 1999.

Rothbard, Murray. *America's Great Depression* 5th ed. (Ludwig von Mises Institute, 2000)

Rothbard, Murray N. *Man, Economy, and State, Scholar's Edition*. Ludwig von Mises Institute, 2009.

Rothbard, Murray N. *The Progressive Era*. Ludwig von Mises Institute, 2017.

Strachan, Hew. *The First World War: Volume I: To Arms*. Oxford University Press, 2001.

Sutton, Antony C. *Wall Street and the Bolshevik Revolution: The Remarkable True Story of the American Capitalists Who Financed the Russian Communists*. Clairview Books, 2012.

Tames, Richard. *Last of the Tsars: The Life and Death of Nicholas and Alexandra*. Pan Books, 1972.

Tanielen, Melanie S. *The Charity of War: Famine, Humanitarian Aid, and World War I in the Middle East*. Stanford University Press, 2017.

Taylor, A. J. P. *Bismarck: The Man and Statesman*. Vintage, 1967.

The Henry Ford Museum. "No One Ever Wins a War." Henry Ford Quotes. Accessed September 30, 2025.

The New York Times. "Flying Machines Which Do Not Fly." October 9, 1903.

The Times History of the War. With Robarts—University of Toronto. Vol. XXI. The Times Printing House Square, 1920.

Toussaint, Eric, and Nathan Legrand. "The French Press in the Pay of the Tsar." CADTM, August 4, 2017.

Tuchman, Barbara W. *The Proud Tower: A Portrait of the World Before the War, 1890-1914*. Barbara W. Tuchman's Great War Series. Random House, 1966.

Tuchman, Barbara W. *The Guns of August: The Outbreak of World War I*. Barbara W. Tuchman's Great War Series. 1962; Ballantine Books, 1990.

Turner, L. C. F. "The Russian Mobilization in 1914." *Journal of Contemporary History* 3, no. 1 (January 1968): 65–88.

Vanderlip, Frank A. *From Farm Boy to Financier*. With Boyden Sparkes. D. Appleton-Century Co., 1935.

Vego, Milan N. *Joint Operational Warfare: Theory and Practice*. 1st ed. Government Printing Office, 2009.

Wagener, Volker. "Germany's Role in the Russian Revolution." DW, November 7, 2017.

Warburg, Paul. "Defects and Needs of Our Banking System." *The New York Times*, January 6, 1907.

Warnes, David. *Russia: A Modern History*. Collins Educational, 1992.

Warth, Robert D. *Nicholas II: The Life and Reign of Russia's Last Monarch*. Praeger, 1997.

Weintraub, Stanley. *Edward the Caresser: The Playboy Prince who Became Edward VII*. The Free Press, 2001.

West, Louis C. *Gold and Silver Coin Standards in the Roman Empire*. Numismatic Notes and Monographs. American Numismatic Society, 1941.

Wiegand, Karl H. von. "Frederick Wilhelm Exclusive Interview with United Press." United Press International, November 20, 1914.

Wikipedia. "Origin of the Palestinians." Last modified August 29, 2025. Accessed September 30, 2025.

Willis, Henry Parker. *A History of the Latin Monetary Union: A Study of International Monetary Action*. University of Chicago Press, 1901.

Witte, Sergei. *The Memoirs of Count Witte*. Translated by Abraham Yarmolinsky. Doubleday, 1921.

Woodward, EL, and Rohan Butler, eds. *Memorandum by Mr. Balfour (Paris) Respecting Syria, Palestine, and Mesopotamia*, Memo on British Foreign Policy, 1919-1939. 1919; HM Stationery Office, 1952.

Index

(Note: Key terms are highlighted.)

www.ingramcontent.com/pod-product-compliance
Lightning Source LLC
Chambersburg PA
CBHW070347200326
41518CB00012B/2162